P9-ANZ-169

AFRICANISMS IN AMERICAN CULTURE

BLACKS IN THE DIASPORA

Founding Editors	Darlene Clark Hine
	John McCluskey, Jr.
	David Barry Gaspar
Editor	Claude A. Clegg III
Advisory Board	Kim D. Butler
	Judith A. Byfield
	Leslie A. Schwalm
	Tracy Sharpley-Whiting

Africanisms in American Culture

Second Edition

Edited by Joseph E. Holloway

INDIANA UNIVERSITY PRESS

Bloomington and Indianapolis

This book is a publication of

Indiana University Press
601 North Morton Street
Bloomington, IN 47404-3797 USA

http://iupress.indiana.edu

Telephone orders 800-842-6796
Fax orders 812-855-7931
Orders by e-mail iuporder@indiana.edu

First edition published by Indiana University Press 1990
© 2005 by Indiana University Press
All rights reserved

No part of this book may be reproduced or utilized in any form or by any means, electronic
or mechanical, including photocopying and recording, or by any information storage and
retrieval system, without permission in writing from the publisher. The Association of
American University Presses' Resolution on Permissions constitutes the only exception to
this prohibition.

∞ The paper used in this publication meets the minimum requirements of the
American National Standard for Information Sciences—Permanence of Paper for
Printed Library Materials,
ANSI Z39.48-1992.

Manufactured in the United States of America

Library of Congress Cataloging-in-Publication Data

Africanisms in American culture / edited by Joseph E. Holloway.
p. cm. — (Blacks in the diaspora)
Includes index.
ISBN 0-253-34479-4 (cloth : alk. paper) — ISBN 0-253-21749-0 (pbk. : alk. paper)
ISBN 978-0-253-34479-3 (cloth : alk. paper)
ISBN 978-0-253-21749-3 (pbk. : alk. paper)

1. African Americans—History. 2. African Americans—Social life and customs. 3. United
States—Civilization—African influences. 4. African diaspora. I. Holloway, Joseph E.
II. Series.
E185.A26 2005
973'.0496073—dc22
2004020284

3 4 5 6 7 16 15 14 13 12 11

Roll Jordan roll, roll Jordan roll
I want to be in de kingdom,
To heah old Jordan roll.

You see dat falcon a-lighting,
You see dat falcon a-lighting
To heah ole Jordan roll,

You see ole massa Jesus a-coming,
You see ole massa Jesus a-coming,
To heah ole Jordan roll,
I want to go to Heaven when I die
To heah ole Jordan roll.

Contents

Contents

viii

Acknowledgments

In my culture, as in many other cultures, the ancestors are important because they serve as a bridge between this world and the world to be. Their memories guide us through life's journey. I give praise to their memory and to my mentors, living and dead. I dedicate this revised edition to my late mother, Elsie Mae Holloway, who lived her dreams through me. Uncle Gus (Harris), who laid the foundations of my cultural understandings, and who, through the stories of Brer Rabbit and John Henry, "Steel Driving Man," taught me ethics, and morals. Aunt Leola Harris-Lewis, who kept her "eye" on me. Professor Boniface I. Obichere, who mentored me, and Jacques Maquet, who taught me the value of African culture and folklore.

Last, but not least, I dedicate this new volume on Africanisms to the pioneers of the field, Melville J. Herskovits and Lorenzo Dow Turner, whose writings inspired me and an entire new generation of scholars.

AFRICANISMS IN AMERICAN CULTURE

Introduction

Africanisms in American Culture has been an important work in the field of diasporic studies for the past decade. It has inspired scholars and others to explore a field blazed originally by Melville J. Herskovits, the father of New World African studies. Since its original publication, the field has changed considerably in that Africanisms have been explored in their broader dimensions, particularly in the field of white Africanisms originally explored by John Philips in the first edition (ch. 13 in this edition).

We know more now than we did then. The new edition has been revised to include some recent essays based on research done two decades ago. One might ask why publish essays based on research at least twenty years old. Originally, the plan was to write the definitive work looking at the subject of Africanisms in American culture since Herskovits's classic study, *The Myth of the Negro Past,* came out in 1941. The volume on Africanisms in America was intended to break the ice and pave the way for a larger study on African transformed continuities in North America, updating Herskovits's seminal work. Needless to say, it was never completed.

Recently, the opportunity came around again and Indiana University Press suggested that an updated and revised edition would continue to be useful and important for another decade. I have written three additional essays for the new volume. The first (ch. 2), "What Africa Has Given America," was written in honor of Melville J. Herskovits, whose original six-page article with the same title changed the field. This chapter uses a transnational framework to examine how African cultural

1

survivals have changed over time and readapted to diasporic conditions while experiencing slavery, forced labor, and racial discrimination. This new focus uses a linguistic metaphor of creolization to demonstrate African transformed continuities in the New World. The second essay (ch. 4), "Africanisms in African American Names in the United States," originally appeared in *The African Heritage of American English* by myself and co-author Winifred Kellersberger Vass. The third essay (ch. 7), "The Sacred World of the Gullahs," is based on research done, as already mentioned, more than two decades ago. Some of the same people who served Lorenzo Dow Turner in his classic study, *Africanisms in the Gullah Dialect* (1949), also served as my informants. This chapter reconstructs Gullah history, citing numerous Africanisms not previously identified by others, thus illustrating that research in any era is timeless.

Finally, "The African Heritage of White America" by John Philips has been revised and presents a new synthesis of approaches. When this essay first appeared, no one had taken seriously the study of Africanisms among white Americans. Researchers in the decades since *Africanisms* was first published have found far more instances of African cultural survivals in white America. Philips's revised chapter reflects this new development in the field in response to his original essay. Chapter 14, by Selase Williams, provides the definitive work on African American Language (AAL) (Ebonics). Williams demonstrates that Ebonics is a language and not simply a dialect of English as some linguists have argued, and that African American Language structure resembles or is identical to features found in African languages.

This revised collection of essays grew out of the need to update the original volume with new materials reflecting changes in the field of Africanisms since 1990. This new edition, like the first one, focuses on Africanisms in North America, especially the United States, from historical, linguistic, religious, and artistic perspectives. The goal and purpose of the new volume is to add to the influential findings of Melville J. Herskovits of a half-century ago. These essays intend to do just that, looking particularly at African cultural survivals in North America not previously described by Herskovits or other researchers exploring New World Africanisms.

The Herskovits-Frazier Debate

The study of Africanisms—those elements of culture found in the New World that are traceable to an African origin—has been a neglected yet controversial area of inquiry in the United States since Herskovits's pioneering study, *The Myth of the Negro Past.*[1] Studies following in Herskovits's wake focused on Africanisms retained in the Caribbean, Suriname, and Brazil, where an abundance of living African culture is still apparent. In North America the most direct remnants of African culture are found in a number of isolated communities, mainly in Florida, Georgia, and South Carolina. In many ways these hemispheric and geographic differences fueled the debate over the survival of African culture in North America.

The opposing sides in this scholarly debate were led by Melville Herskovits and E. Franklin Frazier. Frazier believed that black Americans lost their African heritage during slavery; thus, he postulated, African American culture evolved independently of any African influence. In short, Frazier argued that slavery was so devastating in America that it destroyed all African elements among black Americans. For Frazier, black American culture began without any African antecedents. In *The Negro Church in America* (1963) he stated most forcefully his opposition to Herskovits, arguing that "because of the manner in which the Negroes were captured in Africa and enslaved, they were practically stripped of their social heritage." Slavery in the United States destroyed the African family institution and social structure, he asserted, while at the same time putting blacks in close contact with whites, from whom they learned new patterns of thought and behavior which they adapted to their own use.[2] At the time Frazier wrote this, blacks were attempting to blend into mainstream America and were reluctant to identify with anything that emphasized cultural differences.

It would be wrong to dismiss Frazier as someone with an irrational fear of African identification. A pioneer in African and African American sociology, he did not hesitate to discuss African societies in a positive light. He recognized pervasive African cultural survivals in the West Indies and Latin America but pointed out that even Herskovits had found such survivals in North America to be general rather than specific and pervasive. The culprit, he concluded, was the tremendous repression and social disruption Africans encountered in North America rather than any inferiority of African culture. Although Frazier was incorrect in arguing that North American slaves suffered a complete loss of African culture, he did recognize the strong role played by black churches in helping blacks reorganize their culture after slavery ended.

Herskovits, in *The Myth of the Negro Past*, illustrated many significant African contributions to American culture. Unlike Frazier he emphasized the continuity of West African carryovers in African American culture. But as more historical and ethnographic data on the African cultural background became available, the limitations of the Herskovits model became evident. Although Herskovits spoke of Africanisms in the United States in a global sense, he looked for evidence to prove his theory almost exclusively in the Caribbean and South America. Moreover, his concept of Africanisms was based on a notion of West African cultural homogeneity that is not supported by more recent scholarship, which suggests a Bantu origin for many facets of African American culture. Nevertheless, Herskovits established a baseline theory of African retentions from which other researchers could assess African survivals in the New World and expand into areas he did not take into account.

Herskovits emerged from this debate as one of the most important scholars of Africanisms in North America. *The Myth of the Negro Past* not only confirmed that African traditions had survived in black cultures in the Americas but also revealed the presence of a distinctive African American culture in the United States. And the Herskovits-Frazier debate, though an old one, is still central to an understanding of developments in the field of New World Africanisms.

The Study of Africanisms

One of the early studies aimed at recording and documenting Africanisms in the United States was *Folk Beliefs of the Southern Negro* (1926) by Newbell Puckett. Puckett's book was the first anthropological study to examine African carryovers found in southern society. It presented some ten thousand folk beliefs of southern blacks, showing their origin when possible and indicating some general principles governing the transmission and content of folklore in general. Puckett discussed the preservation of African traits in African American burial customs, folk beliefs, and religious philosophy, including belief in ghosts, witchcraft, voodoo, and conjuration.[3]

Other early scholars examining African carryovers in American society were Carter G. Woodson and W. E. B. Du Bois. In *The African Background Outlined* (1936), Woodson listed several major African survivals—technical skills, arts, folklore, spirituality, attitudes toward authority, a tradition of generosity—and called attention to African influences in religion, music, dance, drama, poetry, and oratory. Du Bois presented the results of a similar study in *Black Folk, Then and Now*.[4]

In 1940, with scholarly research on Africanisms in its second decade, Guy Johnson, in *Drum and Shadows*, produced an extensive examination of African retentions in the Georgia Sea Islands and nearby mainland Gullah communities. This study was part of the Federal Writers Project that recorded the testimony of ex-slaves. It was the first to that character and to adopt an exclusively Anglo one. In the process of his comparative analysis, he discovered that an undocumented naming system among African Americans has developed since the 1960s that not only presents further validation of the existence of the African character in AAL but also opens the door for an entirely new line of research in the areas of African continuities in African diasporic communities.

Molefi Kete Asante's essay (ch. 3) describes the continuity between certain communicational styles of African Americans and West Africans. Tracing the relationship between West African languages and certain African American linguistic patterns, Asante argues that by and large black Americans have retained the basic linguistic structures of their African origins. The linguistic features discussed support this proposition and reveal that African American speakers have maintained this fundamental aspect of West African culture despite their relative acculturation into the language patterns of mainstream American culture. According to Asante, African Americans have retained a linguistic facet of their Africanness, and this African style generally persists even as Anglicization occurs. For example, almost every language spoken in Africa south of the Sahara is tonal, using pitch distinctions to differentiate words in much the same way the European languages use stress. The more evident the African rhythm, tone, and pitch are in vocalization, the more distinctly African is the intonation.

Another example of an African language retention observed in African American speech is that certain tense distinctions can be traced to the Yoruba, whose speakers do not distinguish between the past and present indefinite forms of a verb. When it is necessary to make a distinction between past and present, the Yoruba use an adverb of time. Asante shows that the English language spoken by imported Africans was greatly influenced by the phonological and syntactic structures of their language origins. He concludes that whatever semblances of English they learned bore the unmistakable imprint of an African linguistic pattern.

Religion

Religion, the dominant element in many cultures, reveals much about a people. Religion forms the core foundation of the African world and is central to understanding the numerous Africanisms that have carried over into the New World. Some of the most visible Africanisms are found in such African American religious practices as the ring shout, the passing of children over a dead person's coffin in the Sea Islands, and the placement of objects on top of graves. Many Africans believe that a Supreme Being, or God, exists and is present in all things, both the inner and outer universes, and that a person's life experiences evolve around a world filled with spirituality.

In this tradition, Jessie Ruth Gaston describes the spiritual world of voodoo, once recognized as a state religion in New Orleans (see ch. 5). In her essay Gaston provides valuable insights into the African survivals among blacks in New Orleans. African religious survivals and retentions are defined as those religious beliefs, activities, cults, deities, and rituals that can be directly traced back to Africa. The Dahomean religion of *vodu*, as it is called in many parts of West Africa, is a highly structured and complex religious and magical system, inclusive of duties, symbols, rituals, and faithful supporters. The term *vodu*, variously spelled *voodoo* and *hoodoo* in the United States, is Dahomean, originally meaning "spirit" or "deity" in the Fon language. Gaston's discussion is centered on five topics: the history of *vodu* in North America; the African religious system, with special reference to Dahomey; the cult initiations among voodoo practitioners in New Orleans; the role of songs and prayers in voodoo worship in West Africa, Haiti, and New Orleans; and the historical reconstruction of voodoo practices and practitioners in New Orleans. This original study shows how the voodoo religion was transplanted almost intact from West Africa.

Margaret Washington's essay (ch. 6) explores the cosmic world of the Gullahs. Washington shows that Gullah Christianity is a vital folk religion filled with peculiar patterns and beliefs that link its worshippers with their traditional past. This West and Central African view is consonant with the idea that in a cohesive society each member has a place and the spirit world cannot be set apart from secular or communal concerns. The Gullahs, for example, believed that God offered an explanation for life and provided a model for virtue. Their religion instilled confidence in their eventual freedom on earth and helped them maintained a passionate love for humanity.

Furthermore, Washington shows that the Gullahs attached a tremendous significance to death and encouraged a zest for living. She found little evidence of any apprehension or fear of dying, for death was not considered an end of life but the beginning of a new life as an ancestor. In other words, death did not signal a break with the community of the living; it represented a continuity between the communities of the living and the dead. Washington also shows that the African view of religion encouraged the Gullahs to live as rich and full a life as possible. Although the Gullahs did not fear death, they recognized its power and attempted in their customs to please both God and the "power of darkness." Night vigils, singing, and praying around the bedside of the dying were believed to strengthen a person as he or she passed "through death's door." The same practice is found in the Kongo (Zaire) and Angola, most noticeably among the Bakongo and the Ovimbundu, and is common in most Bantu-related cultures.

Robert Hall's essay (ch. 8) raises a number of issues in African American culture and religion by examining the religious experiences of blacks living in Florida during the eighteenth and nineteenth centuries. Hall addresses certain distinct elements of African American culture by placing spirit possession and ritualistic dancing at the heart of the African survivals controversy in the United States. Because the cultural transformation of African Americans is best viewed as a dynamic process occurring over a long time, a consideration of early American history, particularly the pivotal eighteenth century, is crucial to understanding the relevance of African cultures to African American culture in more recent times. After a brief examination of the formation of African American culture during the eighteenth century, the bulk of his essay describes, in considerable detail, African survivals in nineteenth century Florida. Although ritual scarification, naming practices, magical beliefs, and material culture are mentioned, emphasis is given to ecstatic religious rituals, musical styles, and funeral rites.

The crux of Hall's essay is his demonstration through literary evidence (newspapers, black diaries, autobiographies, travel accounts, and the like) that belief in spirit possession persisted in many parts of Florida throughout the half-century following emancipation. Hall's demographic profile of Florida's black population in 1870 (only eighty-eight black Floridians had been born in Africa) requires an explanation of how possession and other African-influenced cultural traits could have persisted long after the death of African-born blacks in Florida. The oral traditions of black Floridians suggest that vivid memories of African-born parents and grandparents served as conduits of African cultural influences. These African ancestors, no longer in the earthly world when the census takers made their rounds in 1870, passed along their songs, sayings, basket-weaving techniques, and aesthetic learnings to their descendants. Among these legacies was the penchant for ritualized spirit possession, a tradition that remained quite strong among black Floridians even at the turn of this century.

George Brandon's essay (ch. 9) focuses on religious retentions that came to the United States as recently as the 1940s. Santeria, a neo-African cult indigenous to Cuba, has increased its following since it arrived in the United States. A key Africanism preserved in Santeria is the practice of sacrifice. Brandon examines the concept and the elements used in Santeria sacrifices and briefly compares them with traditional

Yoruba practices. He examines how these sacrificial practices bring Santeria devotees into conflict with the culture and laws of the United States and concludes that Santeria is basically African in its rituals and that the ritual of sacrifice has a central role in this religion. He further suggests that the United States is undergoing a slow but significant infusion of African-based religious forms as a result of African emigration and ongoing relations between Africans and African Americans.

The Arts

Aesthetics, folklore, and music are areas of artistic creativity. The persistence of Africanisms in these areas suggests that a vibrant culture is still being transformed into newer forms. Culture is sometimes judged by its existing artifacts and legacy from the past. In African American culture, folklore and musical forms have retained evidence of strong African influences.

Robert Farris Thompson's essay (ch. 10) contributes to our understanding of Africanisms found in African American aesthetics, revealing that the majority of African retentions in African American folk art are Bantu in origin. Thompson shows that the impact of the Kongo on African American culture contributed to the foundation of black American aesthetic and musical culture in the New World. The Kongo influence contributed to the rise of the national music of Brazil (the samba) and to one of the most sophisticated musical forms in the United States, jazz.

Thompson demonstrates that Kongo influences were widespread. For example, in the northern Kongo there are specialized ritual experts, *nganga nkodi* and *nganga nsibe,* who cut designs on the bodies of living fish or turtles and release them back into their element, water, hoping that the ancestors will receive the messages and act upon them on behalf of their descendants. In South Carolina, on the island of St. Helena, when preparing fish the residents make three incisions. I am told that the tradition survives even though the local people have forgotten the meaning of the incisions. Other Kongo survivals are the Charleston dance pattern, which strongly resembles a dance pattern in northern Kongo, and *pakalala,* a pose with both hands on the hips that forms the challenge stance in the Kongo. To stand with hands on hips in the Kongo proclaims a person ready to accept the challenge of a situation. In the United States this akimbo pose has become a classic black woman's challenge pose. In addition, the African Haitian ritual dancing based on a dance form found in northern Kongo was adopted by the baton-twirling "major jonc" called *rara.* Its members twirl batons and strike a Kongo pose when confronting a ritual group. It is hypothesized

that in Mississippi, where many Kongo slaves reside, such group
a major impact. Mississippi has become a world baton-twirling ess

Portia K. Maultsby's essay (ch. 11) shows that Africanisms survived
in American music over time and were transformed into newer forms,
the result of new experiences and a reshaping of European American
idioms to conform to African aesthetic norms. Africanisms survived in
the music of the New World because blacks maintained ties to their African past. This supralingual bond enabled African Americans to survive
and create a meaningful existence in a world where they were not welcome. They adapted to environmental change and social upheaval by relying on familiar traditions and practices. Music played a major role in
this process. Although specific African songs and genres eventually disappeared from the culture of American blacks, they created new ones
using the traditional African styles, vocabulary, and idioms. Maultsby
shows that the fundamental character of culture and music created by
slaves persisted into the twentieth century and was reinterpreted according to the demands of the social setting. Africanisms in African
American culture, therefore, exist as conceptual approaches—unique
ways of doing things and making things happen—rather than as specific cultural elements.

The essay by Beverly Robinson (ch. 12) explores the full range of
African American folk culture, from the epic hero Henry to dance,
drama, food, and medicine. She shows that Africans carried vestiges of
their material and nonmaterial culture on board the slave ships and that
some of this culture resurfaced in the New World in the form of such
folktales as Brer Rabbit. Robinson further describes how many North
American black traditions, songs, and musical styles were rooted in Africa and later emerged on the plantation. Songs sung by Africans on
slave ships while being transported to the New World resurfaced in the
form of spirituals. The popular cakewalk dance, an expression of the
early 1900s, had roots in the folklore of the slave culture, as did juba, a
slave food, and a dance called juba, which later became known as the
Charleston.

New Directions

For too long scholars have focused on African cultural retentions in
black culture only and have neglected to examine vestiges of the African cultural heritage among white Americans. John Philips reassesses
the Herskovits-Frazier debate and suggests that partisans on either side
of the issue ignored the presence of African cultural survivals among
white Americans as they arrived at their respective theoretical positions.

Philips asserts that Herskovits was correct in believing that significant African influence is pervasive in American culture. Philips also believes that Frazier was correct in putting emphasis on the legacy of slavery and segregation rather than on the degree of African cultural survivals as factors that distinguish African American culture from European American culture. His essay (ch. 13) is historiographical, concerned primarily with identifying some sources for definitively exploring Africanisms in white American culture.

Philips supports his thesis by giving evidence from music, cooking, agriculture, folklore, linguistics, religion, and social structure. He shows that despite the reluctance of scholars to investigate the matter, much African culture has already been found in white American culture, some facets of which appear to exist no longer among black Americans. Philips further explores possible avenues of cultural transmission and arrives at certain theoretical implications for the study of cultural influences. These theories also have underlying implications for racial relations in the United States. Philips's essay is groundbreaking in that it prepares the way for future research in a neglected area.

A Note on Nomenclature

The study of Africanisms in the New World has sparked much debate over the survival of African culture in America. Historically, part of the debate has been over the use of the term *African*. The name controversy begins with the landing of Africans in Jamestown, Virginia. More recently, this argument has come full circle with the call for black people to adopt *African American* as a descriptive instead of *black* because the term will give black people their proper historical-cultural base with reference to a homeland. The name controversy is central to understanding black culture in America because its history reveals much about ideological and cultural developments in black life.

In 1619, when the very first Africans were brought to Jamestown, John Rolfe wrote in his journal that "a Dutch ship sold us twenty Negars." This was the first non-African reference made to blacks in North America, even though the term *African* had been used since the thirteenth century to identify black people from Africa. The English word *Negro* is borrowed from the Spanish meaning "black."

From the eighteenth century through the first third of the nineteenth century, black religious and educational organizations used the prefix *African* in their names, providing a sense of cultural integrity and a link to their African heritage. The first black religious organization established in Savannah in 1787 was the First African Baptist Church. The second oldest black denomination in North America, founded in 1787, was the African Methodist Episcopal. In 1806 blacks constructed the first African Meeting House in Boston. This pattern also is seen in such names as African Free School, African Clarkson Society, African Dorcas Society, Children of Africa, and Sons of Africa. The first mutual beneficial societies that had direct roots in African secret societies called themselves African as late as 1841. One such society was the New York African Society for Mutual Relief.

Identification with Africa was strong in both the North and the South. In the North, African cultural institutions were established in the black governor's parade during the Pinkster celebration, where African dances and songs were performed. In New Orleans a corresponding African extravaganza at Congo Square took place every weekend.

Also in the 1800s a movement was started by blacks who worked as house servants, many of whom had white as well as black forebears. The term *colored* was used by these offspring to distinguish themselves from the Africans who worked in the fields. The light-skinned children who were the product of relationships between planters and house servants formed themselves into a distinct class. In Charleston in 1794 the Brown Fellowship was established, admitting members of mixed heritage. A similar society in New Orleans was called the Blue Vein Society; membership was based on skin color so light that the blue veins could be seen.

By the 1830s the term *colored* was no longer used exclusively by blacks of mixed heritage but was common in black leadership circles that included abolitionists, integrationists, and nationalists. Many blacks sought to disassociate from their African identification because of the activities of the American Colonization Society, which wanted to send free blacks back to Africa. Fearing both lost status and the possibility of a forced return to Africa, the black leadership moved away from African identification. From 1830 to 1860 integrationism and nationalism began to ascend over the forces of African cultural identification. A major thrust was to remove the word *African* from both educational and organizational titles. The idea was to fight the colonization scheme by denying that blacks were Africans.

Beginning in the 1890s, the age of Booker T. Washington, strong support arose for black nationalist ideas and linkage with Africa. Marcus Garvey's back to Africa movement of the 1920s contributed to strong nationalistic feelings. The term *Afro-American* gained popularity in the titles of black organizations. Washington himself played a role in getting the U.S. government to use the word *Negro* to refer to African Americans instead of *colored* and *mulatto*. He fought for *Negro* as a unity word.

In the 1960s and 1970s the term *black* finally gained respectability with the coming of the civil rights, African independence, and black power movements. These movements helped elevate black status and pride throughout the world. The word *Negro* became outdated.

Race in the modern world is defined by land of origin: Japanese American, Mexican American, and Chinese American. But there is no land mass called Negro, Black, or Afro. These terms are hybrids, with no real reference to the African continent. The term *African American* defines black people on the basis of identification with their historic place of origin. Backed by Jesse Jackson and Ramona Edlin, among others, the term *African American* has been gaining in usage among the black leadership, including artists, poets, and a variety of intellectuals.

Thus this debate has come full circle, from *African* through *brown*, *colored*, *Afro-American*, *Negro*, and *black* back to *African*, the term originally used by blacks in America to define themselves. The changes in terminology reflect many changes in attitude, from strong African identification to nationalism, integration, and attempts at assimilation back to cultural identification. This struggle to reshape and define blackness in both the concrete and the abstract also reflects the renewed pride of black people in shaping a future based on the concept of one African people living in the African Diaspora.

Notes

1. Melville J. Herskovits, *The Myth of the Negro Past* (Boston: Beacon Press, 1958; originally published in 1941).
2. Edward Franklin Frazier, *The Negro Church in America* (New York: Schocken, 1963).
3. Newbell Niles Puckett, *Folk Beliefs of the Southern Negro* (New York: Dover, 1969; originally published in 1926).
4. Carter Godwin Woodson, *The African Background Outlined* (New York: Negro Universities Press, 1968; reprint of 1936 edition). W. E. B. Du Bois, *Black Folk, Then and Now* (New York: Holt, 1939).
5. Guy Johnson, *Drum and Shadows: Survival Studies Among the Georgia Coastal Negroes.* Savannah Unit, Georgia Writers' Project, Work Projects Administration (Athens: University of Georgia Press, 1940).
6. Lorenzo Dow Turner, *Africanisms in the Gullah Dialect* (New York: Arno Press, 1968; reprint of 1949 edition).

7. Norman E. Whitten and John F. Szwed, eds., *Afro-American Anthropology: Contemporary Perspectives* (New York: Free Press, 1970).

8. Sidney Wilfred Mintz and Richard Price, *An Anthropological Approach to the Afro-American Past: A Caribbean Perspective* (Philadelphia: Institute for the Study of Human Issues, 1976).

9. Peter H. Wood, *Black Majority: Negroes in Colonial South Carolina from 1670 through the Stono Rebellion* (New York: Knopf, 1974).

10. Lawrence W. Levine, *Black Culture and Black Consciousness: Afro-American Folk Thought from Slavery to Freedom* (New York: Oxford University Press, 1977).

11. John W. Blassingame, *The Slave Community: Plantation Life in the Antebellum South* (New York: Oxford University Press, 1972).

12. Winifred Kellersberger Vass, *The Bantu Speaking Heritage of the United States* (Los Angeles: UCLA, Center for Afro-American Studies, 1979).

13. Robert Farris Thompson and Joseph Cornet, *The Four Moments of the Sun: Kongo Art in Two Worlds* (Washington, D.C.: National Gallery of Art, 1981). Thompson, *Flash of the Spirit: African and Afro-American Art and Philosophy* (New York: Vintage Books, 1983).

14. Roger D. Abrahams and John F. Szwed, eds., *After Africa* (New Haven, Conn.: Yale University Press, 1983).

15. Charles W. Joyner, *Down by the Riverside: A South Carolina Slave Community* (Urbana: University of Illinois Press, 1984).

16. Sterling Stuckey, *Slave Culture: Nationalist Theory and the Foundations of Black America* (New York: Oxford University Press, 1987).

17. Margaret Washington Creel, *"A Peculiar People": Slave Religion and Community-Culture among the Gullahs* (New York: New York University Press, 1988).

18. William S. Pollitzer, *The Gullah People and Their African Heritage* (Athens: University of Georgia Press, 1999).

One

The Origins of African
American Culture

Joseph E. Holloway

The history of the New World is a story of cultural interaction, integration, and assimilation. The rediscovery of the New World by Columbus in 1492 opened the gate to world powers and prompted colonialists and private individuals to search for wealth. The fertile land attracted farmers, especially from Spain, Portugal, France, and England. The new immigrants needed cheap labor to mine precious metals and to work on plantations. Their desire led to the transatlantic slave trade, in which millions of Africans were brought to the New World to meet this new labor demand.

The transatlantic slave trade established a permanent link between Africa and North America as Africans sold into slavery transplanted their cultures to the New World. The largest forced migration in history, the slave trade brought an estimated half-million Africans to what is now the United States over some two hundred years. This total is thought to represent about 7 percent of the entire transatlantic slave trade, though the exact figures are in dispute and the total volume of the slave trade may never be known. If one considers those who perished in the stockades and on the cargo ships in estimating the volume of traffic to the New World, the total may well be between sixty and one hundred million. So great was this traffic that "by 1850 a third of the people of African descent lived outside of Africa."[1] African slaves came from diverse regions of Africa but particularly from those areas stretching along the coast through West Africa to Central Africa (see map on page 20).

Scholars over the years, in their endeavors to define an African American culture separate from European American culture, discovered a sig-

18

nificant number of cultural and linguistic properties of African origin and labeled them Africanisms. Until recently scholars used the term *Africanisms* synonymously with *West Africanisms*, implying that the cultural heritage of the majority of the North American slave population was West African in origin and that this culture was homogeneous. This essay argues against the assumption of West African cultural homogeneity. Instead it sees the culture as conglomerate and heterogeneous.

Focusing on the example of South Carolina but not limiting its overview to that state, this essay also sheds light on the theoretical controversy that arose from scholars' attempts to identify the major African cultural groups that contributed to the development of African American culture. I will show that although the West Africans arrived in North America in greater numbers, the Bantu of Central Africa had the largest homogeneous culture among the imported Africans and the strongest impact on the development of African American culture. I will also address the problem of multiplicity in the origins of Africanisms in North America by identifying the contributing African cultural areas.

Geographic Areas

The historical literature shows little agreement on regional and coastal names along the West African coast. Melville J. Herskovits used the term *Guinea Coast* to include the southern portions of the Gold Coast (Ghana), Dahomey (Republic of Benin), and the Bight of Benin (the Niger Delta).[2] Philip Curtin noted that *Guinea* as a geographical designation was always an unstable concept, changing in usage with each century. Early in the sixteenth century it referred to the whole western coast of Africa from the Senegal River to the Orange River. Later it included the coast from Cape Mount to the Bight of Benin. Curtin concluded that during the eighteenth century *Guinea* roughly designated present-day Gambia, Senegal, and Guinea-Bissau.[3]

For clarity I will follow Curtin's definition of Guinea, roughly designating the area between the Senegal River and the Sherbro estuary, including the Canary and Cape Verde Islands, Guinea-Bissau, and present-day Gambia, Senegal, and Sierra Leone. The term *Grain Coast* refers to what is known today as Liberia. *Windward Coast* represents all of present-day Sierra Leone. *Ivory Coast* represents all of present-day Ivory Coast. *Gold Coast* identifies the coastal stretch from Assini in the west to the Volta River in the east, equivalent to the coast of the present-day Republic of Ghana. *Slave Coast* designates what is currently Togo and Benin and a small coastal portion of Nigeria. *Bight of Biafra* refers roughly to the Niger Delta.

Map 1. The Guinea Coast

Map 2. People flow from West and Central Africa to the Americas

Cultural Areas

Herskovits was the first scholar to identify the cultural zones of Africa.[4] His model is useful, but his cultural regions are too large to apply to specific cultures. Thus the cultural areas from where the enslaved Africans came must be revised into smaller cultural clusters: Mande, Mano River, Akan, Sudanic, Niger Cross River, Niger Delta, and Bantu. The Bantu cluster is further divided into Bakongo, Ovimbundu, and Luba Lunda. The cultural map on this page shows these areas in relation to the percentage of Africans arriving in South Carolina from each cultural cluster.

According to Herskovits the areas that furnished the greatest numbers of Africans were the "basin of the Senegal River," the "Guinea Coast" (including especially the southern portions of what are today known as Ghana and the Republic of Benin), and the Niger Delta. Herskovits noted that Africans from the Guinea Coast, Sierra Leone, Liberia, the Ivory Coast, the Bight of Benin, the Gold Coast, Dahomey, and the coastal ports of Nigeria were most often cited in the historical literature of slavery. He identified these cultural zones as the most significant in the formation of the patterns of New World "Negro" behavior.[5]

While historical documents are vague in terms of precise ethnic distribution, they do give the regional points of origin, designating cultural areas. It is likely that cultural groups living near the centers of trade rather than on the peripheries found their way into the slave trade. We can assume that groups living within a radius of two hundred miles of the ports of departure made up the Africans taken to North America. According to Herskovits the locale of the slave trade was the restricted region of West Africa rather than the continent as a whole. Recent research indicates, however, that Africans arrived from much of the Atlantic Coast of Africa, from the Senegal River to the ports of Angola, where buyers learned and became familiar with the diversity of Africans living on the coast and in certain parts of the interior.[6]

The Slave Trade in South Carolina

In 1670 a permanent settlement of African slaves arrived in South Carolina from the English colony of Barbados in the West Indies. Peter Wood concludes that this Caribbean background contributed to the colony's initial distinctive mixture of African and European elements.[7]

The transatlantic slave trade was in full-scale operation by the late

1600s. Documents from 1700 to 1730 are vague in identifying African ethnicity, but we do have data on total importations. Between 1706 and 1724, 5,081 Africans arrived in colonial South Carolina (table 1), and between 1721 and 1726, 3,632 were imported (table 2). Even though relatively few Africans were imported during the early years of the colonial period, they outnumbered the white population. In just twenty years after the original settlement the African population in the Carolinas was equal to that of Europeans. By 1715 Africans outnumbered Europeans 10,500 to 6,250. By 1720 Africans had outnumbered Europeans for more than a decade.[8] In 1724 the white population in colonial South Carolina was estimated at 14,000, the black population at 32,000.[9] A Swiss newcomer, Samuel Dyssli, observed in 1737 that Carolina "looks more like a negro country than like a country settled by white people."[10]

West Africans

Between 1670 and 1700, Africans were imported to South Carolina predominantly from "Guinea." The majority of these "Guinea" Africans were Wolofs and other Mandes, such as Bambaras, Fulani, and Susus. The Wolofs, the most numerous of the African groups to arrive in the United States in the seventeenth century, were mostly house servants who had extensive and close contact with European Americans. They were, perhaps, the first Africans whose cultural elements and language were assimilated by and retained within the developing culture of America. They also had greater opportunities for admixture and interaction with whites than other African groups in the years before 1700.

The enslavement and transport of large numbers of Wolofs in the seventeenth century is attested by Senegambian history. Around 1670 the Wolof, or Jolof, empire broke up into a number of kingdoms owing to a revolt instigated by Mauretanian marabouts. The disintegration of this one-time large empire caused instability, resulting in prolonged warfare as the Cayor region attempted to dominate other secessionist states. Each Wolof state tried to fill the power vacuum.[11] The long-term effect of this instability and continual warfare was that large numbers of Wolofs were taken as prisoners of war, sold to slavers, and transported to America. But after the seventeenth century the Wolofs were never again to provide such a significant number of Africans to the North American slave market.

The Senegambia region includes the ethnic groups Mandingo, Malinke, Bambara, Wolof, and Fula (plural, Fulani). Bambara, Man-

TABLE 1. Africans Imported into
South Carolina, 1706–1724

Year	Number Imported	Year	Number Imported
1706	24	1716	67
1707	22	1717	573
1708	53	1718	529
1709	107	1719	541
1710	131	1720	601
1711	170	1721	165
1712	76	1722	323
1713	159	1723	436
1714	419	1724	604
1715	81	Total	5,081

Adapted with permission from Elizabeth
Donnan, *Documents Illustrative of the History of
the Slave Trade to America*, 4 (Washington,
D.C.: Carnegie Institution, 1935), 255.

TABLE 2. Africans Imported into South Carolina,
1721–1726

Period	Number Imported
May 30–September 29, 1721	104
September 29, 1721–September 29, 1722	215
September 29, 1722–September 29, 1723	527
September 29, 1723–September 29, 1724	602
September 29, 1724–September 29, 1725	433
September 29, 1725–September 29, 1726	1,751
Total	3,632

Figures reported by Wm. Hammerton, Nav. Officer, Port of
Charles Town; adapted with permission from Donnan, *Documents*, 4, 267.

dingo, and Malinke are related ethnic groups that speak dialects of a
single language and share the same Mande culture. Malinke, however,
are Muslim, the Bambara anti-Muslim. Collectively, these West Africans from Senegambia through the Bight of Benin and Biafra represented 60 percent of Africans imported into South Carolina through
the eighteenth and early nineteenth centuries (table 3). But their heter-

TABLE 3. Origin of Slaves Imported into South Carolina, 1733–1807

Region of Origin	Percent of Slaves
West Africa	
Senegambia	19.5
Sierra Leone	6.8
Windward Coast	16.3
Gold Coast	13.3
Bight of Benin	1.6
Bight of Biafra	2.1
Total	59.6
Central Africa	
Angola	39.6
Mozambique-Madagascar	0.7

Adapted with permission from Donnan, *Documents*, 4, passim.

ogeneous cultures placed them at a disadvantage in influencing African American culture.

Central Africans

As Washington points out, the Donnan and Treasury Report data based on documents from the early period (1733–44) show that 60 percent of the Africans entering South Carolina were from Angola in Central Africa; during the middle period of the trade, 1749–87, the figure dropped to 15 percent because of the Stono Rebellion; and in the final period, 1804–1807, Bantu forced immigration rose to 53 percent (table 4). A summary of these data shows that Angolans made up about 32 percent of the slaves brought into Charleston (table 5). Other data indicate the percentage actually was closer to 40.

Toward the mid-1700s, then, more Angolans than any other African ethnic and cultural group were being imported into South Carolina. Peter Wood found documents showing that between 1735 and 1740, 70 percent of all incoming Africans were Bantu from the Angolan region near the Congo River (table 6). Of 11,562 Africans imported in that five-year period, 8,045 were from Angola. The next largest group listed (2,719) was from "elsewhere in Africa." From Gambia only 705

TABLE 4. Slaves Imported into South Carolina, by Origin and Time Period

Coastal Region	Number of Cargoes	Number of Slaves (Est.)	Percent
Early Period 1733–44			
Senegambia	17	1,031	6.2
Sierra Leone	0	0	0
Windward Coast	0.5	34	0.2
Gold Coast	5.5	1,184	7.2
Bight of Benin	0	0	0
Bight of Biafra	2	609	3.7
Angola	46	9,831	59.5
Madagascar, Mozambique	0	0	0
Others (Africa, Guinea and Unknown)	32	3,844	23.2
Total	103	16,533	
Middle Period 1749–87			
Senegambia	116	16,038	26.3
Sierra Leone	27	4,210	6.9
Windward Coast	64	10,397	17.1
Gold Coast	55	8,604	14.1
Bight of Benin	6	1,394	2.3
Bight of Biafra	3	396	0.6
Angola	37	9,030	14.8
Madagascar, Mozambique	0	0	0
Others (Africa, Guinea, and Unknown)	75.5	10,875	17.8
Total	383.5	60,944	
Final Period 1804–7			
Senegambia	8	506	1.7
Sierra Leone	9	1,383	4.8
Windward Coast	42.5	5,123	17.6
Gold Coast	22.5	3,282	11.3
Bight of Benin	0	0	0
Bight of Biafra	2	909	3.13
Angola	55	15,305	52.7
Madagascar, Mozambique	2	473	1.6
Others (Africa, Guinea, and Unknown)	19.5	2,048	7.1
Total	160.5	29,029	

Adapted with permission from "A Reconsideration of the Sources of the Slave Trade to Charleston, S.C.," an unpublished essay by William S. Pollitzer.

TABLE 5. Summary of Slaves Imported into Charleston, S.C.

Coastal Region	Total Slaves (Estimated)	Percent
Senegambia	17,575	16.5
Sierra Leone	5,593	5.3
Windward Coast	15,554	14.6
Gold Coast	13,070	12.3
Bight of Benin	1,394	1.3
Bight of Biafra	1,914	1.8
Angola	34,166	32.1
Madagascar, Mozambique	473	0.4
Others (Africa, Guinea, and Unknown)	16,767	15.7
Total	106,506	

Adapted with permission from "A Reconsideration of the Sources of the Slave Trade to Charleston, S.C.," an unpublished essay by William S. Pollitzer.

Africans (6 percent of the total) were brought into South Carolina, probably to be trained as house servants.

After 1739, fewer Angolans were brought into the colony, for by then the southern planters were prejudiced against them. In the southern planters' minds, the Angolan dominance contributed to the unrest of 1739, in which Angolans revolted, killing whites while en route to Florida. Documents describing the Stono uprising mention that "amongst the Negroe Slaves there are a people brought from the kingdom of Angola in Africa."[12] In 1739-40 only 692 Angolans were imported into Charlestown, the Carolina port, and during the rest of the century Angolan importation dropped to 40 percent of the Africans imported into South Carolina (table 7). But even with this 30 percent drop, Bantu speakers still made up the majority of Africans employed in the fields in South Carolina.

Unlike the Senegambians, the Bantus brought to South Carolina a homogeneous culture identifiable as Bantu, the cover term used to capture the generic relationship of this large African cultural group. This homogeneity is indicated by a common language. According to Guthrie, Bantu languages have a common core lexicon of five hundred or more vocabulary items.[13] In forming the Bantu nucleus, the twenty-eight tested languages were ranked in accordance with the percentage of basic lexical items they contained. Among the twenty-eight languages, Tshi-

TABLE 6. Origin of African Slaves Arriving in Charlestown, March 1735–March 1740

Year	From Angola	From Gambia	From Elsewhere in Africa	From West Indies, etc.	Total
1735–36	2,029	—	612	10	2,651
1736–37	2,891	188	224	23	3,326
1737–38	827	—	228	7	1,062
1738–39	1,606	314	575	12	2,507
1739–40	692	203	1,080	41	2,016
Total	8,045	705	2,719	93	11,562
(%)	(69.6)	(6.1)	(23.5)	(0.8)	

Adapted with permission from Peter H. Wood, *Black Majority* (New York: Knopf, 1974), 340–41.

TABLE 7. Origin of Slaves Imported into South Carolina, 1752–1808

Origin		Number of Slaves
Direct from Africa		65,466
"Africa"	4,146	
Gambia to Sierra Leone	12,441	
Sierra Leone	3,906	
Liberia and Ivory Coast (Rice and Grain Coasts)	3,851	
"Guinea Coast" (Gold Coast to Calabar)	18,240	
Angola	11,485	
Congo	10,924	
Mozambique	243	
East Africa	230	
Via West Indies		2,303
Total		67,769

Adapted with permission from Donnan, *Documents*, 4, 310, passim.

TABLE 8. Origin of African Cargoes in South Carolina, 1732–1774

Origin	Number of Cargoes	Origin	Number of Cargoes
Gambia	70	Whydah	4
Angola	55	Bance Island	3
Africa	40	Grain Coast	3
Sierra Leone	24	Bassa	1
Africa via West Indies	24	Benin	1
Gold Coast	21	Cape Coast	1
Windward Coast	15	Congo	1
Senegal	14	Gabon Coast	1
Guinea	8	Gambia River	1
Cape Mount	7	Tortola	1
Rice Coast	6	West Coast	1
Anamabo	4	Total	306

Adapted with permission from Donnan, *Documents*, 4, 276.

Luba, or Luba Kasai, had 47 percent of the basic vocabulary, Luba-Katanga had 50 percent, and Bemba 54 percent. For the Africans in South Carolina, the first stage in the acculturation process was the melding of numerous West and Central African elements in a culture such as Gullah. The creation of this creole culture allowed these Africans to form a kind of lingua franca, enabling them to communicate with each other as well as with the planters.

The Bantus, then, had the largest constituency in South Carolina and possibly in other areas of the southeastern United States as well. Herskovits noted that the Bantu center in North America was the Sea Islands off the Carolina coast. Elizabeth Donnan gives us a clear picture of the regions they came from in a listing of the sources of African cargoes advertised for sale from 1732 to 1774 (table 8). Given the homogeneity of the Bantu culture and the strong similarities among Bantu languages, this group no doubt influenced West African groups of larger size. Also, since the Bantus were predominantly field hands or were used in capacities that required little or no contact with European Americans, they were not confronted with the problem of acculturation, as the West African domestic servants and artisans were. Coexisting in relative isolation from other groups, the Bantus were able to maintain a strong sense of unity and to retain a cultural vitality that laid the foundation for the development of African American culture.

TABLE 9. Origin of Slaves Imported into Virginia, 1710–1769

Origin		Number of Slaves
Direct from Africa		45,088
"Africa"	20,567	
Gambia (including Senegal) and Goree)	3,652	
"Guinea" (Gold Coast, Windward Coast)	6,777	
Calabar and Bonny	9,224	
Angola	3,860	
Madagascar	1,011	
Via West Indies		7,046
Via other North American ports		370
Total		52,504

Adapted with permission from Donnan, *Documents*, 4, 175–244, passim.

The Slave Trade in Virginia

The picture is somewhat different in colonial Virginia. According to Herskovits's tabulation of data from Elizabeth Donnan's *Documents Illustrative of the History of the Slave Trade to America*, Virginia imported some 52,000 slaves between 1710 and 1769, but the origin of some 20,000 was given only as "Africa" (table 9). This shows that Virginia had no strict selective policy or strong preference for any particular African ethnic group. While Virginians showed some preference for Africans from the Senegambian coast and hinterland, they lacked the prejudice the South Carolina planters had against Igbo males and Africans from the Bight of Biafra, as indicated by the large numbers of Igbos Virginia imported. It is quite possible that South Carolina's merchants sent their male Igbo cargo exclusively to Virginia because of the refusal of local planters to purchase Igbo men.

These data indicate that many of the slaves coming into Virginia came from the West Indies, where they had already undergone an initial process of acculturation. By the time they settled in Virginia or North Carolina they had undergone a second stage of acculturation, losing more and more of their African heritage and culture with each stage of acculturation.

More recent data on slave importation into Virginia reveal, however, that Virginia imported a large number of Africans directly from Africa. A report to the Board of Trade showed that between June 1699 and October 1708, 6,607 Africans were brought in, only 679 by way of the West Indies (Barbados). Between 1699 and 1775 Virginia imported 69,006 blacks, and Virginia was second only to South Carolina in the direct African importation of slaves.[14]

The African Heritage in America

Jacques Maquet divided the cultural areas of black Africa into six civilizations—the civilizations of the bow, the clearings, the granaries, the spear, the cities, and industry. The ones that concern us here are the civilization of the clearings, which includes the Guinea Coast, part of Sierra Leone, Liberia, the Ivory Coast, the Bight of Biafra, and the Congo-Angola region, and the civilization of the cities, which encompasses the Guinea Coast, including parts of Senegambia and the Niger Delta. The people of the clearings were familiar with the cultivation practices for rice, indigo, cotton, yams, maize, sorghum, okra, and sesame. The urban dwellers based their civilization on trade and commerce, and they had strong centralized political authorities. They were also excellent cattlemen and agriculturalists, familiar with the cultivation of yams, maize, corn, okra, palm oil, and sorghum. The Ashanti and Dahomeans in particular perfected artworks in stone, bronze, and iron.

The African slaves' cultural heritage was based on numerous West and Central African cultures brought together collectively from Senegambia (Wolof, Mandingo, Malinke, Bambara, Fulani, Papel, Limba, Bola, and Balante), the Sierra Leone coast (Temne and Mende), the Liberian coast (Vai, De, Gola, Kisi, Bassa, and Grebo), and the Slave Coast (Yoruba, Nupe, Benin, Dahomean [Fon], Ewe, Ga, Popo, Edo-Bini, and Fante). From the Niger Delta came Efik-Ibibio, Ijaw, Ibani, and Igbos (Calabars). From the Central African coast came Bakongo, Malimbo, Bambo, Ndungo, Balimbe, Badongo, Luba, Loanga, Luango, and Ovimbundu.

African cultural patterns predominating in southern states clearly reflect the specific cultural groups imported. That is, the upper colonies tended to be most heavily populated by West Africans and the lower colonies by people from Central Africa. The upper colonies included New York, New Jersey, Massachusetts, Rhode Island, Connecticut, Maryland, Virginia, and North Carolina. The lower colonies included South Carolina, Georgia—eastern coastal areas that were a part of the original thirteen colonies—and northern Florida. The Deep South included the fertile delta region of Mississippi, central Alabama, and Louisiana.

TABLE 10. North American Slaveholders' Occupational Preferences in African Slaves

Occupation	African Ethnicity Preferred	Culture
House servant	Mandingo	Mande
	Yoruba (Nagoes)	Cross River
	Dahomean (Fon), Fanti	Akan
Artisan	Bambara, Melinke	Mande
	Whydah, Pawpaw (Popo), Coromantee (Asante-Fante)	Akan
Rice cultivator	Temne, Sherbro, Mende, Kishee (Kisi), Papel, Goree, Limba, Bola, Balante	Mande
	Vai, Gola, Bassa, Grebo	Mano River
Field slave	Calabar, Ebo (Igbo), Efik, Ibibio	Niger Delta
	Cabinda, Bakongo, Malimbo, Bambo, Ndungo, Congo, Balimbe, Badondo, Bambona, Luba, Loango, Luango, Umbundu, Ovimbundu, Pembe, Imbangala	Bantu

Data from U. B. Phillips, *American Negro Slavery* (New York: D. Appleton, 1940), 42; Phillips, *Life and Labor in the Old South* (Boston: Little, Brown, 1929), 190; and Daniel Littlefield, *Rice and Slaves* (Baton Rouge: Louisiana State University Press, 1981); Gilberto Freyre, *The Masters and the Slaves: A Study in the Development of Brazilian Civilization* (New York: Knopf, 1946).

An examination of contemporary sources makes it obvious that slave owners in America had specific preferences concerning the regional origin of potential slaves (table 10). Guinea, Old Calabar, Bonny, Calabar, Whydah, Pawpaw (Popo), and Nagoes were the names used in the historical literature to indicate the place of origin of slaves to be purchased for the American market. Whydah was the capital city of Dahomey. Pawpaw served as a common name for Popo, a port city in Dahomey. Nagoes commonly stood for the western Yoruba, and Old Calabar and Calabar were names for the Igbo region. The table shows that North Americans preferred Senegambians (Mandingos, Fulani, Bambaras, and Malinkes) as house servants—butlers, maids, nurses (nannies), chambermaids, and cooks. They wanted slaves from the West African region—Whydahs (Fons), Pawpaws (Fantes), Yorubas (Nagoes), and Coromantee (Asante-Fante)—to work as domestic servants and artisans. These groups were also employed as carriage drivers, gardeners, carpenters, barbers, stablemen, wheelwrights, wagoners, blacksmiths, sawyers, washers, and bricklayers. The North Americans imported Africans from the Windward or Grain Coast (Mande and Mano River groups) because of their familiarity with the cultivation of rice, indigo, and tobacco.

The Yorubas, Whydahs, and Pawpaws were sold exclusively to the American market because they were considered less rebellious than the Coromantees (Asante) of the Gold Coast (Ghana). According to U. B. Phillips the Whydahs, Pawpaws, and Nagoes were generally considered the most esteemed of all because they were "lusty and industrious, cheerful and believed to be submissive." These qualities and their "disposition to take floggings . . . made them ideal slaves for the generality of masters."[15]

The planters in North America were known to purchase slaves specifically from these groups in West Africa to serve as house servants and artisans. The Africans that were considered most suitable for the American market were the Senegambians, particularly Fulani, who "had a strong Arabic (Muslim) strain in their ancestry." Because they were believed to be of mixed heritage with an infusion of Arabic blood, they were considered the most intelligent Africans and were to be trained especially for domestic service and as handicraft workers. Phillips, quoting Edward Long, noted that "they are good commanders over other Negroes, having a high spirit and tolerable share of fidelity: but they are unfit for hard work, their bodies are not robust nor their constitution vigorous." The Mandingos were considered gentle in manner but prone to be thieves. Since they were believed to fatigue easily because of a delicate physique, they were employed in the distilleries and boiling houses and served as fire watchmen.[16]

West Africans selected to work in the fields generally came from Senegambia and included the Goree, Serer, Fula, Balante, and Papel. Groups preferred from the Sierra Leone region were the Mende and Temne. Africans from the Grain Coast chosen for agricultural labor were the Bassa, De, Gola, and Grebo. In South Carolina the Igbos were at the bottom of the preference list, imported primarily to be common field laborers. For still unknown reasons, Igbo women were highly sought after.

The Mandes also worked as rowers, transporting crops and supplies as they did in their traditional watercraft on the Senegal and Gambia Rivers. These coastal Africans imported the art of netcasting, which became an established tradition in the tidal shallows of Carolina. Men who could handle nets were also able to make them; in 1737 a runaway named Moses was regarded as "well known in Charleston having been a Fisherman there for some time and has been often employed in Knitting of nets."[17]

Evidence supporting the fact that house servants were recruited from specific ethnic groups from West Africa is found in Myrtie Long Candler's reminiscences of life in Georgia. She tells us that her family's house servant Black Mammy was said to be "descended originally from the Guinea tribe."[18] That Black Mammy was a house servant and came from Guinea was no accident.

A document showing a preference for Guinea Africans is a letter the Reverend John Urmstone wrote on December 15, 1716, from North Carolina, asking his correspondent to arrange for the purchase of Guinea Negroes, "three men of a middle stature about 20 years old and a Girl of about 16 years." He soon wrote again "insisting that he could not remain in North Carolina without two field workers and a domestic servant."[19] That Urmstone wanted Guinea Negroes to work as house servants and field workers suggests that Africans from the Guinea Coast were used both for field and domestic work, particularly in the cultivation of rice after the 1740s.

Igbos and Angolans from Central Africa were selected primarily for the field. Gilberto Freyre noted that "for the English colonies the criterion for the importation of slaves from Africa was almost wholly an agricultural one. What was preferred was brute strength, animal energy, the Negro . . . with good powers of (physical) resistance." Technological skills were also important, and planters were primarily concerned with how to apply such skills to agricultural pursuits in America.[20] Thus the majority of Angolans were used as field slaves because they were large and robust. The whole plantation system was supported by field slaves; they did the bulk of the work that made slavery efficient and economical.

The first preference in South Carolina was for Africans from the Gambia region, the Windward Coast, the Grain Coast, the Bight of Benin, and Angola. While Africans from the upper Guinea Coast were mostly pursued, planters were willing to invest in Angolans as prime field slaves. Historical documents show a strong relationship between type of agricultural cultivation and the various African ethnic groups being imported.

Maryland merchants also concluded that Gambia slaves were well suited to life in the Chesapeake area, and their preference was shared by other North American colonies.

In colonial Louisiana the French authorities favored Bambara slaves, much like the South Carolina planters. Africans were imported from Senegambia primarily because of their agricultural skills and familiarity with the cultivation of rice, millet, and maize, which they were assigned to cultivate in North America. The Mandes also were believed to be suited for house service in that they had been city dwellers throughout the Sudanic empire of western Africa. The women were trained to perform tasks similar to those they had performed in their home villages; they were wet nurses, cooks, and washer-women. According to

McGowan, "those slaves who did adapt were prepared by their background because of the similarity of the tasks they had performed in Africa." In other words, plantation tasks in North America did not place any new technological demands on African labor, and the Africans' familiarity with the cultivation of rice, corn, yams, and millet in the Senegambian hinterlands prepared them for the kind of labor that was required in the Mississippi Valley.[21]

Fulani accustomed to cattle raising in the Futa Jallon area of their homeland "oversaw the rapid expansion of the colonial cattle herd from a total of 500 in 1731 to 6,784 thirty years later." These Fulani, expert cattlemen, were responsible for introducing the husbandry patterns of open grazing practiced in the American cattle industry today. This African innovation allowed efficient use of abundant land and a limited labor force. The Europeans' initial attempts at raising livestock in North America had followed their custom of raising small herds confined to pastures. While settlers felt uneasy about open grazing at first, numerous Africans coming into South Carolina had witnessed and understood the success of this practice from their African experience. Peter Wood believes that from this early relation between cattle and Africans the word *cowboy* originated in the same way that a slave who worked in the house became known as a houseboy.[22]

Senegambians were also employed as medicine men, blacksmiths, harness makers, carpenters, and lumberjacks. They brought with them highly developed skills in metalworking, woodwork, leatherwork, pottery, and weaving. Other slaves "on most plantations were taught with systematic care to excel in cabinet-making, iron crafts, blacksmithing, various domestic work and tailoring," Edith Dabbs reported. "It is not uncommon for slaves to be taught by an apprentice-type association with skilled African craftsmen."[23]

Slave merchants took great care in their advertisements to inform potential buyers of the African region and geographic point of origin of the slaves being sold. This was noticeable throughout the history of the trade. Many of the advertisements referred to the southern planters' familiarity with African ethnic origins. Advertisements for slave cargo occasionally gave the source from which the Africans originated, and runaway notices clearly indicated that planters distinguished the Africans by the various parts of Africa they came from: "he is a young Angola Negro," "a very Black Mundingo [Mandingo] negro man," "a native Madagascar," "a Congo Negro Slave," "of the Suso Country," "New Negro Fellow . . . calls himself Bonna [Bonny] and says he came from a place of that name in Ibo country, in Africa."[24] A cargo from Angola was advertised as "mostly of the Masse-Congo country and are esteemed equal to the Gold Coast and Gambia slaves."[25]

American planters were also knowledgeable about the agricultural cultivation practices in various regions of West and Central Africa. The fact that they could identify the different African ethnic groups showed their familiarity. Generally we have been led to believe that North American planters were not very sophisticated about African ethnicity, but the sources suggest that they were familiar with rice, cotton, and indigo production in Africa and were often able to relate the various African ethnic groups to the types of cultivation found in Africa.

One notice of sale contains a clause referring to the African region and evidences a familiarity by the plantation owners with the "Negroes" experienced in rice planting: "the Negroes from this part of the coast of Africa are well acquainted with the cultivation of rice and are naturally industrious." Another states that Gold Coast Negroes "just arrived in the Brig Gambia . . . directly from Anamaboo. . . . A Cargo of very healthy prime Negroes, the greatest part of them are fit to be put into the field immediately."[26] Here we find the African place of origin identified with the type of labor task to be performed in America. Anamabo was a village of the Gold Coast, an area inhabited by the Fanti, a major Akan ethnic group. That the majority of this cargo would be assigned to the field was directly attributed to their acquaintance with the cultivation of rice, South Carolina's principal crop during the colonial period. Other slave advertisements mentioned other regions.

Conclusion

Slave artisans and domestic servants, mainly West Africans, worked in close proximity to European Americans and were forced to give up their cultural identities to reflect their masters' control and capacity to "civilize" the Africans. By contrast, field workers—largely Central Africans —were relatively removed from this controlling, "civilizing" influence. Given the constraints imposed on artisans and domestic servants by plantation owners, one may logically conclude that the cultures of the Congo-Angola region of Central Africa rather than those of West Africa were dominant in North America. West African culture nevertheless supplied mainstream southern society with Africanisms through a process of reciprocal acculturation between Africans and European Americans.

In the area of folklore, the Brer Rabbit, Brer Wolf, Brer Fox, and Sis' Nanny goat stories were part of the Wolof folk tales brought to America by the Hausa, Fulani, and Mandinka. Other West African tales of trick-sters and hares were also introduced. The hare story is also found in parts of Nigeria, Angola, and East Africa. The tortoise stories are found among the Yoruba, Igbo, and the Edo-Bini peoples of Nigeria. Other examples of folklore from West Africa are such tales as "Hare Tied in the Bean Farm" and "Three Tasks of the Hare." These tales, wide-spread among the Mandinka and Wolof, are common in black folklore in the United States. The Anansi (spider) stories were Akan in origin and remained completely intact in the New World.[27]

The Senegambians were the first African slaves to arrive in South Carolina, bringing with them a unique cultural heritage. The Wolofs' skills became an integral part of the practices of the North American plantation, where numerous African carryovers of Wolof origin were found. Mande and Wolof were the two most widespread languages of Senegambia. Bilingualism was important for trade and commerce in the region. In the 1700s Wolof was by far the dominant African culture on both the upper Guinea Coast and the coast of South Carolina. Abd al-Rahman Ibrahim (known as Prince on the plantation), a West African prince from the kingdom of Tambo in the Gambia, was sold into slavery in New Orleans in 1788 at the age of twenty-six. He was Fulbe (Fula) and spoke fluent Arabic and possibly Wolof and Mande as well as other African languages. That suggests that Wolof was the lingua franca of the plantations before the 1730s, after which large numbers of Bantu were imported into the American South.[28]

Because the Wolofs were predominantly house servants and arti-sans, having extensive contact with European Americans, they were the first Africans to have elements of their language and culture re-tained within the developing culture of America. David Dalby identified certain early linguistic retentions among this group and traced many Americanisms back to Wolof, including such words as *OK, bogus, boogie woogie, bug, john, phoney, yam, guy, honkie, dig, fuzz, jam, jamboree, hip-pie,* and *mumbo jumbo.*[29]

Many other enslaved Africans were employed as field slaves. This oc-cupation, in fact, was engaged in by the majority of Africans, suggesting that it was among the field slaves that much of African American culture and language evolved. These field slaves were mainly Central Africans who, unlike the Senegambians, brought a homogeneous culture identifi-able as Bantu. The cultural homogeneity of the Bantu is indicated by a common language.

Once the Bantu reached America they were able to retain much of their cultural identity. Enforced isolation of these Africans by plantation owners allowed them to retain their religion, philosophy, culture, folklore, folkways, folk beliefs, folk tales, storytelling, naming practices, home economics, arts, kinship, and music. These Africanisms were shared and adopted by the various African ethnic groups of the field slave community, and they gradually developed into African American cooking (soul food), music (jazz, blues, spirituals, gospels), language, religion, philosophy, customs, and arts.

Notes

This research was supported by the Ford Foundation Postdoctoral Fellowship for Minorities Program and with a Faculty Institutional Grant from California State University at Northridge. It was sponsored by the University of California at Los Angeles Center for Afro-American Studies and the UCLA Department of History.

1. Philip D. Curtin, *The Atlantic Slave Trade: A Census* (Madison: University of Wisconsin Press, 1969).

2. Melville J. Herskovits, *The New World Negro: Selected Papers in Afro-American Studies* (Bloomington: Indiana University Press, 1966), 117.

3. Curtin, *Atlantic Slave Trade*, 103–104, 128.

4. See Melville J. Herskovits, "A Preliminary Consideration of the Cultural Areas of Africa," *American Anthropologist* (1924).

5. Herskovits, *New World Negro*, 116.

6. See Winifred Vass, *The Bantu Speaking Heritage of the United States* (Los Angeles: UCLA, Center for Afro-American Studies, 1979).

7. Peter H. Wood, *Black Majority: Negroes in Colonial South Carolina from 1670 through the Stono Rebellion* (New York: Knopf, 1974), 6.

8. Ibid., 31.

9. Fayrer Hall, *The Importance of the British Plantations in America to This Kingdom* (London: J. Peele, 1731).

10. Wood, *Black Majority*, 132. Samuel Dyssli, December 3, 1737 (SCHGM), 90.

11. D. P. Gamble, *The Wolof of Senegambia* (London: International African Institute, 1957), 173.

12. Peter H. Wood, "More Like a Negro Country: Demographic Patterns in Colonial South Carolina 1700–1740," in Stanley L. Engerman and Eugene D. Genovese, eds., *Race and Slavery in the Western Hemisphere: Quantitative Studies* (Princeton, N.J.: Princeton University Press, 1975), 153.

13. Malcolm Guthrie, *The Bantu Languages of Western Equatorial Africa* (London: Oxford University Press, 1953).

14. Walter Minchinton, Celia King, and Peter Waite, eds., *Virginia Slave-Trade Statistics 1698–1775* (Richmond: Virginia State Library, 1984), xv.

15. U. B. Phillips, *Life and Labor in the Old South* (Boston: Little, Brown, 1929), 190.

16. U. B. Phillips, *American Negro Slavery* (New York: D. Appleton, 1940), 44.

17. Sir Harry H. Johnston, *The Negro in the New World* (London: Methuen, 1910), 31.

18. Mrs. Myrtie Long Candler, "Reminiscences of Life in Georgia during the 1850s and 1860s," *Georgia Historical Quarterly* (June 1949), 33(2):110.

19. Elizabeth Donnan, *Documents Illustrative of the History of the Slave Trade to America*, 4 (Washington, D.C.: Carnegie Institution, 1935), 235.

20. Gilberto Freyre, *The Masters and the Slaves: A Study in the Development of Brazilian Civilization* (New York: Knopf, 1946), 298.

21. James Thomas McGowan, *Creation of a Slave Society: Louisiana Plantations in the Eighteenth Century* (Rochester, N.Y.: University of Rochester, 1971).

22. Wood, *Black Majority*, 30–31.

23. Edith M. Dabbs, *Sea Island Diary: A History of St. Helena Island* (Spartanburg, S.C.: Reprint Company, 1983), 50.

24. *Virginia Gazette*, November 5, 1736; April 21, 1738; August 17, 1739; December 8, 1768; January 15, 1767; August 13, 1772.

25. *South Carolina Gazette*, June 6, 1771.

26. *South Carolina Gazette*, July 23, 1785.

27. Interview by author with David P. Gamble, December 5, 1985. D. J. Muffett, "Uncle Remus Was a Hausaman?" *Southern Folklore Quarterly* (1975), 39:151–66.

28. Terry Alford, *Prince among Slaves: The True Story of an African Prince Sold into Slavery in the American South* (New York: Harcourt Brace Jovanovich, 1977).

29. David Dalby, "The African Element in Black English," in Thomas Kochman, ed., *Rappin' and Stylin' Out* (Urbana: University of Illinois Press, 1972), 170–86.

Two

"What Africa Has Given America"[1]

African Continuities in the North American Diaspora

Joseph E. Holloway

Scholars attempting to define African American culture and language, as separate from Euro-American culture, have found a significant number of Africanisms in American culture. Scholars have long recognized African origins in the linguistic forms and cultural traits of African Americans, and assumed that these Africanisms derive principally from West Africa. This essay argues against the assumption of African cultural homogeneity and proposes, instead, that Africa possessed a conglomerate and heterogeneous culture. While West Africans arrived in North America in greater numbers, the Bantu of Central Africa had the largest homogeneous culture among the imported Africans and thus contributed significantly to the development of African American culture.

Although the usual assumption is that these Africanisms derive from West Africa, this assertion of African cultural homogeneity should be questioned. Africa has always had a conglomerate and heterogeneous collection of cultures. West Africans of a variety of origins came to North America in greater numbers, but the Bantu of Central Africa brought in the largest homogeneous culture. Thus Bantus as well as West Africans contributed significantly to the development of African American culture.

Enslaved Africans, not free to openly transport kinship, courts, religion, and material cultures, were forced to disguise or abandon them during the middle passage. Instead, they dematerialized their cultural artifacts during the middle passage to rematerialize African culture on their arrival in the New World. Africans arrived in the New World capable of using Old World knowledge to create New World realities.

Africans, and their descendants, contributed to the richness and fullness of American culture from its beginnings. Their contributions in early America, for which they have received little or no credit, are as varied as the development of the American dairy industry, open grazing of cattle, artificial insemination of cows, the development of vaccines including vaccination for smallpox, and cures for snake bites.

African stories and folklore, such as the Brer Rabbit, Brer Fox, and Chicken Little tales that originated in Africa, were absorbed into America's culture of childhood and laid a foundation for American nursery culture. Despite the limitations imposed by slavery, Africans and their descendants made substantial contributions to American culture in aesthetics, animal husbandry, agriculture, cuisine, food culture, folklore, folk medicine, and language. This chapter examines African contributions to American culture, beginning at the time of the transatlantic slave trade.

The Early Transatlantic Slave Trade

The transatlantic slave trade to the future United States was in full-scale operation by the late 1600s. Between 1650 and 1700, as a result of political disturbances in Senegambia, the dominant group of Africans imported to South Carolina were from "Guinea." Most were Wolof and other Senegambians such as Bambara, Fula, and Susu. The Wolof were the largest group of Africans to come to the American colonies in the seventeenth century and were predominantly house servants or indentured servants, as the legal status of slavery had not yet been formalized.

Having extensive, close contact with Euro-Americans, they were presumably the first Africans whose cultural elements and language were assimilated into and retained within the developing culture of America. They also had greater opportunity for admixture and interaction with other races than any other African groups in the early years.

At some time around the 1670s, the Wolof or Jolof Empire broke into a number of separate kingdoms because of a revolt instigated by Mauritanian Marabouts.[2] The disintegration of this once-large empire caused instability and eventually prolonged warfare. The long-term effect was that many Wolofs were taken as prisoners of war, sold to slavers, and transported to America. Thereafter, however, the Wolofs never again provided such a significant number of Africans to the North American slave markets.[3]

Angolans and the Eighteenth-Century
Slave Trade

By the 1700s, Angolans were the largest African group being imported to South Carolina. Peter Wood has found documents showing that during the five-year period between 1735 and 1740, 70 percent of all incoming Africans were Bantu in origin and came from the Angolan region. Out of a total importation of 11,562 Africans, 8,045 were from Angola. In addition, 705 Africans (6 percent of the total) were brought into South Carolina from Gambia, probably to be trained as house servants.[4]

This large number from Angola may have been one reason why Africans revolted and killed whites while trying to escape to Spanish Florida in 1739. Fewer Angolans were brought into the colony thereafter, as Southern planters mistrusted them after what became known as the Stono Rebellion.

Even with a 30 percent drop in their entry numbers, Bantu-speaking Africans still represented the majority of Africans working in the fields of South Carolina. Wood estimates that roughly seven out of every ten Africans imported into Charleston during this period came from the areas then called Angola, near the Kongo River. Most of these Bantus originated in Cabinda, Ambriz, Ambrizete, Luanda, Benguela, and other Kongo-Angolan ports.

The evidence suggests that the Bantus were the largest constituency of Africans in South Carolina, and possibly in other areas of the southeastern United States. Given the homogeneity of Bantu cultures and their strong similarities in language, this group doubtlessly dominated and influenced surrounding larger West African groups. Also, inasmuch as the Bantus were predominantly field hands or used in activities that required little or no contact with Euro-Americans, they did not confront the problem of acculturation as directly and intensely as did the West African domestic servants and artisans. Coexisting in relative isolation from other groups, the Bantus were able to maintain a strong sense of unity, a cultural heritage, which they passed on to their American descendants.

Elizabeth Donnan's collection of the records of slave importing companies (1935) shows the number of Africans carried by each vessel and the ports from which they were received. These data indicate that planters in South Carolina and Virginia showed some preference for Africans from the Senegambian Coast and its hinterland. It is quite possible that South Carolina merchants sent their male Igbo cargo to North Carolina because of the refusal by local planters to purchase Igbo men and Africans from the Bight of Biafra. However, Igbo women were highly desired as concubines.

In the early years of the slave trade, Senegal was the most important region in the trade. In the late eighteenth century, however, slave ships turned their attention increasingly to Central Africa, a shift that accelerated with British suppression of the Atlantic slave trade in 1807. By the 1780s, Kongo-Angola traffic was already exceeding West African traffic. The Bantu regions of Africa (Angola, Congo, Benguela, and Cabinda) sent significant slave cargoes to South Carolina. These Africans brought a homogeneous culture identifiable as Bantu.

Once the African Bantus reached the Sea Islands of South Carolina, they were able to retain much of their cultural identity because "New Africans" (many Bantus among them) were continually brought from Africa as field slaves to reinforce the labor supply. The strong African tradition of the Sea Islands of South Carolina is a result of this continued influx directly from Africa (not from the West Indies as was once commonly believed).

Curtin identified the African coastal region as the place of origin of slaves imported into Virginia and South Carolina. Senegambia, Windward Coast, and Gold Coast people represented 49 percent of the Africans brought into South Carolina. Collectively, West Africans from Senegambia through the Bight of Benin represented 60 percent of the Africans imported into South Carolina. Still, the Angolans clearly formed the largest single ethnic group (40 percent) imported into South Carolina, and they also formed a culturally homogeneous group on North American plantations.[5]

African cultural patterns predominating in Southern states clearly reflected the specific cultural groups imported into the United States. That is, the Upper South tended to be populated by Africans from West Africa, and the Lower South by Africans from Central Africa. The Upper South generally reached from Maryland and Virginia west into Kentucky and North Carolina. The Lower South, or Deep South, included South Carolina and Georgia as well as the fertile Delta region of Mississippi, central Alabama, and Louisiana. North Carolina and Tennessee were culturally intermediate areas. Southern Virginia and South Carolina were centers of dense African American populations that were derived from different regions of Africa and spread west with the western expansion of the United States following the Revolutionary War.

The Bantu versus the Mande
on the Plantation

Africans transported during the colonial period were from the Guinea Coast, largely Wolof, Fulani, Mandingo, and Bambara. Africans from the Senegambia were considered taller and of lighter complexions. "A preference for light-skinned slaves to work in the house existed in Charleston, New Orleans, and some other cities."[6] While the Mandes were often enslaved as craftsmen, artisans, and house servants, the field slaves were mainly Central Africans who, unlike the Senegambians, brought a homogeneous, identifiable culture. The Bantus often possessed good metallurgical and woodworking skills. They had a particular skill in iron working, which they used in making the wrought-iron balconies of New Orleans and Charleston. As field workers, the Bantus were kept away from the developing mainstream of white American culture. This isolation allowed Bantu culture to escape acculturation and maintain homogeneity.

Certain ethnic groups from the Kongo-Angola region had a reputation for being adept at acquiring mechanical skills. Also, many were trained in, and even dominated, the barbering trade in South Carolina and performed the same tasks as free barbers, shaving, dressing hair, and setting wigs. They worked as personal body servants and also were employed in shops owned by their masters.

Bantu contributions to South Carolina and Louisiana include not only the popular wrought-iron balconies but also forms of woodcarvings, basketry, woven cloth, and early aspects of ceramics such as clay-baked figurines and pottery. Cosmograms, grave designs and decorations, and funeral practices, including the wake, are also Bantu in origin. Distinctive Bantu musical contributions include Bantu instruments such as banjos, drums, diddley bows, mouthbows, quilts, washtub bass, jugs, gongs, bells, rattles, idiophones, and the lokoimni, a five-stringed harp.

The Bantus constituted the largest African group in South Carolina, and possibly in several other areas of the southeastern United States, including Alabama and Louisiana. Melville J. Herskovits noted that the Bantu center in North America was the South Carolina Sea Islands off the coast of Carolina.

Given the homogeneity of Bantu culture and the strong similarities among Bantu languages, this group no doubt influenced West African groups of larger size. Also, since the Bantus were predominantly field hands or did other work that required little or no contact with European Americans, they were not confronted with the same problems of acculturation West African domestic servants and artisans experienced. Coexisting in relative isolation from other groups, the Bantus were able to maintain a strong sense of unity and retain a cultural vitality that laid a foundation for American culture. That is, whereas the Mande had a greater influence on the developing white American culture, the Bantu had the greatest influence on the developing black American culture.

African Ethnicity on
the American Plantations

The planters' preference in South Carolina was for Africans from the Gambia region, the Windward Coast, the Grain Coast, the Bight of Benin and Angola. One possible reason why Africans from Dahomey

were rare in Charleston might be their notoriously strong military tradition, which aroused fear of possible insurrections in the mind of
Charleston's planters. South Carolinians liked Gold Coast Africans
(Akan), but not as much as Virginia and Maryland did. Although Africans from the Upper Guinea Coast were highly prized, planters were
more willing to invest in Angolans as prime field slaves.

   Slave merchants took great care, throughout the entire history of the
South Carolinian trade, to inform potential buyers of the African region
and geographic point of origination of the slaves being sold. Many advertisements refer to the Southern planters' familiarity with African
ethnic origins, and advertisements for slave cargo occasionally gave the
source from which the Africans originated. A cargo from Angola was
advertised in the June 6, 1771, *South Carolina Gazette* as "mostly of
the Masse-Congo country and are esteemed equal to the Gold Coast
and Gambia slaves."[7] Also, a notice in the *Virginia Gazette* during the
eighteenth century gives clear evidence that planters distinguished escaped enslaved Africans by the various parts of Africa they came from,
describing the escapees as "a young Angola Negro," "a very Black
Mundigo [Mandingo] negro man," "a native Madagascar," "a Congo
Negro Slave, of the Suso Country," "New Negro Fellow . . . calls himself Bonna (Bonny) and says he came from a place of that name in Ibo
country, in Africa," or "marked in the face as the Gold Coast slaves
generally are."

   It was once believed that North American planters were unsophisti-
cated about African ethnicity, but an examination of sources suggests
they were familiar with the rice, cotton, and indigo production in Africa
and were often able to relate the various African ethnic groups to the
types of agricultural cultivation found in Africa. It seems clear that
South Carolina planters did not purchase Africans blindly to work
on their plantations. Instead, planters knew and understood cultural
backgrounds and purchased with the expectation of using agricultural
knowledge and skills on the North American plantations, for example,
tending cattle, fishing, boating, house service, and blacksmithing.

   The planters in North America were known to purchase Africans
from West Africa to serve as house servants and artisans. Senegambians
(Mandingo, Wolof, Serer, Fulani, and Bambara) were considered the
most intelligent of Africans (because they were believed to be of mixed
heritage, with Arabic ancestry) and were trained for domestic service
and as handicraft workers.[8] Mandingoes were considered gentle in manner but prone to thievery. Since they were thought to tire easily because
of their delicate physiques, they served as watchmen against fires rather
than as field slaves.

Africans transported during the colonial period were from the Guinea Coast, largely Wolof, Fulani, Mande, Bambara, and a few Yoruba during the early period. Africans from the Senegambia were taller and lighter in complexion. "A preference for light-skinned Africans to work in the house existed in Charleston, New Orleans, and some other cities."[9] While the Senegambians (Mandes) were preferred as house servants, the Kongos, Angolans, and Igbos were preferred for the field, except for Igbo women, who were highly sought after as concubines. The possession of technological skills was also important, and planters explored ways to apply such skills to agricultural pursuits.

The majority of Angolans were used primarily as field slaves because they were large and robust. They were imported in large numbers, especially in the eighteenth century, and were the dominant group in South Carolina and Louisiana. Because they were primarily field slaves, they had little contact with the planter class. Their acculturation during the colonial period was long and slow in contrast to house servants, who lived in close proximity to whites.

In short, South Carolina's planters wanted Gambians first and, next, "Heathy young Fantees, Coromantines, Negroes from Bassa on the Windward Coast, from Bance Island," and Angolans from Central Africa. Africans from the Bight, Igbos, and Calabar (Efik-Ibibio) were the least desired of all, and "captains were frequently urged not to bring them to the South Carolinian market."[10]

African Crops to the New World

Crops brought directly from Africa during the transatlantic slave trade include rice, okra, tania, blackeyed peas, and kidney and lima beans; Africans ate them on board the slave ships. Other crops brought from Africa included peanuts (originating from South America), millet, sorghum, guinea melon, watermelon, yams (Dioscorea cayanensis), and sesame (benne).[11] These crops found their way into American food ways and appeared among the ingredients in the earliest cookbooks written by Southern American whites.

As early as 1687, a young physician, Sir Hans Sloane, living in the West Indies, found many of these crops growing on the island of Jamaica. These plants reached the mainland of North America either directly from Africa, or with enslaved Africans destined for North America by way of trade with the West Indies. These crops may have found a home in North America even before Sloane's encounter. Eventually, however, these crops went from use exclusively by Africans in North America to being part of white Southern cuisine.

Blackeyed peas first came to the New World as food for slaves during the transatlantic slave trade, arriving in Jamaica around 1675, spreading throughout the West Indies, and finally reaching Florida by 1700, North Carolina in 1738, and Virginia by 1775. Slave planter William Byrd mentions blackeyed peas in his writings in 1738. By the time of the American Revolution, blackeyed peas were firmly established in America as a part of the general cuisine.

George Washington wrote in a letter in 1791 that "pease" (blackeyed peas) were rarely grown in Virginia. In 1792 he brought forty bushels of seeds for planting on his plantation. Blackeyed peas became one of the most popular food crops in the southern part of the United States. George Washington later referred to them as "callicance" and "cornfield peas" because of the early custom of planting them between the rows of field corn.

Okra arrived in the New World during the transatlantic slave trade in the 1600s. Okra, or gumbo as it is called in Africa, found exceptional popularity in New Orleans. In French Louisiana, Creole cuisine and African cooking came together to produce the unique cuisine of New Orleans. Gumbo is a popular stew or soup, mixing other vegetables with okra, the main ingredient, and thickened with powder from sassafras leaves (gumbo file). One observer in 1748 noted that thickened soup was a delicacy liked by blacks. Okra was already commonly used by American whites before the American Revolution.

Enslaved Africans used the young fruit that contains the vegetable mucilage to eat by boiling. The leaves also were used medicinally to soften a cataplasm, and on the plantations of South Carolina seeds were used to make a coffee substitute. Okra was popular among women to produce abortion by lubricating the uterine passage with the slimy pods. In West Africa, women still use okra today to produce abortion, using the same method.

The next important crop to arrive to the United States by way of Africa was the peanut. The peanut is known by several names, including groundnut, earth nut, and ground peas. Two other words of African origin are pindar and goober. Thomas Jefferson and George Washington called peanuts peendar and pindars (1794, 1798). The word was in use before the Revolutionary War. The word goober was used principally in the nineteenth century. The period of its greatest popularity was the 1860s, when the Civil War song, "Goober Peas," appeared. After the war, when published, its words were attributed to "A. Pindar" and its music to "P. Nutt."

The American peanut has an interesting history. Although indigenous to South America as a crop, it was first brought to Africa by Portuguese sailors and then to Virginia from Africa by enslaved Africans. The peanut was used to feed Africans on the middle passage. One New World observer noted, "The first I ever saw of these [peanuts] growing was the Negro's plantation who affirmed, that they grew in great plenty in their country." In Africa, peanut stews, soups, and gravies serve as an important part of any meal. However, nut soups in the American South, although of African origin, are no longer enjoyed by the descendants of Africans but are associated with European Americans instead.[12]

George Washington Carver researched the peanut as a crop, and from his experiments he found that they contained water, fats, oils, gums, resins, sugar, starches, pectins, pentosans, and proteins. From these compounds he identified over three hundred possible peanut products, including "Jersey milk," which could produce butter and cheese. Other products were instant coffee, flour, face cream, bleach, synthetic rubber, and linoleum.

Dr. Carver found rubbing peanut oil on muscles helped rejuvenate them. Dr. Carver also created for Gandhi peanut milk and a soybean formula that he found to be a healthful part of his diet.

Sesame first arrived from Africa to South Carolina by 1730, and in the same year a Carolinian sent sesame and sesame oil to London. This was a matter of considerable importance in Colonial America and England because table oil was one of the products England hoped to obtain by colonizing the New World. To avoid importing olive oil for cooking, Britain encouraged production of table oils by offering bounties on edible oils. By 1733, a book on gardening published in London noted the cultivation of the sesame plant and its usefulness as a source of "sallet-oil." Enslaved Africans also grew sesame for other uses. Thomas Jefferson noted in the 1770s that benne (another name for sesame) was eaten raw, toasted or boiled in soups by African slaves. Jefferson also noted that slaves baked sesame in breads, boiled it in greens, and used it to enrich broth. Today sesame is used primarily as bread topping.

The first successful cultivation of rice in the United States was accomplished in the South Carolina Sea Islands by an African woman who later taught her planter how to cultivate rice. The first rice seeds were imported directly from the Island of Madagascar in 1685, with Africans supplying the labor and technical expertise.[13] African experts in rice cultivation were brought directly from the island of Goree to teach Europeans how to cultivate this cash crop.

House servants, while learning from the planters, also brought African culinary taste into the plantation mansions. African cooks in the "Big House" introduced their native African crops and foods, thus becoming intermediaries in the melding of African and European culinary cultures. African cooks introduced deep fat frying, a cooking technique that originated from Africa. Long before refrigeration, Africans understood how deep fat frying of chicken or beef could preserve these foods for a time.

Using their indigenous crops, enslaved Africans recreated traditional African cuisine. One such dish is fufu. In South Carolina this dish is called "turn meal and flour." This meal is prepared by boiling water and adding flour while stirring the ingredients, hence the name. Throughout Africa, fufu is a highly favored staple, a traditional West and Central African meal eaten from Senegambia to Angola. Africans prepare fufu by mixing palm oil and flour. From these fufu mixtures, slaves made hoecake in the fields that later evolved into pancakes and hot water cornbread. Corn bread, prepared by African slaves, was similar to African millet bread.

In the reports of slavers found in the journal entry from the ship *Mary*, June 20, 1796, "Cornbread" was mentioned as one of the African foods provided for their cargo. The report also mentions a "woman cleaning rice and grinding corn for corn cakes." Corn fried into cakes is still prepared throughout Africa today.

As early as 1739, naturalist Mark Catesby noted that slaves made a mush from the corn meal called pone bread. He also noticed that slaves took hominy Indian corn and made grits, a food similar to the African dish called Eba. Catesby observed in 1747 that Guinea corn (sorghum vulgare) and Indian corn were used interchangeably by blacks. He wrote that "little of this grain is propagated, and that chiefly by negroes, who make bread of it, and boil it in like manner of firmety. It [*sic*] chief use is for feeding fowls. . . . It was first introduced from Africa by the negroes."[14] Lawson noted that Guinea corn is used mostly for hogs and poultry (by whites), adding that enslaved Africans ate nothing but Indian corn.[15]

From their food traditions, Africans contributed greatly to the culinary taste of America, and Southern cooking is therefore a cultural experience to which both blacks and whites contributed. Today's black American cuisine is strongly influenced by the African style of cooking, a carryover of this antebellum period. "Soul food" itself goes back to days when plantation owners gave slaves discarded animal parts, such as hog maw (stomach), hog jowl, pigs' feet, ham hocks, and pig intestines. Blacks took this throwaway and added a touch of African culinary technique to create tasty dishes. Collard greens and dandelion greens were first recorded in 1887. Poke greens, turnip greens, and blackeyed peas were first brought to Jamaica from Africa in 1674 and arrived in North

America in 1738. All of these African foods contributed to the great diversity of American cuisine.[16]

Mande and Wolof on the Plantation

Mande and Wolof were the two most widespread languages of the Senegambia. Bilingualism was important for trade and commerce in the region. During the 1700s, Wolof was by far the most dominant African culture found in the upper Guinea Coast and the coast of South Carolina. The West African traders traded between Sierra Leone and Liberia, transmitting folklore, cuisine, and language.

Because of their Civil War between 1685 and 1700, many Wolof arrived in Colonial America as war captives, the only time that they came into North America in such numbers. Later, in 1772, Fenda Lawrence, a Gambian slave trader, visited the American South as a free tourist and to conduct business. The government of Georgia issued her a certificate stating that "a free black woman and heretofore a considerable trader in the River Gambia on the Coast of Africa, hath voluntarily come to be and remain for some time in this province," with permission to "pass and repass unmolested with the said province on her lawful and necessary occasion."[17] Fenda Lawrence probably spoke Wolof and some creole pidgin English, the trade language of the West African Coast. She apparently moved through the South without any problems and returned back to the Gambia to continue her trade in slaves and other commodities.

Another African from the Gambia, Job Ben Solomon, spent a brief time as a slave in Maryland. He attracted the attention of James Oglethorpe by means of a letter written in Arabic (which indicated the slave was literate in the Arabic language). Oglethorpe had Solomon purchased from his master and sent to England, where he was presented at Court, given gifts and later, in 1734, sent home as a free man. He returned as a celebrity among his fellow Foulahs and neighboring Jolofs (Wolofs) and Mandingoes.

Abd al-Rahman Ibrahim (known as Prince on the plantation), a West African prince from the kingdom of Tambo located in the Gambia, was not as fortunate as Fenda Lawrence. Instead of seeing the South as a tourist, he was sold into slavery in New Orleans in 1788 at the age of twenty-six. He was Fulbe (Fulani) and spoke fluent Arabic, Wolof, and Mande as well as several local dialects. Wolof was the lingua franca of the American South prior to the 1730s when Bantus were brought in. Following the intercession of President John Quincy Adams, Ibrahim was set free after forty years of bondage. Southern planters generally accorded Muslims a greater degree of respect than Africans from non-Muslim regions.[18]

Tales Out Of Africa

Brer Rabbit, Sis' Nanny Goat, and others were characters in Wolof, Hausa, Fula (Fulani), and Mandinka (Mandingo) folklore transported to the New World. Other West African tales, such as those involving a Trickster Hare, were also introduced. The Hare (Rabbit) stories also can be found in parts of Nigeria, Angola, and East Africa. The Tortoise stories are found among the Yoruba, Igbo, and Edo-Bini people of Nigeria.

Other examples of folklore from West Africa are tales such as the "Hare Tied in the Bean Farm," or the "Three Tasks of the Hare" (where he goes to ask God for more Wisdom). These tales are widespread among the Mandinka and Wolof of West Africa and also common in black American folklore.[19] Most of the Uncle Remus stories, as retold in the Sea Islands (cf. Walt Disney's "Song of the South"), are African in origin, especially Hausa and Mandinka. These African tales, especially such stories as "Chicken Little," laid the foundation for American nursery tales. More recently, the influence of Brer Rabbit on contemporary America's most famous trickster rabbit, Bugs Bunny, has been noticed.[20]

The Anansi (Spider) stories, Akan in origin, remained intact in the New World. In Surinam, these stories are referred to as Anansitori. The West Indian black people of Curacao call them Cuenta de Nansi. The Spider Trickster Anansi tales maintain a peripheral existence as the "Aunt Nancy" stories of the Georgia and South Carolina Sea Islands. The Anansi stories were told in nineteenth-century United States among a limited group of people, mainly Gullahs. After the twentieth-century influx of West Indians into America, the Anansi tales again became widespread.

The Hare and Hyena tales correspond to Brer Rabbit and Brer Fox tales as Trickster figures brought to North America by the Wolof. These tales from the Mandinka heartland spread south to countries such as Liberia, Sierra Leone, and Cote d'Ivoire. As the Mandinka Jula traders migrated, they brought these tales with them. The Africans who came from those areas during the transatlantic slave trade brought the folklore and tales as part of their oral tradition. African slaves who fled to the Creek Indians introduced these West African Trickster tales, and the Seminoles in Florida also adopted them.[21]

African Dances in North America

Dance is part of folk tradition. Enslaved Africans maintained continuity in their music, song, and dance cultures, as well as in the religions that influenced those cultures, as they adapted to life in North America. Many African dances survived because they were reshaped and adopted by European Americans, while others remained intact, or changed with the new circumstances. For example, the ring shout started as a sacred Kongolese dance but later found expression in nonsacred dance.

In both Africa and the New World, the circle ritual meant different things in different cultures. In the Kongo, the ring shout-circle is identical to the Gullah counter-clockwise dance, which is linked to the most important African ceremony—rites of passage. Among the Mande, the circle dance is a part of the marriage and birth ceremonies, and in Wolof culture, the ring circle is central to most dancing. The Bamboula and the Calinda, variations of voodoo dance, became popular forms of dance expression in early New Orleans. The Cakewalk and the Charleston traveled from Africa to become integral to American dance forms on the American plantation.

The Calinda, also known as La Calinda, is one of the earliest forms of African dance seen in America. This Kongo/Angolan dance first became popular in Santo Domingo, then in Haiti and New Orleans. La Calinda is first reported by Dessalles in 1654 and by a French monk, Jean Baptiste Labat, who went to Martinque as a missionary in 1694. The Calinda is a variation of a dance used in voodoo ceremonies, and is always performed by male and female dancers in couples. The dancers move to the middle of the circle and start dancing. Each dancer chooses a partner and performs the dance, with few variations, by taking a step in which every leg is straightened and pulled back alternatively with a quick strike, sometimes on point, sometimes with a grounded heel. This dance is performed in a manner slightly similar to that of the Anglaise. The male dancer turns by himself or goes around his partner, who also makes a turn and changes her position while waving the ends of a handkerchief. Her partner raises his hands in almost clenched fists up and down alternately, with his elbows close to his body. This dance is vivid and lively. In 1704, records show that a police ordinance was issued prohibiting night gatherings from performing the Calinda on plantations.[22]

The dance now known as the Charleston had the greatest influence on American dance culture of any imported African dance. It is a form of jitterbug dance, which is a general term applied to unconventional, often formless and violent, social dances performed to syncopated music. Enslaved Africans brought it from the Kongo to Charleston, South Carolina, as the Juba dance, which then slowly evolved into what is now the Charleston. This one-legged sembuka step, over-and-cross, arrived in Charleston between 1735 and 1740. Similar in style to the "one-legged" sembuka-style dancing found in northern Kongo, the dance consists of "patting" (otherwise known as "patting Juba"), stamping, clapping, and slapping of arms, chest, and so forth.

The name "Charleston" was given to the Juba dance by European Americans. In Africa, however, the dance is called the Juba or Djouba. The word Juba was used for many things, such as songs sung on the plantation, the food given to the field slaves, and the dance that later became known as the Charleston. The Juba dance itself was primarily a competitive dance of skill.

Later, the Charleston dance, which had evolved over the centuries, spread northward as African Americans migrated north. At first, the step was a simple twisting of the feet to rhythm in a lazy sort of way. When the dance hit Harlem, a new version surfaced. It became a fast kicking of the feet both forward and backward, later done with a tap.

The Charleston and other African dances started out as spectator dances, then became participant dances. Nevertheless, the Charleston became so popular that a premium was even placed on hiring of black domestics who could dance it well enough to teach the lady of the house. The dance also can be seen in other parts of the world, such as in Haiti, where it is called La Martinique. Josephine Baker, the famed black entertainer, introduced this dance to European audiences. It became increasingly popular during the 1920s and today, when we hear of the Charleston, it is usually associated with the "Roaring Twenties."[23]

The Ombliguide was a dance performed by slaves in la Place du Congo, Kongo Square, in old New Orleans. An ordinance of the Municipal Council, adopted on October 15, 1817, made the name of this traditional place law. It was considered one of the unique attractions of old New Orleans, ranking second only to the Quadroon Ball. At the square, women wore dotted calico dresses, and brightly colored Madras headgear tied about their hair to form the popular headdress called the tignon. Children wore garments with bright feathers and bits of ribbon.

Slaves came regularly to Kongo Square to perform the Ombliguide and other Kongo dances, such as the Calinda, Bamboula, and Chica, all transplanted directed from Central Africa.[24] The Ombliguide was criticized in 1766 by the New Orleans City Council. Performed by four men and four women, it involves sensual movements with navel-to-navel contact, a common trait of Angolan traditional dancing.

Figure 1.   The Bamboula. Courtesy of The Historic New Orleans Collection.

Folk Medicine and the Root Doctor

African medical knowledge of diseases in both the Old and the New
Worlds crossed the Atlantic Ocean and contributed to the medical well-
being of Americans. Although African American practitioners as a group
were considered folk and root doctors as compared to their European
counterparts, African American medical practices were generally superior in that era.[25] For example, Africans are credited with introducing
certain folk treatments for small pox. Famed anthropologist R. S. Rattray reported that variolation (use of the serum from lesions) of smallpox was practiced "from time immemorial by the Akan of Ghana."
Likewise, the Scottish explorer Mungo Park, during his travels to the
windward Coast at the end of the eighteenth century, was informed by
a European doctor stationed there that the people of the Gambia practiced inoculation for small pox as their traditional prevention.[26]

In 1729 Lieutenant Governor William Gooch of Virginia manumit-
ted a slave named Panpan for his secret concoction of roots and herbs
because it was a cure for yaws and for syphilis.[27] He was freed from
slavery at a cost of sixty pounds. Bryan Edwards, listening to one of his
Akan women, learned that vaccination was a medical technique used on

the Gold Coast to inoculate children with infectious matter from yaws, thus giving them a mild case of the disease and providing resistance later in life. "Mothers inoculate their infants about the period of weaning, that they may be indulged in nursing them until their recovery; and many believe, from an African opinion and custom in that country, that children should undergo the disease at an early period of life."[28]

In another example, an African slave by the name of Caesar was known to have cured several persons who had been poisoned. One, an overseer named Henry Middleton, found Caesar's antidote effective. Caesar cured Middleton from intolerable pain in the "stomack and bowels" after he had found no cure or relief in the medicines of the "most skilful doctors of the country."[29] Caesar also cured a person bitten by a rattlesnake and a man afflicted with yaws with his body covered from "top to toe" with scabs. The cure for yaws required the use of flowers of sulphur and burnt niccars. He also cured those afflicted with the deadly symptoms of pleurisies.[30] For Caesar's antidote to poison and snake bite,[31] he was given his freedom and financial compensation for life.

Sampson, another African slave, gained his freedom as a reward for discovering a cure for rattlesnake bites.[32] His cure was said to have been even more effective than Caesar's. Colonial planters generally had more respect for their enslaved Africans' knowledge of herbs, medicines, and poison than did the so-called doctors of the era. Enslaved Africans brought indigenous skills and knowledge to North America directly from Africa. They contributed these cultural traditions concerning the uses of plants, as well as the new flora they encountered in South Carolina, in many ways similar to that of West and Central Africa.

Sampson walked into the Commons House of Assembly of South Carolina on May 9, 1754, and offered a cure for rattlesnake bites. To demonstrate the effectiveness of his medicines, he held in his hand poisonous snakes and then pressed them against his flesh and was bitten several times. He was bitten by so many venomous snakes that it was doubtful if he would recover. Sampson declared that he would return in three days alive and well. To everyone's surprise, he returned alive and offered the cure. In proof of the efficacy of his medicines, Sampson on several occasions "suffered himself to be bitten by the most venomous Snakes, and once let his Wounds come so near a Mortification, that it was doubted whether he could recover, yet he cured himself with them; he disarmed any Snake of its Venom with some one of the Herbs."[33] He was immediately given his freedom and a cash annuity for life.

Likewise, Africans knew that smallpox inoculation was done by simply taking some of the sap from the scalp and inoculating those who were not exposed. Smallpox was the most feared epidemic in Colonial

America. Charleston, for example, had several smallpox epidemics during that period. However, the outbreak of spring 1760, was the most widespread. South Carolina had adopted the African practice of using individuals who had previously had smallpox to inoculate the population. In Charleston, townspeople had protested that the government had "negroes seized with that Distemper in the country are immediately brought to town and many others Persons are daily inoculated in order to go through the disease in Charles Town." In other words, "Persons are brought in from the Country, to take the Disease by Innoculation, which Practice, it not speedily prevented."[34]

Through the root doctor, Africans brought holistic health practices to American plantations. African healers brought knowledge of treatment for many diseases, and health practitioners such as midwives and nurses contributed to New World health care services. During antebellum plantation slavery, midwives delivered more than 90 percent of children born during the early nineteenth century, as had been the custom in Africa.

Africans contributed to cures of numerous New World diseases based on their knowledge of similar diseases from the Old World. Their gift of medicine enriched the development medical field of America, fusing the worlds of Africa and Europe, adopting practical use as well as a holistic approach to curing and treating diseases.

African Cultural Influences on European Americans[35]

Most people are not aware that one in every five of the cowboys of the American West was black, contrary to the usual media portrayal of white cowboy historical figures. Also, cowboy culture has some African roots, only recently being recognized. The annual north-south migratory pattern followed by the cowboy is unlike the cattle-keeping patterns of Europe but analogous to the migratory patterns of the Fulani cattle herders, who live scattered from the Senegambia through Nigeria and Niger to the Sudan. Texas (African) longhorns were on the first slave ships to Mexico, followed by African cattle egrets that later migrated farther north. Many details of cowboy life, work, and even material culture, such as open grazing of cattle, can be traced to Fulani antecedents, but historians of the American West have rarely investigated this.

The literature on black cowboys, like that for African contributions to American culture in general, is meager. Major works about cowboys and the American West have ignored black Americans. Black cowboys have been left out of most movies and historical accounts of this period. Also omitted are the accounts of African cattle brought with enslaved Africans to the New World.

Even the search for surviving African culture among white Americans has largely ignored cowboy culture. Historian Peter Wood, however, found that the survival of African culture among white Americans was pervasive and specific, reaching almost every aspect of American culture. He has argued that the American cattle industry owes its origins to Africans.

For example, Fulanis from the Futa Jallon, accustomed to cattle raising, oversaw the rapid expansion of the British American cattle herds in the middle of the eighteenth century. They were responsible for introducing patterns of "open grazing," now practiced throughout the American cattle industry. Wood believes that the word cowboy originated from this early relationship among cattle, Africans, and Europeans in the colonial period when African labor and skills were still closely associated with cattle raising. As late as 1865, following the Civil War, Africans whose livestock responsibilities were with cattle were referred to as "cowboys" in plantation records. After 1865, whites associated with the cattle industry referred to themselves as "cattlemen" to distinguish themselves from black "cowboys."[36] The annual north-south migratory patterns followed by the cowboys are directly related to the migratory patterns of the Fulani cattle herders who travel from the Senegambia throughout Nigeria and Niger.

Many words associated with cowboy culture and originating from this relationship have found their way into American English. For example, bronco (probably of Efik/Ibibio and Spanish origins) was used centuries ago by the Spanish and by enslaved Africans working with cattle and horses. Buckra, also deriving from this relationship, comes from mbakara, the Efik/Ibibio word for "white man." Buckaroo, also from mbakara, was used to describe a class of whites who worked as bronco busters. Dogies, a word that even found its way into popular cowboy songs, as in "get along little dogies," originated from the Kimbundu kidogo, a little something, and (ki) dodo, small. After the Civil War, when large cattle roundups became necessary because of neglect during the war, black American cowboys introduced such Africanisms to cowboy language and songs.

Wolof: Influences on American English

As noted earlier, the Wolof arrived in large numbers in the American South between 1670 to 1700 as a result of political disturbances in Senegambia with other Senegambians.[37] The Wolofs were the largest group of Africans to come to the American colonies in the seventeenth century and were predominantly house servants. As they had extensive, close contact with European Americans, they may have been the first Africans whose cultural elements and language were assimilated into and retained within the developing culture of America. They also had greater opportunity for admixture and interaction with whites than any other African group in the early years.

As a result of numerous Wolofs on American plantations in the early years, Wolof served as a lingua franca during the 1700s, and many words of Wolof origins found their way into American English. The Wolof had a greater impact on the language than their numbers would indicate. For example, one Wolof/Mande word now used throughout the world is "okay," or "O.K." Americans were mystified by its origins from the time of its popularization around 1839. Clues were found in the nineteenth-century black English of Jamaica, Surinam, and the Gullah speech of South Carolina, all of which have numerous forms of the word. Two prime examples from Mande and Wolof are o ke, "that's it" or "all right," and Wolof, waw kay, "all correct." "O.K." is recorded in the speech of black Americans from 1776, but was probably used earlier in the 1700s.

Another Wolof word popular in black English is "dig," as in "dig this man." This word originates from Wolof dega, meaning either "look here" or to "understand," used to mark the beginning of a sentence. In black English of the 1960s, "dig" meant "to understand something." The verb dega is similar in sound and meaning to the Wolof verb dega, meaning to understand, pronounced similarly to the English "digger." An example in Wolof is dega nga olof, "Do you understand Wolof?"

David Dalby draws a direct parallel between the Wolof term "gay" and the American term "guys," used informally to mean "persons" or "fellows." In Wolof it is always used as a plural. Other Africanisms found in American English include uh-hum (yes) and unh-unh (no), which occur in various parts of the world but nowhere as frequently and regularly as in Africa and the United States. The word "cush" was used in the American South during the slavery period to describe "cornmeal soaked in water." A similar word is used in Wolof for millet meal soaked in water.

Honkie, a term popular during the 1960s, was first used to describe white men who would drive to the African American community and honk automobile horns for their black dates. The word "hong" in Wolof means red or pink, and whites are described in most African languages as "Red." The word "sambo," considered an abusive term by African Americans, is respectful in Wolof and a common family name through-out West Africa.

Several Wolof words were popularized during the jazz era. For example, "jive" in Ebonics means "misleading talk," which is code language originating from the Wolof word "jey." The American words "hep," "hip," and "hippie" translate roughly into "to be aware or alive to what is going on," including drugs. In Wolof, the verb "hipi" means "to open one's eyes." The American slang "cat" means a person, as in "hep-cat" or "cool cat," and is similar to the Wolof "kai" used as a suffix following the verb. The Wolof lexicon "jamboree" is now a standard part of American language. Originally, a jamboree was a noisy slave celebration. A jam-session in the old days of the plantation was slave musicians and slaves assembling for dance and entertainment. The origin is the Wolof word for slave, "jaam."

The verb "sock" in the sense of "to strike" or the sexual connotation of "sock it to me, Baby" is found in Wolof and has a similar sound and meaning in Wolof, "to beat with a pestle." The word "bug," as in jitter-bug or Bugs Bunny, denotes an enthusiastic person. The word "fuzz" has been used by African Americans to mean "police." Historically, it meant a policeman, or those who patrolled the plantation at night and hunted down runaways on horseback. In Wolof the word "fas," pro-nounced between fas and fuss, means a horse.

Enslaved Africans used the term "Masa" for master. Many planters thought their slaves could not use the King's English properly. The word "mansa" was a title for many kings of West Africa; during the empire of ancient Mali, it meant chief or leader. (One such leader of note was Mansa Musa.) Enslaved Africans saw the masters as persons of authority and simply used their indigenous word for leader, Ma[n]sa. On the American plantation, the "n" in mansa became silent.

A large number of Wolof words survived in American English be-cause many Wolof interpreters were used during the early European voyages along the coast, and they used Wolof names for African food-stuffs, such as "yam" and "banana," that became part of standard En-glish.

African lexical items found their way into American English speech. The American Southern dialect in particular has been greatly influ-enced by Africa. Black servants who raised the children of the Southern aristocracy passed on their distinctive pronunciations, which then be-came uniquely Southern. The musical quality of Southern speech is also believed to have derived from Africa. Generations of interaction with African speech patterns gave white Southerners their distinctive drawl. Charles Dickens, commenting on the speech of Southerners, noted that there was little difference between the speech of whites and slaves. Edward Kimber, a traveler in the South in 1746, wrote that "one thing they [whites] are very faulty in, with regard to their Children, which is, that when young, they suffer them too much to prowl amongst the young Negroes, which insensibly causes them to imbibe their Manners and broken Speech."[38] Black speech patterns are now found in the larger speech pattern of Americans, particularly among the youth.

White Southerners have adopted and assimilated African speech patterns and have retained Africanisms such as baton twirling, cheerleading, and expressions and words that were once Africanisms but are now Americanism, such as O.K. (okay), bowdacious, bozo (stupid), cooter (turtle), dig, goober, fuzz (police), (peanut), guy, honkie, hippie, hullabaloo, hully-gully, jazz, jam, jamboree, jive, juke(box), moola (money), pamper, Polly Wolly-Doodle, wow, uh-huh, unh-unh, daddy, buddy, and tote, to name a few. Other English words first used by Africans include banana, banjo, Kola (as in Coca-Cola), elephant, gorilla, gumbo, okra, tater, and turnip. These African words retained in American English have greatly influenced the richness of the language.

White Southerners also borrowed the elaborate African social etiquette system, with its terms of endearment and kinship in speaking to neighbors, using such titles as "aunty" and "uncle" as signs of respect for elders. This tradition of respect for elders not only continued but also was reinforced by African social etiquette in the New World.

Finally, Herskovits noted similarities between black and white religious behavior, particularly in Pentecostal sects, such as ritual dancing, drumming, trances, and speaking in tongues. He traced many of these behaviors to the Sango cult. That trance form is characteristically African, but it is often found among whites who belonged to churches with large numbers of African Americans and in those of certain Pentecostal sects.

Other Africanisms found among white Americans, according to Peter Wood, are such practices as leaving gourds on poles for birdhouses and using African techniques of alligator wrestling. As late as the 1930s, whites used funerary pottery in a manner identical to blacks. Both African and Europeans cultures contributed fairly evenly, given the circumstances, to what was to become American. Culturally, Americans shared many experiences—some born in Europe and some in Africa.

Conclusion

The African house servants learned new domestic skills, including the art of quilting, from their mistresses. They took this European quilting technique and Africanized it by combining it with their appliqué style, reflecting a pattern and form still found in the Akan and Fon textile industries of West Africa.

The culture of the Mande had a profound effect on European Americans by way of the "Big House." It was the planter who witnessed the transmission of European culture to the Africans and African culture to the Europeans. The acculturation process was mutual, as well as reciprocal. Africans assimilated white culture, and planters adopted some aspects of African customs and practices such as the Africans agricultural method of rice cultivation, African cuisine (southern cooking), open grazing of cattle, and use of herbal medicines to cure and treat New World diseases such as smallpox.

Winifred Vass has documented survival of Bantu vocabulary in American place names, folklore, lexicon, and literature, and Dena Epstein has shown that the banjo is of African origin. Herskovits identified five areas in which African culture influenced the United States: music, speech, social etiquette, cuisine, and religion. African cultural influence has clearly influenced American musical traditions, mainly spirituals, jazz, blues, and bluegrass. All these musical forms have influenced popular American music, with spirituals remaining the most indigenous American music that developed in America. Many Africanisms, such as the banjo, became Americanisms. Indeed, today the banjo is more characteristic of whites than blacks. Appalachian banjo music is now considered as American as apple pie, without any distinguishing African characteristics.

A diversity of Africans, including the Bantu of Central Africa, changed North American culture, contrary to the popular belief that only West Africans contributed. Because West Africans had a great influence on white American culture by their presence in the plantation "Big House," scholars have assumed the same occurred in African American culture. Nevertheless, recent scholarship suggests a Bantu origin for much of African American culture because, unlike the more numerous Senegambians (Mandes), the Central Africans brought a common culture and language. Both these African groups contributed to the richness and diversity of American and African American cultures.

Appendix

Caesar's Cure for Poison

Take the Roots of Plantane [Plantain] and wid Hoarse-bound fresh or dried, three Ounces; boil them together in two Quarts of Water to one Quart, and strain it: of this Decoction let the Patient take one their Part three Mornings, fasting successively, from which if he finds any

Relief, it must be continued till he is perfectly recovered. On the Contrary, if he finds no Alteration after the third Dose, it is a sign that the Patient has either not been poisoned at all, or that it has been with Poison as Caesar's Antidotes will not remedy, so may leave off the Decoction. During the Cure the Patient must live on a spare Diet, and abstain from eating Mutton, Pork, Butter, or any other fat or oily Food.

N. B. the Plantan [Plantain] or Hoar Hound [*sic*] will, either of them, cure along, but they are most efficacious together.

In Summer you may take one Handful of the Roots and Branches of each, in Place of three Ouinces of the Roots of each.

For Drink during the Cure, let them take the following, Take the Roots of the Golden Rod, six Ounces, or in Summer two large Handfuls of te Roots and Branches together, and boil them in two Quarts of Water to one Quart (to which also may be added a little Hoarse Hound and Sassafras); to this Decoction, after it is strained, add a Glass of Rum or Brandy, and sweeten it with Sugar for ordinary Drink.

Sometimes an inward Fever attends such as are poisoned for which he order the followings, Take a Pint of Wood Ashes and three Pints of Water; stir and mix them well together; let them stand all Night, and strain or decant the Lye off in the Morning, of which ten Ounces may be taken six Mornings following, warmed or cold, according to the Weather. These Medicines have no sensible Operation, though sometimes they work in the Bowels, and give a gentle Stool.

The Symptoms attending such as are poisoned are as follows, A Pain of the Breast, Difficulty of breathing, a Load at the Pit of the Stomach, an irregular Pulse, burning and violent Pains of the Viscera above and below the Naval, very restless at Night, sometimes wandering Pains over the Body, a Reaching and Inclination to vomit, profuse Sweats (which prove always serviceable), slimy Stools both when costive and loose, the Face of a Pale and yellow Colour, sometimes a Pain and Inflammation of the Throat; the Appetite is generally weak, and some cannot eat any; those who have long been poisoned are generally very feeble and weak in their Limbs, sometimes spit a great Deal; the whole Skin peels, and likewise the Hair falls off.

Caesar's Cure for the Bite of a Rattle Snake

Take the Roots of Plantene or Hoarse Hound (in Summer Roots and Branches together) a sufficient Quantity; bruise them in a Mortar, and squeeze out the Juice, of which give as soon as possible, one large Spoonful; if he be swelled you must force it down his Throat. This generally will cure, but, if the Patient finds no Relief in an Hour after, you may give another Spoonful, which never fails. if the Roots are dried, they must be moistened with a little Water.

To the Wound may be applied a Leaf of good Tobacco moistened with Rum.

Notes

1. This title was selected in honor of the memory of Melville J. Herskovits, who wrote an article entitled "What Africa Has Given America."

2. D. P. Gamble, *The Wolof of Senegambia* (London: International African Institute, 1957).

3. Philip Curtin, *The Atlantic Slave Trade: A Census* (Madison: University of Wisconsin Press, 1969).

4. Peter H. Wood, *Black Majority: Negroes in Colonial South Carolina from 1670 through the Stono Rebellion* (New York: Knopf, 1974), p. 153.

5. Curtin (1969), p. 157.

6. Eugene D. Genovese, *Roll Jordan Roll: The World the Slave Made* (New York: Pantheon Books, 1974).

7. J. D. Duncan, "Servitude and slavery in colonial South Carolina 1670–1776," Ph.D. dissertation, Emory University, Atlanta, Ga., 1971.

8. Ulrich Bonnell Phillips, *American Negro Slavery: A Survey of the Supply, Employment and Control of Negro Labor as Determined by the Plantation Régime* (New York, London: D. Appleton and Co., 1940), p. 42.

9. Eugene D. Genovese, *Roll Jordan Roll: The World the Slave Made* (New York: Pantheon Books, 1974), p. 324.

10. Elizabeth Donnan, *Documents Illustrative of the History of the Slave Trade in America*, vol. 4. (Washington, D.C.: Carnegie Institute of Washington, 1935), p. 817.

11. Victor Boswell, "Our Vegetable Travellers," *The National Geographic Magazine* XCVI(2) (August 1949):193–211.

12. Helen Mendes, *The African Heritage Cookbook* (New York: Macmillan, 1971).

13. Duncan Clinch Heyward, *Seed from Madagascar* (Chapel Hill: University of North Carolina Press, 1937), p. 4.

14. Mark Catesby, *The Natural history of Carolina, Florida, and the Bahama Islands: containing two hundred and twenty figures of birds, beast, fishes, serpents, insects and plants* [rev. by Mr. Edwards]; with an introduction by George Frick, and notes by Joseph Ewam. (Savannah, Ga.: Beehive Press, 1974 [originally published in 1743]). See appendix, pp. 81–82.

15. John Lawson, *A New Voyage to Carolina* (London: n.p., 1709).

16. For more information on African contributions to American cuisine, see Helen Mendes, op. cit.

17. Ulrich Bonnell Phillips, *American Negro Slavery: A Survey of the Supply, Employment, and Control of Negro Labor as Determined by the Plantation Regime* (New York: D. Appleton, 1990), p. 16.

18. Elizabeth Donnan, *Documents Illustrative of the History of the Slave Trade*, vol. 2; see "Memoirs of the Life of Job Ben Solomon," pp. 420–27, and Terry Alford, *Prince among Slaves: The True Story of an African Prince Sold into Slavery in the American South* (New York: Harcourt Brace Jovanovich, 1977).

19. Interview by Joseph E. Holloway with David P. Gamble, December 5, 1985, and Moffett, "Uncle Remus Was a Hausaman?" *Southern Folklore Quarterly* (1975), 39:151–66.

20. For example, by David Roediger ("The Long Journey to the Hip Hop Nation," *St. Louis Post-Dispatch*, 18 (March 1994) and by Joe Adamson, *Bugs Bunny: Fifty Years and Only One Grey Hare* (New York: Henry Holt, 1990), both cited in Shelley Fisher Fishkin "Reframing the Multiculturalism Debates and Remapping American Studies," *Journal of American Studies of Turkey* (1995) 1:3–18.

21. Joseph E. Holloway and Winifred K. Vass, *The African Heritage of American English* (Bloomington: Indiana University Press, 1993), p. xxiii.

22. Moreau de Saint Mery, *Description topograpique, physique, evile, politique et historique de la partie Francaise de l'ile de Saint Domingue*, Tome 1, pp. 52–56.

23. Robert Farris Thompson, "Kongo Influences on African-American Culture" in Holloway, ed., *Africanisms in American Culture* (Bloomington: Indiana University Press, 1990), p. 151.

24. The partial Europeanization of some of these African movements eventually created the national dances of Latin American countries such as the marcumbi, a dance learned by the Spanish and later brought to the New World through Spain. The fandango, the national dance of Spain, originated in Cuba from African dances. Other dances derived from the Ombliguide are the Chacharara, Cabomba, Melongo, Malamba, Gati, Semba, rhumba, Conga, and Tango. See Joseph Holloway Papers, #4511 Division of Rare and Manuscript Collections, Cornell University Library.

25. William D. Pierson, *Black Legacy: America's Hidden Heritage* (Amherst: University of Massachusetts Press, 1993), p. 99.

26. Bryan Edwards, *The History, Civil and Commercial, of the British Colonies in the West Indies*, 3 vols. (London, 1993–1801) and R. S. Rattray, *The Tribes of the Ashanti Hinterland*, 2 vols. (Oxford: Clarendon Press, 1932).

27. J. H. Russell, *The Free Negro in Virginia* (Baltimore: Johns Hopkins Press, 1913), R3n.; and Todd L. Savitt, *Medicine and Slavery* (Urbana: University of Illinois Press, 1978), p. 76. See *South Carolina Gazette*, May 9, 1740. Also quoted in Ira E. Harrison, "Health Status and Healing Practices:

Continuations from an African Past," *Journal of African Studies* 2(4) (Winter 1975/6) and Peter H. Wood, *Black Majority* (New York: Knopf, 1974), p. 289.

28. James Stewart, *A View of the Past and Present State of the Island of Jamaica* (1808; reprint ed. Edinburgh: Oliver & Boyd, 1823), pp. 303-304, and Dr. David Mason, "A Descriptive Account of Framboesia or Yaws," Edinburgh Medical and Surgical Caribbean, p. 271.

29. *SC-Ars Upper House Journal,* March 16, 1750, p. 478.

30. Ibid., *SCCHJ,* November 28, 1749.

31. See appendix. These cures were published in *SCCHJ, SC-AR Commons House Journal,* November 29, 1749, p. 304; and also in the *South Carolina Gazette; The London Magazine* xix (1750): 367-68, and in *The Gentleman's Magazine* xx (1750): 342-43.

32. Certificate No. 1876 mark by Negro Sampson, August 23, 1775, Treasury Receipts, 1774-1778, South Carolina Archives, p. 280.

33. Terry W. Lipscomb, ed., *The Colonial Records of South Carolina; The Journal of the Commons House of Assembly,* November 21, 1752-September 6, 1754, p. xxviii; John Tobler, *South-Carolina and Georgia Almanack,* p. 177.

34. *South Carolina Gazette,* April 19, 1760.

35. For a groundbreaking study of African cultural survivals among whites in the United States that prepares the way for more research in this important but neglected area, see John Edward Philips's "The African Heritage of White America" in this volume, pp. 372-96.

36. Peter H. Wood, "More Like a Negro Country: Demographic Patterns in Colonial South Carolina, 1700-1740," in Stanley L. Engerman and Eugene D. Genovese, eds., *Race and Slavery in the Western Hemisphere: Quantitative Studies* (Princeton, N.J.: Princeton University Press, 1975). Also see Peter H. Wood, *Majority: Negroes in Colonial South Carolina from 1670 through the Stono Rebellion* (New York: Alfred A. Knopf, 1975).

37. D. P. Gamble, *The Wolof of Senegambia* (London: International African Institute, 1957).

38. "The Speech of Negroes in Colonial America," *The Journal of Negro History* XXIV(3) (July 1939).

Three

African Elements in African American English

Molefi Kete Asante

The almost total absence of visible African artifacts in African American culture led to the general belief that nothing African survived the tyranny of American slavery.[1] Prohibited by slaveholders from participating in traditional ceremonies and rituals, Africans in the United States for the most part did not develop complete, formal African art forms. The functions of African artists were in fact nearly meaningless in such an alien context. But while the visible artifacts of religious sculpture gradually disappeared, subtler linguistic and communicative artifacts were sustained and embellished by the Africans' creativity when any more conspicuous elements of African cultures would have produced even greater repression. This essay surveys some of these complex verbal behaviors, which constitute continuity and relationship between West African languages and African American English.

The Question of Relationship

Despite the preponderance of pidgin and later of creole among early Africans in America, little investigation into the structure, history, context, or possible relationships with West and Central African languages was ever undertaken. Considered a corruption of English or the babbling of children, the language used by African Americans was dismissed as unworthy of investigation. Furthermore, the persistent and prevailing idea among early American scholars as well as laypersons was that Africans had no culture. Such a view successfully impeded a discussion of language relationships.

65

Melville Herskovits, Janheinz Jahn, and other writers on the subject have been vigorously attacked, not so much for their methods as for the inferences to be drawn from their methods. They theorized on the basis of field research in African cultures, diasporan and continental, and challenged many interpretations about the African connection. Along with W. E. B. Du Bois, Alain Locke, and Carter Woodson before them, they provided, in effect, novel interpretations of old substances.

A considerable intellectual meanness had to be combated by the initial cadre of communicationists who examined the continuity of black language behaviors from Africa to America. The racist assumption that black pidgin reflected an innate inability of Africans to learn English was current at one time.[2] In fact, as Herskovits pointed out, the linguists who studied pidgin often had no knowledge of African languages and therefore could not make informed interpretations. Lorenzo Turner augmented this position by exposing inaccuracies in the work of linguists who were quick to give assurance that there were no African survivals among black Americans. Only with the work of Mervyn Alleyne and other sociolinguists did we begin to get a clearer picture of the African contribution to English.[3] Alleyne particularly demonstrated continuity in the West Indies.

Earlier, Ambrose Gonzales, like many white American linguists, misunderstood the Gullah language and arrived at the wrong conclusion. In 1922 he cited a list of words that were purported to be of African origin. Most of the words are either English words misspelled or African words interpreted as English words that blacks could not pronounce. Gonzales was thoroughly confused about what he was studying, as Turner pointed out:

> Many other words in Gonzales' glossary which, because of his lack of acquaintance with the vocabulary of certain African languages, he interprets as English, are in reality African words. Among other Gullah words which he or other American writers have interpreted as English, but which are African, are the Mende *suwangᴐ*, to be proud (explained by Gonzales as a corruption of the English swagger): the Wolof *lir*, small (taken by Gonzales to be an abbreviated form of the English little, in spite of the fact that the Gullah also uses little when he wishes to): the Wolof *benj*, tooth (explained by the Americans as a corruption of bone): the Twi *fa*, to take (explained by Americans as a corruption of the English for). . . .[4]

The point made by Turner is that white American linguists refused to consider the possibility that blacks used African words in their vocabularies. In fact, the evidence demonstrates that whites unfamiliar with either African languages or Gullah made expansive generalizations that tended to support their preconceived notions about black speech habits. Writing in the *American Mercury* in 1924, George Krapp said that "it is reasonably safe to say that not a single detail of Negro pronunciation or Negro syntax can be proved to have other than English origins."[5] Other writers who voiced nearly the same judgment regarding the presence of African survivals in black American speech supported the notion of an absolute break with African culture.[6] It was inconceivable to them that either phonological, morphological, or semantic interference could have existed where Africans retained their language behavior in connection with English.

These writers represented the prevailing American notions about race, cultural retentions, and African intelligence. And while Herskovits and others were gallant in demonstrating the presence of Africanisms in black America, they frequently concentrated on artifacts that proved insufficient to carry the burden of cultural continuity. Despite charges that Herskovits's work had a negative effect on the discussion of culture because he exaggerated differences between blacks and nonblacks, his primary thesis is essentially sound.[7] It was, of course, an unpopular position because several writers, including the sociologist E. Franklin Frazier, were captivated by the idea of more or less nondistinction between cultures and races. The emphasis was on making Africans Anglo-Saxons, as Frazier's student Nathan Hare eventually put it in his study *Black Anglo-Saxons*. But Africans were and are culturally different, and whether or not one argues that this difference resulted from African retention and syncretism of other cultures, the point was unchanged. In fact, what should have occurred, but did not, was a systematic and empirical testing of culture-related data that promised to explicate African American language behaviors.

Continuity of Language Behaviors

That something of the African backgrounds of black Americans survived is not difficult to argue despite intense efforts to prove that blacks were incapable of cultural retention because of slavery. No displaced people have ever completely lost the forms of their previous culture. The specific artifacts may differ from those employed in a prior time, but the essential elements giving rise to those artifacts are often retained and produce substantive forms in the new context.

It is my contention that black Americans retained basic components of the African experience rather than specific artifacts. To seek the distinctive retention of African words in black America as Turner,

Herskovits, and Romeo Garrett attempted to do is to search amiss. What they sought to do is an interesting, provocative, and valuable addition to our knowledge, but it is not convincing from the standpoint of cultural survivals. It is cast in too narrow a mold and often depends on the continuity of specific words from several ethnic regions of Africa. Although African lexical items may be found in limited supply among African Americans, they do not make the argument for a more general retention of African linguistic behavior applicable to most black Americans. What my research suggests is that combinations of classes of sounds, units of meaning, and syntax behaviors are to be considered in regard to survival rather than concentrating on any single one of these factors or on simple lexical characteristics.

Earlier writers seem to have preferred African lexical discoveries in African American language; they are, after all, easily identifiable phenomena. But the relationship between African languages and African American speech behaviors can be more clearly ascertained on a primary level in the "communication style" of the person. While this concept is difficult to define, it means simply the verbal and nonverbal behavior patterns that distinguish one person from another. Even whole groups may be distinguished in such a manner. On a secondary level, there are observable relationships in the substantive social fabric of language behavior—proverbs, riddles, dozens, call-and-response. The combination of communicative styles and "folkloristic modalities" constitutes an approach to the sense of a language. It is this sense of language in African Americans that is uniquely more African than European, other factors aside. This is not a rejection of linguistic structure, inasmuch as I hope to demonstrate that certain structural matters underscore my basic thesis.

Recent linguistic studies define a language variously referred to as Black English, African American English, or, more appropriately, Ebonics. This language has systematic rules different from English as it is popularly learned and spoken. The cohesive grammar of Ebonics has features shared with popular English and other dialects of English. The most significant fact, however, is that some of its features are found only among Ebonics speakers. At least one researcher, Jeutonne Brewer, believes that "systematic differences in Black English which occur only within that language system, may be the result of interaction between coastal West African languages of the Niger-Congo language family and the dialects of English encountered by Black people when they first arrived in America."[8] In such a case, however, it is highly unlikely that no individuation of those unique systematic differences appeared in other dialects of English. The interaction of African languages with English dialects has not been shown to be significant in the singularity of certain grammatical rules present in Ebonics. A more plausible answer is that Ebonics contains structural remnants of certain African languages even though the vocabulary is overwhelmingly English.

If we accept the creolization theory that Ebonics developed as a result of language interference, isolation factors, and nonpopular linguistic models, then it is possible to trace the language from pidgin to the full coming-to-be of another language. According to creolization theory, a pidgin language is characterized by two factors: its grammatical system is sharply reduced, and it is not the native language system of those who speak it. When pidgin becomes the native language of those who use it, it becomes a creole language.[9]

The language spoken by African Americans was greatly influenced by the phonological and syntactic structures of their first languages. Whatever semblance of English they learned had the unmistakable imprint of African languages, much as the English spoken by the average French person is rendered in many instances in terms of French phonology and syntax. These Africans were, for the most part, not linguists learning languages but lay persons acquiring an instrument for their survival. And the limited English vocabulary and few sentences needed for the task of staying alive were extremely useful in dealing with whites. But the mastery of English morphology and syntax lay in the future.

Pidginization as a first step toward creolization occurs throughout the Africans' history in America. Morphological, phonological, and grammatical principles underlying popular English have constantly played havoc with the African past. The accompanying figure shows the process of structural retention in African American speech behaviors.

Inasmuch as African Americans are descendants of a great many ethnic and linguistic groups, it is necessary, if we are to talk about communication styles, constructions, or preverbal forms, to identify as precisely as possible the areas where most African American ancestors originated. Slave trade records provide us with information regarding areas from which slaves were taken. The Atlantic slave trade was permitted for nearly two hundred years in the American colonies and the United States. Every state was affected at some point, although the majority of Africans landed in the southern states.[10]

The languages spoken by most African linguistic groups are considered to be in the Niger-Congo family, which includes Bantu. Several similarities between these languages and Ebonics are so clearly observable as to deserve immediate mention. The verb system of Efik and Ewe differentiate between a customary aspect (habitual) or repetitive aspect and aspect of completion. Thus it is possible in Efik to express an action

West
African Languages
Niger-Congo

Acquisition of foreign vocabulary
Maintains original morphology, phonology, grammar

More words and some grammar
Pidginization
Maintains original morphology and grammar

Creolization
Maintains morphology

Englishization-Ebonics
Maintains original communication style
Maintains some lexical items
Ability to switch

FROM AFRICAN LANGUAGES TO EBONICS

that occurs habitually in the present, past, or future, with time determined by context rather than vocal inflection. Ebonics also uses aspect rather than tense in some verbal constructions.

Perhaps Richard Long's preliminary analysis of the Uncle Remus dialect best demonstrates work done in recent years on the relationship between Ebonics and African languages. Long provided a comparative paradigm of the Niger-Congo verb system and Ebonics:[11]

Niger-Congo tense–aspect	Examples in English translation
Present	he go
Near past	he gone
Remote past	he been gone
Future	he going to go

Aspect of progress	he going
Aspect of completion	he done gone
Past aspect of repetition	he been going

While Long gave us an interesting point of departure, he drew no clear and definite relationship. Furthermore, the future tense-aspect translated in his construct "he going to go" is probably incorrect. Whether this expression appears because Joel Chandler Harris recorded it or because Long wished to hear it so, it is questionable as the sole expression in Ebonics for the future. A more common phrase is "he gon go" to indicate future.

A more useful investigation was made by William A. Stewart, who observed the lack of verbal inflection in Ebonics to show the difference between simple present and past.[12] "I see it" in Ebonics may mean "I see it" or "I saw it," depending on the speaker's context. One cannot surmise from this that the categories are nonexistent, because the present and past negatives demonstrate the presence of both grammatical categories. Examples include *present:* I see it, I don't see it; *past:* I see it (I saw it), I ain't see it.

According to Brewer, "Twi, Igbo, Ewe, Efik—all Niger-Congo languages—Jamaican Creole, and Gullah all exhibit a similar lack of inflection to show time. Present, past, and sometimes future time are indicated by context rather than by verbal inflection."[13] Examples include *Gullah (Ogeeche):* I de go, meaning "I go, I went"; *Jamaican Creole:* Yesterday me buy salt fish; *Ewe:* May, meaning "I go" (no particular time); *Igbo:* Àdà bù abo, meaning "Ada is (was) carrying a basket"; *Twi:* Fa, meaning "He takes" (all times).

The Ebonics verb system has four perfectives, whereas English has only two.[14] The present and past are similar in the two grammars, but Ebonics also has a completive perfect and a remote time perfect. Examples are *completive (near past):* I done walked; *remote time:* I been walked. Dwyer and Smith described West African Pidgin English in a way that makes an interesting comparison with the Ebonics perfectives.[15] The essential point is that two aspect markers occur before the verb: *de* for continuing or habitual action and *don* for completed action. The word *bin* is used as a past tense marker. It is not just West African Pidgin English that possesses the habitual and continuative aspect. One sees similar elements in Efik and Ewe verbal construction. In Efik any verbal construction may have a habitual counterpart. In Ewe *na* is suffixed to the verb: *nayine,* "I generally go."

Clearly the morphological and grammatical connections are demonstrated between Ebonics and West African languages. The primary argument of this essay, however, is that it is in speech communication style generally, even as Englishization occurs, that African Americans retain their essential Africanness. Precise discovery of lexical items is not necessary to argue continuity.

Jack Berry stated that "almost every one of the languages spoken South of the Sahara is tonal, using pitch distinctions to differentiate words in much the same way European languages use stress."[16] That African American language behavior is characterized by a significant control over vocal inflection and modulation is fairly well established.[17] African Americans mean something precise by their pitch, as in speaking such words as *Jesus, man, say*. Vocal color plays a vital role for the black public speaker, particularly the preacher, who utilizes various intonations and inflections to modify or amplify specific ideas, concepts, or emotions.

Harmonizing is a principal function of black speech behavior, and every attempt is made to reach internal harmony, the blending of sounds and ideas, for effectiveness. Thus the audience frequently responds with interjections, such as "Amen," "Speak," "Pray on," and "Tell the truth." Such interjections are similar to the Igbo "He speaks," "Let him speak," "Speak on," and "He has spoken." A certain noticeable communicative style is transmitted in tone, rhythm, or pitch in these cases. In fact, the so-called black voice can be recognized by other Ebonics speakers by pitch and tone. Thus the more prevalent the African rhythm, tone, and pitch in the vocalization, the more distinctly African is the voice.

One is tempted to suggest that whites in some southern communities, having learned the peculiar intonations and sounds of their African nurses, speak with African tone and pitch. On the other hand, some blacks speak with an almost precise European intonation pattern with no trace of African vocal color. This behavior indicates that language interference has affected the speech of blacks and whites alike. One cannot be sure even how long the African communicative styles will remain. The time may come when we will be able to observe only rare instances of the pitch, rhythm, and tone of Africa. In a real sense the linguists' early ecstasy over such African lexical retentions as *OK, okra*, and *go-go* marked the beginning of a general merging of African lexical items into the general American vocabulary.

Indicators of Linguistic Relationship

It is now necessary to expand on the role of syntactical features of Ebonics as indicators of linguistic relationship. Such an expansion will explicate certain communicative processes that cannot be explained by retention of lexical items alone. For this reason greater insight may be gained by a detailed treatment of two types of syntactical phenomena: serial verbal construction and tense-aspect usage.

Serial Verbs

Serial verblike constructions appear in Ebonics quite frequently, and some West African languages also use several verbs to express actions that require only one verb in English. John Bendor-Samuel described this feature in the Gur branch of Niger-Congo:

> Strings of short clauses characterize Gur syntax. Long clauses with a large number of nominal phrases are very unusual. Frequently complex clauses are broken down into a sequence of two or more clauses. Indirect objects, benefactives, and instrumental phrases are avoided. Thus Vagala uses a two verb sequence in a construction such as *u é ù tè n* literally "he did it gave me" for "he did it for me" and Basari similarly has *ù ná kí tu m* literally he did connective gave me.[18]

Ayo Bamgbose said that serial verbs refer to the combination of verbs found in many West African languages where all the verbs share a common subject in the surface structure. For example, he cited *Twi: òdè siké no màà me* (He take money gave me, meaning "He gave me money"); *Vagala: ù kpá kíyzèé mòng ówl* (He took knife cut meat, meaning "He cut the meat with a knife"); and *Yoruba: ó mú iwé wá* (He took book come, meaning "He brought a book").[19]

There are some surface variations in the structure of serialization across languages. The description of Ewe is one example:

> A peculiarity of Ewe is that we often find a row of verbs one after the other. The chief features of this are that all the verbs stand next to each other without being connected, that all have the same tense or mood, and that in the event of their having a common subject and object, these stand with the first, the others remaining bare: should a conjunction stand between two verbs, the subject and object must be repeated.[20]

Furthermore, Bendor-Samuel made generalizations about serialization in the Gur branch of Niger-Congo:

> In most languages this serial construction has certain clear mark-

ers and though there are many differences from language to language usually the following characteristics are marked:

1. The series shares a single common object which occurs before the first verb in the series and is not repeated within the series.

2. There are no conjunctions between the verbs.

3. Nominal phrases functioning as object may occur after any verb in the series when the object changes, though it is not usual to find more than two such phrases. When the object of two or more verbs is the same it is never repeated and usually occurs after the first verb.

4. Adverbial phrases may occur after a verb but only one phrase (nominal or adverbial) usually occurs between verbs in a series.

5. There are severe restrictions on the forms of the verbs in the series. Categories like future, negative, imperative, etc. are only marked once for the whole series and in some instances are never found in such series at all.

Some languages have conjunctions occurring within the series. Dagbani has two conjunctions which occur with such a series, *ka* and *n*. In Dagaari there are two such conjunctions which occur quite frequently. Bemoba has one conjunction that occasionally occurs. In Vagala two conjunctions may occur. Sisala has one conjunction which frequently occurs, and in Konkomba similarly there is one frequently occurring conjunction.[21]

It is apparent, then, that serial verb constructions vary considerably in surface structure but are characterized by the general principle that several verb phrases appear in a single surface structure prediction.

Westermann agreed that semantics is a common principle of serial verb usage:

In English these consecutive verbs are partly rendered by composite sentences. But very often several Ewe verbs may be expressed by a single verb in English.

The explanation of this is that the Ewe people describe every detail of an action or happening from beginning to end, and every detail has to be expressed by a special verb: they dissect every happening and present it in its several parts, whereas in English we seize on the leading event and express it by a verb, while subordinate events are either not considered or rendered by means of a preposition, adverb, conjunction, or a prefix of a verb.[22]

The semantic relationship between the verbs within a given construction is particularly important. It is apparent from the examples cited that the two verbs are used to convey what would normally be expressed by a single verb in English. This is the dissecting quality of African linguistic expression. The West African speakers analyze events by considering their component parts.

The same tendency can be seen in Ebonics. In some sentences Ebonics speakers use several verbs, whereas Standard English has available a single verb to express the completed action. For example, the Ebonics expression *I took consideration and joined de lawd* can be paraphrased as "I accepted religion" or "I became a Christian."[23] The most noticeable difference between this sentence and its English equivalent is that in the English version the fact that the person pondered the issue or thought about joining the church or accepting religion is not evident in the surface structure of the sentence, but by virtue of his having accepted—which is, by definition, to receive with consent something given or offered—the person must have had to think about it and decide whether to accept or reject this particular faith. English usually focuses on the main verb, and it is the main verb that usually surfaces; therefore, on the surface of the English translation we get the verb *accept*.[24] The Ebonics speaker, tending to surface a larger number of words to express the same action, surfaces the verb participle *took consideration* for the act of having thought about or pondered and *joined* for the actual step taken in accepting that faith. The Ebonics speaker here seems to want to express each event, as does the speaker in many West African languages.

We see a similar phenomenon in the Ebonics command *Turn loose and drap down from dar* ("Come down from there"). The Ebonics speaker finds it necessary to tell the person to first turn the tree branch loose and then drop down from it. Again, note the tendency to segment the action and, more important, the fact that this segmentation appears on the surface, in the form of two verbs. For the English speaker it is sufficient to focus on the main action, falling or dropping from the tree.

Another Ebonics example is *I hear tell you went home* ("I hear that you went home"). Again the Ebonics speaker is found describing every action, and each event is expressed by a single verb. The speaker states that he or she has been hearing a certain thing but also states on the surface that someone is telling that which is heard. This construction is a clear example of the use of the serial verb: the verbs stand adjacent to each other without being connected, and only one of the verbs can be inflected for tense, whereas if they were simply two sentences, one embedded in the other, both could be inflected for tense. That also holds true for many serial verbs in African languages. Additional variations may yield *I heard tell you went home* or *I will hear tell, if you do that*. But inflection of the second verb would yield ungrammatical sentences, such as *I hear told you went home* or *I heard told you went home*.

If the sentence, as a result of an embedding transformation on the component sentences, were said to be simply *I hear it* and *Someone tells/says*, producing *I hear that someone tells other people*, then sentences such as the following could be generated, where either verb or both verbs could be inflected for tense: *I hear tell that you went home; I hear it, (somebody) told that you went home; I heard it told that you went home*. A similar analysis can be made for the sentence *I made do with what I had* ("I used what I had"), where only the first verb can be inflected for tense, never the second.

Another example is *Go home go see about those children* ("Go home and attend to those children"). This sentence is interesting in another aspect as well: it is used both with and without the first *go*. Hearing a sentence of this type, one would automatically assume that *go* is an imperative, indicating that the person being given the command should move in a certain direction away from the speaker, while *see about* means to attend to. But here *go*, expressing a command to move away from the speaker, is used in the same sentence with *go see*, showing that some type of serial relationship holds between *go* and *see*. We cannot claim that it is simply the imperative *go* and the imperative *see*, because *go* exists as a command in initial position in the sentence, alone.

Other Ebonics sentences tend to have a serial-like construction and may be evidence of the same function semantically as the serial verb constructions of many West African languages: *He picked up and went to town* ("He went to town"); *I'll take a switch and beat you good* ("I'll beat you with a switch"). Clearly it is a tendency for African American speakers, like some West African speakers, to describe every detail of an action by using a special verb.

Tense-Aspect Usage

The tense and aspect quality in African American English has been cited by several writers. Lorenzo Turner noted that Ogeeche, or Gullah, speakers, much like speakers of many West African languages, attach little significance to the actual time when an event takes place; on the contrary, they stress the manner of the action. Turner offered examples of West African languages that follow this pattern:

> In the Ewe language, for example, the verb is unchangeable. Tense and mood forms are made by a combination of several verbs or of

verbs and nouns, and it is difficult to distinguish between tense and mood. One verb form, designated by many grammarians as the Aorist, does not indicate any particular time, but can represent the present, past, or even future, according to the context.

In Mandika the actual time when an action takes place is of less importance than the nature of the action as regards the completeness or incompleteness. Accordingly, there are three aspects of the verb: the first represents an action without reference to its completeness or incompleteness: the second describes an action which is being continued: and the third describes one which has been completed.[25]

It has been found that there is no distinction between past and present indefinite forms of the verb among Yoruba speakers. Where it is necessary to make a distinction between past and present, the African uses an adverbial of time. For example, *Ó kéré* may be translated "It is small" or "It was small," depending on context. If we add the adverbial *téléri* it would have to be translated "It was small." This form conveys the meaning of completed action. It holds also in Yoruba that the *n* formative, which marks the verb for progressive or iterative action, can be either present or past time, depending on the time referred to in the context.

Tense and aspect thus are not linked in many West African languages. In some cases the syntactical systems are such that they focus on aspect. As in Hausa, aspect is marked by grammatical formatives while tense is marked by either context or the use of adverbials of time. Therefore, aspect can be used without reference of tense in many languages.

Slave narratives from Alabama reveal numerous constructions in which tense is superseded by aspect. Certainly there exist mechanisms in Ebonics whereby aspect may be expressed without tense. In the statement *He clumb de tree to shake de simmons down whilst I be pickin em up,* the speaker, having made reference to tense in the initial clause, does not repeat the tense marker on the verb phrase of the second clause. Nevertheless the speaker has not neglected to indicate the manner of the action of the verb phrase in the second clause. If we consider the English form of this sentence, "He climbed the tree to shake the persimmons down, while I was picking them up," we find that the tense formative is redundant in the second clause.

These sentences employing *done* indicate the extent to which African American English uses the preverbal particle: *All my chilluns done died or wandered away; 'Fore I knowed it I done fell slap to sleep; Hell done broke loose in Gawgy; He couldn't tell us much about what done happen.*

Labov, in writing about similar constructions, said that the meaning is clear already and therefore *done* becomes a perfective particle. He also stated that *done* is used in certain sentences with a meaning of intensification, as in *After I don won all that money.*[26] While there may be cases where the perfective meaning is obscured, in most cases the preverbal particle *done* is an aspect marker in African American English, marking the verb for completed action without reference to time.

Contrary to Labov's claim that *have* and *done* are interchangeable in their roles as perfective particles, most African American English speakers make a semantic distinction between these two perfectives. *Done* appears to carry a consistent meaning of completion. These sentences show the preverbal form marking of *done: I eat anything that's done; It's been done* (stress on *been,* meaning "It's been completed a long time ago"); *I been done went.*[27] In these instances *done* clearly means completed action, and trying to replace it with some other perfective would yield ungrammatical sentences, thus revealing the difference in status between the forms using *done* and those using *have.* For example: *It's been have* and *I been have went.*

There are two forms of the word *been* in Ebonics. One appears without stress. It is used simply as a past perfect, as in *He been married,* connoting that he has been married but is no longer so. The second form provides added stress, as in *He BEEN married,* connoting that he was married a long time ago and is still married. Other sentences from Ebonics demonstrate this use of *been: My ole man been dead goin' on twenty years; Ca' se I been belongin' to de church for fifty-five years; Just left up to dem, I'd ave been dead; All my chilluns done died or wandered away an' my old man been dead goin' on twenty years.*

It appears that *done* is a verbal aspect of completed action, without reference to time, as opposed to the perfective (*have/had/has*), which is marked for time. Salone reasoned that this usage has been overlooked in other studies dealing with Ebonics because something is lost in the translation, so to speak. To translate an Ebonics sentence using *done* into other dialects of English one would of necessity use a perfective form, thereby also marking the form for tense. For example, the sentence *I done ate* in Ebonics means, literally, I completed the action of eating, where the preverbal *done* specifies nothing in reference to time. This form *done* can also exist with the perfective form that is marked for time: *I would have done ate, I had done ate, I will be done ate.* In translating the *done* sentence into Standard English, one would use the perfective, as in "I have eaten," which does carry information about completed action but also carries information about the relationship of the action in time. And in doing this the Standard English speaker assumes that the Ebonics speaker is also implying a specification of time, which according to the evidence is incorrect.

African American English speakers also tend to use a continuation form without reference to time, especially after the time has been referred to in a previous clause of the sentence, as in these examples: *He clumb de tree to shake de simmons down whilst I be pickin em up; I seed sompin a-comin' down de road—hit keep a-comin' an' keep a-gitten bigger.* Contrasting Standard English equivalents, we find additional tense markers: "He climbed the tree to shake the persimmons down, while I was picking them up"; "I saw something coming down the road—it kept coming and kept getting bigger." While the Standard English speaker must inflect all verbs for tense, the Ebonics speaker is not redundant in expressing tense but nevertheless is redundant in expressing the manner or aspect of the action, even to the extent of using such an archaic English form as *a-comin'*, a + gerund, which implies an iterative meaning.

Conclusion

This essay began with the assertion that followers of Turner, Herskovits, and Garrett were too narrow in their perspectives to adequately substantiate the continuity of Africanisms in African American English. I have argued, however, that the communication styles of African American speakers constitute the real continuity with the African sense. The linguistic factors analyzed support the basic proposition.

African American speakers have maintained this fundamental sense of culture despite the imposition of European cultural values and styles. Retention of lexical items constitutes one part of the continuity, but the major burden of African American English has been carried by such communicative processes as the African American manner in expression, supported in the main by serialization and a unique usage of tense and aspect. Neither phenomenon has any analogue in the English language, providing further proof that Ebonics derived in large part from the genius of West African languages.

Notes

1. The work of Robert Farris Thompson demonstrated the survival of West African carving and sculpturing techniques. Particularly apparent in the coastal regions of Georgia and South Carolina, these techniques are generally considered to be among the major African retentions of African Ameri-

cans. Thompson, a historian of African American art at Yale University, has strong belief in artistic retention; see his essay in this volume. For a similar view, see Judith Chase, *Afro-American Arts and Crafts* (New York: Van Nostrand, 1971). Karimu Asante's work on the survival of movement, as in dance, further demonstrates continuity.

2. Melville J. Herskovits, *The Myth of the Negro Past* (Boston: Beacon Press, 1958), 276.

3. See Mervyn Alleyne, "The Linguistic Continuity of African in the Caribbean," in *Topics in Afro-American Studies*, ed. by Henry J. Richards (Buffalo: Black Academy Press, 1971), 119–34. Alleyne argued that if African elements appear in African American speech it is inescapable that they belong to the African base.

4. Lorenzo Turner, "West African Survivals in the Vocabulary of Gullah," paper presented at the Modern Language Association, New York, December 1938.

5. George Krapp, "The English of the Negro," *American Mercury* (1924) 2:190.

6. See, for example, H. L. Mencken, *The American Language* (New York: Knopf, 1936), 112, 523; Reed Smith, "Gullah," Bulletin of the University of South Carolina, no. 190, 1926, 22–23; Thomas Jackson Woofter, *Black Yeomanry, Folk Culture on St. Helena Island, South Carolina* (Chapel Hill, N.C., 1930), 49–51.

7. See Norman Whitten and John Szwed, eds., *Afro-American Anthropology: Contemporary Perspectives* (New York: Free Press, 1970), 29.

8. Jeutonne Brewer, "Possible Relationships between African Languages and Black English Dialect," paper presented at the Speech Communication Association, New Orleans, December 29, 1970.

9. Robert Hall, *Pidgin and Creole Languages* (Ithaca, N.Y.: Cornell University Press, 1966), xii. See also Ian Hancock, "West African and the Atlantic Creoles," in John Spencer, *The English Language in West Africa* (London: Longmans, 1971), 113–22.

10. Herskovits, *Myth*, 47. Philip Curtin, *The Atlantic Slave Trade: A Census* (Madison: University of Wisconsin Press, 1969), is perhaps the most reliable work on the number of slaves brought to America. Before Curtin, estimates had ranged from 10 to 50 million. Curtin's view is that about 9.5 million slaves arrived in the New World. Considering the mortality rate for captives, nearly 50 million people probably were taken from Africa. James A. Rawley recently revised Curtin's figure upward to 11,345,000.

11. Richard A. Long, *The Uncle Remus Dialect: A Preliminary Linguistic View* (Washington, D.C.: Center for Applied Linguistics, 1969), 6.

12. William A. Stewart, "Urban Negro Speech: Sociolinguistic Factors Affecting English Teaching," *Florida FL Reporter* (Spring 1969), 7:50.

13. Brewer, "Possible Relationships."

14. Ralph Fasold and Walt Wolfram, "Some Linguistic Features of Negro Dialect," in *Teaching English in the Inner City* (Washington, D.C.: Center for Applied Linguistics, 1970), 61–62.

15. David Dwyer and David Smith, *An Introduction to West African Pidgin English* (East Lansing: Michigan State University Press, 1969), 132.

16. Jack Berry, "Language Systems and Literature," in *The African Experience*, ed. by John Paden and Edward Soja (Evanston, Ill.: Northwestern University Press, 1970), 87.

17. For a discussion of the generative uses of vocal inflection, see Arthur L. Smith, "Socio-Historical Perspectives in Black Oratory," *Quarterly Journal of Speech*, October 1970, 264–69.

18. John T. Bendor-Samuel, "Niger-Congo, Gur," in *Current Trends in Linguistics* 7 (The Hague: Mouton, 1969).

19. Ayo Bamgbose, "On Serial Verbs and Verbal Status," paper read at the Tenth West African Language Congress, Ibadan, 1970.

20. Dietrich Westermann and M. A. Bryan, *The Languages of West Africa* (London: Oxford University Press, 1952), 50.

21. Bendor-Samuel, "Niger-Congo, Gur," 22–24.

22. Westermann and Bryan, *Languages of West Africa*, 51–52.

23. Examples used in this section are from the Federal Writers Project film "Slave Narratives—Alabama," University of California Research Library.

24. Sukari Salone, "The Case for an African Influence in African American English," paper read at linguistics seminar, University of California at Los Angeles, 1972.

25. Lorenzo Turner, *Africanisms in the Gullah Dialect* (Chicago: University of Chicago Press, 1949), 34.

26. William Labov, *A Study of the Non-Standard English of Negro and Puerto-Rican Speakers in New York City* (New York: Columbia University Press, 1968).

27. Salone, "Case for an African Influence," 15. The sentences are from Salone's interviews with Charlie Smith in 1972. Smith died in 1974 at over 130 years of age.

Four

Africanisms in African American Names in the United States

Joseph E. Holloway

African Names in Colonial America

The purpose of this chapter is to make available a comprehensive list of linguistic Africanisms drawn from a wide range of domains. The focus in on names and words borrowed from African languages and found in Ebonics and American English.

Scholars searching for linguistic Africanisms in African American names have not been successful establishing a direct relationship between African and black American naming practices. Turner, *Africanisms in the Gullah Dialect* (1949), is the exception. Other scholars who have searched for Africanisms and focused on the phonology, morphology, semantics, and syntax of Black English in relation to African languages include Herskovits (1941), Stewart (1969), Baratz and Shuy (1969), Labov (1970), Wolfram (1969), and Dillard (1972).

This chapter explores the historical relationship between African and African American naming practices and the search for Africanisms in black names. It begins by examining runaway slave advertisements for possible Africanisms. The focus is on African names in Colonial America, Africanisms in black naming practices, and African American nicknames.

At the end of this chapter is a list of African lexicon found in American English compiled from a number of word lists, including Turner (1949), David Dalby (1972), and Holloway and Vass (1990). This chapter does not duplicate their works but seeks to correct the mistaken assumption that only West African languages contributed to the linguistic varieties found in American English. This essay demonstrates that both West and Central African languages contributed to the diversity of linguistic Africanisms found in American English.

In the colonial period, African linguistic survivals were numerous because the memory of the African past was still very much alive. Planters were aware of African ethnicity and attempted to prevent a continuation of African culture and customs on the American plantations they controlled. This actually accelerated the acculturation process among house servants, who were forced to learn English as the only medium of communication with one another and the planters.

The level of English proficiency among enslaved Africans was generally related to the slaves' jobs. House servants, because of their close contact with the planters in the "Big House," learned English more rapidly than field slaves, who had little contact with European American culture and remained unacculturated for a longer period. African acculturation in South Carolina took place at two levels, in the house and in the field.

The first Africans in North America were not completely unaware of English and other European languages. For instance, Africans arriving in South Carolina from the coastal communities of Africa generally spoke some form of pidgin or Creole English prior to coming to America. Many Angolans coming from the Congo-Angola areas spoke Portuguese. Le Jau reported in 1710, "I have in this parish a few Negro Slaves . . . born and baptized among the Portuguese,"[1] and an account in 1739 declared that "amongst the Negro Slaves there are people who spoke Portuguese."[2] Some "Spanish Negroes" were mentioned among the runaways in the *South Carolina Gazette* as heading toward Spanish Florida, while others attempted to seek out other Spanish-speaking slaves.[3]

Peter Timothy's "Negro Named Pierro" could speak "good English, Chickasaw, and perhaps French."[4] A runaway mulatto, Antoine, could speak "very good French and English," whereas Clase spoke "good English, and a little Spanish." Phobe spoke "French and English" and Jupiter could speak "good English and some French."[5] In 1772 Fenda Lawrence, the Gambian slave trader in West Africa who came to the American South as a tourist, must have had some knowledge of English to move around the South as she did.[6] Obviously these Africans who spoke multiple languages had prior contact with Europeans on the western coast of Africa.

A brief survey of advertisements of runaways' slaves revealed that in some cases Africans were speaking Creole or pidgin learned on the coast of Africa. An advertisement read that he or she spoke "good English," a sign of acculturation. If the enslaved African spoke "bad English" it was a sign the African had been in the colony for only a brief period and was probably an adult at the time of arrival.

During the colonial period, African ethnicity played a strong role initially in the development of plantation life. The *South Carolina Gazette* revealed that the majority of "New Negroes" arriving in South Carolina spoke little or no English unless they had been imported from the West Indies or central Africa. A sale advertisement in the *Gazette* read as follows: "A likely Negro Boy about 13 years of Age and speaks good English to be sold."[7] That he spoke good English meant that he was probably "country-born"—raised in the colony and acculturated. Africans born and raised in the colony had little trouble learning the language. For example, a fourteen-year-old Angolan spoke "pretty good English,"[8] a seventeen-year-old Angolan spoke "broken English,"[9] and a nineteen-year-old spoke "good English."[10] An Angolan woman, two Gambian men, and an Igbo man could speak "pretty good English."[11] Obviously, acculturation and the learning of English among younger Africans were quite rapid, whereas older Africans learned English with greater difficulty.

An example of older and unacculturated Africans can be found in this advertisement: "Ran away from the Plantation farm belonging to Capt. Douglas, near Dorchester, a tall Negro fellow named Tower-hill and talks bad English."[12] Many of the Charleston newspapers revealed this slow progress in learning English. Four new Negro men were reported in the *Gazette* of January 22, 1737, out of the ship *Shepherd* from Angola in the beginning of November as "speaking no English and not knowing their master's name." Four other could speak "no English," and an Ebo runaway could "speak no more English other than his name is Jack."[13]

Thomas Wright advertised that his slave Paul "had been one year in my plantation near Silk Hope" and still spoke "little English."[14] Another African could not speak any English when he ran away almost a year earlier,[15] and three Angolan men had been in Carolina three years and still spoke "little English."[16] But "country-born" Africans such as Jacob could speak only English.[17]

African cultural and linguistic acculturation into the American culture took several generations. In each generation less and less of the African culture was retained. After about eight generations of country-born Africans, successful Americanization had taken place. But the linguistic exchanges were mutual and reciprocal: the process also brought about the Africanization of the South. Generations of interaction with African speech patterns produced the distinct white Southern accent. Edward Kimber, a traveler in the South in 1746, noticed the impact of Black English on white Southern speech, writing that "one thing they are very faulty in, with regard to their Children, which is, that when young, they suffer them too much to prowl amongst the young Negroes, which insensibly causes them to imbibe their Manners and broken speech."[18] In other words, the English of Southerners resembled the African version.

Africans arriving in Colonial America, especially South Carolina, continued to give their children African names well into the nineteenth century. In the seventeenth and eighteenth centuries, African American slaves had retained Africanisms in their naming practices. The greatest percentage of African names occurred among male slaves in the eighteenth century, when the majority of the black population was still unacculturated. African names gave them a sense of cultural integrity and a link to their African past and heritage.

The Africans did not forget their traditional naming practices at first. During the colonial period, the practice of naming children after the days of the week, months, and seasons was retained. In some cases the African Americans retained the original African version of their day names, but as generations passed they substituted the original African name for their English equivalent. The following table lists Akan day names found in the *South Carolina Gazette*.[19]

DAYS OF THE WEEK WITH CORRESPONDING AFRICAN NAMES

Day	Male Names	Female Names
Monday	Cudjoe	Juba
Tuesday	Cubbenah	Beneba
Wednesday	Quaco	Cuba
Thursday	Quao	Abba
Friday	Cuffee	Phibba
Saturday	Quamin	Mimba
Sunday	Quashee	Quasheba

Temporal names such as January, April, May, June, September, November, March, August, Christmas, and Midday are also found in the *Gazette* and other publications. There are numerous examples of English equivalents of African day names such as Monday, Tuesday, or Friday. According to Cohen, male names derived from the season are Spring

(Ebo or Calabar) and Winter. Moon and Thunder are names connected with the state of the weather at time of birth. Other names which are probably English equivalents of African words are Arrow ("of the Pappa country"), Boy (Guiney), Huntsman (new), Little One (Ebo), Plenty (Gambia and Mandingo), and Sharper (Bambara).[20] This Akan naming was practiced in the Sea Islands of Georgia and South Carolina until the 1930s.

After the first and second generation, Africans began to substitute African day names for the English translations. Paul Cuffee, a wealthy shipbuilder, came from this African naming system. Cuffe, the seventh of ten children of Paul and Mary Slocum, was born on January 17, 1759, on Elizabeth Island near New Bedford, Massachusetts. When he was nineteen years old, nine of the children dropped the slave name Slocum (the surname of their father's master) and adopted their father's slave name, Cuffe.[21] This word is Ashanti, meaning "male child born on Friday," and comes from Kofi. Linguist Joel Dillard points out that female day names followed practices similar to the male day names and that Cuba was among the most common names given to female children born on Wednesday. The name often given to a female child born on Friday was Phibba, which later transformed into Phoebe. Abby came from Abba, the female day name for Tuesday. According to Dillard, the name Benah, from Gubena (Tuesday), was frequently misanalyzed as "Venus." Cudjoe, the male day name for Monday, might be Cudjoe in the first generation, Monday in the second generation, and Joe in the third generation.[22]

The Georgia Writers' Project during the 1930s found that among the Georgia coastal blacks, a number of people had been named for weekdays or the month in which they were born. One ex-slave who was interviewed in regard to this practice, Thursday Jones, explained:[23]

> Dey name me dat way jis cus uh happen tuh be bawn on Tursday, I guess. Sech things seem tub be in our fambly. I had ah uncle who name tis Monday Collins. It seem tuh come duh fus ting tuh folks' mine tuh name duh babies fuh duh dey is baw on.

Here we see how the English equivalents of African day names were being used. By the nineteenth century, the African day names often had lost their meaning, but African Americans continued to give their children African day names.

Quaco, the male day name for Wednesday, was also commonly found during the colonial period. But, later, Quaco became Jacco, Jacky, and Jack. Martin Jackson of Texas decided to become Jackson because one of his relatives had a similar African name:

The master's name was usually adopted by a slave after he was set free. This was done more because it was the logical thing to do and the easiest way to be identified, than it was through affection for the master. Also, the government seemed to be in an almighty hurry to have us get names. We had to register as someone, so we could be citizens. Well, I got to thinking about all us slave that was going to take the name Fitzpatrick. I made up my mind I'd find me a different one. One of my grandfathers in Africa was called Jeaceo, and so I decided on Jackson.[24]

By 1734, when the *South Carolina Gazette* was established, names of African origin included Bowbaw, Cuffee, Ebo Jo, Ganda, Quaquo, Quomenor, and Quoy for males, Africans and Auba, Bucko, Juba Mimba, Odah, and Otta for females. African names common in the eighteenth century were Sambo, Quash, Mingo, and Juba. The most widely used day names were Cuffee (Kofi) and Cudjoe for males and Abba and Juba for females.[25]

According to Cohen, African day names and their English counterparts existed side by side. Two male slaves named Friday, one of them "this country born" and the other from the "Angola Country," and two male slaves named Monday, one from "Bomborough" (Bambara?) and the other "A Barbian (Bambara) Negro," are mentioned in the *Gazette.*[26]

Blanche Britt supplied Mencken with this list of African names taken from Southern newspapers from 1736 to the end of the eighteenth century: Annika, Boohum, Boomy, Bowzar, Cuffee, Cuffey, Cuffy, Habella, Kauchee, Mila, Minas, Monimea, Pamo, Qua, Quaco, Quamina, Quash, Warrah, and Yonaha.[27]

Cohen gives a list of African names found in the *Gazette* between 1732 and 1775 (table 1).[28]

A list of slave names from a 1656 land patent record suggest that these slaves came from the "Bight of Guinea" to Virginia on a Dutch ship, the *Wittepaert,* by way of New Netherlands. The Virginia importer was Edmund Scarburgh. The names are given in table 2.[29]

TABLE 1. African Names from *South Carolina Gazette,* 1732–1775

Male Names

Ankey	Folee	(Kuamania)*
Assam (Asane)*	Footbea	Quaow
Assey (Ase)*	Gamone(Ngamone)	Quash
Bafey (Bofe)*	Goma (Ngoma)*	Quaw

Continues on the next page

Balipho
Banjoe
Beay (Mbiya)*
Beoy
Bobodandy
Boo (Mbo)*
Boswine
Bram
Bury
Chopco (Tshikapu)*
Claes
Clawes
Chockcoose
(Tshikusa)*
Congo
Crack
Cudjoe
Cuff
Cuffee (Kofi)
Culley
Cumin (Kumina)*
Dago
Dembow (Ndembu)*
Dibbie
Donas
Doney
Easom

Gunnah (Kuna)*
Haloe (Halue)*
Homady
Hughky (Huki)*
Jamina*
Jellemy
Jobny
Ketch
Mahomet
Mallay
Mambee (Muambe)*
Mamena (Maminu)*
Manso
Marmillo
Massery
Mingo
Mobe
Mollock
Monvigo (Muvinga)*
Morrica
Musce Jack
Mussu (Musue)*
Okree
Pherco
Fouta (Fula)*
Quacoe (Kuaka)*
Quammano

Rente
Saffran
Sambo
Sandico
Sango
Santry
Saundy
Savey
Sawney
Serrah
Shampee
Sirrah
Sobo
Sogo
Stepney
Tokey
Tomboe
Wabe (Webe)
Whan
Wholly (Hola)
Woolaw
Yanke
Yanki
Yonge
Zick (Tshika)*
Zocky (Nzoko)
Zoun

Female Names
Aba (Aba)*
Abey
Affrey
Agua
Arrah
Banaba
Binah (Bena)*
Body (Mbudi)*
Plaeby
Quant (Kamu)
Rino

Camba (Kamba)*
Choe (Njo)*
Cuba (Nkuba)*
Dye (Ndaye)*
Eley (Elayi)*
(Ban' Aba)*
Famtame (Patane)*
Fortimer
Rynah
Sack (Seka)*
Sard

Juba
Juda
Mabia
Mamadoe
Mawdlong
Embro (Walongo)*
Minda (Minda)
Nea (Neaye)
Sibby
Tinah
Windy (Wende)

*Luba words identified by Vass

TABLE 2. Names Listed on the Dutch Slave Ship *Wittepaert*

Tony	Tubuno (Tubu'enuk, your hole)*
Ufoler (uhola-harvest)*	Tabortha
Aiquera	Janna (Tshiana, fat child)*
Ambe (let him tell)*	Ommo
Aura	Jihur
Assone (Asune, let him bring water)*	Curmer
Ay (Aye, let him send)*	Dondo (Ndondo, ritual term,
Monafunke (Mona nfunke, see I'm	depths)*
pointing)*	Taryi
Eare	Jonara
Messon (Mesu-eyes)*	Jomora
Roundells	Sango (Sanga, unite)*
Wortells	Croila
Johney	Jurna
Angora (A'Ngola)*	Rommo
Margarretta	Wingoe
Monque	Elloren
Veco	Corle
Ogombe (Ngombe-cow)*	Murrom
Werrye	Agoe (Angue, let him seek)*
Ottonco	Dony

*Luba words identified by Vass

Africanisms in African American Names

Names are of great importance in West and Central Africa. Names are given as stages in an individual's life and, as among all people for whom magic is important, the identification of a real name with the personality of its bearer is held to be so complete that this real name, usually the one given at birth by a particular relative, must be kept secret lest it come into the hands of someone who might use it in working evil magic against the person. That is why, among Africans, a person's name may in so many instances change with time, a new designation being assumed on the occasion of some striking occurrence in the person's life. When the person goes through one of the rites marking a new stage in his or her development, a name change also occurs to note the event.[30]

Stuckey, in *Slave Culture: Nationalist Theory and the Foundations of Black America* (1987), noted that black naming practices were African in origin, in that African Americans changed their names just as Africans did, corresponding to major changes in the life of the individual. The name shifting is clearly demonstrated by the experience of Frederick Douglass, who, soon after escaping slavery, began a series of name changes.[31]

> On the morning after our arrival at New Bedford, while at the breakfast-table, the question arose as to what name I should be called by. The name given me by my mother was Frederick Augustus Washington Bailey. I, however, had dispensed with the two middle names long before I left Maryland so that I was generally known by the name Frederick Bailey. I started from Baltimore; I found it necessary again to change my name. . . . I gave Mr. Johnson, Mr. Nathan Johnson of New Bedford, the privilege of choosing me a name, but told him he must not take from me the name of "Frederick," I must hold on to that a sense of identity.

Sojourner Truth, a crusader for black emancipation and feminine equality, was known as Isabella until about the age of twenty, when she was freed and left her master's plantation. She had a vision in a dream that told her about her new name and her mission to free her people. And Malcolm X, through various stages of his life, was known as Malcolm Little, Homeboy, Detroit Red, Big Red, Satan, Malcolm, El-hajji, and Malik El Shabazz.[32]

Such name shifting is common throughout West Africa and particularly Central Africa. In many parts of Africa every man who leaves his traditional setting and family is given or takes a new name when he turns or walks away from home. This situation parallels that of enslaved Africans who were brought to the Americas, away from their ethnic groups, but who remained in contact with others who shared a similar ethnic background.[33]

Nowhere is this tradition as vivid as in the jazz world, where name shifting is common, signaling a major event in the life of the musician: Jelly Roll Morton (Ferdinand La Menthe), Satchmo (Louis Armstrong), Yardbird (Charles Parker), Lady (Billie Holiday). The story of these name changes follows the African pattern of using a new name to adapt to new circumstance and changes in the person's new life.

Africanisms in African American Nicknames

A more direct African survival is the use of nicknames. Almost every black person is known by two names: a given name and a name used only within the family circle. Lorenzo Dow Turner found a dual naming system among the Gullah in the Sea Islands of South Carolina. This system consists of an English (American) name given at birth and a more intimate name used exclusively by the family and community.

Turner was surprised that previous scholarship had failed to note this practice or the importance of Africanisms in Gullah nomenclature. Slaveholders recognized this dual naming practice among enslaved Africans in the eighteenth century. In their advertisements of runaways in the *South Carolina Gazette*, owners always included "proper" (given) names and "country names," the African names retained.[34]

This naming practice still exists among the Gullahs and in the general African American population. In black naming practices, every child receives a given name at birth and a nickname that generally follows the individual throughout life. Some examples of these nicknames are Jo Jo, June, Tiny Baby, O.K., John John, Mercy, Baby Sister, "T," Sunny Man, Main, Bo, Boo, Bad Boy, Playboy, and Fats.[35]

Among enslaved Africans this practice also was evident in names used by slaves, such as Pie Ya, Puddin'-tame, Frog, Tennie C., Monkey, Mush, Cooter, John de Baptist, Fat-Man, Preacher, Jack Rabbit, Sixty, Pop Corn, Old Gold, Dootes, Angle-eye, Bad Luck, Sky-up-de-Greek, Cracker Jabbo, Cat-Fish, Bear, Tip, Odessa, Pig Lasses, Rattler, Pearly, Luck, Buffalo, Old Blue, Red Fox, Coon, and Jewsharp.

Turner found that Gullah-speaking people preserved their language and nicknames by what they called basket names or day names. Their children always had two distinct names, an English one for public use and an authentic African name for private use by the extended family alone.

Here are a few examples of Gullah basket names which are also straight, unchanged, present-day Tshiluba names: Ndomba is the name given a Gullah child whose hand protrudes first at birth. It means "I am begging (with my outstretched hand)." Mviluki has a Gullah meaning of "a penitent." Its Luba source word is Mvuluki, a rememberer, one who doesn't forget his sins. The basket name Siungila means "to save, help, deliver," while Kamba, a very common Luba name, comes from Munkamba, meaning "ancestor." The Gullah meaning of Kamba is "a grave." Anyika, a Gullah name meaning "to praise the beauty of." Sebe, a Gullah name meaning "a leather ornament," comes from the Mesu (eyes), Kudima (to work or hoe), and Kudiya (to eat) are all Gullah day names, exactly the same in Gullah and Luba.[36]

In the Sea Island of South Carolina, children sometimes have not only their given names but also community names. The community gives the child a name that characterizes or is characteristic of the individual, that is, Smart Child, Shanty (showoff).[37] This practice parallels Bantu naming practices in Zaire. Net's basketball center Dikenibo

Mutombo from Zaire illustrates this point. His full name is Dikambe Mutombo Mpolondo Munkamba Diken Jean-Jean Jacque wa Mutombo. In order, these names are his uncle's name, his family surname, his grandfather's name, his nicknames given by his village, his name given at birth, and his hometown village, wa Mutombo (which means "from the village Mutombo").[38]

Other creolized Gullah pet names (nicknames) so typical of Bantu practices are names of animals or fish: De Dog, Doggie, Kitty, Fish, Yellowtail, Croker, Frog Spider, Boy, Gal Jumper, Tooti, Crocki, Don, Cuffy, Akebee, Dr. Buzzer, and Dr. Eagle.[39]

In Gullah naming practices, as in African naming practices, children are named after parents because they are believed to be the parent spirit residing in the children. The same name might appear in several generations in a family. In the Sea Islands, the name Litia appeared in four generations of female children.[40]

An integral part of Bantu culture is the unchanging secret "spirit name," something that the individual has which is uniquely his or her own from the past and is carried on to the next generation, given to a new baby so that it may remain incarnate. Thus, by a strange interweaving of religion and language, the "inner soul" of the speech of a cultural group is preserved. As Munday reported:[41]

> Investigation brings to light the fact that the Africans of these parts, whether man or woman, have two classes of names: (a) spirit-names and (b) names of manhood or womanhood. Each has one (a few have two) of the names of the first class, and one or more names from the second class. It is by these names of manhood or womanhood that they prefer to be called; some are traditional African names of these parts, some are debased European words, some are European given or family nicknames, some are nicknames, given owing to some peculiarity, some are names given at baptism. All of these names of manhood and womanhood (except the last) can be, and are, changed for any and no reason, and according to who is changed, once it is finally given. It is of this spirit-name that the Lala aphorism says: The name is the Spirit.

Officials now prefer the African to be registered under his spirit name, because it is never changed, but there are two practical disadvantages which weigh against its being used for registration purposes. A Bantu with which we are concerned is exceedingly shy of using it for himself or another, and in some parts, the spirit names are so few in number that the majority of persons in one area may share half a dozen. However, for the Bantu the spirit name is never changed from the mother's back to the grave.

The giving of the spirit name (literally, "of birth" or "of the navel") is regarded as an event of the greatest importance. Every child born is regarded as the "come back" of some dead person, either of the same or of the opposite sex. The person has to be given the spirit name of the dead person.

Munday points out that the spirits of the dead are immortal only as they become incarnate again in another human being that bears their name. If a name is forgotten so that it cannot become incarnate, it wanders through the world as a ghost.[42] This naming practice of spirit names and given names still exists with the African mother continent and African Americans in the North American Diaspora:

AFRICANISMS IN CONTEMPORARY AMERICAN ENGLISH

adobe[43]	Twi (Akan) a palm tree, leaves or grass used for roof covering.
ananse[44]	Twi (Akan) and Ewe, spider; Bambara *nansi*, chameleon.
bad[45]	Very good, used esp. in emphatic form, *baad*. Cf. Michael Jackson's "I'm baad!" Similarly are *mean*, in the sense of satisfying, fine, attractive; *wicked*, in the sense of excellent, capable. Cf. African use of negative terms, pronounced emphatically, to describe positive extremes: Mandingo (Bambara) *a ka nyi ko-jugu*, it's very good! (lit. "it is good badly!"); Mandingo (Gambia) *a nyinata jaw-ke*, she is very beautiful! Also West African English (Sierra Leone) *gud baad*, it's very good!
bad-eye[46]	Threatening, hateful glance. Common African–African American colloquialism. Cf. Mandingo *nyejugu*, hateful glance (lit. "bad eye") and similar phrases in other West African languages.
bad-mouth[47]	In Gullah, slander, abuse, gossip; also used as v. Cf. Mandingo *da-jugu* and Hausa *mugum-baki*, slander, abuse (in both cases, lit. "bad mouth").
bambi[48]	Bantu *mubambi*, one who lies down in order to hide; position of antelope fawn for concealment (cf. Walt Disney, Bambi).
bamboula[49]	African drum used in New Orleans during the nineteenth century. Also, a vigorous style of dancing there, early twentieth century. "Drum" in early jazz use. Cf. *bambula*, beat, hit, or strike a surface, a drum. Similar terms in other West African coastal language groups.
banana[50]	Wolof word for fruit and was first recorded in 1563, and en-

tered British English in the seventeenth century via Spanish and Portuguese.

banjo[51]   Kimbundu *mbanza*, stringed musical instruments, whence also Jamaican English *banja* and Brazilian Portuguese *banza*.

be with it[52]   Mandingo expression, to be *a la* (lit. "to be with in, in it") to be in fashion.

bidibidi[53]   Bantu *bidibidi:* a small bird; a small yellow bird. Ebonic: "a little biddy bird."

biddy[54]   Baby chick, chicken, fowl.

big eye[55]   Igbo *anya uku*, covetous, greedy (lit. "big eye"). Cf. West African and Caribbean English *big yay, big eye*. Same in Gullah and Black English.

bo[56]   Temne and Vai (Sierra Leone), friend; informal term of address for an equal. West African and Caribbean English *bo, ba*.

bogue, bogus[57]   Hausa *boko, boko-boko*, deceit, fraud, West African English (Sierra Leone) *bogo-bogo*, Louisiana French *bogue*, fake, fraudulent, phony. The ending of bogus has an analogy with *hocuses pocus*.

booboo[58]   Bantu *mbuku*, stupid, blundering act; error, blunder. Common nickname found in black English.

boody[59]   Bantu *buedi*, act of emission, sex. Cf. black American slang: "give me that booty."

booger[60]   Bantu *mbukku*, divination, consultation of the spirits; ghost, spirit.

boobaboo[61]   Bantu *buka lubuk*, conjure, enchant, divine; consult a medicine man; imaginary cause of fear, worry; nemesis.

boogie (woogie)[62]   Bantu *mbuki-mvuki*, to take off in dance performance. Hausa *buga* (*bugi* after n. object). Mande *bugs*, to beat, to beat drums. West African English (Sierra Leone) *bogi*, to dance. To dance fast blues music, eight beats to a bar; *boog*, to dance.

bowdacious[63]   Bantu *botesha*, pulverize, grind to powder; extremely, exceedingly, to the ninth degree. Cf. Uncle Remus usage.

bozo[64]   Bantu *boza*, knock things over in passing; a strong, stupid person, a stumblebum. Common in black American slang: "Don't be a bozo!"

brer, buh[65]   Mandingo *kckc*, elder brother; title used before animal names in fables, tales. Cf. Uncle Remus usage.

bronco[66]   Term of Ibibio origin, used centuries ago to denote Spanish and African slaves who worked with and cared for cattle.

buckaroo[67]   Ibibio *buckra*, poor white man; a white person bucking a bronco. See *Buckra*.

buckra (1)[68]	Efik and Ibibio *mbakara*, master. Used by enslaved Africans to refer to and address their masters. By 1730s, enslaved Africans and colonists used it to mean "white man." Often pronounced and spelled *buccara* and *boccra*, by 1775 it had come to mean "gentlemen" and even, by 1860s, the color "white."
buckra (2)[69]	Poor or mean white man, now rare in the United States, except in the South Carolina Sea Islands. Still current in Jamaican English. Convergence with Spanish *vaquero;* hence *buckaroo, bucker* (cowboy).
bug[70]	Mandingo *baga*, to offend, annoy, harm (someone); Wolof *bugal*, to annoy, worry. Note also West African and Caribbean English *ambog*, to annoy; this form; pronounced in eighteenth century with stress on second syllable, may reflect the nominal prefix m-in Wolof *mbugal*, hindrance, annoyance. The same element may be contained in British and American English humbug, to hoax, impose upon.
cat[71]	A person, man, fellow, just a "cool dude." Same as hipi cat.
chance[72]	Bantu *tshianza*, hand, handful; a certain number, several.
chick[73]	Girl, pretty young woman, one especially "hip," or attractive. Cf. Wolof *jigen*, woman. Note convergence with English chicken.
chigger[74]	Wolof *jiga*, insect, sand flea. First recorded in 1743, via Caribbean. Originally pronounced and spelled *chigo, chego,* or *chiego.*
cowboy[75]	Originated in Colonial period when African labor and skills were closely associated with cattle raising. Africans stationed at cow pens with herding responsibilities were referred to as "cowboy," just as Africans who worked in the "Big House" were known as "houseboy." As late as 1865, following the Civil War, Africans whose livestock responsibilities were with cattle were referred to as "cowboys" in plantation records. After 1865, whites associated with cattle industry referred to themselves as "cattlemen" to distinguish themselves from "cowboys."
coob[76]	Bantu *kuba*, care for, take care of, watch over, a hutch, pen, or coop for fowls or small domestic animals: a chicken "coob."
cool[77]	Mandingo cool, slow, and *gone not;* hence fast. Terms applied to music and dancing: calm, controlled, slow tempo and the opposite, hot, fast, and energetic. Corresponding terms found in other African languages.
cooter[78]	Kongo *nkuda*, a box turtle. Also West African *kuta*, turtle, use recorded 1832. Came into southern U.S. dialect via Gullah heard mainly in Georgia, South Carolina, Alabama, and Louisiana.

daskiki

Yoruba *danshiki*, a loose, colorfully patterned, bottomless pull-on shirt. Garment and word were introduced during the civil rights movement of the 1960s, when young black men wore dashikis to reassert their identity with African culture. Made famous by (Ron) Maulana Karenga in the 1960s.

day-clean[79]

Bantu *kutoka kulu*, dawn, "clean sky"; Wolof *ba set na*, it has dawned (day is clean); Mandingo *dugu jera*, it has dawned (day has become clean, clear). Found in Gullah, West African and Caribbean English *do-klin*, day-clean, and black Caribbean French *ju netye* (lit. "day-cleaned").

diddle[80]

Bantu *dinga:* deceive, trick, cheat; cheat, swindle.

diddy-wa-diddy[81]

Bantu *wadid-wadid:* you eat and eat; legendary place of plenty to eat.

dig[82]

Wolof *deg*, *dega*, understand, appreciate, pay attention to. Convergence with Black English to "dig," understand.

dinge[83]

Mandingo *den, din*, child, young person, younger than the speaker, *den-ke*, male child, young man. A black person, *dingey*; a black child, *dinkey*.

dirt[84]

Akan *dote*, earth, soil. Common in U.S., as in "dirt road" or "dirt track." West African and Caribbean English *doti*, dirty, earth. Convergence with British English in its original sense of "filthy."

doll-baby[85]

Yoruba *omo langidi*, little child; *oyedeji*, wooden images. Southern dialect idiom common in black English, distribution mainly along Atlantic Coast.

do one's thing[86]

Mandingo *ka a fen ke* (lit. "to do one's t'ing"), to undertake one's favorite activity or assume one's favorite role.

done[87]

Wolof *doon*, past completive marker, "he done go"; Mandingo *tun*, past completive marker. Cf. also black West African English *don*, as past completive marker. Convergence with English *done*.

fat-mouth[88]

Mandingo *da-baa*, excessive talking (lit. "big, fat mouth"). Same as *bad-mouth*.

foo-foo[89]

Akan *foforo*, new, fresh, strange. An outsider, a newcomer, one who does not belong or is not accepted, a fool, a worthless person. Convergence with English fool. Cf. black Jamaican English *foo-foo, fool-fool*, credulous, easy to take advantage of, stupid.

fuzzy[90]

Wolof *fas*, horse (*fas wi*, the horse, *fas yi*, the horses). "Horse" in two specialized senses: "range horse" and "sure bet at a horse race." Hence, perhaps, *fuzz, fuzzy*, policeman,

	from an earlier use of horse patrols. Convergence with English *fuzzy-tail*.
gam[91]	Hausa *gama*, boastfulness, showing off.
geechee[92]	Originally meant an African from the Guinea coast. Later, it meant a black not yet fully acculturated during slavery. In 1789, applied to Africans brought to Ogeechee River plantation under coercion.
goober[93]	Bantu *nguba*, peanut; use recorded 1834. Another word for peanut is *pinder*, or *pinal*, from Congo *mpinda*, peanut; use first recorded in Jamaica 1707, South Carolina 1848.
goofer-bag[94]	Bantu *kufwa*, to die; v. common to all Bantu languages. A charm to protect from death.
goofer-dust[95]	Bantu *kufaw*, to die. Refers to grave dirt. In Congo (Zaire), earth from a grave is considered at one with the spirit of the buried person. Used by "root workers" on American plantation.
goose[96]	Wolof *kus*, anus. To nudge someone in the anus. "Your goose is cooked." (Originally from Arabic?)
gris-gris[97]	Object worn as protective charm against evil, or used to inflict harm. An amulet in place of and with the power to remove voodoo curses. Associated with voodoo rites in Louisiana. Used by Marie Laveau, noted voodoo queen. She concocted a *gris-gris* of salt, gunpowder, saffron, and dried dog dung. A *gris-gris* that protected from evil or brought good luck was a dime with a hole in it, worn about the ankle. Mende in origin, via Hausa.
gullah[98]	Bantu *Ngola*, an ethnic group in Angola. Refers to African Americans living in the Sea Islands and regions of South Carolina, Georgia, and northern Florida. Also refers to their language.
guy[99]	Wolof *gay*, fellows, persons. Used as a term of address, including "you guys," addressed even to a single man or woman. Convergence with English personal name Guy.
he[100]	Undifferentiated third-person sing. pron., he or she. Similar usage is found in most West African and in all Bantu languages, as well as in most forms of black West African and Caribbean English. In Gullah, he remains undifferentiated, referring to either a male or a female. For reverse African influence in differentiation between second-person sing. and pl. pron.
hear[101]	Mandingo *n mu a men*, I didn't understand (lit. "I didn't

hear it"), hearing in the sense of understanding. Cf. similar application of v. meaning "to hear" in other West African languages.

hep hip[102] Wolof *hepi, hipi*, to open one's eyes, to be aware of what is going on. Hence *hipi-kat*, someone with eyes open, aware of what is going on.

honkie[103] Wolof *hong*, red pink; color used to describe white people in African languages. Cf. also *pink*, a white man, and *redneck*, a powerful white farmer in the U.S. In Ebonics *honkie* referred to whites who would come to the black community, park and honk their horns for their black dates. This term was used before the 1960s.

hoodoo[104] Hoodoo, as opposed to voodoo, is less centrally organized as part of voodoo religious practices. It generally connotes the mystic and magical aspects, usually evolved for negative purpose. "To hoodoo someone" implied that an individual was made to do something against his will by the use of various concoctions, which could be drunk, eaten, or worn, in order to make someone fall in love or to cause a death.

hulla-ballo[105] Bantu *halua balualua*, when those that are coming arrive. Hence noise, uproar, racket of greeting.

hully-gully[106] Bantu *halakala*, compare (the hands, to ascertain the one holding the rock). A child's game.

jam[107] Informal gathering of jazz musicians, playing for their own entertainment. Same element may be contained in *jamboree*, noisy revel, celebration, a full hand of cards, first recorded in 1860s. Possible convergence of Mandingo and black West African English *jama* (from Arabic), crowd gathering, and Wolof *jam*, slave (in U.S., a gathering of slaves or former slaves for their own entertainment). A related Wolof term is *jaambuur*, freeman, freed man.

jamboree[108] Celebration by emancipated slaves made famous with *Juneteenth* celebrations.

jazz[109] Bantu *jaja*, to make dance. Obsolete forms *jas, jasy*. The numerous applications of this term center on basic v. sense of "to speed up, excite, exaggerate, act in an unrestricted or extreme way." Note corresponding use as n. and as adj., "jazzy." Applied to copulation, frenzied dancing, fast music, exaggerated talk, gaudy patterns and colors, excessive pleasure-seeking. Cf. Mandingo *jasi*, to become abnormal or out of character, either diminished or excessive. Cf. similar Wolof *yees* and Temne *yas*, to be lively or energetic to an extreme degree, applied to exaggerated styles of dancing or music, excessive love-making, etc.

jelly, jelly-roll[110]   Mandingo *jeli,* minstrel, who often gained popularity with women through his skills in the use of words and music. A virile man who curries sexual favors of women. Epithet applied in U.S. to several black musicians, including "Jelly Roll Morton" (piano), "Jelly" Williams (bass), and "Jelly" Thompson (guitar). Convergence with English items of food, jelly and jelly-roll.

jenk[111]   Bantu *njika,* reserve, reticence, inhibition. "To spread my jenk": relax, have a good time.

jiffy[112]   Bantu *tshipi,* short. In a second, in a moment.

jigger[113]   Bantu *njiga,* sand flea, insect.

jiggaboo[114]   Bantu *tshikabo,* they bow the head docilely. Derogatory term for black person. In black English a *jiggaboo* is someone who is extremely black, with strong African features, as opposed to high yellow, or light-skinned.

jitter-(bug)[115]   Mandingo *ji-to,* frightened, cowardly, from *ji,* to be afraid. *Jitobaga,* a frightened, cowardly person. To tremble and shake, have "the jitters"; nervousness, fear, cowardice. *Jitter bug:* an excited swing addict, who shakes and trembles in dancing.

jive[116]   Wolof *jev, jew,* to talk about someone in his absence, esp. in a disparaging way. Misleading talk; to talk in a misleading or insincere way. Applied to sexual and musical activity. Ct. semantic range of *jazz.* Convergences with English jive, jibe, to sneer at, disparage.

john[117]   Mandingo *jon,* slave, a person owned by someone else. An average man, esp. one who can be exploited or easily taken in; a male lover, a prostitute's client. Also used in black American folklore, as in John Henry, name of hero-slave frequently in conflict with "massa." The term *massa* provides a convenient convergence of English master and Mandingo *massa,* chief. That Mandingo speakers in U.S. were conscious of this convergence is suggested by the cycle of black American tales involving John-versus-Massa, which corresponds to a similar genre of Mandingo tales in West Africa involving *jon,* the slave, versus *massa,* the chief.

juba (1)[118]   A group dance with complex rhythmic clapping and slapping of knees and things, as done by plantation slaves (1834). Both dance and word are of African origin.

juba (2)[119]   One of the earliest records of the term *juba* dates to American minstrel days. Both Juba and Jube consistently appeared as names of enslaved Africans who were skilled musicians and dancers.

juba (3)[120]

Bantu *juba, jiouba,* or *diubu,* to beat time rhythmically. Used to describe an African dance step, the Charleston; recorded particularly in South Carolina and West Indies. Juba is also the Akan female day name for a child born on Monday.

juba (4)[121]

Traditional slave food. Refers to the food that enslaved Africans working in the plantation house collected from the massa's leftovers. Such leftovers were called *juba, jibba,* or *jiba.* On Saturday or Sunday the leftovers were thrown together; no one could distinguish the meat from the bread and vegetables. This juba was placed in a huge pot and those working in "de big House" shared it with those working in the fields.

juba (5)[122]

Bantu *nguba, kingooba,* peanut, groundnut, "goober," from which an old African melody is derived. The Juba dance was originally performed on plantations but became so popular that whites gave it the name Charleston, after the southern city and major slave port. The dance was introduced in 1926 to the American stage in an all-black production by E. F. Miller and Aubrey Lyles entitled *Runnin' Wild,* and as the "Charleston" it became the dance craze of the 1920s.

juke[123]

Wolof *dzug,* to misbehave, lead a disorderly life; Bambara *dzugu,* wicked. Brothel, cheap tavern, low dive. Mainly Gullah and black use in South. To *juke* (1939), to make the rounds of taverns and low dives, go drinking; used mainly by Southerners. By early 1940s *to juke* came to mean "to make the rounds drinking and dancing to jukeboxes." (1939) *Juke joints,* taverns or roadhouses that featured jukeboxes. *Juke Juke-joint,* a hand-out bar. Cf. also Bantu *juka,* rise up, do your things.

ju ju[124]

Bantu *njiu,* danger, harm, accident. A charm or fetish against such.

kakatulu[125]

Bantu *kukatulu,* to take off, remove; v.i., to be still, immobile. Name of a large bird, mockingbird.

kelt, ketch[126]

Bantu *keleja,* filter, strain; catch the drippings, pale stuff. A light-skinned black person.

kickeraboo[127]

The Americanisms "to kick the bucket" evolved from *kickeraboo* and *kickatavoo,* killed or dead. Term has two African sources: Krio (the English-based Creole of Sierra Leone) *kekrebu, kekerabu,* dead, to wither (as leaves or fruit); Ga (West Africa) *kekre,* dry, stiff; and *bo,* to befall, end. "Kicking the bucket" was used in American blackface minstrel songs, regarding the death of a black person, until about the mid-nineteenth century, when it moved into Standard American English.

kil[128] — To affect strongly, as in "you kill me!" Similar usage in a number of West African languages, including Wolof and Mandingo, or verbs meaning lit. "to kill."

kook, kooky[129] — Bantu *kuku*, dolt, blockhead. A strange, peculiar person.

kong[130] — Bantu *nkongo*, mixture, conglomeration. Bootleg whiskey.

lubo[131] — First used in America in 1732 to identify slaves from Niger Delta. Use of African name indicated a first-generation African or a newly arrived "saltwater" African.

mahoola[132] — Bantu *mahula*, secrets, divulged matters, indiscretions. Silly talk.

man[133] — Mandingo *ce*, man, the man; power, authority. Term of address.

massa[134] — Mande (Mandingo) *masa*, chief.

mat[135] — Hausa *mata* or *mace*, woman, wife.

mean[136] — Similar to bad, as "don't be mean to me."

mojo[137] — Fula moca, to cast a magic spell by spitting. Hence *mocore*, magic spell, incantation uttered while spitting. Originally, magic spell, charm, amulet, spell cast by spitting. Mainly used today in sense of something working in one's favor: "I got my *mojo* working!" Also, narcotics. Cf. Gullah *moco*, witchcraft, magic. Black Jamaican English *majoe, mojo*, plant with renowned medicinal powers.

moola, mula[138] — Bantu *mulambo*, receipts, tax money. Money, wealth. Cf. black English "give me some moola!"

mother yo' mama[139] — West African, esp. Wolof; used as term of severe abuse or of jocular abuse between friends. Includes use of explicit insults, such as "motherfucker."

mouse[140] — Mandingo *muso* and Vai *musu*, woman, wife. Attractive girl, young woman, girlfriend, wife. Convergence with English mouse. Of several terms for "woman" taken over into black English from major West African languages.

nana[141] — Bantu *nana:* grandmother; Akan: *nana:* grandmother or grandfather.

ofay[142] — White man. Extended form: *ofaginzy*. Occurs as a nominal/adjectival prefix in many West African languages. Term for "white," beginning with "f," also occurs widely: *Bama fe, Gola fua, Ndoh fowe*, etc. It has been suggested that ofay represents a rearrangement of the letters of the English word *foe* into pig Latin, but from its form, the word is more likely to have an African origin.

okay (1)[143]

Mandingo *o-ke;* Dogon *o-kay;* Djabo *o-ke;* Western Fula *eeyi kay;* Wolof waw *kayk,* *waw ke,* all meaning "yes, indeed!" "That's it, all right." Note widespread use in languages of West Africa of *kay* and similar forms as confirmatory markers, esp. after words meaning "yes." Recorded use of *oh ki,* indicating surprised affirmation, in black Jamaican English 1816; predates by over twenty years the popularization of OK in white speech of New England. Affirmative use of *kay-ki* in black speech in U.S. is recorded from as early as 1776. Early attempts were made to explain OK as initial letters of misspelling of English words "all correct" or as French words *au quai,* on the quayside. Subsequent attempts have been made to derive term from German, Greek, Scots, English, Finnish, and Choctaw, but little consideration has been given to possibility of origin in black speech.

okay (2)[144]

Mandingo *o-ke-len,* after that (lit. "that being done"). Use of this syntactic construction is widespread in West African languages. "After that" serves as link between sentences in running narrative or discourse, serving to confirm the preceding and anticipate the following sentence.

okra[145]

Bantu *kingombo,* okra, main ingredient of gumbo. Food plant indigenous to Central Africa and brought to New World by enslaved Africans. Known to most Southerners by 1780s.

palooka[146]

Bantu *paluka* (tshiseki), to have a fit, spasm, convulsion. A stupid person; an inferior prizefighter.

pamper[147]

Bantu *pamba,* be worried, upset, afraid, disquieted. To scold or "bless out" someone.

peola[148]

Bantu *peula,* peel off outer skin. A light-complexioned black girl.

pharaoh[149]

Kanuri *fero,* girl. Girl, girlfriend, blues term.

phoney[150]

Mandingo *fani, foni* (to be) false, valueless; to tell a lie. Counterfeit, sham, something false or valueless. Note also *bogue, bogus.*

pin[151]

Temne *pind,* to stare at, see. Black West African English (Sierra Leone) *pin,* staring, as an intensifying adv. After v. denoting "to see." Convergence with English *pin.*

pinto[152]

Temne *(a-) bentho,* bier for carrying corpse. In South Carolina and Georgia, means "coffin."

plat-eye[153]

Bantu *palatayi,* scratch like a dog at the door. Malevolent, supernatural being thought to haunt Georgetown area of South Carolina. Female, animal-like ghost, feared in South.

poke[154]

Bantu -*poko*, deep bag, socket, cavity. A sack, bag, wallet. Cf. "a pig in a poke."

poon tang, puntang[155]

Bantu *mu ntanga*, under the bed. Sexual intercourse with a black person. Sexually attractive (black) woman, vagina. Cf. Lima *puntuy*, vagina. Convergence with French *putain*, prostitute.

poop[156]

Wolof *pup*, to defecate, of a child. Convergence with similar forms in European languages, including Dutch. Cf. black English *pup pup*.

poor jo[157]

Vai dialect work of Liberia and Sierra Leone (1736), heard mainly in Georgia. Colloquial name for great blue heron.

rap[158]

West African English (Sierra Leone) *rap*, to con, fool, get the better of someone in verbal play. Descriptive of a variety of verbal techniques: to speak to, greet; flirt with, make a pass (at a girl); speak in a colorful way; tease, taunt; con, fool. Used also as n. Recently popularized black American usage of *rap* is, in fact, old. Note *to rap*, meaning "to speak or talk."

rooty-toot[159]

Wolof *rutu-tuti*, rapid drumming sound. Old-fashioned music. Also *rootin-tootin*, noisy, boisterous.

ruskus[160]

Bantu *lukashi*, sound of cheering and applause. Informal, noisy commotion, rumpus.

sambo[161]

Bantu -*samba*, to comfort, cheer, console. Cf. Also widespread West African personal name: Wolof *Samb, Samba;* Mandingo *Sambu;* Hausa *sambo;* similar names among Bantu. Black man, male child, popular Southern use of the name. "Little Black *Sambo*" story appears to be a corruption of a West African folk tale.

say, says[162]

Mandingo *ko . . .*, say. Similar use of items meaning lit. "Say" found in numerous West African languages, black West African, and Caribbean English. Term used to introduce reported speech, "that . . . ," "he tell him, say. . . . " Cf. black speech "say, man . . . ," "he say this, and he says that."

shucking[163]

Bantu *shikuka*, hold the head high, be willful, be obstinate. Lying, bluffing, faking.

skin[164]

Temne *botme-der*, put skin; Mandingo *I golo don m bolo*, put your skin in my hand. Cf. black speech "give me some skin, man!" (shake hands with me!). Used in 1960s by African Americans before it moved into white American speech.

tabby[165]

Bantu *ntaba*, muddy place from which mud for building walls is taken. Building material composed of oyster shells, lime, sand, and saltwater, commonly used in building slave houses in Georgia and South Carolina.

too-la-loo[166]   Bantu *tullualua*, we're coming! Words of a song.

tote[167]   Kikongo *tota*, to pick up; Kimbundu *tuta*, to carry, load. Black West African English (Sierra Leone) *tot*, Cameroon *tut*, to carry. Similar forms meaning "carry" found in a number of western Bantu languages.

uh-huh[168]   *Uh-hum*, yes; *mhm*, no. Cf. widespread use throughout Africa of similar responses for "yes" and "no." Scattered use of such forms occurs elsewhere in the world esp. for "yes," but nowhere as regularly as in Africa, where, in many languages, they constitute regular words for "yes" and "no." Note also occurrence of intonational variants of these forms to indicate differing intensities and situations of response, both in African languages and black American English, as well as in black African and Caribbean English. African origin of these items is confirmed by their much wider use in American than in British English.

voodoo[169]   Fon (Dahomey) *vodu*, *vodun*, fetish, witchcraft; to bewitch. Entered English via black French of New Orleans.

wyacoo[170]   Mandingo epithet for a bad but powerful chief. Arabic *Yaqub*, Jacob. Also Yacub, described by Malcolm X as creator of white race. A white racist.

Yah (yo)[171]   Crebo *ya*, used after commands; Temne *yo*, used after statements or commands. An emphatic concluding particle: "Indeed!" Often said in endearing tone, thus softening a statement or command. Also black West African and Caribbean English *ya*, said after statements or command.

yam[172]   Wolof *nyam*, taste; Serer *nyam*, eat; Fula *nyama*, eat; black West African and Caribbean English *nyam*, to eat. Also Bantu *nyambi*, to eat.

yackety-yak[173]   Bantu *ya ntata ya ntata*, of the passing moment only temporary. Idle chatter, monotonous talk.

you-uns[174]   You pl.; similar use of you-all. Regular differentiation between second-person sing. And pl. pron. in African languages undoubtedly played a part in introduction of comparable differentiation in American English, esp. in South. Reinforced perhaps by differentiated pron. of French and Spanish. Cf. esp. Wolof *yow*, you sing., versus *yeen*, yena, you pl. Hence convergences with you in sing. And *you + one* as new second-person pl. form. Note first-person *we-uns* by analogy. Cf. black West African and Caribbean English *yu*, you sing. versus *una*, *unu*, you pl. used in Sierra Leone, Cameroon, Jamaica, and elsewhere. In Gullah, *yu* versus *une*, and in black Guyana English, *you* versus *you-all*.

ziggabo[175]   Someone extremely dark in skin color.

zombie[176]   Tshiluba *Nzambi*, God, and *mujangi*, spirit of the dead; Kimbundu *nzumbi*, ghost, phantom. Supernatural force that brings a corpse back to life. Cf. black Haitian French *zombi*, black West African and Caribbean English *jombi*, Sierra Leone and Cameroon *jumbi*, Guyana and Jamaica *zombie*.

Notes

1. Francis Le Lau to Sec. S.P.G., Aug. 30, 1712, S.P.G. MS.A, no. 27 (Propagation of Gospel).

2. "An Account of the Negro Insurrection in South Carolina," p. 234, in Newton D. Mereness, *Travels in the American Colonies*. Edited under the auspices of the National Society of the Colonial Dames of America (New York: The Macmillan Co., 1916), p. 223.

3. *South Carolina Gazette*, Sept. 17, 1737.

4. Ibid., June 14, 1740; Sept. 22, 1737.

5. Ibid., Feb. 8, 1748; Feb. 25, 1749; May 28, 1750; Feb. 18, 1751.

6. Ulrich Bonnel Phillips, *American Negro Slavery: A Survey of Supply, Employment and Control of Negro Labor in the Old South Plantation* (New York: D. Appleton, 1941), 20; also in Mechal Sobel, *Trabelin' on the Slave Journey to an Afro-Baptist Faith* (Princeton, N.J.: Princeton University Press, 1988), 37.

7. *South Carolina Gazette*, July 8, 1732.

8. Ibid., Dec. 21, 1738.

9. Ibid., Oct. 3, 1743.

10. Ibid., Feb. 1, 1746.

11. Ibid., Nov. 8, 1751; June 14, 1742; Jan. 17, 1743.

12. Ibid., Jan. 17, 1743.

13. Ibid., Oct. 26, 1734.

14. Ibid., Feb. 9, 1738.

15. Ibid., Mar. 16, 1738.

16. Ibid., Mar. 30, 1734.

17. Ibid., Jan. 22, 1734.

18. Quoted in "The Speech of Negroes in Colonial America," *Journal of Negro History* 24(3) (July 1939).

19. Edward Long, *The History of Jamaica* (New York: Arno Press, 1972; reprint of 1774 ed., publ. by T. Lowndes, London), 427; Henning C. Cohen,

"Slave Names in Colonial South Carolina," *American Speech* 27 (1952), 102–107, here p. 105.

20. Cohen, "Slave Names," 105.

21. Whittington Bernard Johnson, "Negro Laboring Classes in Early America, 1750–1820." Ph.D. dissertation, University of Georgia, 1970.

22. J. L. Dillard, *Black Names* (The Hague: Mouton, 1976).

23. Guy Johnson, *Drums and Shadows: Survival Studies among the Georgia Coastal Negroes*. Savannah Unit, Georgia Writers' Project, Work Projects Administration. Foreword by Guy Johnson, photographs by Muriel and Malcolm Bell Jr. (Athens: University of Georgia Press, 1940).

24. Norman R. Yetman, ed. *Life under the "Peculiar Institution."* Selections from the Slave Narrative Collection (New York: Holt, Rinehart and Winston, 1970), 13.

25. Inventories 1732–1736 of Charleston, S.C., Probate Court.

26. Cohen, "Slave Names," 104.

27. H. L. Mencken, *The American Language: An Inquiry into the Development of English in the United States* (New York: Knopf, 1936), 524.

28. Cohen, *"Slave Names."*

29. Land Patent Book No. 4, 23.

30. Dillard, *Black Names.*

31. Frederick Douglass, *Narrative of the Life of Frederick Douglass* (Cambridge, Mass.: Harvard University Press, 1960; originally published in 1845), 147–48.

32. Alex Haley, *The Autobiography of Malcolm X* (New York: Grove, 1965).

33. Dillard, *Black Names*, 25.

34. Lorenzo Dow Turner, *Africanisms in the Gullah Dialect* (Chicago: University of Chicago Press, 1949).

35. Carl Lamson Carmer, *Stars Fell on Alabama* (New York: Farmer and Rinehart, 1934), 96.

36. Winifred K. Vass, unpublished materials.

37. Joseph E. Holloway, personal interview with the Rev. Ervin L. Greene, Jr., in Beaufort, Jan. 18, 1984.

38. "A Mutombo by Any Other Name," *USA Today*, March 1989.

39. Joseph E. Holloway, interview with Mrs. Etta Williams (age eighty-six), St. Helena Island, Jan. 18, 1984.

40. Joseph E. Holloway, field notebook.

41. J. T. Munday, "Spirit Names among the Central Bantu," *African Studies* 7(1) (Mar. 1948), 39–40.

42. Ibid., 44.

43. Turner, *Africanisms in the Gullah Dialect.*

44. Ibid.

45. David Dalby, "The African Element in Black English," in Thomas Koch-

man, ed., *Rappin' and Stylin' Out: Communication in Urban Black America* (Urbana: University of Illinois Press, 1972), 171.

46. Ibid.

47. Ibid.

48. Harold Wentworth and Stuart Berg Flexner, *Dictionary of American Slang* (New York: Crowell, 1967), 18; Dalby, "African Element."

49. Source: Winifred K. Vass, linguist of Bantu languages.

50. *Webster's Ninth New Collegiate Dictionary* (Springfield, Mass.: Merriam-Webster, 1988), 127.

51. Dena J. Epstein, "The Folk Banjo: A Documentary History," *Ethnomusicology* (Sept. 1975), reprint 33; Dena J. Polacheck Epstein, *Sinful Tunes and Spirituals: Black Folk Music to the Civil War* (Urbana: University of Illinois Press, 1977), 120–22, 147l; John A. Holm and Alison Watt Shilling, *The Dictionary of Bahamian English* (Cold Spring, N.Y.: Lexik House Publ., 1982); Dalby, "African Element."

52. Dalby, "African Element," 177.

53. Betsy Fancher, *Lost Legacy of Georgia's Golden Isle* (New York: Doubleday, 1971), 45.

54. *Random House Dictionary of the English Language*, unabridged ed., 145; Zora Neale Hurston, *Mules and Men* (New York: Harper and Row, 1970), 64, 132.

55. Holm and Shilling, *Dictionary;* Dalby, "African Element."

56. Dalby, "African Element," 177.

57. Ibid.

58. Ibid.

59. *Random House Dictionary*, 169.

60. Wentworth and Flexner, *Dictionary*, 69.

61. Bradley, "Word-List," 12.

62. *Random House Dictionary*, 169; Dalby, "African Element," 178.

63. Stoney and Sheby, *Black Genesis*, 177.

64. *Random House Dictionary*.

65. Dalby, "African Elements," 77.

66. Texas newspaper article.

67. Julian Mason in *American Speech* 35 (1960), 51–55, gives a detailed discussion of the etymology of *buckaroo*.

68. Holm and Shilling, *Bahamian Dictionary*.

69. Dalby, "African Element."

70. Ibid.

71. Wolof in origin: cf. *hip-kat*.

72. C. M. Woodward, "Word List," 9: Johnson, *Folk Culture*, 44.

73. Dalby, "African Element," 174.

74. Holm and Shilling, *Dictionary.*

75. Peter H. Wood, *Black Majority: Negroes in Colonial South Carolina from 1670 through the Stono Rebellion* (New York: Knopf, 1974), 32.

76. Frank A. Collymore, *Barbadian Dialect* (Bridgetown, Barbados: Advocate, 1957), 26.

77. Dalby, "African Element," 179.

78. Harold Courlander, *Negro Folk Music U.S.A.* (New York: Columbia University Press, 1963), 191.

79. Holm and Shilling, *Dictionary;* Dalby, "African Element," 179; Joseph E. Holloway, "Africanisms in Gullah Oral Tradition," *Western Journal of Black Studies* 13(3) (1989), 119.

80. Wentworth and Flexner, *Dictionary of American Slang,* 125.

81. Stetson Kennedy, *Palmetto Country* (New York: Duell, Sloan, 1942), 154–55.

82. Dalby, "African Element."

83. Ibid.

84. Ibid.

85. Holm and Shilling, *Dictionary.*

86. Ibid., 180.

87. Ibid.

88. Ibid.

89. Ibid.

90. Ibid.

91. Ibid., *Random House Dictionary,* 582.

92. Turner, *Africanisms in the Gullah Dialect,* 194.

93. *Random House Dictionary,* 609.

94. Hurston, *Mules and Men,* 241, 281.

95. Robert Farris Thompson, this volume, chapter 10.

96. Dalby, "African Element," 180.

97. Jessie Gaston Mulira, this volume, chapter 5; N. W. Newell, in *Journal of American Folklore* 2 (1889), 44.

98. Turner, *Africanisms in the Gullah Dialect.*

99. Dalby, "African Element."

100. Ibid.

101. Ibid.

102. Ibid.

103. Ibid.

104. Mulira, "Case of Voodoo," 56.

105. Thomas, "South Texas Negro Folk Songs"; Vass, correspondence with Madge B. MacLachlan, Jackson, Fla., regarding terms used by her childhood playmate on the turpentine "flats."

106. Newbell Niles Puckett, *Folk Beliefs of the Southern Negro* (Chapel Hill: University of North Carolina Press, 1926), 18–19.

107. Dalby, "African Element," 178.

108. Ibid.

109. Ibid., 181.

110. Dalby, "African Element," 181.

111. Source: Winifred K. Vass.

112. *Random House Dictionary,* 767.

113. Ibid., 768.

114. Ibid.

115. Dalby, "African Element," 182.

116. Ibid.

117. Ibid.

118. Beverly J. Robinson, this volume, chapter 12; Mitford McLeod Mathews, *Some Sources of Southernisms* (University: University of Alabama Press, 1948), 145; Winifred Kellerberge Vass, *Bantu Speaking Heritage of the United States* (Los Angeles: Center for Afro-American Studies, UCLA, 1979).

119. Robinson, "Africanisms and the Study of Folklore."

120. Ibid.

121. Ibid.

122. Ibid.

123. Dalby, "African Element," 182.

124. Source: Winifred K. Vass, linguist; informant.

125. Ibid.

126. Ibid.

127. J. L. Dillard, *All-American English* (New York: Random House, 1975).

128. Dalby, "African Element," 182.

129. *Random House Dictionary,* 794.

130. Vass, *Bantu Speaking Heritage.*

131. Ibid.

132. Wentworth and Flexner, *Dictionary of American Slang,* 331.

133. Dalby, "African Element," 182.

134. Ibid.

135. Ibid.

136. Ibid.

137. Ibid.

138. *Random House Dictionary,* 929.

139. Dalby, "African Element," 182.

140. Ibid.

141. W. A. B. Musgrave, "Ananci Stories," *Folk-Lore Record* 3(1) (1880), 53–55.

142. Ibid., 183.

143. Ibid.

144. Ibid.

145. Ibid.

146. *Random House Dictionary*, 1040.

147. Collymore, *Barbadian Dialect*, 63.

148. Wentworth and Flexner, *Dictionary of American Slang*, 382.

149. Dalby, "African Element," 184.

150. Ibid.

151. Ibid.

152. Ibid.

153. Smith, *Gullah*, 28.

154. *Random House Dictionary*, 112.

155. Wentworth and Flexner, *Dictionary of American Slang*, 401; Vass, *Bantu Speaking Heritage*, 113; Dalby, "African Heritage," 184.

156. Dalby, "African Element," 184.

157. Ibid.

158. Ibid.

159. Ibid.

160. *Random House Dictionary*, 1250.

161. Turner, *Africanisms in the Gullah Dialect;* Dalby, "African Elements," 184.

162. Dalby, "African Element," 184.

163. Ibid.

164. Ibid.

165. *Random House Dictionary;* Vass, *Bantu Speaking Heritage*, 114.

166. *Random House Dictionary;* Vass, *Bantu Speaking Heritage*, 114; Dalby, "African Element," 185.

167. Bradley, "Word-List," 67.

168. Dalby, "African Element," 185.

169. William A. Read, *Louisiana-French*, rev. ed. (Baton Rouge: Louisiana State University Press, 1963).

170. Dalby, "African Element," 185.

171. Ibid.

172. Ibid.

173. *Random House Dictionary*, 1652.

174. Dalby, "African Element."

175. See jiggabbo.

176. *Random House Dictionary*, 767; Read, *Louisiana-French*, 128; Dalby, "African Element," 186.

Five

The Case of Voodoo in New Orleans

Jessie Ruth Gaston

This essay provides insight into African religious retentions among blacks in New Orleans. Such survivals include beliefs, activities, cults, deities, and rituals that can be traced directly back to Africa.[1] In particular we are concerned here with voodoo. The Dahomean religion of *vodu*, as it is referred to in many parts of West Africa, is a highly structured religious and magical system. This system is both complex and functional, with duties, symbols, rituals, and faithful adherents.[2] After giving a brief history of *vodu* in North America, I will describe the African religious system with special reference to Dahomey, then investigate cult initiations among the voodoos of New Orleans and the role of songs and prayers in voodoo worship in West Africa, Haiti, and New Orleans. Finally, I will present a chronological review of voodoo practices and practitioners in New Orleans.

Voodoo in North America

The word *voodoo*, which is Dahomean in origin and means "spirit" or "deity" in the Fon language, generally produces one of three responses from most Westerners: fear, laughter, or respect. The response of fear is based on exaggerated negative views of the supernatural world and of Africa. The laughter response is often motivated by an ignorance that associates voodoo with "mere superstition." Respect comes with one's knowledge that voodoo is a functional religious system in West Africa.

The word and the system arrived in North America when the first

Africans landed in Jamestown in 1619 as indentured servants. The number of voodoo worshippers increased as more Africans arrived, first as indentured servants and later as slaves directly from Africa or through the West Indies, where African slaves were introduced as early as 1504. With the influx of more Africans, voodoo became entrenched in the North American colonies and later in the United States.

Although no record of the introduction of voodoo worship in Louisiana exists, we are certain that New Orleans was the birthplace of voodoo in North America.[3] The Louisiana colony received fresh cargoes of slaves directly from Africa as well as seasoned slaves from the French colonies of Martinique, Guadeloupe, and Santo Domingo. All three colonies were known to be hotbeds of voodooism.[4] The Haitian Revolution of 1791 reinforced voodoo in and around New Orleans as hundreds of Haitian refugees, many of whom were voodoo cult leaders and adherents, settled in the area. The most renowned and earliest voodoo leaders in New Orleans came either directly from Africa or by way of the West Indies.

Contrary to popular belief, slave traders made no deliberate attempt to separate slaves who had the same ethnic background and language. Thus these traders unwittingly guaranteed continuity of the African cultural heritage during the middle passage and after the slaves arrived in the New World. The slaves and their descendants underwent common experiences sufficient to enable them to cooperate in fashioning new customs, traditions, and even languages that reflected their African background. But to do so they had to undergo a double acculturation process.

The first acculturation process, characterized by the contact and interaction of various African ethnic groups, resulted in the blending of their customs and practices. Such blending is evident where Africans resided together in large numbers—places such as the Georgia and South Carolina Sea Islands, Jamaica, and Haiti. The second acculturation process took place when African and Western cultures interacted. Furthermore, African survivals flourished in those areas of the New World where European institutions did not exist with a high degree of fixity. Africans attempted to take the Western culture and reinterpret it in terms of their own African experiences. In the Caribbean and Brazil they led revolts, which in the long run made it possible for them to transplant the African lifestyle to a certain degree. Even in the southern United States African cultural survivals remained intact during the colonial period.[5]

It is more difficult to measure and evaluate the persistence of African culture elsewhere, especially in the United States outside the core areas of New Orleans and the Sea Islands. In many "pocket areas" in the southern states and in cities and towns through the United States, remnants of African culture abound: in language patterns and vocabulary, in literature, in techniques of storytelling, in folktales such as Brer Rabbit and Tar Baby, in music and dance forms, singing, and rhythm, in foods, and in ways of eating certain foods. The extended-family concept and respect for elders in many rural areas were African transplants. Africanisms are of course most prevalent among black southerners because the South was the heart of the slavery system in the United States. These people took their traditions outside the South once they migrated.[6]

The most dominant and intact African survival in the black diaspora has proved to be the religion of voodoo. The survival of African religious and magical systems is directly linked to their importance in everyday life. In addition, their ability to accommodate and be associated with various facets of other established religions strengthened their chances of survival. Ancient deities in the African pantheon were often given Catholic saints' names. The most tenacious African religious retentions in the United States are found where Catholicism has been particularly strong, including New Orleans. By appealing to traditional deities and mystical forces, the slaves were able to keep alive their link with Africa.

During the early stages of slavery the link was reinforced by voodoo priests and root doctors who continued to be represented among the newly arrived slaves. The priests in particular led the crusade for the survival of their religious practices by identifying African deities with Catholic saints in Haiti and Brazil. And African concepts of good and evil found counterparts in the Christians' belief in heaven and hell and Christ and Satan. Since the beginning of the twentieth century, the root doctors have been more visible in practicing their craft than the priests. From its beginning, voodoo encompassed certain elements such as divination, manipulation, and herbalism that gave it the appearance of a magical rather than a religious system. In the early days of slavery, magic was often the strongest element because of the suppression of voodoo as a religion by the authorities and slave owners. These antivoodooists managed to limit the number of voodoo meetings among slaves, but they found it impossible to stop the making of voodoo and hoodoo objects in the slaves' cabins. (Hoodoo is the negative component of voodoo.) Magic helped the slaves to cope with their daily situations, to win the affection of the ones they desired, to cause harm to their enemies, and to feel protected from harm themselves. Its main value was and con-

ological. Magic is intimately related to voodoo, as it is
to most religions, but is not its essence. Voodoo contains some elements
of magic, and magic receives much of its strength from the voodoo deities and rituals.

African religious and magical systems also survived because of the
organizational role they played in slave revolts throughout the New World
but particularly in Haiti and Brazil. Revolutionary protest appears to
have been engraved in voodoo upon its arrival in the Americas. Revolts
in the early period of slavery were largely the work of African priests
and medicine men. In conducting insurrectional meetings disguised as
religious ceremonies, voodoo leaders often promised the gods' support
for any rebellion the slaves decided to engage in. The assurance of supernatural support to both leaders and followers and the priests' promise that the ancestors were aiding the struggle for freedom gave the
slaves the necessary inspiration, courage, and determination. Various
charms, gris-gris, potions, and small parcels containing bits of paper,
bones, or potions hung around the necks of the fighting men provided
protection and good luck by warding off bullets. The slave insurrection
in New York in 1712 was led by a conjurer who convinced the fighters
they were invulnerable. A leader in the 1822 insurrection in South
Carolina, "Gullah Jack," also was a conjurer and root doctor; his charms,
chiefly of animal claws, were designed to make the insurrectionists invulnerable. Voodoo priests also helped suicide victims by telling them
what to do to ensure their return after death to their homeland in Africa.[8]

An account recorded after the Civil War suggests that in New Orleans voodoo worked to emancipate the slaves and inspire them to serve
as "Sons of Freedom in the United States," as it had worked in the 1791
Haitian Revolution:

> This society has played an important role in the events that have
> taken place at New Orleans for the past year. It was induced to take
> an indirect but very active part in the war which resulted in the
> freedom of the black race. . . . The uprising was said to have been
> influenced by the voodoos who undertook the challenge to obtain
> the complete emancipation of the slaves and to punish the slave
> masters.[9]

The use of voodoo as an organized force against a common enemy
was prevalent among some African groups. The Mahi of the People's
Republic of Benin (formerly Dahomey) were noted for using their religion as a weapon against the Fon raids in their area throughout the eighteenth and nineteenth centuries.[10]

The African Religious System

Religion was (and remains) a vital part of the lives of most Africans. For some it encompassed their entire existence. It substantiated and explained their place in the universe, their culture, and their relationship to nature and humankind; it also dictated their roles in the community and society at large. Religion among most African ethnic groups was not simply a faith or worship system; it was a way of life, a system of social control, a provider of medicine, and an organizing mechanism.[11]

Vodu has a highly organized hierarchy of deities, with *vodun* priests, priestesses, novices, and other persons devoted to serving and protecting them. At the top is the Supreme Being (Creator or God). Below the Creator, lesser deities serve as intermediaries. Clans, families, and villages also have their own deities to protect them, to justify their claims to power, and to legitimize their rights of occupation. The deities have prescribed methods of worship, certain ceremonial dances, dress codes, foods, and days set aside in their honor.

The religious system is rigid, and its methods of worshipping the various deities appear to be unchanging. Historically, there was no flexibility and no innovation, but a certain amount of interchange took place between some ethnic groups. Yet such borrowing generally made little impact on the already established deities and how they were worshipped.

Becoming a functioning member of a voodoo cult in Africa was not an automatic process. One had to undergo a training program in the confines of a religious learning center. These centers, or convents, were important religious institutions in many parts of Africa. Most were situated in large towns and villages. Each convent was dedicated to either a particular deity or a group of cult deities. In the Mahi village of Savalou in northwest People's Republic of Benin there were convents for at least five of the major deities: Azaka, Lissa, Damballa, Sakpata, and Hevieso. Religious convents had a twofold purpose: they taught the novice, or *vodunsi*, first how to serve the deity and then how best to live for the deity or deities. In other words, the convents were places where the novices learned how to worship the gods or goddesses, including all ritual and religious ceremonies connected with their worship. There they learned how to dance for the deities and became familiar with the sacrificial needs of the fetishes. They learned the dress codes and colors for rituals. Each convent was headed by a fetish priest or priestess who was assisted by the *vodunsi*.

In precolonial times any individual who wanted to join a convent went to see the appropriate priest or priestess with almost no fear of being rejected. Today even small children are accepted, especially if the parents fear that a witch is after the child. Entry is free of charge. Furthermore, to increase the number of devotees, the priest will bring his own children into the convent. In some parts of Africa the students' parents generally send food to them in the morning and evening during their apprenticeship in the convent. Such practices vary from ethnic group to ethnic group.[12]

Novices had to remain at the convent for nine months, or nine moons. During their stay they were restricted to the convent compounds. In fact, the novices were in voluntary seclusion and were not permitted to view a new moon. The new moon was seen as having extreme power over priests, witches, lunatics, and human emotions in general. Therefore, four days before the new moon the novices did not venture out to ensure that their power was not taken away. The only time the novices ventured out before the seclusion period ended was to participate in the ceremonies of their fetish. They would return immediately after the festival.

In the confines of the convent the novices were free to wear their own clothing, but during the coming-out ceremony (rite of passage) and regularly thereafter they wore the special costume of the fetish. This ceremony was paid for by the novices' parents or husbands. Once the novices completed the nine months they were considered *vodunsi*, members of a particular cult. To become priests or priestesses required much more.

Many of the local experts of herbal medicine who played important roles in most African societies were fetish priests; however, priesthood was not a requirement for the role but an option in most societies. In the Mahi villages of Mondji and Aklampka a medicine man was also compelled to be a fetish leader.

The nature of an illness determined the way it was treated by the root men. In most African societies all illnesses without natural explanations were believed to have been the result of supernatural forces. When there were difficulties in diagnosing an illness, Fa was consulted. Fa, the god of divination among many ethnic groups in the People's Republic of Benin, held control over hidden knowledge, especially in areas relating to the spiritual world and the unknown. Fa would provide the medicine man with information about an illness and its cure.

The local herbal doctors, as they are generally referred to because of their reliance on natural herbs in curative medicines, had unique procedures in diagnosing an illness. In one Mahi village in the People's Republic of Benin the juice of a special herb was sometimes rubbed on the patient, permitting him to see the person who was putting *juju*, or bad medicine, on him. The juice itself was viewed as possessing power to unveil the evildoer. The experience of a medicine man also assisted him in labeling an illness, especially an illness with obvious symptoms. Furthermore, herbalists would meet to discuss various medical problems and their most difficult cases. It has also been asserted that some medical practitioners had extrasensory perception and could look at an individual and explain the medical problem. Nevertheless, Fa would also be consulted for verification.

Another powerful element in African society was the witch, or *azéto* in Fon. The witch was the most feared of the individuals who were seen as having supernatural powers among the Mahi peoples. Female and past menopause, witches were considered to be destructive, with no positive role. They were capable of transferring their powers to their daughters, which they usually did. Many African peoples believed that women who had experienced menopause possessed higher powers. This is understandable when one recalls that age is a sign of wisdom and menopause is associated with aging. The witches were generally described as destroyers with power to transform a person into a fowl and eat it. The *azéto* was believed to possess the power to use any object as a medium to represent an individual over whom she wished to exert control. The witch could do whatever she wanted with the intended victim. All illnesses that could not be cured by the fetish or *juju* potions and designs were seen as being the works of the witch.

In the preceding paragraphs, examples were drawn mainly from the People's Republic of Benin in West Africa. The choice of Benin was deliberate, for the majority of the religious retentions in New Orleans are representative of that area and three of its ethnic groups: Fon, Mahi, and Yoruba.

The Voodoos of New Orleans

In New Orleans the West African voodoo cults merged into one major cult, Damballa, the snake cult, referred to in New Orleans as the Grand Zombi or *Vodou*. Methods of training and accepting new members operated differently from those of Haiti and West Africa. Convents were absent in New Orleans, but that did not prevent the training of dedicated individuals as voodoo practitioners.

Initiation into the cult entailed a period of studying and training under an established practitioner. During this period, which ranged from weeks to years depending on the progress of the student, pupils usually remained at home, but in many cases they moved in with the teacher until after the initiation. Voodoo teachers were free to refuse any pupil if they felt there was no potential. With the permission of the teacher, students were advanced to the next stage, novitiate, at which time they were initiated by a collegelike group of voodoo practitioners called together especially to perform the highly organized initiation ceremony.[13]

During the initiation stage pupils were referred to as neophytes. Their duties included running errands or doing chores, such as dusting houses. They would not be told why. Neophytes would also assist the teachers in their ceremonies. If the practitioners were herbal specialists the pupil sometimes would accompany them in search of herbs.

Once novitiates had been accepted by the hierarchical group of voodoo practitioners, they had to be accepted by the Great One, or Spirit, as the voodoo serpent was sometimes called. If the voodoo spirit rejected the novices for whatever reason, they would be denied membership. The ceremony, which varied according to the voodoo teacher practitioner, was complicated by much ritualistic symbolism. Zora Neale Hurston, an anthropologist who was initiated by voodoo priests in the late 1920s while doing research on voodoo in New Orleans, recounted her initiation ceremony under a hoodooist-voodooist named Samuel Thompson.

> He bade me to sit before the altar for an hour. We sat there silently facing each other across the candles and incense for those sixty minutes. . . . I became conscious after awhile of a minute rhythmic tremor that communicated itself to me through his hands on my head.
>
> He murmured in low syllables in some language very rapidly. A violent retching of his body all but threw me from the chair. He held still and stood silent for a minute listening. Then, he answered, yeah, unhunh, yeah.
>
> On Thursday morning at eleven I was at the shuttered door of the ancient house. . . . We dressed the candles and lit them and set three upon tumblers filled with honey, three filled with syrup, and three with holy water and set them in a semi-circle upon the altar. . . .
>
> I was told that I must begin my novitiate. I must sleep for nine nights with my right stocking on. I must have clean thoughts. I must neither defile body nor spirit. Certain monies were necessary for the ceremony. I paid the sum. I was told to be seated before the altar and offer myself with absolute sincerity to the "Great One." But once I was seated I was not to utter a sound. When the spirit was through with me I must leave in silence.
>
> I sat obedient before the altar, shivering unknowingly. . . . I rose and turned from the altar. . . . Then Samuel spoke, "The Spirit

says you must bring three snake skins next time." I passed out with bowed head. At the end of the nine days I returned with the skins and again sat before the altar.

After viewing the skins, Samuel remarked, "Oh you have got the right ones. I did not say what skins to see if the spirit would tell you. You see I teach nothing. I bring you to the 'Great One.' If he takes you, he tell you what to do; if he don't tell you, you are nothing. The 'Spirit' don't want you."

He prepared the skins and placed them before the "Great One." He called him and admonished him to enter into the skins and give them life.

Then I rose from the altar and helped prepare the sacred couch, that is, the moccasin hide was fixed to green cloth and spread over the couch in the altar room. My sacred garments were made excluding the crown. At 3 o'clock naked as I came into the world, I was stretched face downwards with my navel to the serpent and pitcher of water at my head that my spirit might not wander in search of it, and began my three day search for the favor of the "Great One." Three days I must lie silently that is, my body would be there. My soul would be standing naked before the "Spirit" to see if he would have me.

I had five psychic experiences during those three days and nights. . . . Strangely enough I had no sense of hunger—only exaltation.

At eleven o'clock on March 19, St. Joseph's Day, I rose and was led through the running water and again stretched out upon the couch. Samuel approached me with a brother on each side of him. One held a small brush with red paint, the other a brush with yellow paint. . . . Samuel painted a lightning symbol down my back from my right shoulder to my left hip. This was to be my sign forever. The "Great One" shall speak to me in storms. I was now dressed in the new clothes, stockings, underwear, dress and veil. After I was dressed, a pair of eyes was painted on my cheeks just below my eyes as a sign that I could see in more ways than one. The sun was painted on my forehead. Many came into the room and performed ceremonial acts, but none spoke to me. Nor could I speak to them while the veil covered my face. Then Samuel entered and all the others retired. Samuel cut the little finger of my right hand and caught the gushing blood in a wine cup. He added wine and mixed it with the blood. Then he and all the other five leaders let blood from themselves also and mixed it with the wine in another glass. I was led to drink from the cup containing their mingled bloods and each of them in turn beginning with Samuel, drank from mine. At high noon I was seated at the splendid altar. It was dressed with my name, upon it set in sand five large iced cakes in different colors, a plate of honeyed St. Joseph's bread, a plate of serpent shaped breads, spinach, egg cakes fried in olive oil, breaded Chinese okra fried in olive oil, roast veal and wine, two high yellow bouquets, two red bouquets, and two white bouquets, and a bottle of holy water.

Samuel seated me and stood behind me with his ceremonial hat upon his head and the crown of power in his hand. "'Spirit' I ask you to take her. Do you hear me 'Spirit'? will you take her? 'Spirit' I want you to take her, she is worthy." He held the crown poised above my head for a full minute, a profound silence held the room. Then he lifted the veil from my face and let it fall behind my head and crown me with power. He lit my candle for me. But from then on I might be a candle lighter myself. All the candles were reverently lit. We sat down and ate the feast. First a glass of blessed oil was handed to me by Samuel. "Drink this without tasting it." I gulped it down and he took the glass from my hand, took a sip of the little that was left. Then, he handed it to the brothers at his right who did the same, until it went around the table.

"Eat first the spinach cakes," Samuel exhorted and we did. Then the meal began. It was full of joy and laughter even though we knew that the final ceremony waited only for the good hour of twelve midnight. About ten o'clock we piled into the old Studebaker sedan—all but Samuel who led us in a truck. On Road No. 61, we rattled until a certain spot was reached, the truck was unloaded beside the road and sent back to town. It was a little after eleven. The swamp was dismal and damp, but after some stumbly walking we came to a little glade deep in the wood, near the lake. I could hear the occasional slap-slap of the water. With a whispered chant, some twigs were gathered and tied into a broom. Some pine straw was collected. The sheets of typing paper I had been urged to bring were brought out and nine sheets were blessed and my petition written nine times on each sheet by the light from the shaded lantern. The crate containing the black sheep was opened and the sheep led forward into the center of the circle. He stood there dazedly while the chant of strange syllables rose. I asked Samuel the words but he replied that in good time I would know what to say. It was not to be taught. If nothing came to be silent. The head and withers of the sheep were stroked as the chanting went on. Samuel became more and more voluble. At last he seized the straw and stuffed some into the sheep's nostrils. The animal struggled. A knife flashed and the sheep dropped to its knees, then fell prone with its mouth in a weak cry. My petition was thrust into its throat that he might cry it to the "Great One." The broom was seized and dipped in the blood from the slit throat and the ground swept vigorously—back and forth—the length of dying sheep. The sweeping went on as long as the blood gushed. Earth, the Mother of the "Great One," and us all had been appeased. With a sharp stick Samuel traced the outline of the sheep and the digging commenced. The sheep was never touched. The ground was dug from under him so that his body dropped down into the hole. He was covered with the nine sheets of paper bearing the petitions and the earth heaped upon him. A white candle was set upon the grave and we struggled back to the road and the Studebaker.

Among the most notable African religious retentions in this account are the importance of the snake and snake skins, the role of water and animal sacrifices, and the use of the number nine. Whereas initiates among the Fon, Yoruba, and Mahi were usually secluded in convents, New Orleans voodooists-hoodooists were compelled to alter this aspect of their religious training, given the constant danger posed by local authorities. Instead of being in seclusion for nine months, Hurston went into seclusion by sleeping with her right stocking on for nine days. Before 1865 the majority of voodoo-hoodoo leaders and practitioners operating in New Orleans were free persons of color, since slaves were not at liberty to leave the plantation.

A second account of an initiation ceremony was provided by Hurston.

When I became his pupil I was put to running errands such as "dusting houses," throwing pecans, rolling apples, as the case might be, but I was not told why the thing was being done. After two weeks of this I was taken off this phase and initiated. This was the first step towards the door of the mysteries.

My initiation consisted of the Pea Vine Candle Drill. I was told to remain five days without sexual intercourse. I must remain indoors all day the day before the initiation and fast. I might wet my throat when necessary, but I was not to swallow water.

When I arrived at the house the next morning a little before nine, as pre-instructed, six other persons were there, so that there were nine of us—all in white except Father Simms who was in his purple robe. There was no talking. We went at once to the altar room. The altar was blazing. There were three candles around the vessel of holy water, three around the sacred sand pail, and one large cream candle burning in it. A picture of St. George and a large piece of brain coral were in the center. Father Simms dressed eight long blue candles and one black one, while the rest of us sat in the chairs around the wall. Then he lit the eight blue candles one by one from the altar and set them in [a] pattern. . . . Then I was called to the altar and both Father Simms and his wife laid hands on me. The black candle was placed in my hand; I was told to light it from all the other candles. I lit it at number 1 and pinched out the flame and re-lit it at number 2 and so on till it had been lit by the eighth candle. Then I held it in my left hand, and by my right was conducted back to the altar by Father Simms. I was led through the maze of candles beginning at number 8. We circled numbers 7, 5, and 3. When we reached the altar he lifted me upon the step. As I stood there, he called aloud, "Spirit. She's standing here without no home and no friends. She wants you to take her in." Then we began at number 1 and threaded back to number 8, circling 3, 5, and 7, then back to the altar again. Again he lifted me down placing me upon the step of the altar. Again the spirit was addressed as before. Then he lifted me down by placing his hands in my arm pits. This time I did not walk at all. I was carried through the maze and I was to knock down each candle as I passed it with my foot. If I missed one, I was not to try again, but to knock it down on my way back to the altar. Arrived there the third time, I was lifted up and told to pinch out my black candle. "Now," Father told me, "you are made Boss of Candles. You have the power to work with the spirits anywhere on earth."

Then all of the candles on the floor were collected and one of them handed to each of the persons present. Father took the black candle himself and we formed a ring. Everybody was given two matches each. The candles held in our left hands, matches in the right, a signal everybody stopped at the same moment, the matches scratched in perfect time and our candles lighted in concert. Then Father walked rhythmically around the person at his right, exchanged candles with her and went back to his place. Then that person did the same to the next so that the black candles went all around the circle and back to Father. I was then seated on a stool before the altar, sprinkled lightly with holy sand and water and confirmed as a Boss of Candles.

Then conversation broke out. We went into the next room and had a breakfast that was mostly of fruit and smothered chicken. Afterwards, the nine candles used in the ceremony were wrapped up and given to me to keep. They were to be used for lighting other candles only, not to be just burned in the ordinary sense.

After this ceremony I was put to work inside with Father and his wife so that I might learn everything.

This initiation ceremony proved that the Great One had given his approval. The person who wished to advance now entered the stage of an advanced pupil. The use of the number nine again stands out. The prohibition of sexual intercourse during the initiation period of the novice is also stressed. This restriction is especially prevalent among voodooists of the Fon, Mahi, and Yoruba.[14]

In many instances these were the only types of initiation ceremonies a *vodunsi* in New Orleans underwent. Of course, such ceremonies were somewhat removed from those of the Fon, Mahi, and Yoruba. And as time passed the initiation ceremonies underwent further changes.

Songs and Prayers in Voodoo Worship

Among the key elements of a voodoo ritual are its songs and prayers, which are transmitted orally from one generation to the next.[15] Songs and prayers are voiced in the spirit of supplication or placation relating in some way to the deities, referred to in Haiti as *loas*, and in some cases to the priests and priestesses. The complete meaning of voodoo songs in particular may be seen in their liturgical contexts, where they reveal human-spirit relations and are accompanied by music and dance. In Dahomey and Haiti a group of three drums served to lead and keep the rhythms. Voodooists in New Orleans proper were forbidden by law to use real drums in voodoo ceremonies unless they were part of the weekly public ceremony in Congo Square. Hand clapping, leg patting, and foot stomping provided a handsome substitute.

The songs are primarily revelations of spirits to humans. The truly deep meanings of voodoo songs come to individuals as they become more involved in voodoo by acquiring more knowledge and by passing through subsequent initiation rituals affecting upward mobility in the voodoo hierarchy. They illustrate a symbolic relationship between voodoo spirits and the cult members in which spirits are dependent on man for food and man dependent on spirits for protection. These songs give the personalities of the deities, their names, their likes and dislikes, their attributes and functions, their filiation, conjugal states, places of origin, weaknesses, strengths, and responsibilities. They also unveil basic human nature and needs whereby the people call upon the *loas* to perform certain deeds. Sometimes they address the *loas* directly and at other times the words are spoken by the *loas* themselves. There are even cases where songs entertain an implicit dialogue between a specific *loa* and the singers or other spirits. In these cases there is a constant shifting of points of view; sometimes the songs present the words of the deity, sometimes words addressed to the deity. The name of the deity can appear anywhere in the song as both an invocation word and a rhythmic device. One may easily lose the sense and intent of the words if one is not aware of the song structure. All voodoo songs possess a pattern stanza that is repeated. When the theme has been stated the song usually ends.

Some songs in voodoo ceremonies are borrowed from the Catholic Church. Such borrowing is understandable, because the majority of voodoo worshippers, in Haiti and to a lesser extent in New Orleans, are baptized Catholics who continue to attend mass. Sung at a voodoo gathering, such songs generally associate the Catholic saints with the African deities. The majority of voodoo songs are said to have been taught to a leader or a regular practitioner by the *loas* through dreams, and they are usually sung in French patois in Haiti. Songs acquired while sleeping are seen as coming from a spirit's revelation. The melody and words of such a song are later memorized by the congregation. Only then does it constitute a new song in their repertoire. A new song may also be revealed during a possession trance. The possessed might sing it two or three times, asking the people to repeat it until they memorize it. It is unlikely that the person would remember the words once the trance was over. This manner of learning by oral repetition is characteristic of traditional African societies. Since there are songs for each phase of the ceremony, the various phases in a voodoo ritual can be identified by the type of songs sung. There are preparation, invocation, possession, and farewell songs. In Haiti each spirit was saluted with at least three songs if not called upon for possession.

In nearly any faithful voodoo service of the Dahomean nation in Haiti and New Orleans, the first supplication song was addressed to Legba, keeper of the gate, guardian of the crossroads, and go-between who intercedes with other deities in the affairs of humans. The first supplication is to open the gate so that voices of supplication may be heard and understood, as in this example from Haiti:

Attibon Legba, open the gate for me
Open the gate
I will enter when I return
I salute the *loa*.[16]

The opening of the gate also provided access for other deities to the service.

After this appeal or during the time it was being sung, the priest or priestess would spill a little water on the earth (libation) at the base of the altar as an inducement for the *loa* to reside. Libation, always conducted by a priest or priestess, is a voodoo purifying ritual in which wine, oil, water, or a special liquid concoction is poured out in various places—in all four corners of a worship room, by all doors and windows, and by the altar. This ceremony is undertaken in honor of a specific deity, good or bad depending on what the priest or priestess is trying to accomplish.

A second song to Legba usually followed the pouring of the libation.

Papa Legba is in my hounfor
Papa Legba is in my hounfor
Papa Legba is in my hounfor
You who carry the flag
It is you who shade the *loa* from sun
Papa Legba, Papa Legba.[17]

This part of voodoo ritual was usually followed by a general calling for the *loa* of the cult. To appease the *loa*, songs would also be sung describing his qualities, character, behavioral patterns, and needs, as in this song sung to Damballa, the snake deity:

He cannot be drown in the water
Papa Damballa, you are a snake, oh!
Why don't you drown?

He cannot be drown in the water
Papa Damballa, you are a snake, oh!
Why don't you drown?
Damballa, why don't you drown in the water.[18]

As the *loa* arrived in the hounfor to participate in the ceremonies, the devotees would sing another song noting his coming. The words used to describe the *loas'* behaviors and experiences encountered while arriving are often those of the *loas*. These words are of *loa* Soho:

I am passing through
I am passing through
I am passing through
Eithe hounsi bossale call my name.

They are calling me
They are calling me

The hounsi Kanzo are calling
Daho is calling
They are calling me![19]

Other songs, like this one from New Orleans, were often sung at the climax of ceremonies:

He-ron mande
He-ron mande
Tigui li papa,
He-ron mande
He-ron mande
Do se dan dogo.[20]

Among the voodoo adherents of New Orleans Legba was usually referred to as papa.

The giving of food to the *loa* is also a vital part of the voodoo religious rituals. Songs describing the sacrifices signified that the *loa* was waiting for his food. In Haiti and Africa the voodoo songs sometimes dramatized this significant activity. This example is from Haiti:

Damballa asks for the goat he is to be fed.
Damballa wedo, oh, it is blood e!
Damballa asks for the head of the goat.
It is blood he asks for.

Damballa wedo, oh, it is blood e!
Damballa wedo asks for the head of the goat,
It is blood he asks for.
Damballa wedo, oh, it is blood he asks for!
Oh enough.[21]

Special songs for initiation ceremonies included these two from Haiti:

Agoue
Hail to father Agoue
Who dwells in the sea!
He is the Lord of the ships
In a blue gulf
There are three little islands
The Negro's boat is storm-tossed

Father Agoue brings it safely in
Hail to Father Agoue.

Father Legba, open wide the gate!
Father Legba, where are they children
Father Legba, we are here
Father Legba, open wide the gate that we may pass.[22]

Voodoo songs not only serve to educate the devotees to the personalities and characters of the *loa* but also create a favorable atmosphere for possession trances to occur. Moreover, songs have a magical function in that they can be used to entice and force the spirits to come down and possess someone.

Linguistically, voodoo songs can be divided into two categories: those that employ secret words (African terms and African names of deities) and those that make use of English or Creole terms and language. The connection of Haiti to Dahomey and, to a lesser extent, of New Orleans to Dahomey is more evident in the voodoo songs. Many of the songs and prayers contain the African names of the deities, their African countries of origin, and other African words or segments of African languages that the slaves brought with them or created during the middle passage. Here are two examples from Haiti:

Eh! Eh! Bomba Hen! Hen!
Canga bafio, te
Canga moune, de le
Canga do ki la,
Canga li. . . .

A, a bombaia bombe
Lama Samana quana!
Evan vanta a
Vana docki.[23]

Both songs were sung in Creole during the invocation section of the voodoo ceremony. Robert Tallant provided an example from New Orleans that is identical to the first Haitian example. In New Orleans, however, this song was not restricted to initiation ceremonies. It was sung during the invocation as well as the possession stage of the voodoo ritual.

The majority of the voodoo songs in New Orleans were about the voodoo queens. Two examples provide vivid illustrations of this fact;

both speak of one of the greatest voodoo rulers of New Orleans, Marie Laveau. The first, sung by Marie Laveau herself, originally in Creole, boasts of her powers and fearless courage:

They think they frighten me
Those people must be crazy
They don't see their misfortune
Or else they must be drunk.

I, the Voodoo Queen,
With my lovely handkerchief
Am not afraid of tomcat shrieks,
I drink serpent venom!

I walk on pins
I walk on needles,
I walk on gilded splinters
I want to see what they can do!

They think they have pride
With their big malice,
But when they see a coffin
They're as frightened as prairie birds.

I'm going to put gris-gris
All over their front steps
And make them shake
Until they stutter![24]

The second example boasts of how Marie Laveau went to school with the crocodiles and of the power she possessed:

Eh! Ye Ye Mamzelle
Ya, Ye, Ye, li Konin tou, gris-gris
Li, ti, Kowri, avec vieux Kikordi;
Oh, ouai, ye Mamzelle Marie
Kan soleid te Kashe,
Li te sorti bayou,
Pou, apprened le Voudou,

Oh, tingouar, ye hen hen
Oh, tingouar, ye eh eh,

Li appe vini, li Grand Zombi
Li appe vini, pou fe mouri![25]

In some instances the last two lines of this song, with minor alterations, were chanted in New Orleans to invoke or to acknowledge the arrival of Damballa.

Voodoo Practices and Practitioners in New Orleans

Before 1900 voodoo queens and kings of New Orleans appear to have been on an equal footing in the practice of magic and bad *juju*. But in all matters affecting actual worship in the voodoo cults, the queens and priestesses possessed supreme authority. This supremacy was obvious to voodoo adherents because the majority of the voodoo songs were about the deities or queens. Moreover, throughout the period of slavery and for twenty years after the Civil War the most powerful figures among blacks in New Orleans were the voodoo queens. The queens fixed the time and place of every major voodoo meeting held in New Orleans. Furthermore, rituals of voodooism were also in the hands of the queens. In fact, voodooism seems to have been a matriarchy from its first days in New Orleans, but not without key male figures and their influence. That contrasts with the power structure in Haiti and Dahomey, where, although there were a large number of women cult members, mediums, and priestesses, the majority of those who held supreme power were male, as were the majority of the deities. In New Orleans women generally made up 75 to 80 percent of the cultists.[26]

This section will provide insight into voodoo activities in New Orleans before 1900 by examining several of its most important practicing voodoo queens, priestesses, leaders, and *juju* workers, including Sanité Dédé, Marie Saloppé, and Marie Laveau.

Sanité Dédé, the first recorded New Orleans voodoo priestess, was a free quadroon from Santo Domingo.[27] She reigned from 1822 to 1830, reaching her peak around 1825. In New Orleans Dédé operated an interracial voodoo cult. She was also able to increase her income by acting as a procurer for wealthy and influential citizens who lived in or visited the city.

The only eyewitness we have of a cult ceremony conducted by Dédé is a fifteen-year-old white boy who saw one in 1825. One must view the account cautiously for two reasons: the story was recorded only after the witness had become an aged, wealthy planter in Plaquemines Parish, and it was published in the highly sensational *Century* magazine. With these precautions, the account provides us with the most vivid description of any of the pre-Laveau queens and ceremonies. This eyewitness claimed that one night in 1825 he was led by one of his father's female slaves to a brickyard where a voodoo initiation ceremony was in progress.

> An entrance door was opened at the call of Dédé . . . Each man and woman had a white kerchief tied around the forehead, though the heads of the latter were covered by the traditional madras handkerchief . . . with its seven artistic points upturned to heaven. . . . There were males and females, old and young, Negroes and Negresses, handsome mulatresses and quadroons. With them half a dozen white men and two white women. . . . At a given signal the four initiates formed a crescent before Dédé. She made cabalistic signs over them and sprinkled them vigorously with some liquid from a calabash in her hand, muttering under her breath. . . . She raised her hand and Zozo [her helper] dismounted from his cylinder and from some hidden receptacle in or behind the large black doll drew an immense snake which he brandished widely aloft. . . . He talked and whispered to it. At every word the reptile with undulating body and lambent tongue, seemed to acknowledge the dominion asserted over it. In the meantime, with arms crossed and reverent eyes the initiates had now formed a crescent around Zozo. He now compelled the snake to stand upright for about ten inches of its body. In that position Zozo passed the snake over the heads and around the necks of the initiates repeating at each pass the words which constitute the name of this African sect, "Voodoo Magnian."[28]

The remainder of the initiation ritual was divided among several other helpers and consisted of black effigies, a writhing coiling snake, and chanting and dancing, which eventually ended in the possession of the initiates and the rest of the congregation with Dédé leading them in the familiar gyrations.

After 1830 Dédé lost her position to Marie Laveau. Her decreased fame among voodoo practitioners did not undermine her innovations. She fixed the night of June 23 as St. John's Eve, the major voodoo celebration of the year, and designated Lake Pontchartrain as a regular meeting place.

A second important queen in New Orleans was Marie Saloppé, a pure-blood Congolese. She also achieved popularity in the 1820s. Saloppé was a specialist in unhexing people. Here is a description of one voodoo ceremony during her reign:

A tall Negro sprang into the space between the platform and the vodu's cage and began to dance. He whirled with increasing speed as the tom-toms and drums beat faster, leaping into the air his legs spread wide, dropping almost on his toes, it seemed, and springing even higher, until he looked to be almost on his toes, his own height above the earth. Then someone tossed him a live black rooster, its leg bound. The dancer quickly broke its neck and flung it from him. It was a signal. Others began to join the dance until soon they were all part of it. They spun and leaped upward sometimes singly, sometimes two or three, or even more joining hands. But, always in the center was the first dancer whirling faster than others, leaping higher.[29]

Saloppé's ceremonies usually involved the sacrifice of a young goat and the drinking of its blood, followed by the dance and, after the ceremony, the drinking of rum.

Despite her reputation as a voodoo expert, Marie Saloppé was hexed into insanity by her trainee and chosen successor, Marie Laveau. Laveau and Saloppé presided over the St. John's Eve ceremonies together for a brief period. Laveau's impatience and eagerness to rule led to her hexing of Saloppé, who afterward made a small fortune selling portions of brick dust at five cents each on the streets of New Orleans.[30]

Marie Laveau, the most memorable of the New Orleans voodoo queens, reigned as voodoo priestess for some forty years.[31] Like the two queens before her, she had no formal education and was probably illiterate. Marie Laveau was a free mulatto born in New Orleans in 1794 to Charles Laveau and Darcantel Marguerite. On August 4, 1819, Marie married Jacques Paris, a carpenter and a free person of color, who suddenly and mysteriously disappeared in 1822. An official announcement of his death came five years later. Marie was already calling herself Widow Paris, according to custom.

Soon after the disappearance of her husband Marie became self-supporting as a hairdresser to the elite ladies of New Orleans in addition to venturing into voodoo as a profession. By 1826 she had stolen the clientele of other voodoo leaders. She is recorded to have possessed psychic powers, and she did not hesitate to distribute cards that advertised these powers. In addition to receiving her initial training as a voodooist from Saloppé, Marie served a period as a neophyte under Dr. John, a voodoo-hoodoo practitioner who specialized in foretelling the future. In 1826, at age thirty-two, Marie went independent and by 1830 she was the recognized head of the New Orleans voodoos. Tallant, in *The Voodoo*

Queen, gives an excellent imaginative account of her first voodoo ceremony as queen:

The crowd quieted so she imagined she heard their breathing steady and in tune with the rhythmic beating of the hands of Dr. John. As the beat increased, then reached a certain pitch, she stepped into the yard. A loud outcry of approval poured from numerous throats. . . .

She stood in the center of the white sheet, the caged *vodu* just behind her, the rooster to one side, with no one else touching the white sheet and let herself grow tall and rigid. Dr. John ceased his beat and there was complete silence. For more than a minute she let the silence remain. It became agony. A woman far in the back cried out. Marie clapped her hands quickly together. Again, there was silence. Then, Marie suddenly screamed, "Papa La Bas [Legba]!"

Answers came immediately, "Ye! Ye!" She screamed that name again, "Papa La Bas!" She could almost feel them shudder. Marie sprang on top of the cage containing the snake. She felt elation so strongly that her body began to quiver and tremble. She swung from side to side, raising her hands above her head. Like them, she cried, "Oh, Oh, Oh, Ye, Ye." . . . Marie wrapped the snake around her shoulders and began to twist and writhe. The drum affected her as well as the people. Then a man sprang into view before her, a black man wearing only a loincloth, and she realized he was a slave she knew named Daniel whom she had instructed to appear at this moment. In his hands he held the fluttering, struggling black form of the rooster. She opened her eyes more widely and pointed a rigid finger. Daniel seized the rooster's head, swung the creature over his head, and the fowl's neck snapped. He then held the creature before him and tore its neck with his teeth. Blood gushed down his black chest. Marie heard screams, heard her own voice rising above the others. Her legs felt like rubber and she thought for a moment she would collapse in ecstasy. Yet, she remained upright as the vibrations of her body increased and increased, and the drums beat and beat and beat. It stopped and she seemed to return from a place far distant. She lifted the *vodu* and Saija took it and returned it to its cage. She heard the sounds—the wails and mourns, the tearing of garments, the heavy breathing. Some of the people were on the ground prostrate before her. She felt high above them, exalted and alone, far removed. She felt the power, yet, she felt exhausted too, drained of strength.

This account clearly illustrates her strong character, her great showmanship, and her self-confidence. It also presents several distinct Africanisms. For example, two Dahomean deities—Legba, referred to as Papa La Bas, and Damballa, referred to as the *vodu*—were important forces in the ritual; there is also the sacrifice of an animal and the snake dance by the queen.

Marie used a variety of techniques, ranging from trickery and physical force to voodoo charms and powerful gris-gris, to secure her position as head of the voodoos. If she met a rival on the street she did not hesitate to beat her soundly to extract a promise either to abdicate her throne or to serve under Marie as a sort of subqueen.

Her position as supreme head of the New Orleans voodoos was seriously challenged in 1850 by a quadroon voodooist called Rosalie. For many years Rosalie had aspired to dethrone Marie Laveau. To enhance her ceremonies and to attract large numbers of followers, including Marie's clientele, Rosalie supposedly imported from Africa a large, almost life-size doll that had been carved from a single tree trunk. Painted in brilliant colors and with ornamented beads and ribbons, the doll was projected as the source of Rosalie's magical powers. Thus it earned Rosalie much respect and popularity among the New Orleans voodoo community. To retain her dominant position, Marie had to undermine Rosalie's position. She stole the doll, the source of Rosalie's power and fame. Rosalie had Marie arrested. Marie, however, used her private connections to prove to the court that the doll belonged to her.

White politicians, judges, and ladies of high society purchased Marie Laveau's good luck amulets. But blacks, free and slave, were the most devoted of her clientele. They regarded Marie as semidivine and made few moves without first consulting her or one of her many subservient doctors. By the 1850s the majority of black servants not only had connections with the voodoo cult but were also part of the voodoo network.

Because the police were dedicated to suppressing the voodoo cult, Marie covered up her private activities. But she held public ceremonies and invited members of the press, the sporting fraternity, and the magnates of the police force to the annual festivals on St. John's Eve and to Congo Square, the site designated by New Orleans authorities for slaves and voodoos to gather on Sunday afternoons and dance. There she popularized a modernized worship of Damballa. In the backyard of her house on Lake Pontchartrain she usually held her most secret voodoo rites. Neither police nor reporters were welcome to these rituals, held every Friday night either in Marie's house or before one of the dozen altars which the cult maintained in New Orleans. At these ceremonies

Marie departed from her modernization of the voodoo rituals. Devotees were permitted to return to the ancient practices, the real voodoo of the earlier immigrants from Africa by way of Santo Domingo. The lips of the initiates were smeared with the blood of freshly slaughtered animals and fowl as they took oaths. The snake was presented to Marie Laveau, the queen, as the practitioners sang:

Eh Ye Ye Mamzelle Marie
Ya Ye Ye le konin fon, gris-gris
Li te kouri leka aver veux koko dril
Oh ouai, ye Mamzelle Marie. . . . [32]

This documented account of a Friday night voodoo meeting attests to Marie's complete control over the ceremony:

Like the caller of a country square dance, she called the figures she wanted to dance telling the dancers exactly what to do and yelling incomprehensible phrases in between. At times she would take a mouthful of whiskey and blow it in the face of a dancer, as she would call her snake and make it crawl over the dancers' legs. The snake lived in the watermelon patch she had planted there and sup-posedly lived off the melon.

As the tempo increased the dancers fell, were revived with whis-key, and continued. Then there was a dance that Marie did by herself. Wrapping the snake around her shoul ders she shook and twisted herself like the snake she was wearing though her feet never moved. [33]

The dance that Marie did with the snake was identical to that done by the Damballa worshippers in the People's Republic of Benin. Only on rare occasions were favored whites or nonbelievers allowed to attend such secret rites without destroying the sense of awe essential to the cult.

During the forty years in which Marie Laveau reigned as a priestess, voodoo in New Orleans underwent a series of changes. It penetrated every level of society by reaching beyond the darkness of the slaves' minds to overwhelm even the minds of their masters. And it became an interesting mixture of Catholicism and African–West Indian voodoo worship. This mixture clearly illustrates the Africans' survival abilities. Prayers, incense, candles, holy water, and a host of Catholic saints were added to voodoo paraphernalia. St. John the Baptist became the patron saint of voodoo in New Orleans. St. Michael became "Daniel Blanc," St. Anthony "You Sue," St. Paul "On za tier," and St. Peter "Legba." Some saints not recognized by the Catholic Church were invented for the specific experiences of blacks. For example, St. Marron, or Maroon, became the black patron saint of runaway slaves, who were called marrons or maroons. Other Catholic saints were accorded new powers—for instance, St. Raymon for favors and St. Rita for children. These developments were excellent examples of the Africans' accommodating abilities.

Yet Marie continually called upon the old Dahomean and Haitian deities such as Damballa and Legba in her ceremonies. Information attesting to this was provided by one of Robert Tallant's informants, Josephine Green:

> My ma say that woman used to strut like she owned the city, and she was tall and goodlookin', and wore her hair hangin' down her back. She looked just like an Indian or one of those gypsy ladies. She wore big full skirts and lots of jewelry hangin' all over her. All the people with her was hollerin' and screamin', "We is goin' to see Papa Limba!" My grandpa go runnin' after my ma then, yellin' her, "You come in here Eunice! Don't you know Papa Limba is the devil?" But after that my ma find out Papa Limba meant St. Peter, and her pa was just foolin' her.[34]

Legba or Limba, as the name was often spelled, was viewed as the devil by early missionaries in Africa and Haiti because of his trickster nature. Marie generally called upon Papa Legba at the beginning of the voodoo ceremonies. The overwhelming majority of her ceremonial rituals were borrowed from the voodoos of Haiti, the New World guardians of Dahomean voodoo.

Cult members held meetings in 1869 to discuss the future of Marie Laveau as leader of the voodoos. They decided that her age no longer permitted her to perform the duties of her high post. Marie was informed that she had to relinquish her leadership to someone younger. She presided over her last major ceremony in the first quarter of 1869. This ceremony at the lake chapel was reported in the *New Orleans Times* on March 21, 1869. The central attraction of this ceremony was a young white woman seeking to regain the affection of her lover. Most of the participants were women, with a few quadroon men, each carrying a burning candle. Although the reporter's attitude was obviously negative regarding the voodoo ceremony, he did provide the reader with an inside view:

> These women were all dressed elaborately, some of them in bridal costumes, and with an extraordinary regard for the fineness and purity of their linen. At one end of the chapel a corpse was exposed. The rites having been commenced, an elderly turbaned fe-

male dressed in yellow and red [Marie Laveau] ascended a sort of dais and chanted a wild sort of fetish song, to which the others kept up an accompaniment with their voices and with a drum-like beat of their hands and feet. At the same time they commenced to move in a circle, while gradually increasing the time. As the motion gained in intensity the flowers and other ornaments disappeared from their hair, and their dresses were torn open and each one conducted herself like a bacchante. Everyone was becoming drunk and intoxicated with the prevailing madness and excitement. As they danced in a circle, in the center of which stood a basket with a dozen hissing snakes whose heads were projecting from the cover, each Corybante touched a serpent's head with her brand. In the midst of this saturnalia of witches, the pythoness of this extraordinary dance and revel was a young girl, with bare feet, and costumed *en chemise*. In one hand she held a torch, and with wild maniacal gestures headed the band. In this awful state of nudity she continued her ever-increasing frantic movements until reason itself abandoned its earthly tenement. In a convulsive fit she finally fell, foaming at the mouth like one possessed, and it was only then that the mad carnival found a pause. The girl was torn half-dead from the scene, and she has never yet been restored to her faculties.[35]

This description vividly shows that whites as well as blacks and quadroons formed part of the voodoo community in New Orleans. Moreover, it illustrates the musical improvisations made by the participants with the use of their hands and feet and the importance of the Damballa cult represented by the pythons.

Marie's life as a voodooist did not conclude with the loss of her position as head of the voodoos. Thousands of clients continued to seek her help in spite of her age. One source reported that Marie was still going strong in 1878 and was very capable of engaging in all voodoo activities. She would have been at least eighty-four years old; one would hardly expect her still to be capable of performing the dances that were so much a part of her renowned voodoo ceremonies. One of Marie's daughters who took up her profession at times substituted for her mother.

According to evidence, Marie lived in seclusion from 1875 until she died at home on June 15, 1881. She was buried in St. Louis Cemetery Number One. To this day, strange items continue to be found at her tomb, placed there by those who come requesting from her a special favor, to put a hex on someone or to take a hex off. All requests entail the performance of a certain ritual. The cemetery guide, Buddy, explained to a researcher in 1945 that as part of this ritual an individual was obliged to

> pick up a piece of brick chalk (which always seems to be in abundance in front of the grave), make an "X" mark on the tomb, tap the left foot three times in the "goopher dust" (soil or marble dust from the tomb), knock on the tomb three times with the left hand, flatten the left hand over the "X" mark, silently make the wish, keep the chalk as a charm.[36]

Charles M. Gandolfo, owner of the Voodoo Museum in New Orleans, gave me another version of the graveyard ritual: "Draw an 'X,' place your hand over it, rub your foot three times against the bottom, throw some silver coins into the cup, and make your wish." Some devotees place their hands on the tomb to absorb Marie's magic as they whisper with their lips against the tomb.

By the end of the nineteenth century voodoo had undergone many changes in New Orleans. Leaders who reigned after Marie Laveau proved incapable of holding the cult together. New and old leaders, male and female, established independent voodoo sects. Organized voodoo ceremonies became less public and more secretive. To the general public they were events of the past. Most citizens of New Orleans, like the tourists who ventured into the city, knew voodoo only as a magical act, i.e., hoodoo, which was less centrally organized than voodoo. Subsequently, many practitioners did not emphasize the worship of African deities or voodoo dances to any significant degree. They stressed gris-gris, the placing and removing of curses, or simply those works normally associated with witchcraft. Nevertheless, hoodoo, like bad *juju* or *bó* in Dahomey, is also part of the African religious system. Moreover, hoodoo was not always negative in a violent sense. "To hoodoo someone" implied that an individual was made to do something against his or her will. The process was done by the use of various concoctions and potions. People could obtain potions to be drunk, eaten, or worn in order to make others fall in love with them, for example, or to cause their deaths.

In many respects the voodooist and the hoodooist have much in common. This point is clear if one understands that voodoo connotes the positive religious rites while hoodoo generally connotes the mystic and magical aspects that are usually evoked for negative purposes. There are many instances when voodoo has been evoked to achieve a negative purpose, such as the "death dance." Conversely, hoodoo has occasionally been used to protect against evil or impending danger. Many voodooists have also incorporated their knowledge of hoodoo into their practices. For example, Marie Laveau, though a voodoo queen, was also a hoodoo practitioner. To be a good voodoo priest or priestess, in fact, one had to have a working knowledge of hoodoo. This was confirmed by an informant in summer 1979 when he stated that a voodoo priest or priestess must know how to put on a curse in order to be able to remove one. It is also true that all professional voodooists claim to know various ways of killing people with black magic.

The emphasis on hoodoo caused a revolutionary change within the world of the voodoo. The predominance of female rulers was undermined. Even though women remained part of the religious sects and were numerically well-represented in the fields of magic and medicine, the majority of cult leaders and hoodoo practitioners were men, generally referred to as hoodoo or voodoo doctors, medicine men, root doctors, or conjurers.

Descriptive accounts of voodoo ceremonies from the close of the nineteenth century clearly illustrate the changes in the voodoo rituals that were so prevalent at the turn of the century. Dancing and singing remained important, but the songs very seldom referred to the African deities or to the reigning voodoo kings and queens. Religious worship and healing by incantation were more likely to take place at the same ritual ceremony. Most important, the term *voudou* was often used to denote the male leader and not the snake of Marie Laveau. In many instances blood sacrifices were replaced by various foods and liquids.[37]

Joe Goodness, a black informant of James Haskins, claimed to have witnessed voodoo rites at the turn of the century when he was young. His description illustrates the degree to which voodoo as a religious system had changed:

> In my day they didn't even drink blood that I know of, but only ate things like gumbo and chicken and drank a lot of liquor. In my uncle's day they ate worse things. They used to tear chickens to pieces and eat 'em while they are still alive. They wore all kinds of gris-gris on their bodies—dolls made out of feathers and hair, skins of snakes and pieces of human bones. I heard people say hoodoos are cannibals and used to eat babies but I can't believe that unless it was way back even before my uncle was alive.[38]

Such changes did not alter the fact that voodoo was and is an African religious retention. In fact, the way in which the changes were woven into the overall religious system of New Orleans reflected yet another tradition and practice that was common among certain West African groups. The Fon of the Kingdom of Dahomey were known to incorporate certain religious practices of the peoples they conquered or who conquered them. Moreover, when the French colonized the kingdom, human sacrifices were outlawed and the Fon adjusted to the change by holding "mock" sacrifices or by altering their religious traditions to exclude the sacrifices. These adjustments guaranteed that the tradition survived at least to some degree. Still other practitioners simply went underground, as in New Orleans, and continued to practice their religious rituals.

Information concerning the activities of voodoo practitioners in New Orleans proper is sketchy for the first twenty years of the twentieth century. Most information comes from newspaper articles and police reports. The arrival of Dr. Koko in New Orleans was announced in a local newspaper in 1902. Dr. Koko, claiming to come from the Congo, boasted of discovering the seal of Solomon on the shores of Syria. Such claims were of course designed to give him respect in the voodoo and hoodoo community. He rented a small cottage a few blocks from the house of Marie Laveau and opened a business. Unfortunately for the naive, most of those claiming to be voodoo and hoodoo experts of the early twentieth century were more interested in making money than in observing religious rituals and rites. In fact, many were regarded as swindlers and thieves. In 1906 a group of voodoos asked the New Orleans police to arrest their pastor, J. V. Larson, on a charge of embezzling the funds of the sect. He headed an organization called the Voodoo Church.[39]

Dr. Kat, alias Joseph M. McKay, also flourished during the first quarter of the twentieth century. A dentist by profession, he used voodoo and hoodoo to supplement his income. In 1914 he was operating a mail-order business in New Orleans through which he sold advice, candles, and gris-gris to all parts of the United States. He is credited with starting the first large-scale mail-order racket in marketing voodoo and hoodoo merchandise. He was arrested in July 1914 by federal authorities in Birmingham and later charged with using the mails to defraud and with violating the Mann Act.[40]

Many hoodooists and voodooists openly and boldly publicized themselves and their trade despite legal restrictions and penalties. In 1913 one notorious hoodoo practitioner, Emile Laile, not only signed his name with a P.H. (Professor of Hoodoo) but had cards printed that set a new record for frankness:

Emile Laile, P.H.
Meaning Professor of Hoodoo
All Manner of Hants and Hoodoo Removed
with neatness and dispatch

No witch doctor is too strong for my power
References exchanged
Special attention to emergency calls
Office 2928 Orleans Street
My Office Hours Anytime
All Mail Order Filled[41]

Emile found himself in trouble after accepting a fee from a white woman who marked a fifty-cent piece with a pin and notified the police. The court found him guilty of obtaining money under false pretenses and sentenced him to jail.

The greed of a few did not erase the sincerity of other practitioners and leaders. Nor did it mean that voodoo adherents had forgotten the powers of the ancient African deities or that the faithful hoodoo clients no longer believed in the effectiveness of gris-gris. The interns and nurses at Charity Hospital in New Orleans could attest to the continued existence of voodoo and hoodoo in 1920. They had been treating patients for years who not only insisted that they had been hoodooed but who brought their gris-gris to the hospital and kept it in bed with them. The April 13, 1924, edition of the *New Orleans Item* reported on page one that the hospital attendants found "metal pieces shaped like devils' souls, coins, colored and knotted strings with fish scales, obas or bags filled with mystic stones and teeth, bones and mosquito bar rings."

The most important eyewitness of voodoo activities in the 1920s was Zora Hurston, a member of the inner voodoo circle. From her detailed descriptions we know the names of the most important sect rulers of that time. The list includes hoodooists and voodooists Samuel Thompson, Father Simms, Dr. Grant, Dr. Barnes, and Dr. Albert Frechard. Samuel Thompson, who initiated Hurston into his cult in the 1920s, was one of the most acclaimed voodoo-hoodoo doctors of the Catholic faith in New Orleans. Thompson claimed that his remote ancestors had brought the power with them from the rock (Africa). He also contended that his forebears lived in Santo Domingo before coming to the New Orleans area. Hurston's account gives invaluable data on the initiation rituals of the cult during this time, and the various responsibilities and duties of the neophytes.[42]

Lyle Saxon, noted for his writings on early twentieth century New Orleans, claimed to have attended a voodoo service around 1926 that would have given credit to Marie Laveau. According to him such ceremonies were rare compared with the number of cases in which people were hoodooed.

Documentation on organized voodoo activities in the 1930s is rarer than for the 1920s. Most of the information deals with hoodoo activities. In 1931 hoodoo activities were heavily associated with the intensified use of goober dust (graveyard dirt), denoting bad magic. In March 1931 two women went to the St. Rochelle Cemetery in lower New Orleans to put flowers on the grave of their mother, who had passed away fifteen years earlier. They were about to place their flowers in the vase when they noticed a stump of a black candle almost concealed in a small mound of freshly turned earth in the center of the grave. The women dug into the ground beneath the candle, bringing forth an old tobacco can sealed tightly and bound with a string. Inside they found a photograph of a man unknown to them, a package of needles, and some charred scraps of paper. The picture was also charred along the edges and punctured with numerous needle holes symbolizing the fate of the man. The two women reported their find to the police but the offender was never found.[43]

A much more bizarre case was told to Robert Tallant by Sexton, the graveyard attendant:

> The chicken we found was a big rooster . . . and it was all dressed up in a coat and pants, a hat, a collar and a tie. His legs were tied wit' about a hundred yards of white cord. On the tomb where he was we found three nickels . . . left food and water where couldn't reach it. . . .

Being ignorant of its meaning, Sexton decided to ask an elderly black woman to interpret the findings. She stated:

> Somebody was in jail and he ain't the right one to be there, so his friends took a rooster, dressed it like a man and tied it up in the cemetery so it would suffer. As long as that rooster suffered the guilty man was supposed to suffer and in the end he was supposed to confess and give himself up.[44]

Another gruesome find was unearthed one morning in the summer of 1939. While walking through one of the old New Orleans graveyards, a worker found the strangled nude body of a young black woman. The body was on its back and in each of the breasts was a black hat pin sticking upright. In one hand was a curious gris-gris consisting of a wasp's nest and some horsehair wrapped in red silk. There were other negative reports of hoodoo practices outside the graveyard setting. For example, in 1938 in a New Orleans parish, Reverend Howard Randle cut his wife's throat because he believed she had put a spell on him.[45]

By 1936 enormous quantities of charms, amulets, and magical powders were being sold to both whites and blacks. Love potions of various
powders guaranteeing to charm an employer into granting a raise, more
time off, or some other special favor were most preferred. One white
victim of hoodoo was Lyle Saxon, who was preparing to go on a trip to
New York when his house servant, wishing to accompany him, decided
to purchase Boss Fix powder to be used to persuade Saxon to take him
along. This powder was put in Saxon's food and coffee for a week.[46]

During the 1930s most of the information on voodoo practitioners
was very negative. Voodoo had virtually disappeared from the public eye.
Many voodooists resorted to becoming vendors of hoodoo merchandise.
In 1934 Wanda Carter, an African American, was arrested in her home
in uptown New Orleans. She claimed to be a voodoo queen even though
evidence failed to place her above a hoodooist. In her first room, on a
center table, was a white bowl filled with cranberries, which she had
blessed. These cranberries were supposed to have special curative power
and sold for a handsome fee. The police also found a varied assortment
of gris-gris in her home.[47]

The outstanding voodooist of the 1930s was Dr. Rockford Lewis.
Born in Thibodaux, Louisiana, in 1905, Lewis moved to New Orleans
in 1920.[48] He was first employed as a yard boy and later as a chauffeur
for white residents of the city. He began his voodoo career in 1929 when
he opened a drugstore on lower Royal Street dealing in voodoo-hoodoo
paraphernalia—herbs, roots, powders, and so forth, not prescription
drugs. Dr. Lewis was known as the most powerful voodooist of fire, but
he was best known for his hoodoo works. Among his clients were some
of the most respected white citizens of New Orleans. He excelled in a
mail-order business specializing in hoodoo and voodoo charms and
powders. After his initial success he expanded his business and hired at
least five secretaries and several other assistants.

Dr. Lewis denied knowledge of voodoo when he was arraigned in federal court in 1934 on mail fraud charges. His case received much pub-
licity. The *Item* printed Lewis's statement to the court: "I handles medals, sachet bags, lucky beans, lucky medals. Yes, sir, I believe in luck. I
believes in helping people. But mostly I handles 'Save Your Life Rheumatic Oil.' I sells a lot of that." He claimed that the oil had nothing to
do with voodoo but was a valuable aid to suffering invented by himself
in his own laboratory. One of his secretaries testified that the mail orders authorized by Dr. Lewis to be sent out of town had consisted almost entirely of the rheumatic oil. A circular letter that Lewis had
mailed to all of his clientele and prospective clients was also presented
in court:

Dear Friend:

I am writing you just to find out if you would like for me to do anything for you? I can do any kind of work you want done. Let me help you out of trouble and give you luck and success in anything you undertake to do. I have helped peoples all over the world just by sending them stuff to do all the work. Anyone can tell you my hands and tobies are good. Mail $5.00 and I will send the order. Anything you want done cost $5.00, state what you want done. Anybody in the world will tell you I am good.

NOTICE

If you tell your friends to write me I will make a discount for you.

This letter, and specifically the Notice section, clearly illustrates the religious and business levels that voodoo and hoodoo practitioners had reached by the 1930s. Dr. Lewis lost his case and received a two-year sentence in the federal penitentiary in Atlanta. When he returned to New Orleans in 1936 he reopened his Royal Street business. For a while he was content with local trade. But, desiring to increase his income, he reopened his mail-order business in 1938 and was eventually arrested again.

By 1940 voodoo ceremonies were still rarely visible to nonmembers. Moreover, many of the overt practitioners concealed their voodoo affiliations under the guise of hoodoo doctors or by mingling with such sects as the spiritualists. The selling and purchasing of gris-gris and other hoodoo paraphernalia were done through specific stores or the local grapevine. There were few outward signs attesting to the presence of voodoo and hoodoo in New Orleans. Yet throughout the 1940s any early-morning stroller in Congo Square could come upon a rooster tied to a tree, still alive, feathers plucked, and nine silver pins stuck in its breast, or a plate of black-eyed peas and rice cooked with sugar surrounded by silver coins. Furthermore, six voodoo-related murders were reported around New Orleans between 1940 and 1945.[49]

The most important source for voodoo and hoodoo activities during the 1940s is Robert Tallant.[50] One informant told him about the continued power of hoodoo over its believers:

Right now there is more hoodoo around this town than there ever was. . . . But, it sure has changed. I'll say this though, it's a good thing to keep away from. It has just as much power over the people now as it ever did, and it can do some funny things. Hoodoo is somethin' peoples shouldn't even talk about. It might be changed but it's just as bad as it ever was.

It is obvious that by 1940 the majority of blacks in New Orleans were more familiar with hoodoo than voodoo.

Tallant also provides us with the names, specializations, and activities of various hoodoo and voodoo practitioners who flourished in New Orleans and environs during this period. Among female hoodoo-voodoo practitioners were Lola, Julia Jackson, Madame Cazounoux, and Grandma Beavois. Lola and Julia were the most important voodoo queens.

Lola, a tall, very lean black woman with high cheekbones and prominent eyes, began her work as a child and was known to mix spiritualism with voodoo. When Tallant questioned her on the use of the snake, associated with eighteenth- and nineteenth-century New Orleans voodoo, she replied:

> I ain't got no more snake. . . . You really ought to have one to do hoodoo work, but them mean niggers around here reported me and the policemens came and make me give it to the zoo at Audubon Park. It sure made me mad. If I still did bad work I would fix 'em. How I gonna work at all wit'out no snake?

The symbol and manifestation of the African deity Damballa was still viewed as important to work strong voodoo-hoodoo.

Lola was known to attend hoodoo meetings held by a fisherman every Friday night; however, no detailed description of any public or private ceremony conducted by her was recorded. She claimed to move her residence at least three times a year because too many people came to ask her questions. She was a strong believer in spirits and swore that she conversed with them daily. She also possessed an endless store of hoodoo knowledge. An example of one of her formulas "To Make a Person Go Away" is:

> Make a black candle and knead the wax like dough. Write the person's name on a piece of paper four times backward and five times forward. Roll your wax into a ball and put this paper in the middle of it. Then stick nine pins in the ball. Get on the ferry and go out to the middle of the river and throw it in. Snap your finger and say St. Epedite, make him go quick.

Julia Jackson was a contemporary of Lola's. Julia was reputed to have been able to detect from vibrations whether an individual had signed up with the devil. By 1946 Julia had accumulated enough money to buy half the property on her block and a car to take trips into the country, where she acquired an extensive trade in gris-gris. To save money she made her own ingredients and claimed to use all kinds of things in her work—chicken feathers, earthworms, red pepper, coffee grounds, nails, beef tongues, oils, and powders. Julia asserted that faith was the essential part of hoodoo. She claimed to have the knowledge to kill people with hoodoo but denied having killed anyone. Her "To Kill Someone: Formula I" was as follows:

> Catch a rattlesnake, kill it, hang it in the sun to dry. Write the person's name on a piece of paper and put it in the snake's mouth. Just like that snake dry up the person gonna dry up too. If you keep that snake in the sun long enough the person's gonna die.

Various of her voodoo and hoodoo death dances were also said to have been very effective.

Male dominance of the world of hoodoo was particularly evident by the 1940s. Among the most famous were Dr. Hawkins, Dr. Butler, Dr. Johnson, Dr. W. L. Berry, Dr. Nathan Barnes, Bert Ellis, and Dr. Thomas Byron.

Dr. Byron, one of the most outstanding, claimed to have the power to cure illnesses, heal cripples, and bring love to lonely lives. He further asserted that his one claim in life was to help humanity and to give advice to troubled peoples in this troubled world. Father Byron, as he was often called, was a serious-looking man, and this quality was enhanced by the Catholic priest's robe he wore. In addition to his noble claim to help humanity, Father Byron operated a small establishment on South Rampart Street. On the window of his establishment a sign was painted: "Public Consultant, Personal Advice, Public Stenography, Magazines and Novelties."[51] Among the novelties sold were beauty preparations, patent medicines, candles, incense, and milder types of gris-gris.

Dr. Nathan Barnes practiced hoodoo and voodoo throughout New Orleans, distributing his business cards widely:

> Have any kind of trouble? I can solve them for you. Want a mate? Need a lover? Seeking new friendship? Win a lawsuit? I can do all this and more for you. Try my special herbs, oils, and incenses, and other powerful voodoo specialties. Will make any kind of good luck charm on request. Wanga dolls expertly made. See Dr. Zawambe at anytime seven days a week. Special rite performed on request.[52]

The special rites included voodoo ceremonies.

In 1945 the World Order of Congregational Churches designated voodoo as a bona fide religion. This recognition put voodoo on a better standing with nonvoodoo worshippers in New Orleans and environs. Faithful voodoo worshippers, however, did not have to be informed that they practiced a justifiable faith. By 1940 there were approximately one thousand voodoo churches of varying types in the area, but the inner voodoo meetings and ceremonies were becoming more secretive. Many were by invitation only, while others could be entered by paying a fee.[53]

Throughout the 1940s hoodoo doctors did a prosperous business with their claims of being able to do almost anything, from removing curses and tumors to giving out lucky numbers and restoring sexual powers. Their fees ranged from five to five hundred dollars and their ranks included ex-GIs and ex-convicts.[54] By 1947 the term *voodoo* had been virtually replaced with *hoodoo* when referring to the money-making traffic of talismans, luck powders, and bottled love.[55] Nevertheless, the nonreligious elements of voodoo are by-products of voodoo as a faith system whose origins are African.

Conclusion

The cruel conditions of slavery, its adherence to a rigid working system, and its rules against any African tradition that threatened the slave system guaranteed the destruction of many African political, social, and economic institutions among the slaves. Many artistic skills were also forgotten because the new slave system provided no leisure time to engage in such activities. The slaves were forced to abandon the outward material things while preserving the inward nonmaterial things such as religion and magic, the most retained African survivals. These two retentions not only survived but underwent an expansion in parts of the New World, including the West Indies, South America, Central America, and to a lesser extent North America.

Religious retentions among blacks in New Orleans were as strong or as intense as those in areas such as Haiti, where Africans were a majority of the population and often of the same ethnic group or related linguistic group. Voodoo rituals and ceremonies in New Orleans were composed of remnants of various religious practices found among several ethnic groups. Given the diverse ethnic groups found among the slaves, especially in the United States, the African slaves were forced to create a synthesis of their religious beliefs. In New Orleans *vodu* survives as a conglomeration of various African rituals, beliefs, and practices. Two Dahomean deities, Legba and Damballa, the serpent deity often referred to as the *Voudou* or Zombi, continue to reign supreme among the voodooists of New Orleans who emphasize this Dahomean religious pantheon. Ogun of the Yoruba Orisha cult is also very important. Other worshipped deities appear to be secondary.

Today in New Orleans the most vivid and common signs of voodoo are its magical and mystical elements, but one should not be misled; voodoo as a religion is still very strong. One has only to read New Orleans newspapers. In almost every neighborhood south of Canal Street evidence can be found in ordinary homes and makeshift offices set up by practitioners that hoodoo and voodoo are alive in the black community. Oral evidence that I have gathered through personal interviewing also supports the contention that voodoo religious ceremonies with animal sacrifices continue to be practiced among the true believers of voodoo in New Orleans and Algiers. Such services and rituals are often performed in flats around the city or in people's backyards as well as in established voodoo churches. The ceremonial rites remain secret because of their nature. Of course, the number of those faithful to voodoo is lower than the figures claimed by self-styled doctors and reverends who have chosen to foster hoodoo. One only has to look deep enough and to ask the right questions to find evidence that voodoo believers, both black and white, continue to flourish in New Orleans and Algiers.

To survive, voodoo had to become a religion practiced in secret in spite of its designation as a bona fide religion in 1945. As a result of this designation a distinct division emerged in New Orleans between those who practiced voodoo as a religion and those who practiced hoodoo. As early as the nineteenth century the separation of voodoo and hoodoo had been heavily influenced in New Orleans by police pressure. Police harassment forced voodooists such as Marie Laveau to hold weekly public ceremonies in Congo Square. These public ceremonies stressed hoodoo. Hoodoo had become an economic opportunity for many. The cooperation of the voodooist leaders was designed to camouflage their real activities. But not all of the voodoos were willing to accept the actions of the police. Many hoodooists and voodooists retaliated by intimidating the police. In February 1956 a bomb was sent through the mail addressed to police headquarters. It exploded prematurely in the post office. The day before, the assistant police superintendent had received a letter containing threats, signed by a female calling herself Marie Laveau:

> We are so high you cannot climb over us—so low you cannot get beneath us—and so broad you cannot go around us—so you must go through or by us. . . . You must go straight and keep your word or else. . . . You get all kinds of help and now you want to run out on your pledges. . . . Your name has been handed to us as a rat and double crosser. . . . To this we give you ten days warning to get back in line or to where you just left or else stand the consequences. You may run but you can't hide. . . . We will make you melt away like dry ice in vapor on a hot day and lose everything. . . . No one will be able to help you.[56]

This letter not only shows the power and influence of the hoodooists and voodooists in 1956. It also indicates that whites in high places were their clients with whom they had a habit of making deals. Such alliances with the officials of New Orleans can account in part for the African religious survivals that have continued to thrive underground in New Orleans.[57]

Notes

The research for this project was made possible by grants from the Center for Afro-American Studies and the Institute of American Cultures at the University of California at Los Angeles and the National Fellowship Fund of the Ford Foundation, Atlanta.

1. John Hope Franklin, *From Slavery to Freedom: A History of Negro Americans* (New York: Knopf, 5th ed., 1980), 28–29. Melville J. Herskovits, *The Myth of the Negro Past* (Boston: Beacon Press, 1958), 1–32.

2. Jessie Gaston Mulira, "A History of the Mahi Peoples from 1774 to 1920," Ph.D. dissertation, University of California, Los Angeles, 1984, interviews held throughout Mahiland, February 3–April 28, 1981, 17–30. Pierre Saulnier, *Le vodun Sakpata: Recherche sur le vodun Sakpata* (Porto-Novo: [n.p.], 1974). A. Akindélé and C. Aguessy, "Contribution a l'étude de l'histoire de l'ancien royaume de Porto-Novo," *Mémoires de l'Institute Français d'Afrique Noire*, no. 25 (Dakar: IFAN, 1953). Melville J. Herskovits, *Dahomey: An Ancient West African Kingdom* (Evanston, Ill.: Northwestern University Press, 1967; reprint of 1938 ed.), vol. 1, 132–34, 228–29, 242–43, 265, 375–78; vol. 2, 100–288, 305–306. J. A. Skertchly, *Dahomey as It Is* (London: Chapman and Hall, 1874), 147. Sir Richard Burton, *A Mission to Gelele, King of Dahome* (London: Routledge and Kegan Paul, 1966), 297. R. Le Herisse, *L'Ancien royaume du Dahomey: Moeurs, religion, histoire* (Paris: Larose, 1911), 118–19. Christian Merlo, "Hierarchie fetichiste d'Ouidah: Inventaire ethnographique, demographique, et statistique des fetiches de la villa d'Ouidah, Dahomey," *Bulletin de l'IFAN* (1940) 2(1–2):12–20. Maximillien Quenum, "Au pays des Fons," *Bulletin du Comité d'Etudes Historiques et Scientifiques de l'Afrique Occidentale Française* (1935) 18(2–3):218–19, 239. Maurice A. Glele, *Le danxome: Du pouvoir Aja a la nation Fon* (Paris: Nubia, 1974), 67, 68, 77–79, 82, 112, 121–22, 134–35, 149, 160, 164, 169–70, 234, 244. Julien Alapini, *Les initiés* (Avignon: Aubanel père: 1953), and *Les noix sacrées: Etude complète de Fa-Ahidegoun* (Monte Carlo: [n.p.], 1950). Judith Gleason, *Agotime: Her Legend* (New York: Grossman, 1970), 10–38. Boniface I. Obichere, "Women and Slavery in the Kingdom of Dahomey," *Revue Française d'Histoire d'Outre-Mer* (1978) 238:11.

3. Robert Tallant, "Voodoo Articles," New Orleans Collection, Tulane University, box 18, folder 9, 1945, 8.

4. Herbert Asbury, *The French Quarter: An Informal History of the New Orleans Underworld* (New York: Knopf, 1936), 254.

5. Franklin, *From Slavery to Freedom*, 28–29. Melville J. Herskovits, *Accul-*

turation: The Study of Culture Contact (New York: J. J. Augustin, 1938). Sidney W. Mintz and Richard Price, *An Anthropological Approach to the Afro-American Past: A Caribbean Perspective* (Philadelphia: Institute for the Study of Human Issues, 1976). Norman Whitten and John Szwed, eds., *Afro-American Anthropology: Contemporary Perspectives* (New York: Free Press, 1970).

6. Nathan Irvin Huggins, *Black Odyssey: The Afro-American Ordeal in Slavery* (New York: Pantheon, 1977), 57–85. Harold Courlander, *A Treasury of African Folklore* (New York: Crown, 1975), 5. James Haskins, *Witchcraft, Mysticism, and Magic in the Black World* (Garden City, N.Y.: Doubleday, 1974), 36–37, and *Voodoo and Hoodoo: Their Tradition and Craft as Revealed by Actual Practitioners* (New York: Stein and Day, 1978), 52.

7. Haskins, *Witchcraft*, 32, 34, 37, 73–74, and *Voodoo and Hoodoo*, 52. Melville J. Herskovits, "African Gods and Catholic Saints in New World Belief," *American Anthropologist* (1937) 39:635–43, and *Life in a Haitian Valley* (New York: Knopf, 1937), 31–32. Susan M. Slemons, "The Possibility of an Aesthetic in Haitian Vodun," honors thesis in anthropology, Newcomb Comb College, 1965, 52.

8. Haskins, *Witchcraft*, 32–34, and *Voodoo and Hoodoo*, 52. J. B. Hollis Tegarden, "Voodooism," dissertation, University of Chicago, 1924, 6.

9. The passage is translated from the French found in Tegarden, "Voodooism," 13. See also Theodore Lothrop Stoddard, *Religion and Politics in Haiti* (Washington, D.C.: 1966), 38; William Buehler Seabrook, *The Magic Island* (New York: Blue Ribbon Books, 1929), 312; Henry Gilfond, *Voodoo: Its Origins and Practices* (New York: Watts, 1976), 12–13; Haskins, *Witchcraft*, 63–65; Kyle Kristos, *Voodoo* (Philadelphia: Lippincott, 1976), 102.

10. Interviews by the author in Mahiland; see Gaston Mulira, "History," 27.

11. Ibid., 17. Additional references are in note 2 above. See also Melville and Frances Herskovits, "An Outline of Dahomean Religious Beliefs," *Memoirs of the American Anthropological Association*, no. 41, 1933, 7–77, and Melville Herskovits, "Some Aspects of Dahomean Ethnology," *Africa* (July 1932) 5(3):266–96.

12. Information in this paragraph and the rest of this section comes from Gaston Mulira, "History," 19–22, and Herskovits, *Dahomey*, vol. 1, 38, 228–29, 242–43, 265, 375–78; vol. 2, 133, 152–66, 170, 174–75, 179–88, 215–22, 225–29, 305–306. For more details, see Alapini, *Les initiés* and *Les noix sacrées*.

13. Information in this and the next several paragraphs is from Zora N. Hurston, "Hoodoo in America," *Journal of American Folklore* (October–December 1931) 44(174):358–60, 381–82.

14. Gaston Mulira, "History," 23–25. Obichere, "Women and Slavery," 6. For additional information, see Alapini, *Les initiés* and *Les noix sacrées;* Max Gluckman, "The Individual in a Social Framework: The Rise of King Shaka of Zululand," *Journal of African Studies* (Summer 1974) 1(2):113–

14; Robert Sutherland Rattray, *Ashanti* (Oxford: Oxford University Press, 1923), and *The Tribes of the Ashanti Hinterland* (Oxford: Clarendon Press, 1932).

15. Information in this section comes from Harold Courlander, *The Drum and the Hoe: Life and Lore of the Haitian People* (Berkeley: University of California Press, 1960), 22, 75–81; Michel S. Laguerre, *Voodoo Heritage* (Beverly Hills, Calif.: Sage, 1980), 17–18, 22–23, 27–31, 37–38, 139–40; Robert Tallant, *Voodoo in New Orleans* (New York: Putnam, 1956), 23, 30–32, 41; Robert W. Pelton, *Voodoo Secrets from A to Z* (South Brunswick: A. S. Barnes, 1973), 79–80; and Seabrook, *Magic Island,* 56, 58, 319.

16. Courlander, *Drum and Hoe,* 77.

17. Ibid., 78.

18. Ibid.

19. Ibid., 80.

20. Tallant, *Voodoo,* 30.

21. Courlander, *Drum and Hoe,* 81.

22. Seabrook, *Magic Island,* 58, 56.

23. Ibid., 319.

24. Tallant, *Voodoo,* 30–31.

25. Ibid., 31–32.

26. Haskins, *Witchcraft,* 69. Asbury, *French Quarter,* 255, 259–60. Tallant, *Voodoo,* 29–31. Robert W. Pelton, *The Complete Book of Voodoo* (New York: Arco, 1972), 16.

27. Information on Dédé comes from Pelton, *Complete Book,* 16, 55, and *Voodoo Secrets,* 114; Jacques d'Argent, *Voodoo* (Los Angeles: Sherbourne Press, 1970), 90–91; Asbury, *French Quarter,* 261–63; J. W. Buel, *Metropolitan Life Unveiled, or the Mysteries and Miseries of America's Great Cities* (St. Louis: Historical Publishing Co., 1882), 522–30; W. A. Roberts, *Lake Pontchartrain* (Indianapolis: Bobbs-Merrill, 1946), 193–94; and Tallant, *Voodoo,* 55.

28. Asbury, *French Quarter,* 261–63.

29. Robert Tallant, *The Voodoo Queen: A Novel* (New York: Putnam, 1956), 55–59.

30. Pelton, *Voodoo Secrets,* 63, 93. Tallant, *Voodoo,* 58, and *Voodoo Queen,* 24. Haskins, *Witchcraft,* 72.

31. Information on Marie Laveau comes from Tallant, *Voodoo,* 62, 63, 65–67, 70, 74–79, 82; Raymond Joseph Martinez, *Mysterious Marie Laveau: Voodoo Queen, and Folktales along the Mississippi* (New Orleans: Hope, 1956), 5, 8, 13, 14, 17, 24, 27; Tallant, *Voodoo Queen,* 4, 5, 67, 103, 109–11, 138, 176; Tallant, "Voodoo Articles," 8, 19, 32, 169; Haskins, *Witchcraft,* 101, 130, 132, 133, 135; Roberts, *Lake Pontchartrain,* 175, 195, 196; Jerry and Charles Gandolfo, *Le voodoo: A la Nouvelle Orleans* (New Orleans: Voodoo Museum, 1975), 2; Asbury, *French Quarter,* 265, 268, 269–70; Kristos, *Voodoo,* 97; Henry C. Castellanos, *New Orleans as It Was* (Baton Rouge: Loui-

siana State University Press, 1978; facsimile of 1895 ed.), 97, 98–100; John W. Blassingame, *Black New Orleans*, 1860–1880 (Chicago: University of Chicago Press, 1973), 5; Gaston Mulira, "History," interviews in New Orleans and Algiers, Louisiana, 1979, and in the People's Republic of Benin, West Africa, 1981; Haskins, *Voodoo and Hoodoo*, 60–61; and Julie Yvonne Webb, "Superstitious Influence (Voodoo in Particular) affecting Health Practices in a Selected Population in Southern Louisiana," dissertation, Tulane University, New Orleans, La., 1971, 100.

32. Tallant, *Voodoo*, 75–76.

33. D'Argent, *Voodoo*, 101.

34. Tallant, *Voodoo*, 67.

35. Asbury, *French Quarter*, 269–70.

36. Tallant, "Voodoo Articles," 32.

37. Ibid., 39–43.

38. Haskins, *Witchcraft*, 104–105.

39. Tallant, *Voodoo*, 167.

40. Pelton, *Complete Book*, 18. Tallant, *Voodoo*, 213–14.

41. Tallant, *Voodoo*, 214.

42. Hurston, "Hoodoo in America," 357, 362, 368–71, 380–81, 387–88, 390–91.

43. Tallant, *Voodoo*, 169–70.

44. Ibid., 171.

45. Ibid., 241.

46. Asbury, *French Quarter*, 282–83.

47. Tallant, *Voodoo*, 215.

48. Information on Dr. Lewis comes from Pelton, *Complete Book*, 18; Edward Clayton, "The Truth about Voodoo," *Ebony*, April 1951, 54–61; and Tallant, *Voodoo*, 215–17.

49. Tallant, *Voodoo*, 20, 146; Haskins, *Witchcraft*, 105.

50. Information in this and the next several paragraphs is from Tallant, *Voodoo*, 146, 178, 180, 182–83, 188, 189, and Hurston, "Hoodoo in America," 369–71.

51. Tallant, *Voodoo*, 212, 213.

52. Pelton, *Complete Book*, 18–19.

53. Tallant, *Voodoo*, 161–63. Interviews held by the author in New Orleans and Algiers, Louisiana, summer 1979.

54. Clayton, "Truth about Voodoo," 56.

55. Interviews held by the author in New Orleans, summer 1979. Roberts, *Lake Pontchartrain*, 199.

56. Martinez, *Mysterious Marie Laveau*, 38–39.

57. David Crosby, "Voodoo Thrives Underground in New Orleans," *Times Picayune*, Sept. 16, 1979, section 1, 5.

Six

Gullah Attitudes toward Life and Death

Margaret Washington

The coastal region of South Carolina, bounded on the north by George-town and on the south by Port Royal and St. Helena Sound, is the land of the Gullah slave population. Halfway between Charleston and Savannah a fringe of fertile islands borders these coastal lowlands and stretches out into the arms of the sea. Here, as slaves, the most isolated Gullah people lived, first cultivating indigo and later the famous long–staple fine-quality cotton. More significantly, the Gullahs created a distinct, original African American cultural form.[1]

Diversity of African ethnic origins was limited in the Sea Island region because Carolina planters paid particular attention to the geographical sources of their black cargoes. White Carolinians preferred Gold Coast Africans, but they were difficult to obtain because West Indian sugar planters usually got first choice. Still, the first African-Carolinians were probably of Gold Coast origin (Akan speaking), since West Indian planters who settled the colony brought about a thousand slaves with them. Next in demand were Africans from the Kongo-Angola area. But in 1739, when African-born Angolans rose up against Carolina masters, slaves from this region were no longer so desirable. Following the 1739 Stono Rebellion a nonimportation act was in effect for ten years.[2] Afterward a preponderance of Mande-speaking Africans from the Windward Coast (Sierra Leone and Liberia) was imported. Many of these Africans went to the Sea Islands during a period of extensive settlement and agricultural expansion twenty-five years before the War for Independence. The postwar years witnessed another period of massive importations, and the Kongo-Angolan region once again supplied the majority of Africans to slave coffles. Some of them peopled the Carolina low country, but an even larger number went to up-country plantations and to planters in states refusing to import.[3]

Thus some cultural homogeneity was retained as Africans passed from the Old World to the New. In the Sea Island region of South Carolina, cultural similitude was coupled with relative isolation and resulted in a tendentious process of African provenance, American acculturation, and intergroup socialization.[4] The prevalence of Akan names in Gullah Creole language certainly indicates Ashanti and Fanti influence and supports the "hearth area" concept, emphasizing the lasting effects of first "settlers" whose influence far exceeds their numbers. But evidence demonstrates that the dominant African presence in the Sea Island region derives from the Kongo-Angolan and Windward Coast ethnic groups.[5]

Kongo-Angola was the home of BaKongo civilization and Bantu-speaking peoples whose language is KiKongo.[6] KiKongo linguistic presence in Gullah Creole is demonstrative. Gullah *ndoko* is Bobangi (Ki-Kongo), meaning "a bewitching that is said to cause illness." *Ndoko* is also a version of what in KiKongo is *ndoki*, meaning sorcerer or witch. Also the Gullah name *n'zambi* is KiKongo for God. Many scholars even suggest that the name Gullah is a shortened form of Angola. The Central African Mbundu ruler was called the Ngola, from which the Portuguese named the colony. There is obvious similarity between Ngola and Gullah (which went through various spellings).[7] But equally significant and generally overlooked is the African influence from the Windward Coast region.

Gola (sometimes spelled Goulah) is the name of a large group of Africans from the Liberian hinterland. Golas were heavily preyed upon by neighboring Mende, Vai, and Mandingas, and were imported into the Sea Island regions of South Carolina and Georgia at the height of rice and indigo cultivation. Africans from Upper Guinea (Gola, Vai, Mende, Kissi, Kpelle, and so on) shared a common socioreligious bond that provided a certain cultural uniformity through mandatory secret societies.[8] Names related to these societies appear in Gullah Creole.

Lorenzo Turner wrote extensively on African influences in Gullah Creole but identified no Gola language terms. As P. E. Hair notes, however, the majority of Turner's Gullah words in stories, songs, and prayers are Mende and Vai, and the Sierra Leone–Liberian influence is also prominent in Turner's list of personal names. Hair further believes that Turner missed these relationships because "no dictionary or informant" from this region "was available." Several Gullah personal names identified by Turner and listed with West African equivalents relate to Windward Coast secret societies. For example, Turner lists Gullah *beri* and *berimo* as Vai, stating that these words refer to "a branch of the society known as pora, a 'ceremonial rite.'" The Gullah name *pora* Turner determines is Mende, meaning "the great secret society of men." These relationships appear correct. *Beri* is one name used to refer to the secret society institution found in the Sierra Leone–Liberian region, and *Poro* is the more generally used name for the same male organization. Similarly, Turner's African equivalent for the Gullah name *zoe* is a Vai term, "the wearer of the mask in Sande Society." *Sande* was the most common name (Bundu was another) describing the mandatory female secret society of the Upper Guinea region. Among these groups, secret society leaders, who hid behind masks, were the spiritual leaders called *zoe*.[9]

The purpose of this essay is threefold: to offer some original interpretations of Gullah attitudes toward life and death, to suggest how an African cosmological and ontological heritage could impact the Gullah culture, and to show how the Gullahs forged African Christianity into a liberation theology.

Little attention was focused on Gullahs in antebellum days, and much of their early cultural history appeared lost. During the post-Civil War era and the early twentieth century, however, Gullahs became the focal point of a large body of research, writing, and fictional literature. Although much of this literature is filled with sociological bias, the studies of Gullah music, folklore, linguistic patterns, and lifestyle reveal a North American example of African retentions within black society.[10] Several more recent works on Gullah culture have been published.[11] Yet the cultural realm that provides some of the clearest examples of African American syncretism among Gullahs has received little attention. For indeed, the sphere of "things of the spirit" reveals how Gullahs synthesized the old and new into African American. Despite the paucity of published material on the Gullahs' spiritual beliefs,[12] most observers who studied or lived among the Gullahs attest to religion's importance in Gullah life. Gullah African Christianity was a vital folk religion, filled with peculiar patterns of beliefs linking them with their traditional past. The Gullahs' original interpretation of religion included viewing spirituality as a means of communal harmony, solidarity, and accountability.

Christian proselytization of Lowcountry slaves did not seriously begin until 1830. The primary motive of this instruction was to use Christianity as a conservative element in plantation life and slave conduct. Sporadic and intermittent exposure to Christianity occurred during the colonial and early national periods. But Methodist missionaries sent among the Gullahs in the 1830s provided their first organized exposure to Christianity.[13] Later, Baptist planters dominating the region took over this activity. Their efforts consisted chiefly of occasional preaching on plantations and building plantation praise (or pray's) houses,[14] mainly to keep slaves on numerous estates from mingling. Even today praise houses are found on some plantations. The desire to cloister the slaves actually encouraged them to fashion their own version of Christianity more suited to their circumstances. And this was done under the "watchcare" of black elders ostensibly responsible to white deacons. The fulcrum of the bondspeople's folk religion was spiritual and psychological autonomy. Baptist planters unwittingly contributed to its continued development. Hence, while energetic Methodist missionaries were somewhat influential among Gullahs up until 1844, most slaves united with the white Baptist church through the praise house. But the majority never saw the inside of Baptist churches until the Civil War.[15] Thus memories of African social and spiritual traditions were often nestled within Christianity but were still making a forceful impact on Gullah life, thought, and culture.

An African worldview, an African theory of being, and some African customs were significant in Gullah religious tendencies and communal existence. These features of Africanity sometimes superseded, sometimes coexisted with the Christian influence. Elements of syncretism were especially pronounced in Gullah attitudes toward life and death. The African traditional worldview was consonant with the idea that in a cohesive and integrated society each member had a place. This was true even though traditional religion, unlike Christianity, was not primarily an individual experience. Emphasis was on total well-being of the community of which an individual was only a part. For the Africans—and this was also true for the Gullahs—religion was a process of total immersion. Spiritual concerns could not be set apart from secular or communal ones. Religion assumed a meaning outside of a "holy" building, a "sacred" day of the week, or a set of dogmas and creeds to be accepted at face value. In the traditional worldview, spirituality affected one's whole system of being, embracing the consciousness, social interactions and attitudes, fears and dispositions of the community at large. As John Mbiti expressed it,

> in traditional society there are no irreligious people. To be human is to belong to the whole community, and to do so involves participating in the beliefs, ceremonies, rituals and festivals of that community. A person cannot detach himself from the religion of his group, to do so is to be severed from his roots, his foundation, his context of security, his kinships and the entire group of those who

make him aware of his existence. To be without one of these corporate elements of life is to be out of the whole picture. Therefore,
to be without religion amounts to a self-excommunication from the
entire life of society, and African peoples do not know how to exist
without religion.[16]

In traditional African society, codes of ethics also stemmed from religiosity. Moral defects were spiritual flaws as well as character blights.
Individuals were guided by the ethics characteristic of God, the ultimate upholder of moral order. Ancestral patriarchs, matriarchs, diviners,
the living dead, and other spirits were daily guardians of human behavior. Punishments and retribution for breaches in morals and ethics were
not the province of a future world judge but were dealt with on earth.[17]
Thus, although Africans were not adherents of the Christian concept of
a future tribunal, they believed that evil activities and failure to obey
social regulations warranted earthly censure and punishment according
to the degree of the depravity. This was perhaps a more efficient method
of controlling deviant social behavior, since immediate repercussion and
ostracization from society were more realistic threats than fear of a remote world beyond.

Inherent in an African worldview with religion foremost as a unifying force was an anthropocentric philosophy. John Mbiti, an adherent of
this point of view, divides the categories of African ontology into five
parts: God as the ultimate explanation of the genesis and sustenance of
all things; spirits, made up of superhuman beings and the spirits of
those who died long ago; humans, including those who are alive and
those about to be born; animals and plants, or the remainder of biological life; and phenomena and objects without biological life.[18]

While God is the apex in this African theory of being, humankind is
the center, as everything is viewed in relation to life. This anthropocentric approach also expresses affirmation of life as ontological categories
of human existence and environments integrate, from the highest to the
lowest form of being. Human spiritual activity encourages justification,
preservation, protection, and enrichment of life. God is a supreme all-
knower who explains creation and provides a model of virtue. Lesser
spirits are intermediaries, representing an assurance of human perpetuity beyond the grave. While human actions represent confirmation that
earthly life is the nucleus of existence, the recognition of ancestors and
tributes to lesser gods represent the Africans' endeavor to have an impact on the natural and supernatural processes believed to govern life
and death.

Relationships between the pivotal position of humanity and spirituality in African ontology are demonstrated in general concepts regarding life on individual as well as on communal levels. Religion accompanied one from conception to physical death and in the afterlife. Significant events in individual life activities were enveloped in beliefs and rites with deep spiritual connotations: each person's introduction into various states of life was accompanied by a sacred observance. Marriage rites were festive, socioreligious commemorations of human life and community longevity. African women's participation in numerous religious ceremonies was to ensure bringing healthy children into the world. The fate of the unborn was in the care of spiritual beings and forces. When only a few days old an infant was honored with a naming ceremony and was blessed by the priest who invoked God to direct the child through a life of good habits and industry and toward a meaningful occupation. At childhood's end a sacred rite expressed appreciation for care received from God and the spirits. Upon entrance into puberty, the send-off into the bush for initiation was a sacred and spiritually charged event. After initial bush training, a religious commemoration welcomed the neophyte into the community as a citizen. Death called for a sacred send-off of major proportions. This passage into the unseen (but not remote) spiritual world was the climax of one existence, which continued through contact with the living, and the beginning of another.[19]

African religion and spiritualism thus emphasized a celebration of human life. To life fully and robustly, to be esteemed by the community, was basic to African thinking and was incorporated into Africans' particular ontology. Sacred observances were often a fusion of the festive and the solemn. But their meanings to community living and social responsibility reveal the seriousness of the services. That which threatened the will to live, this "vital force," was dangerous to the individual and hence to society. Inhabitants of the spiritual world were the guardians of life, appealed to in periods of crisis, such as illness, environmental disaster, and the malice of others, or under normal stress of adult life. Often spiritual forces were placated as a precautionary measure for the preservation of the person, the clan, the village, and the ethnic group.

An underlying and dynamic force operative in Gullah folk religion and spirituality was rooted in an African worldview. Some pristine elements of traditional religious thought that remained with Sea Island slaves, although not inconsistent with Christianity, largely account for the vigor of their African American culture.

During the Civil War some observers were appalled at what they interpreted as resignation among Sea Island slaves. A northern teacher, Arthur Sumner, wrote from St. Helena Island in 1863: "I am astonished that they should be fit to live after such generations of mere animal life. A higher race would have lost all moral sense."[20] Even one of the Gullahs' staunchest Yankee advocates, Elizabeth Botume, remarked that "the patience of the freed people in sickness was so general and remarkable, it seemed like apathy."[21] This attitude might be attributable to the Gullahs' affiliation with the fatalistic features of Christianity. Yet it also came from the sense of protection that spiritual association offered, since religious and community membership together forged social ties, strengthening the Gullahs' resolve and their belief in collective survival. Thomas Wentworth Higginson, Civil War commander of the First South Carolina Volunteers composed mainly of Gullah men, was "surprised" to find the black soldiers so little demoralized. He attributed it to religion:

> I learned to think that we abolitionists had underrated the suffering produced by slavery among the negroes, but had overrated the demoralization. Yet . . . it must be admitted that this temperament, born of sorrow and oppression, is far more marked in the slave than in the native African.[22]

Higginson recognized the significance of slave religion. But the personality and "religious temperament" of Gullahs owed much to a non-Christian tradition and hence was not as much "born of sorrow and oppression" or as foreign to the "native African" as he imagined. If traditional African religion celebrates and affirms human life, with God as the apex of being and humankind as the center or pivotal point, it could also function thusly for Gullah slaves in the New World. On the conscious level, perhaps, the pillar of their faith rested on an association with Christ. But this faith may primarily have helped shape their Old World thinking into an organized, plausible New World perception. Paul Radin insightfully wrote that the Christian God provided the African American slaves with a "fixed point," and rather than being converted to God they converted God to themselves.[23] The Gullahs converted Christianity to their African worldview, using the new religion to justify combating objective forces, to collectively perpetuate community-culture, and as an ideology of freedom. Thus it was less a case of Christianity instilling a sense of resignation because of beliefs in future rewards than of an African philosophical tradition being asserted in the slave quarters.

Life on earth was not negated by Gullahs, as is illustrated by their desire for freedom and their capacity to create. Freedom was a continuous topic of conversation among them.[24] It was often expressed thematically in Gullah spirituals. While spirituals appear to be a portent of heavenly futurity in a Christian sense, the ambiguity in many Gullah "prayer songs" implies otherwise. Double meanings and surrogates abound in them. For example:

Jesus made de blind see,
Jesus made de cripple walk,
Jesus made de deaf to hear.
Walk in, kind Jesus!
No man can hinder me.[25]

When northern teacher Laura Towne heard this impressive spiritual she believed that the refrain "No man can hinder me" meant that "nothing could prevent access to Jesus."[26] Yet Charles Nordhoff, a journalist sent to Port Royal in 1863 to write about the freedpeople, heard the song and attributed to it "an aspiration for liberty."[27] Nordhoff was probably closer to the mark. Some observers reported that the phrase was sung as "No man can hinder *we*." Certainly both interpretations have an element of truth—a combination of mystical belief in the miraculous powers of the Christian God, a deep sense of pride that was a heritage of the Gullahs' African past, and feelings of nationalism developed over generations as similar social and cultural traditions merged under slavery, creating one people with common interests, ambitions, and beliefs.

The Gullahs' Marseillaise was the spiritual "New Jerusalem":

De talles' tree in Paradise
De Christian calls de Tree ob Life,
An' I hope dat trumpet blow me home
To my New Jerusalem.

Blow Gabriel! Trumpet, blow louder, louder!
An I hope dat trumpet blow me home
To my New Jerusalem!

Paul and Silas jail-bound
Sing God's praise both night and day,
An' I hope dat trumpet blow me home
To my New Jerusalem![28]

This song was triumphant not tragic and was a favorite Gullah "shout" song. Thus it was not sung with a "heby heart" or a "troubled speerit." When a freedman named Maurice, who had been blinded by his master in a fit of rage, sang "New Jerusalem" at the praise house his mind turned toward heaven and gaining his sight in a future world. But when the freedpeople sang "New Jerusalem" at the Emancipation Jubilee on

New Year's Day in 1866 their earthly future and enthusiasm for long-awaited freedom filled their thoughts and expectations. The tree of life was apparently the tree of liberty, as paradise was a land free of bondage. The meaning behind the spiritual was not lost on Elizabeth Botume. She wrote:

> The streets of the city were filled with happy freed people. According to their spiritual, they had "fought for liberty," and this was their "New Jerusalem," of which they so often sang. Even the poorest, and those most scantily clothed, looked as if they already "walked that golden street," and felt "that starry crown" upon their uncovered hands. It was indeed a day of great rejoicing, and one long to be remembered. These people were living their "New Jerusalem."[29]

God, personified as Jesus, and an African worldview offered the Gullahs an explanation for life and provided a model of virtue. Gullah religion contained a fervent zest for life, and the cornerstone of their faith was a confidence that freedom on earth would come to them or their progeny.

Gullahs, as realists, did not accept all religious teachings imposed upon them and were not beguiled by stealthy attempts to "make them better slaves." From their African heritage Gullahs possessed a proclivity for rising above their near-tragic situation for the sake of community. That was more important than blindly striking out and possibly committing racial suicide. Gullahs also considered the issue of insurrection in practical terms. They believed that successful armed rebellion was possible but impractical. Still, the Gullahs were not without great courage. Men, women, and children risked their lives for freedom when the Union Army occupied part of South Carolina. Gullah soldiers also served in that army under the most unfair circumstances. Furthermore, Gullahs did not merely survive and persevere. They taxed creative talents to a maximum by developing a community, perhaps seeing that as one way to maintain their dignity. This development of a community may be the truest example of their valor and vitality. Gullahs maintained a passionate love of humanity and confronted the masters without motives of revenge. Yet they also displayed a keen sense of revolutionary rationalism through a calm realization that masters and slaves were natural enemies. In observing the Gullahs' capacity to endure pain and their tendency to transcend individual situations, the surgeon in Higginson's black regiment referred to them as "natural transcendentalists."[30] While that is true to some extent, perhaps a more accurate characterization is that these African American slaves were natural humanists who believed in the integration of the human personality on a collective level, placing cultural considerations first, sometimes at the expense of practical, personal ones.

While the African tradition from which the Gullahs were descended emphasized the preservation, protection, and enrichment of life, the phenomenon unifying this anthropocentric philosophy was religion. Hence it is not difficult to understand why Gullah life was expressed from an essentially religious perspective. Christianity and traditional African religion combined, providing the Gullahs with an ideology of freedom and a lofty, mystical explanation of their existence as a people. The optimism present in traditional West African religion and spiritualism provided a necessary ingredient in the creation of Gullah culture. Slavery did not erode the African sense of pride, the love of home and family. Yet how long could these attributes alone sustain cultural life among slaves, no matter how their spirits struggled against degradation? Christianity offered cohesion of a kind needed to develop a homogeneous people. The heritage from Upper Guinea and from the BaKongo tradition also inspired social cohesion.

The Upper Guinea region of Africa (Senegal, Gambia, Sierra Leone, and Liberia) contained a multiplicity of ethnic groups, mixed kinship systems, and languages. Non-Moslem societies there did not possess high degrees of political centralization. Nor were community groups usually as large or territorial holdings as extensive as those in the Niger Delta or Western Sudan. Yet early explorers, travelers, and traders were struck by what H. Baumann called distinctive culture circles on the West African coast. Upper Guinea exemplifies Baumann's conceptual framework. There peoples historically had common cultural features, the most significant being secret societies that regulated the social, political, and, to some extent, economic life of the communities. The Poro (or Beri) society for men and the Sande (or Bundu) society for women were almost universal and, where they existed, always mandatory. The area of the "Poro Cluster" on the inland African coast included the Lokko, Temne, Kono, Mende, Bullom, Krim, and Limba in Sierra Leone. On the Malguetta Coast (today Liberia), Poro and Sande groups included the Gola, Vai, De, Kpelle, Kissi, Gbande, Belle, Loma, Mano, Gio Ge, Bassa, and Kru. Sixteenth-century Portuguese traders observed similarities among various groups belonging to these associations. Affinity was so strong that traders viewed these people as one society. They dressed alike, had the same system of justice, and understood each other. Although they lacked political centralization, these groups possessed social homogeneity through their common secret societies. Ostensibly these societies were a way of training youth. They introduced all members into adulthood after isolating them from the community for years in a special "sacred grove."[31]

While Poro and Sande represented transformation from childhood to citizenship, membership was much more than a puberty rite of passage. Sylvia Boone writes that "Sande is a socially consolidating force," and "a religion with the power to make life good and to inspire the highest aspirations among its members." According to Kenneth Little, Poro's function as a puberty rite was secondary to the main one, "to impress upon the new member the sacredness of his duty to the Poro" and hence to the community. To this end the youths underwent a *travel*, a series of terrifying dreams in which they were symbolically eaten by the Poro or Sande spirit—the devil—and were then reborn by the same spiritual force. Once rebirth in the bush occurred, each individual was bound to the society and vowed to uphold secrecy of the initiation and to abide by Poro-Sande authority. Allegiance was no longer to parents and kin but to the secret society as foremost arbiter. Thus Poro-Sande instituted a regulatory process with sociopolitical duties implemented to fulfill collective and societal goals. The Poro council was supreme. It stopped village quarrels, tried and condemned social criminals, intensified holiday spirit, and gave permission to declare war. Although the chief was the nominal ruler, real power rested with the council, which was composed of senior members of both Poro and Sande societies and could even depose a chief. Thus the secret society functioned as the primary psychological and physical coercive agent for the common good. The institution's power, however, was derived from its affinity with the spirits and from other religious manifestations. Poro-Sande was law. Poro-Sande was order. And Poro-Sande came from God.[32]

No aspect of West African life was completely secular, and Poro-Sande sociopolitical power symbolized relationships between the sacred and the temporal. The foundation of Poro-Sande prerogative was mystical in nature, since the institution was considered to be made by God. Thus Poro-Sande spiritual significance was pervasive. Spirits dwelled in the sacred grove; among them were ancestral spirits, bush and water spirits, spirits of associations, and Poro-Sande spirits, all with particular functions. Ancestral spirits, for example, explained life after death, were concerned with family and the larger group's well-being, and were protectors. Poro-Sande spirits, of whom the "bush devil" was the most important, were worldly representations of supernatural forces, personifying the will of God and mysteries of life. While other spirits in the pantheon were of the unseen world, Poro-Sande spirits represented the supernatural sphere and earthly manifestations of supernatural power. All spirits remained hidden behind masks, and the chief spiritual leader's identity was an especially guarded secret. The leader's authority was intergroup, and his or her standing was recognized even in distant chiefdoms where a language barrier existed. Bush initiates were often taken from several surrounding villages, adding to the strength of communal regulation and superseding immediate kinship ties.[33]

Hence one aim was spirit control, mainly through ceremony, ritual, meditation, medicine, and exclusive contact. Essentially, as Harley writes, Poro-Sande was a means of reducing the pervading spirit world to an organization in which humans might become spirits and take on "godhead." This transformation allowed secret society religious leaders to "contact the spirit world and interpret it to the people." The initiates' capacity to withstand the sacred bush experience and uphold its secrets extended functionally into the secular realm. Society was organized around allegiance to and belief in the power of Poro and Sande. Reverence for the symbolically sacred led to obedience, accountability, and respect for what was generally its identical secular arm, the Poro council.[34]

Nearly all Africans brought to North America came from groups that practiced some type of initiation process. While none contained the distinctive structurally inclusive elements of Poro and Sande, one can still argue for the tenacity of the practice. The bush experience was a shared memory instilling loyalty, bonds of attachments, and unity that neither Christianity nor Islam could destroy, even today.

In the antebellum period Methodist missionaries found some Gullahs "professing" Christianity and nearly all of them organized into "black societies." "The society exerts its influence against us which is remarkably strong," wrote one missionary in 1844. "This 'society' is altogether in the hands of the colored people who are actively engaged against us."[35] Thus Gullahs struggled to exercise spiritual and communal independence and missionaries attempted to fragment black control. Another Methodist wrote to the *Southern Christian Advocate* in 1846, bemoaning the "deplorable exhibition of pseudo religion" among the slaves on large plantations in coastal South Carolina:

The superstitious notions prevalent here and there . . . probably . . . reflects . . . more ancient superstitions, handed down by tradition and propagated by so called *leaders*, who prior to the preaching of the gospel by . . . the missionaries . . . wielded a fearful amount of spiritual influence among their followers, and the negro communities of the plantations generally. And it is with remarkable tenacity these superstitious actions still maintain their hold in spite of a better teaching. Instead of giving up their visionary religionism, embracing the simple truth . . . our missionaries find them endeavoring to incorporate their superstitious rites with a purer system of instruction, producing thereby a hybrid, crude, and undefinable medley of truth and falsehood.[36]

Unlike Methodist missionaries, Baptist planters did not try to destroy the black societies but organized them into plantation churches. "Subsidiary to the church," wrote Civil War observer Edward Channing Gannett, "are local 'societies,' to which 'raw souls' are admitted after they have proved the reality of their 'strivings.'" Gullah slaves rarely saw the inside of a white church prior to their taking them over when owners fled during the Civil War. Gullahs embraced Christianity through praise house membership and maintained complete loyalty to these "invisible institutions" in both a spiritual and communal sense. Elders and members scrutinized personal behavior, and the praise house functioned as a religious court. Plantation membership and praise house membership were synonymous and were termed "catching sense." According to Patricia Guthrie, who did field work in the Sea Islands, "entrance into the religious and politico-jural domains parallels the time when plantation membership becomes fully realized," and in antebellum days joining the praise house formally expressed initiation into the plantation domain of the bondspeople. An individual was no longer only a household member but was also a citizen of the slave quarters through church membership. Personhood was attained through praise house membership, and all members answered to its religious court whenever internal discord arose. Praise house law was "just law," and membership demanded that disputes be settled within its jurisdiction. The "unjust law" was white law or forces outside praise house authority. Harmony, morality, justice, leadership, and dignity were upheld by the praise house. Thus plantation societies were the nucleus of the Gullah socioreligious community, perhaps just as the West African secret society was the communal and spiritual center of village life.[37]

Gullah methods of admission to church membership further demonstrate the relationship to secret society initiation. The time between an expressed desire to become a Christian and acceptance by the elders of one's religious experience was called "seekin'." It was a time when "raw souls" began their "striving." The phrase "to seek Jesus" was introduced to bondspeople by Methodists, but the seekin' process represents a Gullah interpretation. Gannett noted: "This 'striving' is a long process of self-examination and solitary prayer 'in the bush,' and so unremitting must be the devotion during this stage that even attendance at school is thought to interfere with the action of the spirit." Seekin' began with a personal decision not devoid of community pressure, followed by the choosing of a lifelong "spiritual parent," usually a female elder pointed out in a dream. The spiritual parent taught the seeker correct conduct and "how to pray." A seeker shunned social contact and went into "de wilderness" for prayer, solitude, and meditation. Night vigils (usually unapproved by plantation authority) were common, occurring in graveyards, cotton or cornfields, and marshes. Seekers often prayed to nature objects.[38]

The most important indication of spiritual transformation was the vision or *travel* as interpreted by the spiritual parent. "This word *travel*," wrote one Methodist missionary, "is one of the most significant in their language, and comprehends all those exercises, spiritual, visionary and imaginative which make up an 'experience.'" While the *travel* might differ in some things, "in others they all agree. Each seeker meets with warnings—awful sights or sounds," and has a vision of a white man who warns and talks with the seeker and eventually leads the seeker to the river. The spiritual parent decides when "de trabbel" is complete and when the seeker is ready to be presented to the praise house. The praise house elder and his committee further examine the candidate, asking spiritual and communal questions and finally approving baptism. Following baptism and church fellowship, new members engaged in a "ring shout." This counterclockwise dance involves people moving around in a circle, rhythmically shuffling their feet and shaking their hands while bystanders outside the ring clap, sing, and gesticulate. This religious circle dance is a spiritual outpouring which symbolizes community integration.[39]

The mystical nature of the Gullahs' conversion and its importance in community accountability has African antecedents. Sterling Stuckey argues that "movement in a ring during ceremonies honoring ancestors" was an integral part of life in central areas of Africa. According to Stuckey, the circle ritual of BaKongo peoples was "so powerful and elaborate" that it "gave form and meaning to black religion and art." Community initiation through spiritual metamorphosis, symbolic death, and rebirth in "de wilderness" or "the bush" was germane to both societies. The role of slave women in seekin' correlates to the influence of female altar parents in African secret society. The head of the Sande society also wore white. Additionally, once African neophytes returned to the village they were given a water burial and new clothing, just as Gullah Christian seekers were baptized in old clothes and dressed in their "best" afterward for their communion and fellowship service.[40] Both processes, of a journey into the world of the ancestors (i.e., death) and subsequent return, represented an end of individualistic tendencies inimical to group interests. Both initiates were in the power of a spiritual leader who would not condone or overlook frailties. In each case the initiate or seeker entered into a state of wildness, helplessness, and irresponsibility, having no social sense. Guided by the altar parent, a physical, mental, and moral test was undergone to prove the individual's worth. In Africa, if transformation was not evident, the initiate did not return. In both societies, initiation represented efforts either to transcend what could not be controlled or to control elements of human variance and division.

Like Islam and Christianity, traditional African religions adhered to monotheism, though for non-Moslem Africans the Supreme Being or Sky God had many names. Akan-Ashanti referred to God as Onyame. Bantu peoples called God Nzambi. Among the Mende God was Ngewo and to the Gola, Daya. The Supreme Deity was generally considered omniscient and omnipotent, the creator of all life forms. God represented the highest values—kindness, justice, sincerity, and mercy. Thus in African perceptions God was no fomentor of mischief or ill will. Unlike Jehovah, the African God was not to be feared, and no prayers needed to be offered. Evil came from other sources, not the Creator. Although God was not accorded worship through libation and was invisible, allegiance was rendered, and the deity's ultimate power over humans was recognized. "Nzambi possesses us and eats us" or "He is gone, Nzambi has willed it," were central themes in some BaKongo proverbs and songs.[41]

Belief in afterlife was integral to traditional African religion. But Africans did not view the future world with fear nor as a place of dispensations for rewards and punishments in a Christian sense. In this land of the dead, where life continued, there was no sickness, disease, poverty, or hunger. But underworld inhabitants retained the positions of their earthly hierarchy. Death was a journey into the spirit world, not a break with life or earthly beings. The idea of the perpetuity of life through time, space, and circumstance was common to African religious culture, and the complexity of this belief system is typified by BaKongo cosmology and concepts of the four moments of the sun. Using the sun through its course around the earth, the BaKongo pointed out the four stages that make up one's life cycle: rising (birth, beginning, or regrowth), ascendancy (maturity and responsibility), setting (death and transformation), and midnight (existence in the other world and eventual rebirth). Life was a continuum, and the sign of the four moments of the sun symbolized "spiritual continuity and renaissance" through a spiral journey. The crossing of the four solar moments, though similar to the Greek cross and the Christian cross, was not introduced to the

BaKongo by early Christianity. Long before the arrival of Europeans this geometric statement, the Kongo cruciform, adorned funerary objects and in other ways reflected BaKongo aesthetic perceptions of their relationship to the world. Robert Farris Thompson (see his essay in this volume) and Joseph Cornet brilliantly demonstrated this fact through BaKongo visual traditions in Africa and the New World.[42]

Belief that one's spirit consciously exists after death was also common. "New" Africans, once they learned English, found reinforcement, in Christian principles taught by white ministers, of the belief that everyone possessed a soul apart from one's human form, with its own destiny. In certain ways African concepts were more complicated.

BaKongo peoples probably had the most elaborate and complex system of afterlife beliefs, and these beliefs were central to their religious traditions. Humans were double beings, consisting of an outer and inner entity. Each entity in turn had two parts. One part of the outer being, the shell, was visible. After death it was buried and rotted. The second part was invisible and could be "eaten" by bad medicine, *kindoki*, but helped by good medicine, *minkisi*. The inner being's two parts were both necessary for continued existence. One signified personal life and, although expressions differed among groups, there was continuity in meaning. Some BaKongo peoples expressed the personal entity as *kivuumunu* (breathing). *Kivuumuni* was the agent of life and breath, hidden and protected from bad medicine. Death could not destroy it. The second part of the inner being, the *belly*, was different. It took food, which had to be provided for the entity to continue living. Both contributed to continued existence, one through breath and the other through nourishments. In the world of *mpemba* (land of all things white), the dead, through powers commensurate with the goodness of their previous earthly life, are expunged of earthly acquired impurities and reenter the world as reincarnated spirits (in grandchildren) or as immortal *simbi* spirits. Notions of the afterlife practiced by BaKongo peoples and their neighbors and reinforced by similar beliefs among other Africans parallel some Gullah "Christian" ritualistic customs of death and burial.[43]

Gullahs attached a tremendous significance to death, but there was little evidence of apprehension at the prospect of dying. Slaves lived in the presence of death constantly and seemed to feel that the phenomenon was as much a part of living as their continuous labor. That they often reflected on the subject is evident in their spirituals. Yet these songs do not indicate that Gullahs thought of death with fear, foreboding, or morbidity. Perhaps it was partly this stoicism in the face of earthly demise that some observers viewed as resignation or the effects of demoralization. All African ethnic groups believed in life beyond physical death. Possibly Gullahs retained the West African bush-initiation experience in their attitude toward death. This idea of a symbolic journey to the world of the dead and a triumphant return might explain the Gullahs' ability to transcend feelings of dread about death and to disavow its ultimate power over them. But perhaps an equally strong influence was the BaKongo, since these societies had the most elaborate afterlife beliefs. In the four moments of the sun, earthly death, the setting of the sun, is only the third moment. Thus death was not the end of life nor the cemetery a final resting place; it was a door (*mwelo*) between two worlds. The fourth moment is midnight on earth, when the sun is shining on the world of the dead. There rebirth takes place.[44]

No matter what the unconscious motivation, however, what many considered to be a weakness among these bondspeople was actually a source of strength. They overcame a fear of death in light of the reality of its dominant presence among them and through their realization that they, more than most other people, were often powerless to alter its course. Thus while Gullahs did not shrink from death they were aware of the degree to which their lives were exploited and of the oppression that often caused an untimely end to life.

The depth of their understanding was sometimes grippingly demonstrated. Teacher William Allen was struck by how much the children sang of pain and death. Little "Margaret" came to the well to draw her pail of water. Putting it on her head, she walked off singing, "Shall I die—shall I die." She was followed by Tom and Abraham, "galloping along on bamboo horses and shouting, 'my body rock 'long feber.'"[45]

Charlotte Forten was much affected by one of the hymns which she heard Gullah children singing:

I wonder where my mudder gone;
  Sing, O graveyard!
Graveyard ought to know me;
  Ring, Jerusalem!
Grass grow in de graveyard;
  Sing, O graveyard!
Graveyard ought to know me;
  Ring, Jerusalem!

"It is impossible," Forten wrote, "to give any idea of the deep pathos of the refrain, 'Sing, O graveyard.'"[46] The pathos is there certainly, but the sense of hope, so characteristic of the Gullahs, is also present in the words "Grass grow in de graveyard." This statement might indicate that in the BaKongo tradition, although there was death, there was also life and rebirth. The refrain "Graveyard ought to know me" might refer to the slaves' previous journey to the world of the dead as "seekers." The phrase might also recognize the omnipresence of death among the slaves.

Another spiritual expressed a sense of optimism and a superior attitude toward death:

O Massa Death,
He's a very little man,
He goes from door to door;
He kills some souls,
And he woundeth some.
Good Lord remember me;
Good Lord remember me;
Remember me as the years roll round,
Good Lord, remember me.[47]

In Christian belief the finality of death was often negated. One of the most appealing aspects of Christianity for Gullahs was the expectation of a better life after death. This afterlife was not visualized in the African sense, which held that an individual's status would not differ from one's mortal position. Instead, Gullahs strongly adopted the Christian concept of heaven, where all "true believers" would sit on "Christ's right side." For obvious reasons this was the tenet of Christianity they cherished most. While their African worldview encouraged Gullahs to take a positive attitude toward life, through the Christian influence they expected a better life as payment for their suffering. As one person expressed it:

De harder me cross to bear down here de better I go be prepare to tek me place in dat Happy Land where all is 'joicin, an' when I git dere, I want de Lord to say, "Ophelia . . . come an' rest wid de elect ob de Lord!"[48]

There was little in the prayers or songs of the Gullahs to indicate they feared the tribunal expected to reward the "faithful" and damn the "sinners." Thus they disregarded that portion of their religious instruction that strenuously emphasized a judgment day when "every theft or falsehood" would be brought to light and held against them. What was more important to the Gullahs was a change in their conditions. A Baptist slave master, Daniel Pope, asked Marcus, the praise house elder, whether the Gullahs really believed Christ wanted "black nigger in heben." But so were the slaves convinced that the "Kingdom of God" would have almost no white subjects. Gullah Christianity was one of recompense. Slaves accepted the Christian doctrine of eternal life but modified it so that heaven was an exclusive place, primarily available to sufferers of the right hue, as expressed by a former slave:

It is impossible to reconcile the mind of the native slave to the idea of living in a state of perfect equality, and boundless affection with white people. Heaven will be no heaven to him, if he is not to be avenged of his enemies. I know, from experience, that these are fundamental rules of his religious creed; because I learned them in the religious meetings of the slaves themselves. A favorite and kind master or mistress may now and then be admitted into heaven, but this rather as a matter of favor, due to the intercession of some slave, than as a matter of strict justice to the whites, who will, by no means be of an equal rank with those who shall be raised from the depths of misery, in this world.

The idea of a revolution in the conditions of the whites and the blacks, is the cornerstone of the religion of the latter; and indeed it seems to me, at least, to be quite natural, if not in strict accordance with the precepts of the Bible.[49]

Although the Gullahs did not fear death, they recognized its power, and the passing of one of their number had a profound effect on the community. Methodist missionaries observed this effect and often tried to use the drama of death among the Gullahs to "bind them to the cross."[50] But while the Gullahs' perception of life after death was essentially of Christian origin, many practices associated with the dying and the dead were derived from African antecedents.

When death was expected the plantation community members felt compelled to enter into the spirit of the event and vicariously involve themselves in the death throes of the individual. Otherwise, when their time came they might have to face the ordeal alone, or the deceased, dissatisfied with the sendoff, might return and bring evil. The dying person was surrounded by the community, which offered comfort and support. "We got tuh help him cross de ribber," the Gullahs would say. Friends of the dying were expected to bring gifts even though the sufferer could not use them. Such offerings were usually edibles "tuh taste de mout'," but never flowers. Singing, praying, and pious conversation filled the cabin nightly. It was not a solemn time, unless sad or obscure circumstances caused the death, but rather was somewhat cheerful, and the subject of death itself was not neglected. Everyone was expected to hold forth as part of the ritual of coaching the dying person to report a heavenly visit or some other evidence of "dying good." When the sufferer drew the last breath, everyone present gave a loud shriek as notification that another soul "done crossed ober." Many northern teachers were repulsed at the Gullah "death-watch":

This practice of sitting up all night with the dying, H. W. [Harriet Ware] justly enough condemns as "heathenish." The houses cannot hold them all, of course, and they sit round out-of-doors in the street, the younger ones often falling asleep on the ground, and then they "hab fever."

But of course it was useless to expostulate with them; to their minds the omission of the watch would be a mark of great disrespect.[51]

Like their African forebears, Gullahs believed in the presence of evil almost as much as they believed in the forces of good, and their attempts to please both God and the "powers of darkness" explain much about their customs regarding death. Although Gullahs professed to believe that God "called" his servants to heaven, they still viewed death as an instrument of the powers of darkness. Thus night vigils, singing, praying, and preaching around the bedside of the dying were supposed to strengthen the dying as they "passed death's door." The loud shriek as the last breath was drawn was a formal announcement of the death, but it also "scares off the spirits of hell who are always lurking around to get possession of another soul."[52]

Gullahs believed that one could not always know whether demise had come through natural causes because "God called," which was a "good" death, or by witchcraft, a "bad" death. That was also true of many African peoples. Among those of the Windward Coast, death was said to come to people because God or the ancestors wanted them or because of witchcraft. Among the BaKongo the concept of a bad or a good death was also important. A bad death would be indicated if the sick person quarreled with those present, had severe pains, or suffered a prolonged death agony. If a person could not speak properly when dying or turned his or her head toward the wall, a bad death was also suspected. A bad death meant a person was "shot with nkisi-guns" and was considered an *ndoki*, or witch. A good death was a calm ordeal, peaceful and easy, with the person lying on his or her back.[53]

Though Gullah attitudes about good and bad deaths were infused with African customs, the death watch was viewed in a Christian context. An individual was said to "die good" by praying out loud, reporting a heavenly vision, or giving some evidence that peace had been made with God on the deathbed. A pious life counted for little if such things were not observed. Nor did an evil life mean damnation if the dying could satisfy spectators with an appropriate heavenly vision. What was probably more important to Gullahs was that the deceased be at peace with the world, assuring the community that he or she was not a witch or bewitched and would not return to "haant" the living.[54]

Spirits destined for hell did not actually go there until judgment day, according to Gullahs. Instead these "on-easy speerits," having no resting place, roamed the earth and tormented the living. Some Gullahs believed that good spirits went straight to heaven, but most seemed to think that even these spirits remained on earth, close to the place of their burial. Unlike those who "died bad," good spirits would normally not harm the living; nor would they roam. They appeared only in dreams, giving messages and warnings to the living. Thus Gullahs had a real concern for coaxing an individual to "die good" and a real superstition about those who "died bad." The slaves devised various mechanisms of defense against the latter spirits.[55]

Much of the Gullah attitude toward death and belief in spirits was inherited from the African respect for and honor of the living dead and from the African belief in the power of sorcery. Consider a description of death among the Mende:

> When a dying man is panting for breath, the Mende say "Taa ha ha yiyei le ma" ("he is climbing the hill of death"). As soon as death is announced, the members of the family all begin to wail. The body of the deceased is then washed, and messages are sent to call the absent members of the family. . . . Members of the family will bring money, cloth, wine and rice as their contribution towards the funeral expenses. . . . On the fourth day for a man (the third day for a woman), the "crossing-the-river" ceremony takes place. . . . If these ceremonies are not properly performed, the evil will fall on those responsible.

Similarly, for Temne people the underlying idea of funeral rites is to appease the spirits of the dead so they will not trouble the living. Mende also believe that separation of good and bad people takes place after crossing the river. While there is no clear-cut idea as to who bad people are, they are chiefly thought of as those who dealt in bad medicine or witchcraft. These evil ones in their spirit form will vent their feelings by sending disease and will haunt the living and take possession of them. Among the BaKongo the curse of the dying is much dreaded, especially that of a relative, for the deceased will soon enter the spirit world. A dying person may admonish those around to take care of his or her affairs. "If you do not, I shall fetch you, and you will not become old here on earth." The dying one may also request the living to "wrap me well in the cloth that I leave" and may insist that the living hold many lamentations after the death and care for the deceased's family. If not properly buried the deceased might bring *kindoki* (evil).[56]

A curious example of the application of both African and Christian practices among the slaves is provided by a former South Carolina bondsman. A good-looking and popular slave girl named Mary died after a lingering illness of a few months. The slaves on the surrounding plantations were sure that Mary had been conjured (poisoned) by a rival in a love triangle. The plantation proprietor, a Methodist minister, had Mary treated by his brother, a practicing physician. While the white doctor was attending Mary the slaves appealed to their own doctor, a plantation slave, who also treated the young woman. But Mary died and, according to the author, her funeral—which, in line with tradition, took place at night—"was the largest ever held in all that region of the country":

The coffin, a rough home-made affair, was placed upon a cart, which was drawn by an old Gray, and the multitudes formed in a line in the rear, marching two deep. The procession was something like a quarter of a mile long. Perhaps every fifteenth person down the line carried an uplifted torch. As the procession moved slowly toward "the lonesome graveyard" down by the side of the swamp, they sung the well-known hymn of Dr. Isaac Watts:
When I can read my title clear
To mansions in the skies,
I bid farewell to every fear
And wipe my weeping eyes.
Mary's baby was taken to the graveyard by its grandmother, and before the corpse was deposited in the earth, the baby was passed from one person to another across the coffin. The slaves believed that if this was not done it would be impossible to raise the infant. The mother's spirit would come back for her baby and take it to herself.
After this performance the corpse was lowered into the grave and covered, each person throwing a handful of dirt into the grave as a last farewell act of kindness to the dead, and while this was being done the leader announced that other hymn by Dr. Watts:
Hark! from the tomb a doleful sound
My ears, attend the cry;
Ye living men, come view the ground
Where you must shortly lie.
. . . A prayer was offered. . . . This concluded the services at the grave. No burial or commital service was read. At a subsequent time, when all the relatives and friends could be brought together a big funeral sermon was preached by some of the antebellum negro preachers.

The presence of a plantation slave "doctor" is reminiscent of the BaKongo priest, *nganga,* who employed life-affirming *nkisi* to heal and ward off *kindoki.* The charm did not work for the plantation slave, and the large funeral turnout may represent the people's desire to protect themselves from whatever evil had caused Mary's death as well as to express their respect. Passing the woman's baby back and forth over her coffin was a well-known Gullah graveside custom. "Dead moder will hant de baby," Gullahs explained, and "worry him in his sleep." A similar custom among the BaKongo women was crossing back and forth over the graveside of a woman who died in childbirth, hoping that such a fate would not befall them. Singing at the grave was also part of the BaKongo sendoff. The funeral, a lavish affair, would take place when all members of the clan could gather and enough food could be collected.[57]

Thus besides the Christian version of immortality there were elements of African tradition that accounted for the Gullahs' attitude toward death, as indeed it did their philosophy of life. Not only was the existence of deceased spirits central to African ontology, but these beings also constituted the largest group of religious intermediaries. Hence Africans viewed death as perhaps the most important rite of passage rather than as the end of life. Death was a momentous transition, requiring demonstrative evidence that the physical presence of the deceased would be missed. But it was just as necessary to celebrate this passage into the spirit world in a manner indicating a continued existence. Africans believed that the spirit that survived the body was conscious of all earthly events and had the power to exercise influence over the destiny of the living. Consequently, the death of a clan member was observed with greatest respect, and the death commemoration was expressed collectively.[58]

Ancestors retained their normal human passions and appetites, which had to be gratified in death as in life. Ancestors felt hunger and thirst. They became angry or happy depending on the behavior of their living "children." The living dead were vindictive if neglected but propitious if shown respect. Just as filial loyalty prevents one from allowing a parent to go hungry, "so must food be offered to the ancestors." Among the BaKongo, food was put out immediately after the burial and palm wine poured over the grave. Survivors believed the deceased would eat the food and bless those who placed it there.[59]

Among the Gullahs, even for one who "died good" the spirit could not rest if something had been left behind which it desired. Observers noted that Gullahs and other African Americans placed articles on new graves. These objects were usually personal belongings, broken pottery and porcelain, playthings, lighting utensils, objects pertaining to medicine, food, and water. According to the antebellum memories of Telfair Hodgson, a number of her father's slaves came directly from Africa. Their graves were "always decorated with the last articles used by the departed, and broken pitchers, and broken bits of colored glass were considered even more appropriate than the white shells from the beach nearby." Sometimes the slaves also carved "wooden figures like images of idols" or put a "patchwork quilt" on the grave. One twentieth-century investigator, Samuel Lawton, was told by a number of Sea Island ministers that it was also a common custom to bury articles along with the dead:

> You must not think that just because you do not find anything on those graves that the relatives did not put some things in there. It is most likely that they have a number of things buried with the body. I have often, at the burials I have conducted, seen the relatives pour hamper baskets full of things right down on top of the coffin before the dirt is shoveled into the grave.[60]

The custom of putting objects both in and on top of graves can be traced to African origins. The Ovimbundu place such articles as baskets, gourds, and instruments used in the burial on top of grave sites. People in the Kongo were said to "mark the final resting-places of their friends by ornamenting their graves with crockery, empty bottles, old cooking-pots, etc." Many ethnic groups of the Windward Coast believed it necessary to provide the dead with various gifts, domestic articles, and clothing to use in the life beyond the grave. Such articles, along with food and water, would be left at the grave, and it was believed that the spirit of the deceased would come and claim them.[61]

Of the two spirits the Gullahs believed in, it was the "trabblin" spirit rather than the heaven-going spirit that caused the greatest concern. The reasons given for grave adornment clearly indicate the African precedent. One informant related:

> Yo' see, suh, everybody got two kinds ob speerits. One is der hebben-goin' speerit. . . . Den dere is de trabblin' speerit. De hebben-goin' speerit don't gib you no trouble, but de trabblin' speerit, 'e be de one dat gib you worriment. E come back to de t'ings 'e like. E try fur come right back in de same house.[62]

Similarity of beliefs and motives regarding grave adornment is best illustrated by the types of articles found on graves in the Sea Islands. Such objects as partially filled medicine bottles, mirrors, broken pitchers, saucers and cups, mayonnaise jars, cold cream, tobacco, and black pepper were commonly placed on graves. Seashells were also commonly placed on graves. Other personal items included shaving brushes, tooth-brushes, combs, and belt buckles. Twelve Gullah ministers reported to Samuel Lawton that other articles of food, such as grapes, oranges, ap-ples, bananas, bread, and cake, were often placed on graves and soon eaten by animals and birds. Further efforts to satisfy the spirits of the dead included pouring water on the grave during a drought. This cus-tom could have been for the purpose of quenching the thirst of the spirit so that the dead would not disturb the living by seeking water.[63]

Gullah decoration of graves indicates a firm belief in the return of ancestors from the world of the dead. Offerings on graves were state-ments of homage, and in these graveyards one finds the strongest ex-pressions of African-inspired memories. Many objects are associated with or used to hold water. In BaKongo religion, deceased ancestors became white creatures called *bakulu*, who lived in the land of all things white. This village of the dead was located under riverbeds and lakes. The white spiritual transparency of *bakulu* allowed them to return to the world of the living undetected. Seashells used on Gullah graves, for instance, are an important theme in BaKongo metaphysics. One BaKongo prayer that addresses the shells states: "As strong as your house, you shall keep my life for me. When you leave for the sea, take me along, that I may live forever." The essence of this prayer is recap-tured by the late Bessie Jones of St. Simons Island, Georgia: "The shells stand for the sea. The sea brought us, the sea shall take us back. So the shells upon our graves stand for water, the means of glory and the land of demise."[64]

Just as seashells and pottery express immortal existence and the sig-nificance of a water underworld, so the glittering, iridescent mirrors and porcelain on Gullah graves reflect the light that represents the spirit. These objects, like water when struck by sunlight, are intimations of the flash of the separated spirit in symbolized flight. Mirrors, lamps, porcelain, and glass are spirit-embodying once they are placed on the graves. Their presence keeps the spirit away from the living. The signifi-cance of spiritual proximity in brilliance gave rise to the BaKongo cus-tom of lighting bonfires on graves to lead one's soul to the other world. Similarly, Gullah torchlight burials may have a deeper meaning than simply lighting the path. Certainly the presence of lamps on African American graves indicates that perhaps this was a means of lighting the way to the world beyond and keeping away the deceased's spirit. Fur-thermore, the decorations imply the deceased's entrance into the fourth moment, a spiritual existence where all is light and brilliance. Breaking pottery and porcelain was perhaps not done to prevent theft, as some researchers believe, but may indicate the deceased's break with earthly life.[65]

Another interesting continuity between Gullah and African traditions in regard to burial is the positioning of the deceased. In central West Africa the coffin is placed so that the deceased faces eastward. Folklorist Elsie Parsons noted that Gullah graves were "invariably dug east to west, with the head to the west." Thomas Higginson wrote in his diary of a "very impressive" funeral for two black soldiers in his regiment. Just before the coffins were lowered "an old man whispered to me that I must have their positions altered—the heads must be towards the west." Higginson complied without asking why. Gullahs and Africans shared a concept of the cosmos. The world followed the sun from east to west.[66]

The deity empowered Upper Guinea peoples through Poro-Sande, gave *minkisi* to the BaKongo, and transformed the ancestors into spiritual guardians. Hence God was not only a Supreme Spirit but a lawgiver as well. The supernatural existence of Poro-Sande was thus ordained and the pantheon of Poro-Sande spirits, through association with God, decreed laws and set standards and modes of behavior, worship, and customs. The "captured spirit" in each *nkisi* was incarnated power sent directly from Nzambi (similar perhaps to the Christian Holy Ghost). Ancestors were the emissaries of the withdrawn Supreme Deity. This idea of the remoteness of God, noted by writers and observers, is disputed by some recent African scholars. Still, both sides of the debate acknowledge the presence of a Supreme Deity in African spiritual concepts, and that God had agents through which divine will was dispensed. This provided a linkage of spiritual virtue with communal responsibility. The attributes of God corresponded with characteristics of harmony and social order, the antithesis of bush living, which was a wild, antisocial state of consciousness.

Similarly, Gullahs who accepted Christianity associated community socialization with religious piety. The laws of God were synonymous with correct conduct toward other members of the slave quarters. In maintaining this African socioreligious connection in the American ambiance, bondspeople operated on an internal logic that excluded planters, overseers, even white Christian ministers. A parallel existed between the structural configuration of what became Gullah folk religion and the composition of social order in the quarters. African and Gullah theories of being are related. In both, God (Jesus for the Gullahs) was the apex, representing honor, constancy, harmony, and perfection, while humanity occupied the center, ever striving to be godlike through a sense of community, kinship, and cooperation. In addition, the good and bad of the spirit world existed in both traditions, although it was far more complex for Africans than for Gullahs. These beings included superhumans, animals, and objects without biological life. Gullahs applied the African ontology, adapted Christianity and bondage to it, and created a religion that employed spirituality as a means of self-preservation and as a vital component of community life.

It is, then, to the Gullahs' credit that, though circumstances prevented their rising up against slavery physically, they did not succumb to white cultural domination. Instead, the Gullahs successfully rose above deceptive aspects of their Christian instruction while assimilating certain other attributes that were serviceable and syncretistic with African culture. In bondage, Gullahs achieved elevation through personal culture and the molding of community values. The edifying qualities of Gullah African-Christian folk religion must be seen as having contributed much to that achievement.

Notes

1. Mason Crum, *Gullah: Negro Life in the Carolina Sea Islands* (Durham, N.C.: Duke University Press, 1940), 3, 19–22, 78. Paul Quattlebaum, *The Land Called Chicora* (Gainesville: University of Florida Press, 1956), 86–88. Margaret Washington Creel, *"A Peculiar People": Slave Religion and Community-Culture among the Gullahs* (New York: New York University Press, 1988), passim.

2. Peter H. Wood, *Black Majority: Negroes in Colonial South Carolina from 1670 through the Stono Rebellion* (New York: Knopf, 1974), 131, 301–304, 333–41.

3. Elizabeth Donnan, *Documents Illustrative of the History of the Slave Trade to America*, 4, *The Southern Colonies* (Washington, D.C.: Carnegie Institution, 1935), and "The Slave Trade into South Carolina before the Revolution," *American Historical Review* (1927–28) 33:807–808, 816–17. Converse Clowse, *Economic Beginnings in Colonial South Carolina, 1730–1760* (Columbia: University of South Carolina Press, 1971), 206, 230–32. Philip Curtin, *The Atlantic Slave Trade: A Census* (Madison: University of Wisconsin Press, 1969). W. Robert Higgins, "The Geographical Origins of Negro Slaves in Colonial South Carolina," *South Atlantic Quarterly* (1971) 70:42–43. Creel, *"A Peculiar People,"* 29–30, 37.

4. The same is true of the Georgia Sea Island region, home of the "Geechee" slave population; see Creel, *"A Peculiar People,"* 17–19.

5. Lorenzo Turner, *Africanisms in the Gullah Dialect* (New York: Arno Press, 1968; reprint of 1949 edition). Donald R. Kloe, "Buddy Quow: An Anony-

mous Poem in Gullah-Jamaican Dialect Written circa 1800," *Southern Folklore Quarterly* (June 1974) 38(2):82–84. Wilbur Zelinsky, *The Cultural Geography of the United States* (Englewood Cliffs, N.J.: Prentice-Hall, 1973), 20–21. Wood, *Black Majority*, 333–41. Curtin, *Atlantic Slave Trade*, 30–36, 44–45, 134–35, 411. Creel, *"A Peculiar People,"* 29–44, 329–34. Daniel Littlefield, *Rice and Slaves: Ethnicity and the Slave Trade in Colonial South Carolina* (Baton Rouge: Louisiana State University Press, 1981).

6. The spelling of Kongo with a *K* instead of a *C* is used by some Africanists. It refers to the traditional, unitary civilization and way of life of Ba-Kongo peoples. The *C* spelling represents the political shift that occurred with white colonial penetration and partition in Central Africa. Traditional Kongo civilization includes modern Bas-Zaire, neighboring Cabinda, Congo-Brazzaville, Gabon, and Northern Angola. The ancient civilization was once under the suzerainty of the kingdom of Kongo. The language is KiKongo, although dialects vary widely in this Bantu-speaking area of Africa. The numerous ethnic groups and some neighboring ones share cultural and religious traditions. They also share memories of the trials and tears left in the wake of centuries of transatlantic slave trading and subsequent colonial exploitation. John M. Janzen and Wyatt MacGaffey, *An Anthology of Kongo Religion: Primary Texts from Lower Zaire* (Lawrence: University of Kansas Publications in Anthropology, no. 5, 1974), 1–3. Robert Farris Thompson and Joseph Cornet, *The Four Moments of the Sun: Kongo Art in Two Worlds* (Washington, D.C.: National Gallery of Art, 1981), 27. Robert Farris Thompson, *Flash of the Spirit: African and Afro-American Art and Philosophy* (New York: Vintage Books, 1983), 103. Wyatt MacGaffey, *Custom and Government in the Lower Congo* (Berkeley: University of California Press, 1970), 11.

7. Turner, *Africanisms in Gullah*, 63, 136, 138, 151, 189, 194. Winifred Vass, *The Bantu Speaking Heritage of the United States* (Los Angeles: UCLA, Center for Afro-American Studies, 1979), 31.

8. *Southern Christian Advocate*, December 22 and 29, 1843. Creel, *"A Peculiar People,"* 29–44.

9. P. E. Hair, "Sierra Leone Items in the Gullah Dialect of American English," *Sierra Leone Language Review* (1965) 4:79–84, 89–93. Turner, *Africanisms in Gullah*, 63, 150, 189. Creel, *"A Peculiar People,"* 17–19.

10. For an extensive bibliography on works about Gullahs and the need for more modern approaches, see Mary A. Twining, "Sources in the Folklore and Folklife of the Sea Islands," *Southern Folklore Quarterly* (1975) 39:135–50. In 1980 the *Journal of Black Studies* devoted an entire issue to Sea Island culture, edited by Twining and Keith E. Baird.

11. See Willie Lee Rose, *Rehearsal for Reconstruction: The Port Royal Experiment* (Indianapolis: Bobbs-Merrill, 1964), and, more significant, Charles Joyner, *Down by the Riverside: A South Carolina Slave Community* (Urbana: University of Illinois Press, 1984), and Patricia Jones-Jackson, *When Roots*

180

Die: Endangered Traditions on the Sea Islands (Athens: University of Georgia Press, 1987).

12. The current exception is Creel, *"A Peculiar People."*

13. Charles C. Pinckney, *An Address delivered in Charleston before the Agricultural Society of South Carolina, at Its Annual Meeting, 18th August, 1829* (Charleston, S.C.: A. E. Miller, 1829). Charles C. Jones, *The Religious Instruction of the Negroes in the United States* (New York: Negro Universities Press, 1969; reprint of 1842 ed.), 70–71. William Wightman, *Life of William Capters, including an Autobiography* (Nashville, Tenn.: J. B. McFerrin, 1858), 291–92. Luther Porter Jackson, "Religious Instruction of Negroes, 1830–1860," *Journal of Negro History* (1930) 15:83–84. James O. Andrew, "The Southern Slave Population," *Methodist Magazine and Quarterly Review* (1831) 13: 315–21.

14. Most sources refer to the Sea Island plantation churches as praise houses because northerners living among and writing about the Gullahs adopted this spelling. But the term *pray's house* is used to signify its function as a place for prayer on the plantations—hence a house of prayer. The Gullahs' pronunciation of the flat *a* and their failure to pronounce the last syllable on many words probably explains why no difference between *pray's* and *praise* was detected. Yet according to Samuel Lawton, who interviewed Sea Island blacks, many of them former slaves, Gullahs called the plantation churches either "pray house," without the *s* sound, or they pronounced the two syllables very distinctly, "pray-ers house," and stated that it was "Way oner go fur pray." Lawton also observed that the Gullahs freely changed verbs into nouns without adding the extra ending. Thus, at the meeting house, "One pray, Den Annuder lead a pray'—Dat mak' two pray's." Lawton's argument is reinforced by Patricia Guthrie's more recent field work in the 1970s. According to Guthrie, "Praise houses are also known locally and in the literature as prayer and pray houses." The Gullahs' mastering of double meaning may also inform the discussion. They often asked white northerners to "jine praise wid we." Also their anthem, "New Jerusalem," stated, "Sing God praise both night and day." Thus the Gullahs went to the meeting house to praise *and* pray. Samuel Lawton, "The Religious Life of Coastal and Sea Island Negroes," Ph.D. dissertation, George Peabody College for Teachers, 1939, 54–56. Patricia Guthrie, "Praise House Worship and Litigation among Afro-Americans on a South Carolina Sea Island," paper, Sixth Annual Martin Luther King Lecture Series, Purdue University, Feb. 21, 1980, 1.

15. William Pope, Sr., to William E. Baynard, Esq., Jan. 8, 1834, and James Sealy to William E. Baynard, Esq., Jan. 8, 1834, Historical Society South Carolina Conference, Methodist Church Archives, Wofford College, Spartanburg, S.C. *Christian Advocate and Journal*, Jan. 31 and June 20, 1834; July 22, 1836. *Southern Christian Advocate*, June 26, 1840; June 26, 1843; Apr. 8, 1842; Feb. 16, 1844; Sept. 29, 1843. James H. Cuthbert, *Life of Richard Fuller, D.D.* (New York: Sheldon, 1879), 81–106. James W. Busch, "The Beaufort Baptist Church," Beaufort County Historical Society pa-

per, Beaufort, S.C., Township Library, n.d., 14–16. Minutes, Savannah River Baptist Association, Baptist Collection, Furman University, Greenville, S.C. Minutes, Beaufort Baptist Church, Baptist Collection, 271–74 and passim. George P. Rawick, *The American Slave: A Composite Autobiography*, 2, *South Carolina Narratives* (Westport, Conn.: Greenwood Press, 1972 reprint), pt. 1, 274; pt. 2, 185. Diary of Laura M. Towne, 15, Penn School Papers, vol. 1, Southern Historical Collection, University of North Carolina, Chapel Hill.

16. John S. Mbiti, *African Religions and Philosophy* (New York: Praeger, 1969), 1–5, 15. James L. Sibley and D. Westermann, *Liberia Old and New* (London: James Clarke, 1928), 187–88. Willie Abraham, *The Mind of Africa* (Chicago: University of Chicago Press, 1962), 52. Robert T. Parsons, *Religion in an African Society* (Leiden: E. J. Brill, 1964), 173–76, 179, 183–85. Geoffrey Parrinder, *Religion in Africa* (Middlesex, England: Penguin, 1969), chaps. 2–6. Placinde Tempels, *Bantu Philosophy*, trans. from French by Colin King (Paris: Presence Africaine, 1959). MacGaffey, *Custom in Lower Congo*, 261–62.

17. Mbiti, *African Religions*, 210–13. Abraham, *Mind of Africa*, 106. Sibley and Westermann, *Liberia*, 190–91. Parsons, *Religion in an African Society*, 174, 183–84. W. T. Harris and Harry Sawyerr, *The Springs of Mende Belief and Conduct* (Freetown: Sierra Leone Press, 1968), 103–105. Parrinder, *Religion in Africa*, 41, 81–89. Tempels, *Bantu Philosophy*, chaps. 5 and 6. Jahnheinz Jahn, *Muntu: An Outline of Neo-African Culture*, trans. from German by Marjorie Greene (London: Faber, 1961), 110, 114–17. Kwabena Amponsah, *Topics on West African Traditional Religion* (Accra, Ghana: McGraw-Hill, 1974), 70–80. Kofi Asara Opoku, *West African Traditional Religions* (Jurong, Singapore: FEP International Private, 1978), 152–60.

18. Mbiti, *African Religions*, 2–16. Despite the exalted modern application of *ontology* in its reference to abstract being, the word originally referred to that which belongs to existent finite being; see Walter Brugger, ed., *Philosophical Dictionary*, trans. from German by Kenneth Baker (Spokane, Wash.: Gonzaga University Press, 1972), 301–302. With regard to African culture and spirituality, the concept of being cannot be restricted to the physiological as opposed to the psychological or fantastic sphere.

19. Thompson and Cornet, *Four Moments of the Sun*, 27–99. Tempels, *Bantu Philosophy*, 64–66. Jahn, *Muntu*, 121–27. Sibley and Westermann, *Liberia*, 187–202. Abraham, *Mind of Africa*, 48–49, 52, 59–62. Parsons, *Religion in an African Society*, 174–93. Harris and Sawyerr, *Mende Beliefs*, 117–21, 123–24. Mbiti, *African Religions*, 15–16, chaps. 11–14. Parrinder, *Religion in Africa*, 78–83. Opoku, *West African Religion*, 91–139. Amponsah, *Topics on Traditional Religion*, 48–68.

20. Arthur Sumner to Lt. Joseph H. Clark, Jan. 23, 1863, Penn Papers, vol. 4, Southern Historical Collection, University of North Carolina, Chapel Hill.

21. Elizabeth Hyde Botume, *First Days amongst the Contrabands* (New York: Arno Press, 1969; reprint of 1893 ed.), 218.

22. Thomas W. Higginson, *Army Life in a Black Regiment* (New York: Collier, 1962 reprint of 1870 ed.), 231–39.

23. Paul Radin, "Status, Phantasy, and the Christian Dogma," in *God Struck Me Dead: Religious Conversion Experience and Autobiographies of Negro Ex-slaves* (Nashville, Tenn.: Social Science Institute, Fisk University, 1945), i–ix.

24. John W. Blassingame, ed., *Slave Testimony: Two Centuries of Letters, Speeches, Interviews and Autobiographies* (Baton Rouge: Louisiana State University Press, 1977), 377. Dorothy Sterling, *Captain of the Planter: The Story of Robert Smalls* (Garden City, N.Y.: Doubleday, 1958), 32–33. Mary Ames, *From a New England Woman's Diary in Dixie* (New York: Negro Universities Press; reprint of 1906 ed.), 45.

25. Charlotte Forten, "Life on the Sea Islands," *Atlantic Monthly*, May 1864, 588.

26. Rupert Holland, ed., *Letters and Diary of Laura M. Towne* (New York: Negro Universities Press, 1969; reprint of 1912 ed.), 26.

27. Charles Nordhoff, "The Freedmen of South Carolina," in *Papers of the Day*, ed. by Frank Moore (New York: C. T. Evans, 1863), 10.

28. Higginson, *Army Life*, 192. Botume, *Amongst the Contrabands*, 204. Forten, "Life on the Sea Islands," 672.

29. Botume, *Amongst the Contrabands*, 204.

30. Higginson, *Army Life*, 235–38, 267–76.

31. Walter Rodney, *A History of the Upper Guinea Coast, 1545–1800* (Oxford: Clarendon Press, 1970), 32–33, 65–67. Kenneth Little, "The Political Function of the Poro," pt. 1, *Africa* (Oct. 1965) 35:349–56; *The Mende of Sierra Leone* (London: Routledge & Kegan Paul, 1951), 7–8, 240–42; and "The Poro Society as Arbiter of Culture," *African Studies* (Mar. 1941) 7:1. Nicholas Owen, *Journal of a Slave Dealer: A View of Some Remarkable Axedents in the Life of Nicholas Owen on the Coast of Africa and America from the Year 1746 to the Year 1757* (London: George Routledge, 1930), 30–31. John Matthews, *A Voyage to the River Sierra Leone* (London: Frank Cass, 1966; reprint of 1788 ed.), 82–83. Warren L. d'Azevedo, "The Setting of Gola Society and Culture: Some Theoretical Implications of Variation in Time and Space," *Kroeber Anthropological Society Papers* (Berkeley: University of California, 1959), 43–45, 67–68. M. McCulloch, *Peoples of Sierra Leone* (London: International African Institute, 1950), 29–37, 68–69, 81–82, 93. George W. Harley, "Notes on Poro in Liberia," *Papers of the Peabody Museum of American Archaeology and Ethnology* (1941) 19:6. Sibley and Westermann, *Liberia*, chaps. 5–9. Folkways Research Series, *Tribes of the Western Province and the Denwoin People* (Monrovia: Department of Interior, 1955), 17, 24–32. Parsons, *Religion in an African Society*, 140–51.

32. Mark Hanna Watkins, "The West African 'Bush' School," *American Journal of Sociology* (1943) 48:667–71, 674–75. Sylvia Boone, *Radiance from the Waters: Ideals of Feminine Beauty in Mende Art* (New Haven, Conn.: Yale University Press, 1986), 13–18. Little, "Political Function of the Poro,"

pt. 1, 357–58; "The Role of Secret Society in Cultural Specialization," *American Anthropologist* (1949) 51:200–205; and "Poro as Arbiter of Culture," 1, 4–6, 9–10. Richard Fulton, "The Political Structures and Functions of Poro in Kpelle Society," *American Anthropologist* (1972) 74:1222–23. Sibley and Westermann, *Liberia*, 176–86, 217–36. Folkways Research Series, *The Traditional History and Folklore of the Gola Tribe in Liberia*, 2 (Monrovia: Department of Interior, 1961), 10–12, 16–22. S. N. Eisentadt, "Primitive Political Systems: A Preliminary Comparative Analysis," *American Anthropologist* (1959) 61:202–203, 208. Warren d'Azevedo, "Common Principles of Variant Kinship Structures among the Golas of Western Liberia," *American Anthropologist* (1962) 64(3):513–14, and "Gola Society and Culture," 70–76.

33. Little, *The Mende*, 226–27, 240–47; "Poro as Arbiter of Culture," 3; and "Secret Society in Cultural Specialization," 199–201. Fulton, "Functions of Poro in Kpelle Society," 1226–28. Harley, "Notes on Poro," 3–9, 11–12, 29–31.

34. Harley, "Notes on Poro," 7.

35. "Origin of the Colored Societies," Minutes, Beaufort Baptist Church, Oct. 7, 1859, 12, Baptist Collection, Furman University, Greenville, S.C. *Christian Advocate and Journal*, Jan. 31, 1834; Nov. 20, 1835; July 22, 1836. *Southern Christian Advocate*, May 1, 1840; Apr. 8, 1842; June 26, 1843; Feb. 16, 1844; Oct. 30, 1846.

36. *Southern Christian Advocate*, Feb. 16, 1844; Oct. 30, 1846.

37. Edward Channing Gannett, "The Freedmen at Port Royal," *North American Review* (July 1865) 101:9. Thomas J. Woofter, *Black Yeomanry* (New York: Henry Holt, 1930), 243–54. Lawton, "Religious Life," 62–63, 69–72. Guthrie, "Praise House Worship and Litigation," 1, and "Catching Sense: The Meaning of Plantation Membership on St. Helena Island, South Carolina," Ph.D. dissertation, University of Rochester, 1977, chaps. 4 and 5.

38. *Southern Christian Advocate*, Apr. 18 and July 28, 1843; Oct. 30, 1846; Oct. 30, 1847; Sept. 6, 1859. Gannett, "Freedmen at Port Royal," 9. Jenkins Mikell, *Rumblings of the Chariot Wheels* (Columbia, S.C.: The State Company, 1923), 137–39. Higginson, *Army Life*, 194–95. Elsie Clews Parsons, *Folk-Lore of the Sea Islands of South Carolina* (Cambridge, Mass.: American Folklore Society, 1923), 204–205. Diary of William F. Allen, William F. Allen Family Papers, 1775–1937, State Historical Society of Wisconsin, Madison, 155. Charles A. Raymond, "The Religious Life of the Negro Slave," *Harpers New Monthly Magazine* (Oct. 1863) 27:680–81. Botume, *Amongst the Contrabands*, 254–55. Seekin' may also have been practiced by other African American slaves; see Raymond, 680–82.

39. *Southern Christian Advocate*, Oct. 30, 1846; Oct. 30, 1847. Towne Diary, 52. Gannett, "Freedmen at Port Royal," 10. Sterling Stuckey, *Slave Culture: Nationalist Theory and the Foundations of Black America* (New York: Oxford University Press, 1987), 85–90. Creel, *"A Peculiar People,"* 297–302.

40. Stuckey, *Slave Culture*, 11, 13–16, 89–90. Watkins, "'Bush' School," 66–67. D'Azevedo, "Kinship Structures among the Golas," 505. Harris and Sawyerr, *Mende Belief*, 47–49. M. C. Jedrej, "Structural Aspects of a West African Society," 136; Carolina H. Bledsoe, "Stratification and Sande Politics," 143–45; Svend Holsoe, "Notes on the Vai Sande Society in Liberia," 97–107; and Warren d'Azevedo, "Gola Poro and Sande: Primal Tasks in Social Custodianship," 98–104, all in *Ethnologische Zeitschrift Zurich* 1 (1980). Towne Diary, 52. David Thorpe to John Mooney, Jan. 25, 1863, Dabbs Papers, Thorpe Series, Southern Historical Collection, University of North Carolina, Chapel Hill.

41. Opoku, *West African Traditional Religion*, 14–29. Amponsah, *Topics on West African Religion*, 20–30. J. B. Danquah, *The Akan Doctrine of God: A Fragment of Gold Coast Ethics and Religion* (London: Lutterworth Press, 1944), 30–42. Sibley and Westermann, *Liberia*, 192–97. Folkways Research Series, *History of Gola Tribe*, 1–5. Harris and Sawyerr, *Mende Belief*, 2–13, 119–20. Karl Laman, *The Kongo* (Uppsala: Studia Ethnographica Upsaliensia, 1962) 3:1–2, 53–63. Georges Balandier, *Daily Life in the Kingdom of Kongo, from the Sixteenth to the Eighteenth Century*, trans. by Helen Weaver (London: George Allen & Unwin, 1968), 244–45. Edwin Smith, ed., *African Ideas of God* (London: Edinburgh House Press, 1950). Beryl L. Bellman, *Village of Curers and Assassins: On the Production of Fala Kpelle Cosmological Categories* (The Hague: Mouton, 1975), 129–30.

42. Parrinder, *Religion in Africa*, 26. Mbiti, *African Religions*, 159–62. Jahn, *Muntu*, 109–14. Janzen and MacGaffey, *Anthology of Kongo Religion*, 34. Thompson and Cornet, *Four Moments of the Sun*, 27–28, 42–47, 134n.50, and passim. Thompson, *Flash of the Spirit*, 103–58. Balandier, *Daily Life in Kongo*, 245–49.

43. Laman, *Kongo* 3:1–6, 216–18. Thompson and Cornet, *Four Moments of the Sun*, 43.

44. Thompson and Cornet, *Four Moments of the Sun*, 27.

45. Allen Diary, 96.

46. Forten, "Life on the Sea Islands," 666.

47. Nordhoff, "Freedmen of South Carolina," 4.

48. *Southern Christian Advocate*, July 7 and Aug. 11, 1843; Jan. 19, 1844; Aug. 20, 1847; May 5, 1844. South Carolina Folklore Project 1655, D-4-27, W.P.A. Collection, South Caroliniana Library, University of South Carolina, Columbia.

49. Towne Diary, 26. James Ball, *Fifty Years in Chains, or the Life of an American Slave* (New York: H. Dayton, 1860), 150.

50. *Southern Christian Advocate*, July 7, 1843.

51. Elizabeth Ware Pearson, *Letters from Port Royal* (New York: Arno Press; reprint of 1906 ed.), 253–54. Towne Diary, 64, 75. Folklore Project 1655 D-4-27.

52. Pearson, *Port Royal*, 252. Irving E. Lowrey, *Life on the Old Plantation* (Columbia: University of South Carolina Press, 1911), 81–83. Folklore Project 1655 and 1855, D-4-27. T. W. Richardson to Rev. George Whipple, Sept. 14, 1863, American Missionary Association Papers.

53. Harris and Sawyerr, *Mende Belief*, 31–32. Laman, *Kongo* 2:85.

54. Folklore Project 1655 and 1855, D-4-27A, 27B. Janie G. Moore, "Africanisms among Blacks in the Sea Islands," *Journal of Black Studies* (June 1980) 10(41):476–77. John M. Vlach, *The Afro-American Tradition in Decorative Arts* (Cleveland: Cleveland Museum of Art, 1978), 139–40. Parsons, *Folk-Lore of the Sea Islands*, 213–14.

55. Parsons, *Folk-Lore of the Sea Islands*, 213–14.

56. Harris and Sawyerr, *Mende Belief*, 31–32, 89. McCulloch, *Peoples of Sierra Leone*, 74. W. C. Willoughby, *The Soul of the Bantu: A Sympathetic Study of the Magico-Religious Practices and Beliefs of the Bantu Tribes of Africa* (Westport, Conn.: Negro Universities Press, 1970; reprint of 1928 ed.), 86–87. Laman, *Kongo* 2:84.

57. Lowrey, *Old Plantation*, 83–87. Laman, *Kongo* 2:88–92. Moore, "Africanisms in the Sea Islands," 473–76. Parsons, *Folk-Lore of the Sea Islands*, 213. Thompson, *Flash of the Spirit*, 117. John H. Weeks, *Among the Primitive BaKongo* (London: Seeley Service, 1914), 267–68.

58. Mbiti, *African Religions*, 149. Ellis, *Negro Culture in West Africa*, 70–71. Harris and Sawyerr, *Mende Belief*, 14, 50. Laman, *Kongo* 2:95–96.

59. Harris and Sawyerr, *Mende Belief*, 14. Laman, *Kongo* 2:95–96.

60. Lowrey, *Old Plantation*, 85–86. Folklore Project 1655 and 1855, D-4-27. Vlach, *Afro-American Decorative Arts*, 139–40. H. Corrington Bolton, "Decoration of Graves of Negroes of South Carolina," *Journal of American Folklore* (July–Sept. 1891) 4:214. "Notes and Documents: Antebellum and War Memories of Mrs. Telfair Hodgson," Sarah Hodgson Torian, ed., *Georgia Historical Quarterly* (Dec. 1953) 27(4):352. Virginia C. Holmgren, *Hilton Head: A Sea Island Chronicle* (Hilton Head, S.C.: Hilton Head Publ., 1959), 63. Lawton, "Religious Life," 196.

61. Wilfred Hambly, *The Ovimbundu of Angola* (Chicago: University of Chicago Press, 1934), 288. Laman, *Kongo* 2:92–95. Bolton, "Decoration of Graves," 214. Thompson and Cornet, *Four Moments of the Sun*, 181–91. Folkways Research Series, *Tribes of the Western Province*, 25, 27. McCulloch, *Peoples of Sierra Leone*, 74.

62. Lawton, "Religious Life," 214.

63. Ibid., 217. Vlach, *Afro-American Decorative Arts*, 143. Thompson, *Flash of the Spirit*, 132–46. Elizabeth Fenn, "Honoring the Ancestors: Kongo-American Graves in the American South," *Southern Exposure* (Sept.–Oct. 1985) 28:44–45. Hodgson, "Antebellum and War Memories," 352.

64. Vlach, *Afro-American Decorative Arts*, 143. Laman, *Kongo* 3:21, 37. Thompson and Cornet, *Four Moments of the Sun*, 198.

65. Thompson, *Flash of the Spirit*, 139–42. Thompson and Cornet, *Four Moments of the Sun*, 183. Vlach, *Afro-American Decorative Arts*, 141. Laman, *Kongo* 2:95, writes that "the porcelain articles may comprise mugs (with holes knocked in bottom), to prevent their being stolen."

66. Vlach, *Afro-American Decorative Arts*, 147. Parsons, *Folk-Lore of the Sea Islands*, 215. Higginson, *Army Life.*

Seven

The Sacred World of the Gullahs

Joseph E. Holloway

When Prof. John F. Szwed wrote "Africa lies just off the coast of Georgia," he was referring to the mainland coastal areas and adjacent Sea Islands of Georgia and South Carolina where the most direct living repository of African culture to be found anywhere in North America exists.

Until as late as 1858, during the slave trade, there was an undetected traffic in illegally transported Africans brought directly from Africa to the Sea Islands. This was easily accomplished in the complex watery wilderness off the southern coast of the United States. Because of this geographic isolation, African culture has been retained in almost every element of the Sea Island culture, including aesthetics, cuisine, folktales, folklore, language, and oral tradition. In South Carolina, African naming practices, net making, fishing practices, the ring shout, basketry, and burial ceremonies permeate indigenous culture.

The Gullah language is essentially a Krio. It arose out of need on Africa's slave coast for Europeans and Africans to communicate while trading and was brought to the American slave communities along the coastal South. The Gullah speech was able to flourish in the isolated atmosphere of the Sea Islands up until the middle of the twentieth century.

The African influences also can be seen in the decorative use of gourds and shells placed on tombs and graves, in the unique Gullah language, the wearing of charms and amulets, root medicines (herbalists), extended family patterns, musical instruments, cuisine, land tenure practices, and the concept of time.

187

This chapter will focus on the sacred world of the Gullahs, viewing both their temporal and spiritual world with the aim of gaining some insight into how the African experience in the Sea Islands helped to shape the world of the Gullahs and how that world shaped the African American experience.

During the slave period, many of the African traditions that survived reflected the Kongo Angolan culture of the Bantu people from Central Africa. The Bantu accounted for 40 percent of all the Africans brought to the Sea Islands. Their culture was transported through the Middle Passage and rematerialized in South Carolina. Despite the Africans' gradual acculturation into European American life, especially after 1940, they still retained many elements of their original culture.

Africanisms and the Black Family

There has been much debate on African survivals in the structure of the black American family, such as extended family ties, "shipmate" relationships, strong stress of kinship, and use of terms of respect for elders such as "uncle" and "aunty" as a sign of respect for age. Prominent scholars such as E. Franklin Frazier believed that the black family began during slavery, and that there were no African antecedents in the structural reorganization of the African family in North America. According to Frazier, there was no question that the present black family took roots under the institution of slavery.[1] However, Melville Herskovits argued just the opposite, that the African family structure among blacks in the New World did survive, and that many elements of their African past carried over into North America.

One of the major changes in the structure of the black family was the absence of the father playing a strong role as he did in the African tradition. For example, during slavery, the family was easily separated through sale. Children generally were sold with their mothers. The planters contributed to making the black female the dominant sex in the family life of the enslaved African by making her the owner of all common property including the children. For example, the cabin was hers; the children also were listed on plantation records as belonging to the mother. Seldom was the father's name indicated.[2]

Generally, the patterns of sale strengthened the bond between mother and child, and diminished the role of the male as the role of the female became more dominant. Many scholars believed that this female dominance created the "maternal family" in black America.

Herskovits correctly pointed out that "slavery did not cause the maternal family but it tended to continue certain elements in the cultural endowment brought to the New World by Africans." Herskovits further pointed out that families of this type are not African but they show important African survival traits, they illustrate the tenacity of the tradition under change and indicate how new circumstances can reinforce old traditions.[3]

Nanice L. Gonzales disagrees with Herskovits; she believes that matrifocality developed as a result of African migration into the New World under slavery. Gonzales pointed out that matrifocality is broad enough to indicate that that African origins in and of itself is not significant because the development of the condition for matrifocal families evolved in the New World. Gonzales and Herskovits both agreed that matrifocality is common among persons of African descent.[4]

Women in the West and Central African society play a significant role in the family economy by controlling the local markets. It was customary for women to handle and control their own property in many African societies. According to custom, labor was divided according to sex— the male did all the labor-intensive work while women turned their concerns toward planting and some local handicrafts.

In most African societies, women ran the local markets. In North America the slave women also operated similar markets for slaves. It was the women who worked the family patch, and it was the women who marketed the produce. Women sold their hogs, garden vegetables, baskets, boats, and canoes, usually in town on Sundays.[5] In addition to this, the major responsibility for cooking, childrearing, and the transmission of the culture to the children fell to the women.

Despite the artificial structure of the family during slavery, one strong African carryover was the extended family concept. Until recently, the strongest element of this tradition existed among blacks in the southern parts of the United States. In Africa, the immediate family consisted of the male, his wife or wives, and their children. Generally, the extended family consisted of two or more families of different generations united by consequences of kinship ties in a common residence under a single head, and also several brothers in the same compound with their families.

The patrilocal extended family consists of a patriarchal head, his wife or wives, his unmarried children, his married sons, and their wives and children.[6] Among black Americans, the traditional immediate family consists of the father, mother, and their children. The extended family in the southern parts of the United States is similar to the extended family patterns found throughout Africa.

In the Sea Islands, we find a strong and similar pattern of extended family ties. Many of the families own land in common (heir property) handed down from generation to generation. This collective ownership of land is found throughout the South. The land is communal property owned by every member of that family. Land cannot be sold or transferred but remains in the family to be handed down to their descendants. In Africa, it is very common to find that land is held or owned by lineage groups, which are corporate groups.[7] This communal relationship recreates ties of lineage and of the extended family as they exist in Africa. Blood relationships are replaced with community membership.[8]

In the Sea Islands, the elderly parents may live in one residence and their children and grandchildren in another residence. There is easy movement from one household to another and economic support and childrearing activities are closely shared. The family joins in collective activities such as hunting, fishing, and farming.

On Ladies Island, a clear example of this extended family pattern was found. On one parcel of family land the grandmother lived in her own house. Her son with his daughters and their children lived in an adjacent house. Her sons and wife lived in another compound facing his father and their grandmother compound. Four generations altogether were living on the same compound. This pattern was repeated on St. Helena and Hilton Head.[9] The structure of these families were matrifocal in that the woman was the focal point of the family.

From "Shipmate" to Aunts and Uncles

Another phenomenon found in the South is the tradition of calling older males and females "uncle" and "aunty" as a sign of respect, whether or not they were related to the person speaking. According to Newbell Niles Puckett, this tradition represents a possible African survival and points back to African matrilineal conditions in which an offspring stood closer to his maternal uncle than to his actual father.[10] This points back to the matrilineal inheritance from the uncle in which the kings' son was not selected for succession to the throne but, rather, his sister's son was.

Actually, the tradition of calling older males and females "uncle" and "aunty" may go back to the relationships that were established between bond men and women in the coastal African factories that were established on the decks of the slave ships. Mintz and Price point out that this "shipmate" relationship became a major principle of social organization and continued for centuries to shape ongoing social relationships.[11]

In Jamaica, the term "shipmate" was synonymous, according to Steward, with "brother and sister."[12] Kelley asserted that "so strong were the bonds between shipmates that sexual intercourse between them was considered incestuous."[13] According to Kelly, shipmates were said to "look upon each other's children mutually as their own,"[14] and it was customary for children to call their parents' shipmates aunts and uncle.[15] This was where the tradition of calling older people "aunt" and "uncle" originated.

This same process of "shipmate" relation reappeared in the southern portion of the United States. The following passage reflects that tradition:

> Uncle Tom com 'long wid Granny Judith from Africa. Two women folks come wid dem. Aunt Ghang and Daphne. Aunt Ghang and Aunt Daphne was bought by de Frees dat had a plantation near Jonesville. Uncle Tom and "Granny" was by mares Jim Gist, but dere masters Allus 'lowed dem to visit on July 4th and Christmas. When dey talk, no body didn't know what dey was talkin' about. My granny never could speak good like I can. She talk half African and all African when she git bothered. . . . [16]

This passage suggests that the "shipmate" relationship continued from the coastal factories of Africa, to the decks of slave ships, and in the Sea Islands and throughout the American South. Enslaved Africans arriving in the Sea Islands on the same ships held a strong bond with each other, and their children addressed appropriate persons as uncle or aunty as Africans struggled to reorganize the family ties they left in Africa. Africans faced with an absence of any real kinship ties in the Sea Islands were forced to model new social ties based on traditional African relationship as they now remembered them from their African past. Each following generation moved from the African reality to the African American experience. This full transformation from African to African American would take several more generations.

Found in a society with the absence of close kin, the Africans attempted to reconstruct their African social and kinships system on the plantations. The slave master went through great pains to eliminate any elements of African culture. For example, in Georgia old man Oka built a place like he had in Africa. It was about twelve by fourteen feet. He built the side that looked like basket weave with clay plaster on it. It had a flat roof he made from bush materials and palmetto palm. It had one door and no window. But "Mussah" made him tear it down because he did not want any African hut on his place.[17]

Given these limitations, African Americans attempted to reestablish a kinship relationship within the framework of the plantation system. In Africa, the children learned of their customs, traditions, history, folklore, tales, and proverbs from the elders, who played an important role in their communities. These grandparents were essential to the family unity. They were the links with the past and the transmitters of culture.

Enslaved Africans were visible and recognizable on the plantations and they attempted to maintain strong relationships with fellow Africans. One informant recalled, "Doze Africans alluz call one anudduh countrymen. Dey know ef dey come frum duh same tribe by duh mahk dey hab. Some hab a long mahk an some hab a roun un. Anudduh weah eahring in duh eah. Some weaks it in duh lef eah and doze frum anudduh tribe weaks it in duh right eah."[18]

These recognizable distinctions in African culture diminished over time and in each generation. In time, strong ties with fellow Africans became kinship ties based on a broader reorganization of the family structure that now included countrymen and their African American descendants. The enslaved Africans came from highly organized societies in which kinship ties were at the center of all social relationships. Men of the same age group associate together and formed association with others their same age, which lasts for a lifetime. The strong respect and regard for elders was a tradition that continued in North America with reference to "aunts and uncles."

Enslaved Africans imported into North America had generally gone through this "shipmate" relationship, already firmly established by the time the Africans arrived in North America. The extended family became represented by "aunts and uncles," and, because the black family could not maintain extended ties in the African sense, they were "reinterpreted" to reflect their new homeland situation.

This kind of social Africanisms is no longer found in the Sea Islands or in black America. There, however, still exists a strong respect for elders, but the young people no longer address the elders as "uncle" and "aunty" as a sign of respect for age. The older people still communicate with each other as "uncle" and "aunty," but this tradition does appear to be dying out.

African Custom of Polygamy
and Black Americans

While slavery reemphasized a role women had previously played in Africa, slavery by its nature promoted the absence of the father and a tradition of sexually promiscuous relationships. Puckett suggested that "sexual promiscuity among Blacks was the result of the African cultural background in which sexual indulgence of the Negro, so open in Africa and in many parts of the rural South, may conceivably be a racial characteristic developed by natural selection in West Africa."[19] While this statement is racist in nature, it touches on the African system of polygamy with little understanding of African traditional society, culture, and an understanding of the African in his historical and sociological setting.

What planters regarded as a tradition of promiscuous relationship was actually rooted in the African concept of polygamy, which was generally found in African societies in which there was a shortage of men. In a system of polygamy, a man could have as many wives as he could afford to maintain in their separate compounds. Through the colonial period, this African custom continued to have a strong influence over the Carolina enslaved Africans. Planters refused to accept legal marriages between slave and wife who were sometimes sold separately from their mates. Planters for the most part were not interested in the sexual habits of enslaved Africans, as long as it did not conflict with their sexual privileges because their greatest interest was to increase their profits by increasing the number of their slaves.

In 1708 Francis Le Jau, the missionary at Goose Creek for the Society for the Propagation of the Gospel (SPG), noted the "grievous sins dayly committed by all our Slave here, and elsewhere, and tolerated or at least connived at by as under a pretense of Impossibility to remedy them." Le Jau more specifically meant "the constant and promiscuous cohabiting of Slaves of different Sexes and Nation together." Le Jau continued, "When a Man or Woman's facy dos alter about his Party they throw up one another and take other which they also change when they please." Le Jau concluded that this was "a General Sin," and the exceptions were "so few they are hardly worth mentioning."[20] In another letter on the same subject, Le Jau asked the SPG how to prevent "the promiscuous cohabitation" of slaves and the plurality of wives. Le Jau refused to baptize several slaves who still practiced polygamy. However, he did baptize several enslaved Africans with the warning that "the Christian Religion dos not allow plurality of Wives, nor any changing of them" and he made them promise "truly to Keep to the Wife You now havt till Death dos part you."[21]

In the roots to what planters believed was sexual promiscuity among enslaved Africans was a lack of understanding of traditional African society and culture. The sexual life of Africans was well regulated by customary law and social tradition. In West and Central Africa, marriages were arranged by families, whereas in North America enslaved Africans were brought together artificially for the purpose of procreation and not to create strong family ties. In short, the plantation system encouraged separation of families, sexual promiscuity for the purpose of increasing slave population, which created a general moral breakdown in the social cohesiveness of the African American family.

The Burial Societies

Another recognizable Africanism in the United States which was a direct African carryover was the secret societies. There has been no comprehensive study and research on the origin and history of black insurance companies, and yet they are the only indigenous institution that has direct linkage with West and Central African secret societies. The black insurance companies represent one of the few African institutions that have survived in the United States today. The Black mutual aid societies and self-help organization are direct carryover from African mutual aid societies. According to Carter G. Woodson, "drawing on the African penchant for burial pomp secret societies have been developed mainly around the idea of taking care of the sick and dead; and from this as a nucleus these orders have become mainly insurance companies."[22]

Once the Africans arrived in America they were not permitted to continue their African secret functions, so they found suitable substitutes by modifying their African societies into lodges, and according to Herskovits these African secret societies became insurance and burial societies.[23] Carter G. Woodson also pointed out "most of the large Negro insurance companies may be traced to such beginnings. W. W. Browne, an enterprising Methodist Minister of Richmond Virginia, started an insurance company from this early tradition."[24]

According to Herskovits, there were three major black insurance businesses that grew from this tradition. They were the Afro-American, the Knights and Daughters of Tabor, and the Universal Life Insurance Company. The first two are also fraternal orders with appropriate rituals and a pronounced social flavor.

According to W. E. B. Du Bois, there was a direct connection between African secret societies and the founding of Black Insurance companies in the United Sates. Du Bois said:

> No complete account of Negro beneficial societies is possible, so large is their number and so wide their ramification. Nor can any hard and fast line between them and industrial insurance Societies can be drawn some in membership and extent of business. These societies are also difficult to separate from the secret societies; many have more or less ritual work, and the regular secret societies do much fraternal insurance business.[25]

Burial insurance among blacks comes directly from this tradition. The ideal of providing insurance for the dead survivors and burial plans were never in the early years addressed by whites, and African Americans continued this tradition by providing for the collective economic cooperation in times of need for the community.

Burial Societies in the Sea Islands

Burial societies in the Sea Islands are still numerous on Hilton Head, St. Helena, and Beaufort County. Some of the better known burial societies were the Workers of Charity, Lily of the Valley, and Rome of Victory.[26] The Mutual Aid, the Jolly Boys, the Golden Link, the Seaside Branch, and the Union Gospel Travelers were on Hilton Head.[27] On the Island of St. Helena, the Farmer's Club was an important functioning burial society. In Beaufort County, there were the Odd Fellows, Eastern Star, and Weeping Mary.[28] The Knights of Wisemen is a lodge that still assists in burials; Ladies Union, Young Men Social Club, and the Blue Mountain lodge all have similar functions. The Knights of Wise Men is for men only and Rome of Victory is mixed and includes both sexes. The Young Men Social Club and the Blue Mountain lodge also are male societies.[29]

In the Sea Islands people would pay a small amount of money and when a member became ill they would "sit up" with the sick and family and make sure that the home was cleaned and food prepared and all the daily functions taken care of such as cooking and cleaning. If the member died they would sit up (the wake) until the person was buried, generally the next day. The burial society would make all the funerary arrangements. They functioned as a beneficiary society to the community. Only Rome of Victory still performs this function today.[30] In addition to funerary arrangements and the wake, the burial societies in the older days also prepared members' bodies for burial. As one journal article explained it:

> When an Odd-Fellow dies, "de body cover up, nobody mus' touch. Six men come to babe an' dress de body." Similarly, on the death of a Good Samaritan, "de body cover up, no one can touch de body 'til de Sister come. Sen' to de Wordy (Worthy) Chief. Fo' Sisters come was De body an' lay out. Nobody can look at de face widout de Sisters say So."[31]

These beneficent societies were the forerunners of black insurance companies, and they developed particularly out of the need of black people to properly bury their dead and to provide for the families of deceased members. This was a strong African carryover of the belief that the dead person's spirit could not rest until he had a proper funeral and burial. The first of these societies was organized in Philadelphia in 1787. Societies were soon established in other cities both in the North and South. Usually these societies were secret and they were composed of free blacks exclusively because slaves did not have to worry about burial expenses and financial support for their orphaned children. Members paid a fee of twenty-five cents. Part of this money was used to care for widows and orphans, the latter being guaranteed the rudiments of an education. In 1790, the Free African Society in Philadelphia applied for a plot of land in Potters Field, where it might bury its dead.[32]

Organizations of this type still persist in the southern black communities to this day.[33] Black insurance companies sprang from such societies. The first was founded in Philadelphia in 1810 with a capital stock of $5,000. Joseph Randolph, Cavey Porter and William Coleman served as president, treasurer, and secretary, respectively. After operating for about three years, the company collapsed and no other companies were established until after 1820.[34]

Sea Island Burial Practices

From the eighteenth century to around the 1930s in the Sea Island the Gullah and African burial custom were very similar in the preparation of the body for burial. According to observer Sam Doyle, before they started embalming persons "if you died today or at night you would be bury tomorrow." When a person died, the burial societies would send out people to wash and dress the body. The Elders would perform this function for men, and women prepared the bodies of women. The body would be dressed in a white sheet (no clothes) and something would be tied underneath the mouth and the body would then be placed in a casket. The caskets were made from four pieces of wood and it would be covered with black cloth inside the casket.[35]

The Preparation of the Body

In Beaufort County in the community of Dale near Red Hill there was a group of women who would go around and prepare the body when someone died. First they would lay the body in the bed. For the final wash the water would be brought into the room. Soap and towels or a fine cloth would be used to wipe the body clean. They would bring coffee to be placed underneath the arms, legs, and open spaces. Coffee would then be rubbed over the body. The body would then be kept for two or three days. The women would dress the body and then place it in the casket. After the body had been prepared they would begin singing and shouting over the body until the time for the funeral came. This singing and shouting over the body is a direct African carryover into African American burial customs. Even when they began embalming bodies (in the house) the people would sit around the body until the funeral would be held in that person's yard or home. The bodies were generally kept on the outside of the house or in the living room, as was the custom.[36]

The Final Wash

The final wash was a tradition is common throughout West and Central Africa and is found among speakers of the Niger-Kongo language family which includes groups from the Senegambia to Angola. Therefore, this custom came to be reinforced by both Central and West Africans. Among the Kalabari, a Bantu-related group, the washing of the dead is done in a particular spot at night in privacy. For this ritual, water is brought in an earthen pot which may not touch the ground but is kept from touching the earth by means of an Ezikila (a thick roll of cloth wound into the shape of a carrier's pad). A piece of cloth is dipped into the water and then wrung out and with this the body is washed until clean. In this ceremony water must fall to earth.[37]

Among the Igbo in the preparation of the body for the final wash the elder men prepare the male bodies and the elder women prepare the female bodies. They rubbed the body with palm kernel and coconut oil and sometimes rubbed the body with camwood and herbs.[38] This is similar to the ritual in the Sea Islands. The people in Igboland keep an all night vigil until the funeral. The pots used to wash body are later placed on top of the deceased's grave.

The Wake

During the wake, friends, family, guests, and members of the burial society would sit around the dying person "tuh help them cross de ribber." When the last breath was drawn everyone present gave a loud shriek as notification that another soul had "done crossed ober" into the spirit world.[39] During the Civil War, the Gullah "death-watch" or "sit up" was looked down upon by Northern instructors as heathen practices:

This practice of sitting up all night with the dying, H. W. [Harriet Ware] justly condemns as "heathenish." The houses cannot hold them all, of course, and they sit round out of doors in the street, the younger ones often falling asleep in the ground, and they "hab fever." But of course it was useless to expostulate with them; to their minds the omission of the watch would be a mark of great disrespect.[40]

In the Sea Islands they would keep an all-night vigil, singing, praying, and preaching around the bedside of the dying. This was supposed to strengthen the person as they "passed death's door." When the person died they would immediately begin shouting over the body. The loud shrieks were made as the last breath was breathed, as it was believed that loud shrieking "scares off the spirits of hell who are always lurking around to get possession of another soul."[41]

In the Sea Islands the "sit up" around the body, were all-night vigils. Singing, praying, and shouting over the body were very similar to practices in Central Africa. The all-night funeral observances and singing are also common practices in African and European cultures. Observance of a wake is common in both societies. However, vocal and public expression of grief at the wake in the form of shouting, screaming, and dancing is a direct African carryover.[42] While this is common throughout Africa, Sea Island wakes bear more similarity to Central Africa wakes than those of West Africa.

As we attempt to identify the origins of this practice with the possible African ethnic group, we find the same identical practice in Angola among the Umbundu. As soon as a dying person took the last breath, relatives, neighbors, and friends who are gathered around the death bed "pierce the air with lamentations and heartrending cries" and other wild expression of grief. The loud noise and shouting "is supposed to drive away the spirits." Between the wailing and the shouting the assembled guests, friends and society members may drink, dance, gamble and be merry. At the time of death, if the deceased was one of their members, the secret society honored his funeral by spending whatever was found in the cashbox in which the contributions of the members were deposited.[43]

The death ceremony was the most important event in the life of the community and everyone wanted to die in their place of birth. On St. Helena Island, one informant explained: "We all leave in our youth to find work and sometimes many of us stay away thirty or forty years spending our lives working and living in the Big City. But when it's almost time for us to die we come back home."[44] In the Sea Islands they believe: "Fus the spirit tuh rest in the grave folks have tuh be buried at home. They nevuh feel right ef they buried from home the spirit just wanduh around."[45] Another example of this is found in Georgia. "A Combahee Negro of today, never mind how far away he may have wandered, when he comes to die, thinks of the old plantation as his house, and wants to be carried back and buried among his own people . . ."[46] In White Bluff, Georgia, strangers were not allowed to be buried in the local cemetery but in what was known as the "strangers lot." A piece of ground set apart from the cemetery proper. This African custom of bringing the dead back to their original home for interment was found throughout the coastal areas of both Georgia and South Carolina.[47]

This concept is common in many African societies. Bosman reports that "the Negroes are strangely fond of being buried in their own Country; so that if any person dies out of it, they frequently bring his Corpse home to be buried. . . ."[48] "When a man dies at a distance from his home his body is always taken back, when possible, to his home, wrapped up in mats covered by a cloth and placed on a bier or cradle, which is carried on the shoulders of his relatives."[49] Among the Igbo the greatest desire of all men and women is to die in their own hometown. If you are buried in a place other than your home the ancestral spirits of that region will not accept a stranger into their midst and that is why the Igbo bring the body of their dead home for burial. In the case of death in a foreign land the body will be returned home for burial.

An example of this occurred in Los Angeles many years ago when an Igbo student was killed in an auto accident. The uncle, who resided in Los Angeles, had to call his senior brothers in Nigeria to determine where the nephew would be buried. He was told that the body could not be buried in a foreign land, and that it had to be returned to the town of his birth in Awaka, Owerri, Imo State, Nigeria, for interment. He was given a funeral service in Los Angeles, and the body was returned three months later for the funeral and burial in his hometown of Owerri.[50]

Above-Grave Decorations

In the Sea Islands when a person died, everything that person used—plates, spoons, saucers, medicine, and pots—were all placed on the grave. The medicine bottles were then turned down into the grave. There were no flowers or headstones except for the Civil War soldiers. Ole man Gabriel "said tat dis wuz de way dey bury dem in Africa." "If I am sick all de tings they used to care for me with an de bottle to give me medicine. When I'm dead dey place dem on top of de grave. Dis ole slavery time customs."[51] "Dey use tuh put duh tings a pusson use las on duh grabe. Dis wuz suppose tuh satisfy duh spirit and keep ir frum follin yuh back tuh duh house."[52]

After the 1920s things begin to change and they started placing wild flowers or a lily on the grave.[53] In Central and West Africa it is believed that unless the dead person has a proper funeral their spirit will not join with the ancestors and will wander as well as cause problems and harm the community. Part of the proper funeral involves the placement of items used by the dead on top of the grave. This is still practiced in numerous Bantu and West African cultures. In short, great pains are taken to provide for a proper carryover. "Wen a pusson die in duh house, ef yuh take em out fo' duh ministuh say few wuds, den deah spirit will hant duh house, cuz dey jis caahn be happy till de hab ebryting done propuh an right."[54] The Gullahs, like their African ancestors, did everything to pacify the "speerit." They further placated the spirits of the dead by placing their things on the grave. "Dey puts tings on the grave so de be handy for de speerit and he be satisfied."[55] By satisfying the spirit, "dey keep de speerit out en de house."[56]

In Eastern Nigeria, in Onitsha, all the implements of the dead are placed before the corpse: tools, gun, and bag, as well as other implements in accordance with his profession. For a man of wealth, a bowl filled with cowries (money) will be added to the collection. The place of articles is symbolical. They represent the equipment that the man will need in the underworld; the tools to enable him to prosecute his occupation; the money wherewith the rich man will be able to maintain his proper dignity. Small pots and bowls are generally placed on the grave to aid the departed in the spirit world. When the burial is finished, more "omu" (palm leaves) are deposited on the top of the grave. On the grave of a woman, a small pot (oku) alone is placed.[57]

Throughout the South, this custom was found in almost every southern state. In South Carolina "the most common items placed on graves were bleached seashells, broken crockery and glassware, broken pitchers, soap dishes, lamp chimneys, tureens, coffee cups, syrup jugs, all sorts of ornamental vases, cigar boxes, gun locks, tomato cans, teapots, flowers with pots, bits of stucco, plaster image, pieces of carved stone-work from one of the public buildings during the war, glass lamps and tumblers in great number and other kitchen articles are used. . . . "[58]

From early observation of this tradition in the Sea Islands at a grave in Beaufort, the tradition of placing broken crockery and special household items have been substituted with pots and neatly placed artificial flowers—a combination of African pots and European flowers. Today, both blacks and whites bring flowerpots to be placed on top of the graves. The present styles represent new forms of Africanism that have been substituted for more socially acceptable items, such as in Daufuskie and Coosaw islands, where there still exist strong elements of this custom. The more isolated the area, the stronger the Africanism.[59]

Today for the most part, professional morticians now incorporate traditional ideas into Styrofoam and plastic vases. Modern grave decorations incorporate elements of the African tradition of above-grave decorations. New patterns of arrangement reflect the changing forms. In other words, the African forms have been African Americanized. Instead of pots, plates, saucers, cups, and medicine bottles, artificial pots and plaster flowers have now taken their place.

At Coffin Point Cemetery, where the Coffin Plantation is still located, the same graveyard used by enslaved is still being used by their descendants today. Even though, the graveyard is located in an all-white area in St. Helena, some new forms of Africanisms and change in the style of the above grave decoration were observed. On the grave mound rested a single pot, which was placed in the center of the grave between two headstones similar to some Bantu styles. In Charleston, South Carolina, the same pattern appears in a black graveyard in the community of Red Top.

One informant, remembered recently on the Island of Coosaw seeing a candle and pennies all over the grave. When one asked the people what the placement of the pots on the grave meant, the just said, "Ole time slavery ways."[60]

In the older days when making the headstone, they would place the dead person's favorite plate in the cement before it hardened, and if the person had requested some special food before he died, the food was prepared and placed on the grave. "I carry duh kine uh food we use tuh had tuh eat on duh days he wuz off rom work. I take cooked chicken an cake an pie an cigahs."[61] This is still common in most African societies from the Senegambia to Anglo and found in places where Africans were enslaved throughout the New World—Brazil, Venezuela, Jamaica, and most of the West Indies.

The South Carolina grave decorations were similar to the above-grave decorations found among the Bakongo, Luba, and Ovimbundu. From early travel accounts in Central Africa by missionaries, we can reconstruct the origin of placing objects on graves. E. J. Glave, a nineteenth-century explorer, traveled through the Congo and observed this Bakongo burial practice: "The village burial place presented a curious aspect, for the final resting place of a Congo chieftain is marked by grotesque display. All the cheap crockery which the deceased had been able to collect during his lifetime was strewn along in an oblong path on the grave and surrounded by a suggestive little margin of Gin."[62]

This practice seems commonplace among the Bantu of the region. For example, in the Kongo (Zaire), "the natives mark the final resting place of their friends by ornamenting their graves with crockery, empty bottles, old cooking pots, etc. all of which articles are rendered useless by being cracked or perforated with holes."[63] "Also, broken crockery, little flags, images of men or beasts, either carved in wood or molded in clay, are often found tombs."[64]

The custom of placing objects on top of the grave is African in origin. However, the style which survived in the Sea Islands was more closely related to the Bantu, particularly the Bakongo and the Ovimbundu in Angola, which places articles such as baskets, gourds, and instruments used in the burial on top of the graves.[65]

Mrs. Telfair Hodgson in 1850 observed in South Carolina a pattern of above-grave decoration almost identical to what is practiced presently in Zaire:

> The slaves were not allowed to leave the field in the daytime, so night weddings and night funerals were the custom. Negro graves were always decorated with the last article used by the departed and broken pitchers and broken bits of colored glass were considered even more appropriate than the white shells from the beach nearby. Sometimes they carved rude wooden figures—like images of idols and sometimes a patchwork quilt was laid upon the grave.[66]

There are other forms of African grave decoration found. At the Bowen family plot at the Baptist Church Cemetery in Trade Hill section of Liberty County, Georgia, a wooden pole marker carved with the name Bowen on it and other wooden sculptures reveal a unique retention of African wood carving tradition. The Cyrus Bowen sculpture is very African and Robert Farris Thompson credited its use of a branched shape to a similarly branched sculptural technique used and practiced by sculptors of the Congo.[67]

Both the Bowen and Kongo sculptors use natural twisting features of branches to make art and sculptures. Again, this is also common in other parts of Africa but it bears a closer resemblance to the Kongo form. This may be because during the final years of the slave trade more Kongo-Angolan slaves were brought to America. This also would contribute to the dominance of Bantu culture found in the field.

In the Mount Pleasant area of South Carolina, shell-covered graves are commonplace as the grave decoration. While broken glass and crockery were the primary material found on black graves, the use of White Sea shell was common throughout the South. In the St. Helena area, seashells were used with lime to make cement-like material that was also used on graves to make small borders that outlined the graves. This "tappy" was used for the foundation of the Coffin Point Mansion. Only the slaves knew how to make tappy and today the art is completely lost.[68] J. Vlach has proposed a theory about the use of seashells to decorate African American graves. He believes that the seashells are connected with the Congolese beliefs that deceased ancestors inhabited villages of the dead under riverbeds and lake bottoms. The layering of the shells may create an illusion of such a river or lake bottom under which the realm of the dead lies.[69] We can conclude, given our present information, that this primarily originated among the Bantu.

Above-grave decorations are common among speakers of languages in the Niger-Congo language family, and they are found from the Senegambia to Angola. But given the present above-grave ornamentations in Africa and that found in old photographs in South Carolina and Georgia there is more similarity to the Angolan-Kongo style, particularly the Bakongo and the Ovimbundu, in regard to both content, form, and meaning. There exists a more direct correlation to Congo and Angolan forms, particularly with the Bakongo, Luba, and the Ovimbundu in Angola, than with the Mende, Igbo, Yoruba, Akan, Bambara, Wolof, and Fang from West Africa. This cultural survival, which has been documented in South Carolina and Georgia, is still today found in Zaire.[70] This does more than suggest the Bantu of Central Africa as the main point of origination for this custom.

Cooperative Labor Patterns among the Gullah

One African cultural pattern which continued in the Sea Islands was that of gang labor. Gang labor survived because it was reinforced by similarities with the European mode of gang or cooperative labor. African institutions and customs seem to have been able to survive when they did not directly conflict with European customs such as the emotionalism found in religious worship, concept of a Supreme Being, and practices in agricultural cultivation. William Bascom pointed out that when the Africans first arrived, they shared with the Europeans numerous preexisting commonalities in economic systems based on money, markets, middlemen, and similarities in government. What was uniquely African in their pattern of gang labor versus the European pattern was the working in unison to the beat of drums, music and singing.[71]

The institution of cooperative work among the Gullah had it roots in West and Central Africa. In West Africa cooperative work is widespread and common among most groups. Bascom says that among the Yoruba cooperative labor takes two forms. First is the Aro which is a single exchange between two or three farmers. The other form of cooperative labor is more of a social event Owe (working bee). This is when a man calls upon his friends, relatives, or societal members to help him with a task. For example, if the man needs to hoe the field or build a thatch house, the wife calls together her friends and society members to assist her in preparing a large feast for the men with palm wine or gin.[72]

In Dahomey, the pattern of cooperative labor is done by members of the society called dokpwe, equivalent to the Yoruba Owe. Here the host hires a drummer to set the pace for the men working in the field. All the workers work in step and keep pace with the drummer. While the Yoruba work in line, they do not work in unison to music like the Dahomeans. The Dahomean work hoeing in unison to a drummer. This pattern has been retained and observed in Haiti, the Virgin Islands, and Jamaica.

In the Sea Islands, Bascom had observed this pattern of gang labor and with various regional variations. On the Island of Sapelo in Georgia one informant remembered large groups of thirty to fifty people, hoeing side-by-side in the field. He concluded that this was significant because in Sapeloe during slavery work was assigned by the task system. European Americans understood this practice from the African and adopted on the plantations. In the Sea Island gang labor patterns were African in nature; the Gullahs hoe side-by-side in unison to music.

The motor behavior and movements in relationship to hoeing and the planting and cultivation of rice were African. For example, the hole in which the seed was dropped was first made with the heel and then covered with the foot. This practice was first identified in West Africa by Herskovits.[73]

On the Island of St. Helena when the people used to hoe together each took his own row and, as they worked in unison, it was to the beat of spirituals. In St. Helena this cooperative labor was provided by one of their societies called Knights of Wisemen and assisted members only.[74]

This type of labor practice observed by Bascom is no longer required because by 1920s, the islands were inaccessible except by boat because of the many rivers, creeks, and marshes. Some bridge construction was started about 1915, but it was not until 1940 that most of the islands had direct access to the mainland. The bridges marked an end of an era of isolation. Sam Doyle, a long-time resident, remembered the change.

"When the bridges came they brought the automobile and the automobile brought the lights and with the coming of lights all the spirits left never to come back again."[75] The automobile revolutionized farming patterns on the island.

Passing of Children over the Coffin

Puckett observed among the Gullah in 1925 that children of dead parents were passed over the coffin. This ritual appears not to be of African American origin and there appeared to have been no corresponding African custom. This practice is not as common as it was in the past years but it is still practiced from Georgetown to Savannah. All my informants recalled witnessing this custom recently.[76] None of the old people knew or remembered why they did this, except a local minister who declared that young children are passed over the coffin of the dead person to prevent the spirit of the parent or loved one from entering the body of the child. "If the child is very young and don't understand what has happened their soul is still without identity and the dead spirit can enter the body of the child causing it harm. Children can hear the voices of the dead, especially if they where close to the individual which had died."[77]

Recently his daughter was found walking down a country road about the same time her grandfather had died. She was found by a niece wandering in the wilderness and was questioned as to where was she going. "Granddaddy called me!" She replied. The elders were consulted about how to deal with this problem. Their solution was based on what had worked in the past.

They revealed that this was a very serious problem and instructed that the child would have to attend the funeral because she was in danger until the funeral was over. "Kids don't understand what death is all about and because the child is younger their spirit is not as strong as the dead. The child has to witness the funeral and be shown where the grandfather is going—down into the ground." Therefore, the child is passed over the coffin to separate the spirits—the point at which the child is passed over the coffin signals the separation of the two spirits.[78] Two other children who did not attend the funeral and were not passed over the coffin experienced serious psychological problems for about six months.

This custom has been recently identified as originating among the Ubani in West Africa. This same custom is today found in Bonny and Opobo and has remained almost identical in form and meaning, as we shall now see. An informant from Opobo remembered this custom performed when her grandfather died in the 1960s. She recalled that at the funeral the great-grandchildren and grandchildren were passed over the coffin. The ceremony was performed by her cousin, who passed the children from one end of the coffin to the other. One of the children as she was being passed over the coffin landed on top of the coffin and began to scream. The whole community was upset with this very serious error in tradition.[79]

The children were passed over the coffin so that the spirit of the dead would not be attached to the children such that it would keep visiting them. Visitation by the dead loved ones to the children is a serious matter because the children could become alarmed and because they are too young to understand they might become ill and die. This rite is performed to sever the bond between the dead person and the living children. This is done as an act of love and to keep the spirit from coming back into the house. Once the child is passed over the coffin this signal a break in the close bond between the dead loved one and the living relative, and so that the spirit will go on its way and not come back and visit the children. This rite is performed for the sake of the children whose spirit is weak and not yet fully developed as an adult. The person who has passed could love the child so much that they might want to take the child with them.[80]

This phenomenon of passing children over the coffin is still practiced by the Gullahs of South Carolina and by the Ibani of Bonny and Opobo in West Africa. In the historical literature, Bonny was one of the major ports from where Africans found their way to North America. This custom is found in Africa and South Carolina and is completely intact. This suggests that this custom was first introduced into the Sea Islands by the Ubani Bonny.

A close examination of slave importation records into South Carolina show that a total of 1,975 Africans arrived from Bonny in 1739.[81] This was the year of the Stono Rebellion and South Carolinians refused to import Angolans who were brought into the South Carolina Colony as planters temporarily turned from Central Africa to West Africa exclusively.

There were no substantial imports of Africans from Bonny until 1800 when there were again intense slave activities in the Bonny area between 1800 to 1807 just prior to the closing of the legal slave trade. Shipments identified as arriving from Bonny Ports by Elizabeth Donnan were 530 Africans in 1805[82] and only 368 Africans in 1807.[83] These figures show that the core group of Africans from Bonny arrived in 1739. This suggests that the transportation and foundation for this particular custom carryover sometime started in 1739 when the majority of Ibanis imported into South Carolina arrived from the nation of Bonny.

Gullah Religious Carryovers

The Gullahs merged Christianity and African ritual together as they interpreted Christianity and the Christian experience to their daily lives. Probably the strongest connection between the West African water spirit cults and the Baptist Church in the United States are the emotionalisms found in spirit possession, and the emphasis placed on the use of water in the religious ceremonies.

The Gullahs always placed a bowl of water in the house to ward off the spirit and "keept de ghost out de House." Similar to their African ancestors, water was sprinkled around the house in the morning to purify the house and keep evil spirits out.[84]

In the Sea Islands, the Baptist and Holiness Churches dominate the region. According to Herskovits, the reason why the majority of African Americans are Baptist is because of the importance of the association of water with African ritual. In the West African cults emphasis is placed on the immersion of the body in water, as is practiced in the water cults of Ibibio, Calabar, Ijaw, the Yoruba, and Grebo in Liberia. All bear witness to this strong tradition. The water spirit cults of the Yoruba, Ashanti, and Dahomey all visit the river and use water for purification in their religious ceremonies. Herskovits points out those slaves came to the United States with a tradition in which their worship involved immersion in a body of water. The Baptist emphasis on total immersion of the body was similar to the tradition found in the water cult sects. Herskovits concludes that the Baptist "shouting" sect is a direct reinterpretation of the Shango cult.[85]

In African cults, such as the cult of Sango, spirit possession was a part of the religious ceremony. They are parallel to spirit possession found in holiness churches (Church of God and Christ) and Pentecostal Churches found throughout the Western hemisphere. The priest of Sango when in possession of his spirit will perform a holy dance in a circle. In the Pentecostal Churches dancing and speaking in tongues is also a common feature of the service. Herskovits was the first to recognize this close relationship between the "Baptist Shouters" and the Sango cult.

Probably the strongest connection between the West African water spirit cults and the Black Baptist in the United States are the emotionalism found in the spirit possession, and the emphasis placed on the use of water in the religious ceremonies. An area in which little attention has been paid in terms of African survivals or carryovers are what Herskovits note in body movements which lie below the level of consciousness,[86] such as the motor behavior in walking, singing, dancing, speaking, and the behavioristic aspects that give overt expression as in spirit possession. According to Herskovits, these are the most striking and recognizable survivals of African religion.[87]

In the United States, the religious institutions were predominantly Protestant rather than Catholic and slaves sought the sects which resembled their own African religious tradition. Black Americans in large numbers joined into the Baptist churches because the mode of worship more clearly " . . . resembled nearly that religion which they had been accustomed to in Africa."

One informant recalled that her mother said that she was Glebo (Grebo)[88] and another informant recalled an African community or community of Africans that lived on the Wallace Plantation about five miles from the present site of the Penn Center. On St. Helena some of "the old people remembered what their parents and grandparents told them and in turn, they handed down the experience of the race. — Oh, he can remember hearing about the landing of those 'African people.' There at Lonesome Hill. Many died, and many ran away, and I spec dey ran back to Africa."[89] Whether this was a group of Africans that were never acculturated into the general populations is not known. One possible explanation was that they were members of the *Wanderer* or some other illegal slave ship into the area that was recorded.

Another possible connection with the ship *Wanderer* was Isaac Smith. Mrs. Bernice Brooks recalled the African stories and recollections of her great-grandfather who said he came over on a slave ship in his teens and did not remain a slave for long because freedom came soon after arriving. He died in 1932 at ninety years of age. He was born in West Africa in 1842. He recalled being in his teens, about sixteen seasons, at the time of his arrival in Georgia. He remembered being on deck with long horn cattle (probably from the Senegambia), and that it was very hot when he arrived (probably during the summer). The way Africans were smuggled in was to mix them with the legitimate cargo. Africans were hidden and mixed in with the cattle. He was captured in Africa along with his father, but was separated after they landed in Georgia. Isaac Smith never did learn how to speak good English and talked with a strong Gullah accent. In America, he was employed as a "house boy" and never really worked the field. He fished all the time and drank strong coffee. He was probably from the coast [or a river area] and familiar with fishing.[90] Given his age at the time of his arrival and death, it is more than likely that he was a member of the Wanderer. Being too young to work the fields may explain why he saw service as a "house boy." However, the fact that he was Senegambia and employed as a house servant was no accident in that they were preferred over other Africans for house service duty in America. The fact that longhorn cattle were being exported from West Africa is a situation that requires additional examination. It is also known that cattle egrets came with the cattle from West Africa, but whether they were consciously imported to North America or whether they followed the cattle on their own is not known. Today cattle egrets are found in West Africa and the Southern portion of the United States where they now follow tractors instead of cattle.

The fact that slaves were being smuggled in the area on a regular basis contributed to a strong African presence. Slave traders continued to unload their cargoes of slaves directly from Africa into the Sea Islands until the middle of the nineteenth century. The last recorded ship to have landed a cargo of Africans in the Sea Islands was the Wanderer which came to Jekyll Island in Georgia with 420 Africans in 1858. They were unloaded on the Dubigion Plantation and about half of them were taken to the Butler and Tillman Plantation near Hanburg in Edgefield County, South Carolina. Although the majority of the Africans were later scattered throughout the South, a large number of them remained in South Carolina and Georgia, living in a radius of twenty to thirty miles from where they originally landed.[91]

Emory Campbell on Hilton Head Island recalled that his great aunty told him how these illegal Africans were smuggled in wagons that were covered as to keep the authorities unaware of their activities.[92] As late as 1862, Miss Towne noticed that one woman from Gabriel Eddings Plantation had been brought from Africa. Her face was tattooed and she was one of the more "vigorous stock."[93] It is quite possible that this African Community existed since the time of slavery and had preserved a continued African presence as reflected in burial custom, cosmology, basketry, handicraft, and folklore.

In 1893, the local population was very African in their own cultural heritage. Nevertheless the people on the Wallace Plantation were identified as Africans. "Dem people dat can give you moe history dey all gon' now. Dem people on de Wallace Plantation dey we're Africans and I kno' dis to be true. Dey were da people dat know all about Africa and African tings. Dey all gon' now dey wuz wiped out when de storm uh 1893 came."[94]

The fact that the Wallace Plantation was the only plantation with people identified as "Africans" on St. Helena by the local people suggests that Mr. Wallace was in the illegal smuggling business. This suggestion is also substantiated by the State Stature which revealed that L. R. Wallace, on February 19, 1829, incurred penalties for slave trading.[95] During the Civil War, when the white planters fled the Sea Islands before the invading Union troops, the enslaved Africans who lived on the plantation refused to relinquish it, having nowhere else to go. It was then that the Sea Island Blacks began to cultivate the land for themselves. Hundreds more joined the Union Army as part of the First South Carolina Volunteers. On January 16, 1865, General William Tecumseh Sherman issued his famous military decree, Special Field Order No. 15, which set aside "the islands from Charleston South [and] the abandoned rice fields along the river for thirty miles back from the sea"[96] for the freed slaves, who received an average of ten acres of farmland each. Many of those who had been smuggled in prior to 1858 remained on the Wallace Plantation up to the time of the devastation of the storm of 1893.

Time in the Gullah Experience

Americans of African descent in the South Carolina Sea Islands share another major cultural trait which can be directly linked to their African ancestors—their concept of time. Since the majority of Africans coming into South Carolina came from both West and Central Africa, examples of time perception are taken from these areas. However, this concept is shared by the entire African continent and within the African Diaspora in the New World. In other words, many people of color seem to have a common cultural perception of time.

In the Sea Islands, as in Africa, time is episodic and is associated with the forces of nature, the seasons: lunar and solar cycles, and so on.[97] Common climatic factors, particularly the hot, humid Carolina summers, have reinforced the general pace and style of life. From this viewpoint, events are used as dates and are recalled chronologically. Among the Gullah existed historical time, using memorable events such as "de Big Gun Shoot," that is the Civil War, to mark distance in time from the past, present and future. Locational time used the distance from plantations to approximate time, sacred and religious time, and human time.

The Gullah concept of time was strongly rooted in the African concept of time and history. To the Sea Islanders, time is ecological and measured by natural phenomena. Time is based on the natural cycle of nature, and history is episodically based on major events in life. Major events are used as benchmarks for historic time. That is, in African society we can divide time into four categories: ecological time, periodic time, episodic time, and eternal time. Ecological time refers to the environment and time as recorded from natural calamities such as crop failure due to droughts and so forth.

Periodic time records events which occur and reoccur at certain intervals. For example, in West Africa, the Igbo note that locust comes and destroys the crops at four-year intervals. The Igbo record time in reference to this periodic event as history is recalled and retold in relation to the coming of the locust at specific intervals.

A precise time or date is irrelevant because history is remembered in terms of major events. According to John Mbiti, time in African societies is referenced by major episodic events:[98] wars, eclipses, or reigns of former kings. Shany O Munsukhan, Khen Musu, and Shaka are used as markers to recall and record history in the oral tradition.[99] Likewise, a person's age group is also determined from the nearest major event occurring when persons of that age were born.

History in the Sea Islands is essentially African in nature. As one informant put it, "Mine history is what I know and what I had been told."[100] In the African context, history is recorded and retold from generation to generation. In the Sea Islands, history is oral and is recalled in reference to the time of day. Morning "Day Clean" (which is Tshilluba idiom carried over into Gullah from Kutoka Kulu meaning clean sky); Midday, and "fus Night" coming. Among the Gullah, the future, present, and the past are related to natural cycles, such as planting, harvesting, day, and night. Time is not static but cyclical and moves with nature, not apart from it.

Reinforcing this cyclical concept of time in nature, Mrs. Maggie Smalls, a midwife who was trained to time the contractions of women in labor, relied on the physical signs of nature for a time reference. An infallible source was the tide. "Babies are only born on the flood tide," and regardless of the statement of the pregnant woman, she made no attempts to deliver a child if the tide was not in flood stage. She objected to the various instruments used by doctors to deliver children because they are unnatural and more children are lost this way than by nature. "Women get her [sic] baby by nature, I let the baby come by nature." Being at one with the environment and nature, she utilized the tides as a timing device.[101]

The Gullah oral tradition recorded a visit by President Abraham Lincoln to Frogmore in 1863. The old people still claim they can identify the very site and oak tree where President Lincoln spoke.[102] One informant, Sam Doyle, remembered what his great-grandfather told him. "Pablo Rivers was mine great-grandfather, and he told us that Lincoln came and spoke on the Island where Highway 21 is located today before he was inducted into the Union army. I kno' dis to because he told me. He was a soldier in the Civil War—a corporal. He was recruited from the Island here. He told us the story of Lincoln."[103]

In the Kongo, "truth" is what has been transmitted by the ancestors as having really happened.[104] According to Edith Dabbs, President Lincoln had issued an official proclamation for the first time to the thousands of ex-slaves gathered to hear it on a platform under an immense live oak tree.[105] Thomas Wentworth Higginson, commander of the Black Regiment in the Sea Islands, wrote that he received the President's Second Message of Emancipation and he read it to the men.[106]

Obviously, this oral testimony either became corrupted in time or the event was misunderstood by the ancestor. In this case, Pablo Rivers, who heard Lincoln's message being read, apparently made no separation between Lincoln and his words. The testimony was correct in that Lincoln's message was heard, recorded, and passed on to future generations. In other words, the process of oral transmission remained African in that Lincoln's words were as representative as the person. The fact that Rivers did not heard Lincoln personally was irrelevant. The words were Lincoln's and that was recorded. Who said them was not important. A good example of this process works in the African context is found in an interview with a Vai person in regard to the transmission of the history of Borkeza. According to him [they] "told my father, and he told me. . . . So our people, our old-old people, they talked about Borkeza, and we heard it. Even at the time of the war with the Gola that people talk about, I was too small to remember anything, when the old people talked about it, we listened and that's how I know about it today."[107]

The great devastation caused by the tidal wave and hurricane which hit St. Helena Island in 1893, destroying crops and livestock and killing over two thousand people, was also a major event, and remembered by Gullah as a reference point in historical time, part of the living history of the Gullahs.[108] The velocity of the wind prevented them from talking refuge on the limbs of the trees, and in the darkness of night they drowned and were never seen again.[109] Ben Mack, the oldest man on the Island at 105, died in 1984, but before he died, he passed the event to the Penn Center, recording them in a song, recounting all the things that were destroyed by the storm.[110]

Remembered in relationship to the storm of 1911 was an African, turnip-like vegetable called Tania by the local people, which disappeared after this storm. "We had an old-fashioned thing that came from Africa called Tania. . . . It had elephant ear-like leaf and on the bottom was something like turnip. . . . It came from Africa, mine Ma Ma used to grow it. . . . This crop vanished after the 1911 storm. Everything vanished and it don't grow no more."[111]

In the Sea Islands, the people also were familiar with Tania. One informant interviewed in regard to African-born remembered that he [the African] "ate funny kine uh food. Roas wile locus an mushruhm an Tanya root. It lak elephant-eah and tase like Irish potatuh."[112] In identifying this African root plant we know that Tania is a root plant that appears to be indigenous to Central Africa. There are two known varieties; old coco-yam (colocasia antiquorum) called Tania in Central Africa, eddo in the West Indies, koko in Ghana, and in Nigeria. Coco-yam (Tania) probably originated in the Kongo basin as one the indigenous foodstuffs. The earliest citation in reference to Tania on the African continent was made by the Portuguese in the fifteenth century.[113] The other variety is called coco-yam Tania (*Xanthosoma Sagitifolium*).[114]

The Gullah also calculated their age in a manner similar to that of their African ancestors. Age was not numerically calculated but was recorded in relationship to episodic events such as the "Big Gun Shoot." The "Big Gun Shoot" was "de fust gun what shoot on Hilton Head edurin' de Civil war." For example, when the census was being taken the Gullah replied to inquiry about how old they were as follows: "Well Ma'am I can't rightly tell, but I tell you dis when gun shoot—." This meant she was born during the Civil War. Another replied, "When gun shoot I bin so leetle I tink it bin tunder." "I bin jest big 'nuf to tie de cow out." Another ex-slave remembered that, "I birth de berry day gun shoot. I bin a grown 'oman wid chillum." Another ex-slave admitted that, "Dey nebber did told me ma age Ma'am, but when gun shoot I ben a leetle bot in shirt tail." They remembered the "Big Gun Shoot" days and record their ages from that important event in their lives.[115]

Eva L. Ver Dier, who took the Census among the Gullah in 1932, noted that "the coastal Negro does not date time by Anno Domini, but from events of great excitement of danger." Instead of "gun shoot" days the "younger ones reckon from the 1886 earthquake and still younger ones from the 1893 storm when over 2,000 of them lost their lives in this section."[116]

Eternal time is part of nature. Eternal time is unity of time with nature where the past, present and future are seen as part of a continuum. Eternal time never ends because it always renews itself. It is symbolized by the rising and the setting of the sun and by the change from night to day respectively.

The concept of time in the Sea Islands is a direct Africanism. Oral history is how Africans for centuries kept their culture intact by passing on the history of their ancestors to new generations. In West Africa, south of the Sahara, there was no "history" or tradition of writing in an indigenously invented script until the Vai developed writing in the eighteenth century. This oral history tradition is characteristic of pre-literate societies that included black Americans during the slavery period. Preserved by a process of oral tradition were the numerous folktales, folksongs, and basket-weaving techniques that were transmitted from generation to generation, and the like. After the black spirituals developed from the African tradition of call-to-response pattern, they were preserved by slaves through oral tradition until Emancipation.[117] Legislation preventing blacks from learning how to read and write reinforced the importance of oral history and actually helped to preserve this African tradition. As a result of this tradition, black Americans today are an oral people and because of this emphasis writing and reading skills have been substituted by strong oral skills.

Today on the island of St. Helena these old plantation locations are now used to measure time and distance. For example, "I am going to Tombee" translates location, time, and measurement of distance. One person related that "when I tell my wife that I am going to Wallace Plantation she knows that I will be gone for 40 minutes because it takes 20 minutes there and 20 minutes back by auto."[118] The local population still identifies the area according to the old plantation location. There are about fifty plantation locations used to locate distance and the time it will take to arrive at a given point and location. The plantations include: Corner's Plantation, Coffin Plantation, Cedar Grove, Pine Grove, (Thomas Aston Coffin) (Robert) Fuller Plantation, Oak Plantation, 66 Acres, Eustis Plantation, Hazel Farm, Wallace Plantation, Tombee (Tom B. Chaplin) Jenkins' Croof, Cuffie, Mary Jenkins, Daniel Jenkins, William Jenkins, (Gabriel) Caspers, Edding Point, (Joseph D. Eddings) Hope's, Pope Plantation (Joseph J. Pope) Edgar Fripp, Oliver Fripp Plantation, John Fripp, Tom Fripp, and Ann Fripp to name a few.

Melville Herskovits noted that C.P.T.—"Colored Peoples' Time"—was not disregarded for punctuality but that it was an approximation of time rather than punctuality.[119] For example, if an event was scheduled to start at 8 P.M., that meant some time between 8 and 10 P.M. This was strongly rooted in the African concept of time, referred to in Africa as "African Time." There is no abstract numbering of time because time is eternal. The numbering of time was a European introduction into African society.[120] As we have seen, African descendants in the New World reckon time in a similar way.

Summary

Oral tradition, folktales, folksongs, and spirituals were vital in retaining African influence from generation to generation. The slaves used their spirituals as a vehicle of communication. In other words, they had a dual function as an information center, a kind of "grapevine system of communication."

The Gullah, like their African ancestors, acknowledge time as an unbroken circle. From birth, adulthood to death is the completion of life's circle. Death, as in the African context, is not final but a new beginning; unlike the European, conception is a final act that expresses a break with community of the living. In the Gullah concept of time in the circle of life the dead still have an impact on the community of the living as in to the African ancestral cults. South Carolina's Ministers continually invoke the spirits of the dead and those who have passed on because their "presence is still felt."[121] In other words, there exists continuity between the community of the living and the dead. For as long as an ancestor [a person] can be remembered he or she will continue to have an impact on the community of the living.

Also, the oral transmission of one's lineage is extremely important in the Sea Islands, as it is in the African tradition. Kinship is most often established through oral transmission as opposed to birth certificates. In short, one is expected to know his or her family lineage. Younger persons often undergo seemingly intense interrogation by Island residents who might wish to know their family affiliation. This is how kinship relationships have been established and this gives a sense of community over time.

Africanisms in South Carolina, Georgia, and Florida are direct cultural links to the traditions and history of Africa. The various ethnic groups depending on their numbers, either absorbed the less represented groups, or were assimilated by the larger cultural groups, specifically the Bantu. In spite of this blending over time, distinct African characteristic from each ethnic group survived, at least to some extent; this is evidenced in the language, rituals, and crafts of the African Americans from the Sea Islands. The concept of time and the oral tradition are common to all tribal groups; a shared heritage that survived the Middle Passage and gave a sense of continuity and kinship to a culturally uprooted and enslaved people. Today, some four hundred years after the slave trade, despite acculturation into mainstream America, the African link is still manifested in many ways in the lifestyle and culture of the Gullah people of the Sea Islands, where Africa is still present in the life of the and culture of the people.

Conclusion

The sacred world of the Gullah has revealed how the forgotten African has contributed to the worlds of the slave and master and provided a bridge for African Americans and linkage with their African past. Today Brer Rabbit belongs to white culture as much as black, but Uncle Remus kept Brer Rabbit alive in the Sea Islands. Southern social etiquette, particularly the use of terms of endearment such as "uncle" and "aunty" crossed the Atlantic with the enslaved African and found roots in the Sea Islands. The use of such terms no longer distinguishes black from white but is now an important part of southern culture. Many years ago, Melville J. Herskovits was the first to recognize how African culture transformed and gave definition to American culture, and discovered that this cultural exchange process was mutual and reciprocal: Africans assimilated white culture, and meanwhile planters were adopting African customs and practices, including agricultural methods such as rice cultivation, and cuisine ("southern cooking"), open grazing of cattle, and use of herbal medicines and other procedures to cure and treat disease such as smallpox. Herskovits concluded that African culture influenced the United States in four areas: speech, social etiquette, cuisine, and religion. Today, we know much more about how American life in those areas has been affected, and we are discovering the location and nature of African origins for what has now become fully "American."

For example, the African family structure was reorganized by the master class. Planters adopted the African practice of polygamy for themselves and for the most part demanded that the enslaved African remain monogamous when it suited the needs of the master in regards to competition for enslaved women on the plantation. In addition, African Americans were not permitted to continue their African secret societies, so they formed new societies that carried out the function of their African originals. In Africa the purpose of secret societies was to keep certain traditions, culture, histories, and secret information only among its members like the *Sande* and *Poro* societies in Liberia. These societies in Africa conformed to requirements of meeting certain social and religious needs of the community at the time of death and final burials.

Among the Gullahs these African societies were reorganized as burial societies with the purpose of taking care of the sick and dying and providing proper burial for the dead. The Bantu of Central Africa played a dominant role in the culture of the Sea Islands. For example, the "ring shout," the importance of the use of water in black Baptist churches, and the fusion of African belief of "spirits" into an Afro-Christianity in which African religious beliefs and Christianity blended and found new life in the "Pentecostal" experience.

Even the African concept of time found its way into southern "timelessness" and slow pace of life, explaining in part a southern interpretation of time that is strongly rooted in the African concept of time. We can conclude that much which is "American" was at one time "African."

Notes

1. E. Franklin Frazier, *The Negro Church in America* (New York: Schocken Books, 1963).

2. Guion Griffs Johnson, *A Social History of the Sea Island with Special Reference to St. Helena Island* (North Carolina: University of North Carolina Press, 1930), p. 137.

3. Melville Herskovits, *The Myth of the Negro Past* (Boston: Beacon Press, 1941), pp. 181–82.

4. Norman E. Whitten, Jr., and John F. Szwed, eds., *Afro American Anthropology: Contemporary Perspective* (New York: Free Press, 1974), p. 235.

5. Op. cit., Johnson, pp. 140–41.

6. George Peter Murdock, *Africa: Its Peoples and Their Culture History* (New York: McGraw-Hill, 1959), p. 26.

7. A[lfred] R[eginald] Radcliffe-Brown and Daryll Forde, eds., *African System of Kinship and Marriage* (London, New York: Published for the International African Institute by Oxford University Press, 1950).

8. J. Herman Blake, "New Perspectives on the Black Family Heritage" (Santa Cruz, 1977). Unpublished manuscript. I am grateful to J. Herman Blake for giving me the opportunity to consult his unpublished manuscript and his endless discussion of his Sea Island experiences and contacts. Also, I am thankful for the assistance of his brother—once I arrived in Beaufort, South Carolina, the Rev. J. Henry Blake looked out for me and showed me the island. Without their assistance, this research would have been very difficult.

9. Field notes on Ladies Island, St. Helena, and Hilton Head, South Carolina. Jan. 16, 1984, p. 19.

10. Newbell Niles Puckett, *Folk Beliefs of the Southern Negro* (Chapel Hill: University of North Carolina Press; London: H. Milford, 1926), p. 23.

11. J. Stewart, *A View of the Past and Present State of the Island of Jamaica* (Edinburgh: Oliver and Boyd, 1823), p. 250.

12. Orlando Patterson, *The Sociology of Slavery: An Analysis of the Origins, Development and Structure of Negro Slave Society in Jamaica* (London: MacGibbon and Kee, 1967), p. 150.

13. James Kelly, *Voyage to Jamaica and Seventeen Years' Residence in the Island* (Belfast: n.p., 1838), p. 150.

14. Ibid.

15. Op. cit., Patterson, p. 19.

16. George P. Rawick, *The American Slave: A Composite Autobiography*, vol. 3, South Carolina Narratives, parts 3 and 4 (Westport, Conn.: Greenwood, 1977), p. 65.

17. *Drum and Shadows: Survival Studies among the Georgia Coastal Negroes* (Athens: University of Georgia Press, 1940), p. 179.

18. Ibid., p. 106.

19. Op. cit., Puckett, p. 8.

20. Francis Le Jau to S. P. G., Nov. 15, 1708, S. P. G. Ms. A 4 No. 125, pp. 345-46.

21. Francis Le Jau to S. P. G., Nov. 15, 1708, A4 No. 91, p. 236.

22. Carter G. Woodson, *The African Background Outlined or Handbook for the Study of the Negro* (Washington, D.C.: Association for the Study of Negro Life and History, 1936), p. 170.

23. Op. cit., Herskovits, p. 162.

24. Op. cit., Woodson, p. 170.

25. W. E. B. Du Bois, ed., "Economic Cooperation Among Negro Americans," Atlanta University Publication No. 12 (Atlanta, 1907), p. 92.

26. Personal interview with Emory Campbell on St. Helena at the Penn Center, Jan. 1984.

27. William R. Bascom, "Acculturation among the Gullah Negroes," American Anthropology [n.s., 43 1941], p. 48.

28. Personal interview with the Dale Senior Citizen Center in Beaufort County, Jan. 1984.

29. Personal interview with St. Helena Citizen Center in Frogmore, S.C., Jan. 31, 1984.

30. Ibid.

31. Guy Benton Johnson, *Folk Culture on St. Helena Island, South Carolina* (Hatboro, Pa.: Folklore Associate, 1930), p. 215.

32. "The Negro in Business and Professions," *Freedom's Journal*, Feb. 22, 1927, p. 141; Browning, "The Beginning of Insurance Enterprise among Negroes," pp. 417-19.

33. Today there are thirty-three black-owned burial societies located almost exclusively in southern states. They are: Afro-American Life Insurance Co., Jacksonville, Fla.; American Woodmen's Life Insurance Co., Denver, Colo.; Atlanta Life Insurance Co., Shreveport, La.; Benevolent Life Insur-

ance Co., Shreveport, La.; Booker T. Washington Insurance Co., Birmingham, Ala.; Bradfort's Industrial Insurance Co., Birmingham, Ala.; Central Life Insurance Co. of Florida, Tampa, Fla.; Chicago Metropolitan Mutual Assurance Co., Chicago, Ill.; Christian Benevolent Insurance Co., Inc., Mobile, Ala.; Certude Geddes Willis Life Insurance Co., New Orleans, La.; Golden Circle Life Insurance Co., Brownsville, Tenn.; Lighthouse Life Insurance Co., Shreveport, La.; Lovett's Life and Burial Insurance Co., Mobile, Ala.; Majestic Life Insurance Co., New Orleans, La.; North Carolina Mutual Life Insurance Co., Durham, N.C.; Peoples Progressive Insurance Company, Rayville, La.; Pilgrim Health and Life Insurance Co., Protective Industrial Ins. Co. of Ala., Birmingham, Ala.; Purple Shield Life Insurance Co., Baton Rouge, La.; Reliable Life Insurance Co., Monroe, La.; Security Life Insurance Co. of South Jackson, Miss.; Southern Aid Life Insurance Co., Phoenix, Arizona; Virginia Mutual Benefit Life Insurance Co., Richmond, Va.; Winston Mutual Life Insurance Co., Winton-Salem, N.C.; and Wright Mutual Insurance Co., Detroit, Mich.

34. Op. cit., Browning, p. 419.

35. Personal interview with Mr. Sam Doyle on the Island of St. Helena, Jan. 19, 1984.

36. Ibid.

37. P. Maury Talbot, *Tribes of the Niger Delta: Their Religion and Customs* (London: Cass, 1932), p. 232.

38. Ibid.

39. Elizabeth Ware Pearson, ed., *Letters from Port Royal, 1862–1868* (New York: Arno Press and New York Times, 1969), pp. 253–54; Towne Diary, pp. 64–75; Folklore Project no. 1655 D-4-27 W.R.A. SC:28.

40. Pearson, "Port Royal," pp. 253–54.

41. Ibid., p. 252; Irving E. Lowrey, *Life on the Old Plantation* (Columbia: University of North Carolina Press, 1911), pp. 81–83; Folklore Project nos. 1655 and 1855 D-4-27 W.P.A. SC: 28.

42. Op. cit., Herskovits, p. 202.

43. Op. cit., Chatelain, p. 17.

44. Interview with Mr. Leroy E. Brown at the Penn Center, Jan. 1984.

45. Op. cit., Drum, pp. 62–63.

46. Duncan Clinch Heyward, *Seed from Madagascar* (Chapel Hill: University of North Carolina Press, 1937), p. 88.

47. Op. cit., Drum, p. 77.

48. William Bosman, *Description of the Coast of Guinea: Divided into the Gold, the Slave and Ivory Coast,* printed for F. Knapton, A. Bell, R. Smith, D. Midwinter, W. Han, W. Davis, C. Strahan, B. Lintoll, T. Round, and F. Wale, 1705, p. 232.

49. C. K. Meek, *A Sudanese Kingdom and Ethnographical Study of the Jukun-*

Speaking Peoples of Nigeria (London: Kegan Paul, Trench, Trubner and Co., 1931), p. 228.

50. Theodore Chinedum Opara was born in Umukwe, Ndegbelu Awaka, and Owerri on October 2, 1950, and he met his untimely death in a tragic car accident in Los Angeles at the intersection of Vermont Avenue and 43rd Street. He was given one funeral in Los Angeles and his body was taken three months later to Owerri, Nigeria, for his final resting place. In Nigeria he was given several funerals and his body was placed in his bed in his room until he was interred.

51. Op. cit., communication with Mr. Sam Doyle.

52. Op. cit., Drum, pp. 58–59.

53. Op. cit., Sam Doyle.

54. Op. cit., Drum, p. 4.

55. Lawton, "Religious Life," p. 213.

56. Edward Geoffrey Parrinder, *West African Psychology: A Comparative Study of Psychological and Religious Thought* (London: Lutterworth Press, 1951), pp. 17–18.

57. Basden, Niger Ibos, p. 275.

58. Newbell Niles Puckett, *Folk Beliefs of the Southern Negro* (Chapel Hill: University of North Carolina Press; London: H. Milford, 1926), p. 105.

59. The author observed this at an old slave grave site on the Coffin Point Plantation and on the Island of Coosaw in 1984.

60. Communication with the Secretary at the Penn Center in South Carolina in January of 1984.

61. Op. cit., Drum, p. 59.

62. Op. cit., Glave, 1893, p. 397.

63. E. J. Glave, "Fetishism in Congo Land." One of Stanley's pioneer officers. *Century Magazine* 19 (1896), p. 208.

64. Heli Chatelain, "Angolan Customs," *Journal of Folklore* 9 (1896), p. 17.

65. Wilfred Hambly, *The Ovimbundu of Angola* (New York: Kraus Reprint Co., 1968), p. 208.

66. Torian, 1943, p. 353.

67. Thompson, 1969, p. 352.

68. Personal communication with George McMillian in Progmore, South Carolina at the Coffin Point Manson. Note: According to Dr. Archibald Johnson (1819–93), a long-time resident of Beaufort wrote an article in the *Beaufort Republican*, January 23, 1873, explaining how enslaved Africans made tappy. Tabby or tappy is an artificial stone or concrete used extensively, at one time, on the Sea Islands as a substitute for brick and stone in the construction of houses, foundation indigo-vats, and cisterns of all kinds, as well as sea-walls, fortification, and so on. It is composed of shell lime, sand, and drifts or dead oyster shells in the proportions of one part, by measure, of

lime, two of sand, and four to six of shells: quality of the latter depending upon the strength of lime and quality of the sand.

69. Vlach, 1978, p. 143.

70. Communication with Winifred K. Vass.

71. William Bascom.

72. Ibid.

73. Op. cit., Herskovits, "Myth of the Negro Past."

74. Op. cit., Sam Doyle.

75. Interview with Sam Doyle, South Carolina, St. Helena, 1984.

76. Claude and Pat Sharpe, local linguists living in the areas, witnessed this custom taking place at a local funeral. They refused to identify the individual. Later, I found out that the individual in question was the Reverend Green, the minister of the historic Brick Baptist Church. His stepfather had died, and at his funeral this custom was observed because his grandchildren, who were very close to him, saw his spirit at the moment of his death. One granddaughter told Rev. Greene that granddaddy had just died. He phoned his mother and found out that his stepfather had indeed died. He consulted the elders of the community in regard to what it all meant. They instructed him that this was an extremely serious matter, and that at the funeral the children would have to be passed over the coffin in order to separate their spirits from that of the grandfather. I interviewed Rev. Greene about this important matter, and he informed me that "when in doubt you always observed the custom, so you don't have to worry later by second guessing."

77. Personal interview with Rev. Ervin L. Greene Jr. in Beaufort, S.C., pastor of the historic Brick Baptist Church, on Jan. 16, 1984.

78. Ibid.

79. Interview with Ruby Iyman, who was born in Opobo, Nigeria (River States), on Jan. 1, 1954. She was interviewed in 1984 at the University of California at Los Angeles.

80. Ibid.

81. W. Robert Higgins, "The Geographical Origins of Negro Slaves in Colonial South Carolina," pp. 40–41.

82. Elizabeth Donnan, *Documents Illustrative of the History of the Slave Trade to America: Volume IV The Border Colonies and the Southern Colonies* (Washington, D.C.: Carnegie Institution of Washington, 1935), p. 588.

83. Ibid., p. 21.

84. Personal interview with Mrs. Elizabeth Glenn, South Carolina, St. Helena, January 1984.

85. Op. cit., Herskovits, p. 214.

86. Ibid.

87. Ibid.

88. Op. cit., Mrs. Maggie Smalls interview.

89. Op. cit., Sam Doyle, 1984 field interview.

90. Personal interview with Mrs. Bernice Brooks in Los Angeles on Aug. 3, 1983.

91. Juanita Jackson, Sabra Slaughter, and J. Herman Blake, "New Research in Black Culture: The Sea Islands as a Cultural Resource," in *Black Scholar* (Mar. 1, 1974); Du Bois, *Suppression of the Transatlantic Trade to the United States of America 1638–1870* (New York: Schocken Books, 1896), p. 181.

92. Personal communication with Emory Campbell, Director of the Penn Center on the Island of St. Helena. Interview conducted on Hilton Head Island in January 1984.

93. Laura Towne, Diary (Southern Historical Collection, University of North Carolina, Chapel Hill N.C.); Rupert S. Holland, *Letters and Diary of Laura M. Towne, written from the Sea Islands of South Carolina, 1862–1884* (New York: Negro Universities Press, 1969 [Riverside Press, 1912]); Laura Town miscellaneous.

94. Op. cit., interview with Sam Doyle.

95. Op. cit., Du Bois, p. 129.

96. Patricia Jones-Jackson, *When Roots Die: Endangered Traditions* (Athens: University of Georgia Press, 1987), p. x.

97. Jan Vansina, *Oral Tradition: A Study in Historical Methodology* (London: Routledge & Paul, 1961).

98. John S. Mbiti, *African Religions and Philosophy* (Garden City, N.Y.: Anchor Books, 1970), p. 24.

99. Personal communication with John Singler, July 26, 1984, from his interview with Carolina, a settler (Americo-Liberian), in Farmersville, Sinoe County, Liberia, on May 6, 1980. The settler community of African Americans separated themselves from the indigenous Africans by identifying themselves as "Americo-Liberians," meaning "Americans."

100. Personal interview with Mr. Sam Doyle on the Island of St. Helena on Jan. 19, 1984.

101. Interview with Mrs. Maggie Smalls on St. Helena, Frogmore, S.C., and Jan. 19, 1984; also found in J. Herman Black, "'Doctor Can't Do Me No Good': Social Concomitants of Health Care Attitude and Practices among Elderly Black in Isolated Rural Populations." Presented at the National Conference on the Black Aged. Washington, D.C., May 27, 1977, p. 11.

102. Personal communication with Sam Doyle, Elizabeth Glenn, and Maggie Smalls of St. Helena, Jan. 19, 1984.

103. Op. cit., interview, Sam Doyle.

104. Op. cit., Vansina, p. 103.

105. Edith M. Dabbs, *Sea Island Diary: A History of St. Helena Island* (Spartanburg, S.C.: Reprint Co., 1983), p. 171.

106. Thomas Wentworth Higginson, *Army Life in a Black Regiment* (Boston, 1890), p. 40; reprinted by Beacon Press, 1962.

107. Interview with Pinter, a Vai in Robertsport, Grand Cape Mount County, conducted by Boakai Zolunua, on Nov. 29, 1980.

108. Op. cit., Sam Doyle; Elizabeth Glenn; Maggie Smalls. According to Dabbs's *Sea Island Diary,* the total number of residents that died in the storm was three thousand.

109. Duncan Clinch Heyward, *Seed from Madagascar* (Chapel Hill: University of North Carolina Press, 1937), p. 122.

110. Recording master tape Mr. Ben Mack, August 1972. Penn Community Center Tape Archive. St. Helena, Frogmore, S.C.

111. Op. cit., Sam Doyle.

112. *Drum and Shadow: Survival Studies among the Georgia Coastal Negroes.* Savannah Unit, Georgia Writers' Project, Work Projects Administration (Athens: University of Georgia Press, 1940), p. 71.

113. Sir Harry Johnston, *George Grenfell and the Congo* (London: Hutchinson Co., 1908), vol. II, p. 600.

114. Frederick Robert Irvine, *A Text-Book of West African Agriculture, Soils and Crops* (London: Humphrey Milford, Oxford University Press, 1934), pp. 135–41.

115. Eva L. Ver Dier, "When Gun Shoot: Some Experiences While Taking the Census Among the Low Country Negroes of South Carolina," Beaufort Township Library, Beaufort, S.C., 1932, pp. 3–4.

116. Ibid.

117. Jacqueline Cogdell Dje Dje, *American Black Spiritual and Gospel Songs From Southeast Georgia: A Comparative Study* (Los Angeles: Center for African American Studies, University of California at Los Angeles, 1980).

118. Personal interview with Mr. Leroy Brown on St. Helena, Jan. 24, 1984.

119. Melville J. Herskovits, *The Myth of the Negro Past* (Boston: Beacon Press, 1941).

120. Personal communication with Professor Boniface I. Obichere at UCLA, Apr. 24, 1984.

121. Interview with Reverend Ervin L. Greene, pastor of the historic Brick Baptist Church in Beaufort, S.C., Jan. 16, 1984.

Eight

African Religious Retentions in Florida

Robert L. Hall

Knotty issues in African American culture and religion are raised by an examination of the religious experiences of blacks living in Florida from the founding of St. Augustine in 1565 through the early twentieth century. This essay addresses the cultural distinctiveness of African Americans by placing spirit possession and ritual ecstatic dance at the heart of the controversy over African survivals in the United States.

Because the cultural transformation of African Americans is best viewed as a dynamic process that occurred over a long period, a consideration of the eighteenth century is critical to an understanding of the relevance of African cultures to American culture. But the bulk of the essay describes African survivals in nineteenth-century Florida. Although ritual scarification, naming practices, magical beliefs, and material culture are mentioned, emphasis is on ecstatic religious ritual, musical styles, and funeral rites. This analysis regards religion as the matrix of nineteenth-century African American life and the centerpiece of African cultural influences in Florida.

Revisiting a Controversy

When African American religious life is discussed, two troublesome and interlocking concerns usually emerge. First is the question of the degree to which African culture survived in slave communities. Second, and closely linked, is the question of whether slave religion was essentially docile or rebellious. Too often, as David E. Stannard observed, the confrontation of these issues by historians has come with a "sharply dichotomous approach": a given element of antebellum or postbellum black American culture either is or is not African.[1] Such an approach creates several problems. The assumption that a particular aspect of black culture can be neatly pigeonholed as either African or European in origin obscures a fundamental similarity in the general pattern of the cultures of Africa and Europe that anthropologist William R. Bascom believed "justifies the concept of an Old World Area which includes both Europe and Africa."[2] This approach also obscures the cultural blending process that Melville J. Herskovits illuminated.[3]

One unconquered problem of the African survivals theory advanced by Herskovits is identifying, as precisely as possible, the cultural and geographical core areas in Africa that are relevant to the particular local New World black populations being studied. That is where earlier theorists went astray or were stymied by the truncated state of African historical studies in the United States at the time they were working. A significant part of the problem derives from imprecise or shifting labeling of the coastal and geographical areas from which the African ancestors of United States blacks came. Some writers and speakers who say that the African ancestors of black Americans came from "West Africa" mean the entire Atlantic coast from the Senegal River to Angola. Others envision the same area but then proceed to cite ethnographic examples only from the area between the Senegal River and the Cameroons, omitting Kongo-Angola almost entirely, as did George P. Rawick.[4] But recent research has shown that Angola and the Kongo are relevant to studying retentions, not only in the Caribbean and Brazil but also in the southern United States. Robert Farris Thompson, citing linguistic and artistic evidence, raised serious questions about the primacy of Dahomean and Yoruba groups in the New World and suggested that Kongolese and Angolan influences were scarcely less important in either South America or the United States.[5] As Bennetta Jules-Rosette suggested, "many of the ambiguities concerning African musical retentions may be clarified when the Central African cultural complex [as distinguished from the narrowest definition of West Africa] is viewed as a source for Black American expressive form."[6] Linguistic evidence and data summarizing the origins of African newcomers to the lower South during the middle of the eighteenth century suggest that Central African Bantu influences were more prominent in the coastal zones of Florida, Georgia, and South Carolina than heretofore recognized.[7]

The study of African American religious practices and magical beliefs is central to the controversy over African cultural retentions. In *The Myth of the Negro Past*, Herskovits wrote that "African religious practices and magical beliefs are everywhere to be found in some measure as recognizable survivals, and are in every region more numerous than survivals in other realms of culture," such as material aspects of life and political orientation.[8] In Herskovits's scheme of things, then, if one cannot find African survivals or influences in African American religious practices and magical beliefs one cannot find them anywhere. Although subsequent research by historical archaeologists has forced reconsideration of Herskovits's statement that "Africanisms in material aspects of life are almost lacking," it remains accurate to say that religion constitutes the centerpiece of his tapestry of African survivals.

The Eighteenth Century

As Mechal Sobel indicated, "it seems fairly clear that during the eighteenth century large enclaves of several tribal peoples existed from Maryland south, although among each group many languages were spoken."[9] Eighteenth-century planters in the lower South had clear ethnic preferences among African groups and appear to have attached a greater importance to origins than did their counterparts in the Chesapeake area.[10] Ira Berlin argued persuasively that during the seventeenth and eighteenth centuries three distinctive slave systems evolved in North America: the northern nonplantation system, the Chesapeake Bay plantation system, and the Carolina and Georgia low-country plantation system. According to Berlin, "The mass of black people, however, remained physically separated and psychologically estranged from the Anglo-American world and culturally closer to Africa than any other blacks on continental North America." Low-country blacks, Berlin argued,

> incorporated more of West African culture—as reflected in their language, religion, work patterns, and much else—into their new lives than did other black Americans. Throughout the eighteenth century and into the nineteenth century, low country blacks continued to work the land, name their children, and communicate through word and song in a manner that openly combined African traditions with the circumstances of plantation life.[11]

The experience of blacks in Florida during the colonial period was closer to Berlin's Carolina and Georgia low-country slave system than to the two other systems. Indeed, well into the nineteenth century several Florida slaveholders perceived a particular style of speech among slaves as "low country." It was said that Primus, a runaway from Conecuh County, Alabama, "speaks after the manner peculiar to most negroes raised in the low country."[12] Jacob, who escaped from E. T. Jankes in

Florida in 1841, spoke "thick like an African negro."[13] And John, a stout, dark-complexioned man who ran away from Gadsden County, Florida, in 1852, was described as "slow and low country spoken, having been raised in East Florida."[14]

The evidence provided by language and naming practices strongly supports Sobel's notion that "several African languages may well have survived the initial slave trade into the Americas."[15] The "Nine New Negroe Men" from the Gold Coast who were advertised for sale near Savannah in 1764 surely spoke their mother tongues.[16] Over one-fourth of the advertisements for runaways printed in the *Georgia Gazette* during 1765 indicated that the fugitives in question spoke no English.[17] Since over 40 percent of the African slaves who arrived in the British mainland colonies of North America between 1700 and 1775 arrived in South Carolina, the Carolina experience has direct relevance to the history of blacks living in Florida during the eighteenth century. Black fugitives from South Carolina and later Georgia established a maroon tradition in Florida that persisted well into the nineteenth century.[18] Other fugitives from colonial South Carolina sought and received asylum, nominal freedom, and Catholic religious instruction near St. Augustine during the first period of Spanish rule.[19] Fugitive blacks from the Carolinas and Georgia had been seeking and finding refuge in Florida since the late 1600s because, as John D. Milligan pointed out, the area's semitropical climate, sparse white settlement, and chronic political instability made it an ideal haven for runaway slaves.[20] Asserting the particularly aggressive character of the Florida maroon, Milligan concluded: "Quite clearly, if in the first place newly imported Africans had been encouraged by a propitious environment to found the maroon and to mold its activist character, once they had established the tradition, American-born fugitives took advantage of that same environment to continue the maroon."[21]

The peak of the colonial import trade in slaves was probably reached between 1764 and 1773, a period that overlaps nine of the twenty-one years of British occupation of Florida. More narrowly, more than eight thousand black newcomers were landed in Charleston alone between November 1, 1772, and September 27, 1773.[22] Thus the most recently purchased among the slaves brought to Florida by refugee Loyalists during the American Revolution were likely to have come directly from Africa. By 1767 Richard Oswald had more than one hundred blacks on his East Florida plantation, many of them shipped directly from Africa. Probably most of the Africans were secured through Charleston slave traders such as Henry Laurens.[23] It was in 1767 that the first cargo of seventy slaves arrived from Africa during the brief history of British

East Florida.[24] In the same year Governor James Grant estimated that six hundred slaves were working in the province.[25] Thus, even in the unlikely event that none of the remaining 530 slaves was born in Africa, not fewer than 11.7 percent of the blacks in East Florida in 1767 were shipped directly from Africa. Between 1764 and 1772 two ships from Africa arrived at St. Augustine (one in 1769 and the other in 1770).[26] Then on the night of November 18, 1773, the *Dover*, with one hundred Africans aboard, wrecked near New Smyrna, losing two mariners and about eighty Africans.[27] We also know that at least a few slaves residing in Pensacola in the 1760s and 1770s spoke African languages. A fugitive escaping Pensacola early in 1770 was described by his master as speaking African and Indian languages but no English.[28]

The persistence of African naming practices during the era of British control of East Florida (1763–84) underscores the probability that African religious patterns exerted continuing influence among St. Augustine's black population. J. Leitch Wright, Jr., was able to discover the names of fifty East Florida blacks from the British era, roughly half of whom were clearly of African origin, including Qua, who was publicly executed for robbery in St. Augustine in 1777. Qua was a popular West African day-name (Akan group) meaning male child born on Thursday.[29] Even as late as 1840 an occasional Ashanti day-name appears in advertisements for runaway slaves, including another Qua, who had "one front tooth a little shorter than others."[30]

When the government of East Florida was transferred back to the Spanish in 1784, 450 whites shifted their allegiance to the new Spanish government and remained in the colony. Remaining with them were two hundred blacks, who constituted the only surviving nucleus of an East Florida black population that may have numbered more than nine thousand at the peak of the Loyalist refugee period. The immediate geographical and cultural roots for most of them were in the English-speaking colonies of Georgia and South Carolina, especially the coastal region stretching from Cape Fear to Cumberland Sound. They partook of the creole cultures developed during the eighteenth century in those regions.

Evidence of the persistence of African naming practices during the second Spanish period is contained in a 1792 inventory of the estate of Dona Maria Evans, an Anglo-American who had migrated to Florida from South Carolina in 1763. The inventory listed a total of twenty blacks organized into three nuclear family units of four, six, and two members and eight unattached individuals. Some had African-sounding names: Zambo, Pender, Sisa, Fibi, Ebron, Congo.[31]

The eighteenth century, then, was not only the century in which the

United States was launched politically; it was also the incubation period for what some historical linguists have called the creolization of African American culture.[32] Religiously and intellectually the question of whether to convert the African and African American slaves to Christianity was a focal point of debate among white clergy and slave owners. Peter H. Wood took the importance of the eighteenth century one step further by suggesting that the controversy over African American conversion was also a topic of heated debate among African Americans themselves and hence constituted "a forgotten chapter in eighteenth-century southern intellectual history."[33]

The Nineteenth Century

In 1804 about fifty Africans, almost evenly divided between men and women, arrived in Florida and were settled on the St. John's River where their importer and owner, Zephaniah Kingsley, consciously eschewed the imposition of Christianity and other aspects of European culture. Kingsley, who generally purchased slaves directly from the African coast, adopted a policy of nonintervention in all areas of slave culture except manual training: "I never interfered with their connubial concerns, nor domestic affairs, but let them regulate these after their own manner."[34] If these Africans continued their native dances for a number of years after their arrival, as Kingsley asserted, the likelihood is great that they also continued African styles of worship. In fact, most of the "native dances" that they perpetuated probably emanated from their indigenous religious patterns.

Although "salt water Negroes" from Africa became less numerous following the official close of the overseas slave trade by the U.S. Congress in 1807, illegal importees from Africa continued to be found. Some of them entered the United States through Florida, which remained under Spanish control until 1821. In October 1812 Richard Drake, an Irish American and a U.S. citizen, made a slaving voyage from Rio Basso on the Windward Coast to Pensacola Bay.[35] During the waning years of Spanish jurisdiction over Florida, a considerable stir arose over slaving activities from Amelia Island. Toward the middle of January 1818, two privateers, carrying a combined total of 120 slaves, arrived at Amelia Island. A week later a committee of the U.S. House of Representatives issued a report on the illicit introduction of slaves into the United States from the island.[36]

Besides the black populations concentrated around St. Augustine and, to a lesser extent, Pensacola, there were maroons who had managed both to escape their owners in South Carolina and Georgia and to avoid the areas of Florida that were effectively controlled by the Spaniards. Large, quasi-permanent maroon communities thrived in border areas that generated international rivalry. Close relations that had developed between blacks and reds in Florida when it was a Spanish territory continued into the American period. These black fugitives frequently settled among the Indians of northern Florida, usually living in "Negro towns" associated with "Indian towns." Although sources describing their religious behavior are scarce, provocative linguistic clues to their cultural status exist in the form of Florida place names conventionally described as of unknown origin. The river and town of Aucilla are near the site of the old Negro Fort (now known as Fort Gadsden). Variant spellings include Assile, Agile, Axille, Aguil, Ochule, Ocilla, and Asile. Winifred Vass, for twelve years editor of one of the largest and oldest vernacular periodicals in Central Africa, suggested that Aucilla might derive from the Bantu verb *ashila*, which means "to build or construct a house for someone else."[37] Vass also suggested that the name of the Suwannee River might derive from the Bantu word *nsub-wanyi*, which means "my house, my home." A large black settlement along this river was destroyed in 1818 during the Seminole Wars. Perhaps as many as twelve hundred African American maroons were living in the Seminole towns by 1836. Because the black fugitives were better acquainted with the language, religion, and other facets of the ways of white folks than were their Indian hosts and nominal masters, the blacks served as cultural go-betweens for reds and whites. That this was the case in matters of religion is strongly suggested by the Reverend Simon Peter Richardson's stratagem of preaching to the blacks of an "Indian town" as a way of gaining missionary access to the Indians themselves, the principal aim of his visits.[38]

After Florida became a part of the United States in 1821, it was still not unusual to find Africans bearing "tribal" marks. In 1835, for instance, Charles, aged forty, who ran away from Henry W. Maxey near Jacksonville, bore "the African marks on his face of his country."[39] While some "illegal aliens" from Africa may have been shipped directly, others probably arrived in Florida in the clandestine Cuba-to-Florida trade. Despite wildly clashing estimates of the extent and significance of the trade, there is no doubt that some Africans bound for Cuba ended up in Florida. Milo, one of eight slaves transported to Florida on the schooner *Emperor* in 1838, said not only that he was from Africa but "that he was brought here from Havana."[40] There is also the example of the *lucumi* slave encountered by the Swedish novelist Fredrika Bremer during her visit to Florida in the 1850s. When Bremer asked the middle-aged African whether he had "come hither from Africa," he replied yes, "that he had been smuggled hither from Cuba many years ago."[41] Illegal slave trading persisted in South Carolina as late as 1858 with the arrival of the slave yacht *Wanderer*, and small parcels of its cargo of four hundred Africans were sold into Florida.[42]

The African roots of modern African American culture in Florida had been considerably decreased even as early as the Reconstruction era, especially as far as the continued presence of individuals who had actually been born in Africa was concerned. By the middle of this era we clearly are dealing primarily with a U.S.-born black population in Florida, as elsewhere in the South. Only eighty-eight African-born persons were enumerated in Florida in the 1870 U.S. census. Among the more elderly of these Africans was Jeff Martin, aged 102, who had been born around 1768 in some unidentifiable region of Africa. Martin, who resided in Jefferson County at the time of the census, was the sole black Floridian who listed his occupation as "root doctor." He was one of twelve African-born persons residing in Jefferson County in 1870. Of seventeen other Florida counties having African-born residents, only Leon had as many as twelve. Of the 9,645 blacks counted in the entire 1870 census who were born outside the United States, 1,984 (20.6 percent) were born in Africa. Eighty-eight (4.4 percent) of all the African-born residents of the United States in 1870 lived in Florida.[43] If Martin reached American shores at age ten, he would have arrived in 1778, the year Virginia outlawed the overseas slave trade. If he arrived between the ages of ten and twenty and if he arrived legally, he may have entered a port in Pennsylvania, Maryland, South Carolina, or Georgia, which abolished the overseas slave trade after Virginia did.

Martin was by no means the only practitioner of herbalism or the occult. Both before and after the Civil War black and white Christians were embedded in a cultural milieu in which "conjur" and other rural folk beliefs exercised considerable power. In her memoirs Ellen Call Long mentioned Delia, a slave who "began to droop at about age 18" and soon died.

After death the nurse (a character on every plantation), brought to my mother a small package of dingy cloth, in which was wrapped two or three rusty nails, a dog's tooth, a little lamb's wool, and a ball of clay. Trembling with awe, she said: "This is what killed Delia, ole Miss, I most knowed it was jest so. I most knowed as how she was conjured, and jest found dis under her matrass where she die."

On inquiry we found that she was the cause of jealousy to a companion negro girl, who had made threats towards her; and moreover, we learned, that every negro on the plantation had known all the time what power was at work upon Delia, but dared not, as they expressed it, "break the spell," for the evil spirit would have turned on the one that told it.[44]

The slaves on this Leon County plantation obviously believed in the potency of the medicine man who had cast the spell on Delia. If all others in this slave community knew of the spell, it is very likely that the victim also knew. The combination of knowledge that a root doctor was working magic against her and the belief in the power of such magic may have caused her literally to lay down and die. Such appears to be the case in voodoo death as described by anthropologist W. B. Cannon.[45]

Folk belief in sympathetic magic did not disappear overnight after the end of legal slavery. In an account set down in 1892, Ellen Call Long noted that "negro witchcraft" was thriving in Leon County during the early 1870s. The occasion for her observation was the tragic death of five black children between the ages of four and six.

Thus it was that near the end of the first decade of freedom to the negro, I saw one of the most remarkable exhibitions of superstition ever beheld by intelligence—the more so, that what I shall relate occurred in what was considered the purlieu of those most cultured and educated of the middle Florida country.[46]

During and after Reconstruction black ministers contended with the power of both Divine Providence and folk beliefs. When in 1880 the horse of a black drayman died after the fellow had "cussed out" his preacher, the minister interpreted the man's misfortune as "a visitation of Divine Providence for his cussedness."[47] Equally powerful was belief in the abilities of special individuals to cast spells on people who had wronged them. A man in Tallahassee, assisted by an elderly woman, astounded onlookers by appearing to vomit nails, moss, and other debris. "His friends believe strongly in the reality of it all," noted the *Floridian*, "and insist that he had had 'a spell' put upon him by a woman to whom he was engaged but whom he jilted and who now protests that she intends to pay him off for his base desertion."[48]

Most blacks living in Florida during the last half of the nineteenth century had been born neither in Africa nor in the Caribbean but in six southeastern states: Florida, Georgia, South Carolina, Virginia, Alabama, and North Carolina. In 1890, 122,170 individuals, making up 76.3 percent of Florida's total black population, were native Floridians. Only 5.7 percent (7,411) of all Florida-born blacks lived outside the state of their birth in 1890, whereas between 11.1 percent and 25.9 percent of the blacks born in North Carolina, South Carolina, Georgia, Alabama, and Virginia did so. Between 1880 and 1890 Florida experienced a net gain of 30,528 black inhabitants through interstate migration. During the same decade Georgia, South Carolina, Alabama, North Carolina, and Virginia experienced net losses of black population. Put another way, a hefty 23.7 percent of the blacks living in Florida in 1890 were born in other states, compared with 2.9 percent in Virginia, 2.8 in North Carolina, 6.6 in Georgia, 1.7 in South Carolina, and 10.0 in Alabama.[49]

If distinctive cultural patterns bearing traceable African origins are found in postbellum Florida, they cannot be explained simply by the presence of large numbers of African-born individuals in the state's black population. Other explanations must be found for the persistence of such culturally distinctive and widely acknowledged African-influenced elements of culture as basket-making styles, grave markers, mortuary customs, and shouting (spirit possession) in African American religious rituals in the latter half of the nineteenth century. These Africanisms had become Americanisms and persisted in Florida and elsewhere in the Deep South as integral parts of an interconnected circum-Caribbean creole culture that had been forged in Florida, Georgia, and South Carolina during the previous century and had alternately influenced and been influenced by the customs and lifeways of southern whites and Indians.

Dispensing with the possibility of any significant influence by native Africans still alive during the 1870s and 1880s because their numbers and proportions were minuscule does not, however, remove the possibility of indirect and even direct African influence. Some of Florida's older American-born black adults, such as the Reverend Eli Boyd, remembered deceased African-born parents and grandparents. A self-designated "Geeche" interviewed in Miami during the 1930s, Boyd recalled that "my grandfather was brought directly from Africa to Port Royal, South Carolina."[50]

The possibility of vivid memories of African-born parents and grandparents was underscored strikingly in a conversation I had with Richard McKinney, the son of a black Baptist minister who figures prominently in the history of Live Oak's African Baptist Church. The McKinney family oral tradition posits links of kinship stretching from Jacob, an Ashanti African born around 1820, to the present.[51] And while the proportion of Florida's black population born in Africa had diminished to statistical insignificance by 1870, personal memories of African family ancestors had not disappeared even as late as the 1930s, when Shack

Thomas, born a slave in Florida in 1834, recalled that his father was from the Congo:

> Pappy was a African. I knows dat. He come from Congo, over in Africa, and I heard him say a big storm drove de ship somwhere on de Ca'lina coast. I 'member he mighty 'spectful to Massa and missy, but he proud, too, and walk straighter'n anybody I ever seen. He had scars on de right side he head and cheek what he say am tribe marks, but what dey means I don't know.[52]

From these and other African ancestors, no longer in the earthly world when the census takers made their rounds in 1870, some older country-born black Floridians, such as Mrs. Lucreaty Clark of Lamont (Jefferson County), may have learned African basket-weaving techniques handed down across several generations, as did George Brown in South Carolina.[53] Although South Carolina's African American basket-weaving tradition, which Peter H. Wood said "undoubtedly represents an early fusion of Negro and Indian skills,"[54] is widely known and highly visible to tourists along the roadsides of the low country, less attention has been focused on the traditions of basket weaving still practiced by some African American craftspeople in Florida today. In describing the white oak baskets made by Lucreaty Clark, James Dickerson wrote:

> Within her fingertips is carried the memory of an ancient African craft fast disappearing from the face of the Florida Panhandle. African slaves, once brought to the Panhandle to work on plantations, made baskets to hold cotton picked from the fields.[55]

The tendency once was to assume that in those instances where Africans did not bring African-made artifacts with them in the slave ships there was no possibility of reproducing the ancestral material culture. That is an entirely too physicalistic conception of how diffusion, even of material culture, works. The specific materials from which the artifacts are made is one thing; the form and design concepts of the artifact are another matter altogether. The artifact might be most appropriately viewed as the analogue of a phenotype and the ideal traditional form as the genotype. What we see is not necessarily what the craft worker has in his or her head. It is, rather, the end product of an interaction among the craftsperson's image of the cultural tradition or ideal; the materials available to work with; and the craftsperson's skill, practice, and ability to shape the materials in conformity with the ideal image. The ideal image is a mental image carried, not in the hands or on the backs of the African bondsmen, but in their heads. The reappearance of artifacts conforming reasonably well with African cultural ideas for pot, basket, chair, or door is therefore a mental feat before it becomes a physical reality. One archaeologist called the idea of proper form, which exists in the mind of the craftsperson who is fashioning an artifact, "the mental template," an apt phrase.[56]

Spirit Possession and Ritual Ecstatic Dance

High emotionalism has often been considered characteristic of black religious life.[57] The frequency, long duration, and "emotionality" of black church services in Florida have drawn comment from a number of observers. The image of black religionists as vocally demonstrative in their worship was so widespread that finding a group of black worshippers during Reconstruction that was "not noisy" was cause for comment.[58] While traveling in Florida in 1870 G. W. Nichols visited St. Augustine and Jacksonville, where he witnessed "shocking mummeries, which belonged to the fetich worship of savage Central Africa and not of Christian America."[59] If we substitute "traditional African religion" for the ethnocentrically loaded "fetich worship" and bracket the obviously biased adjective *savage*, an important kernel of historical truth may remain in this jaundiced account. What did Nichols mean by Central Africa in geographical terms? Was he making a distinction between West Africa and Central Africa or was this simply his verbal shorthand for "primitive Africa" in general? In 1871 the Jacksonville *Courier* reported the complaints of local whites about the duration of demonstrative services in a revival that continued several weeks.[60] The same year Miss E. B. Eveleth, an American Missionary Association instructor at Gainesville, wrote that "many of those old church goers, still cling to their heathenish habits, such as shouting and thinking the more noise and motion they have the better Christians they are."[61] Eveleth and a colleague attended a service at which a woman jumped up in the middle of a sermon, clapped her hands, screamed, danced up to the pulpit, and whirled around like a top before throwing herself back in the seat. She was followed by another woman with similar motions. In an 1879 article entitled "Begin Worship Earlier," the Tallahassee *Weekly Floridian* reported that white citizens residing in "the neighborhood of the colored people's churches" had complained about "the singing and exhorting at a late hour." Ever helpful, the *Floridian* suggested that "the colored people begin services earlier and preach short sermons."[62]

In 1873 Jonathan Gibbs, a Dartmouth-educated Presbyterian minister who became Florida's first black secretary of state, was apologetic about the ecstatic religious behavior of blacks. They "still preach and pray, sing and shout all night long," said Gibbs, "in defiance of health, sound sense, or other considerations supposed to influence a reasonable being."[63] One seeming example of how some black worshippers shouted in defiance of health was described by James Weldon Johnson. A woman known as Aunt Venie out of respect for her age was "the champion of all 'ring shouters'" at St. Paul's Church in Jacksonville, Johnson recalled.

> We were a little bit afraid of Aunt Venie, too, for she was said to have fits. (In a former age she would have been classed among those "possessed with devils.") When there was a "ring shout" the weird music and the sound of thudding feet set the silence of the night vibrating and throbbing with a vague terror. Many a time I woke suddenly and lay a long while strangely troubled by these sounds, the like of which my great-grandmother Sarah had heard as a child. The shouters, formed in a ring, men and women alternating, their bodies close together, moved round and round on shuffling feet that never left the floor. With the heel of the right foot they pounded out the fundamental beat of the dance and with their hands clapped out the varying rhythmical accents of the chant; for the music was, in fact, an African chant and the shout an African dance, whole pagan rite transplanted and adapted to Christian worship. Round and round the ring would go. One, two, three, four, five hours, the very monotony of sound and motion inducing an ecstatic frenzy. Aunt Venie, it seems, never, even after the hardest day of washing and ironing, missed a "ring shout."[64]

Johnson's speculation that the sounds of the ring shout resembled the sounds his great-grandmother heard in childhood is noteworthy because his maternal great-grandmother, Sarah, was born and raised in Africa. She was aboard a slave ship headed for Brazil when the ship was captured by a British man-of-war and taken to Nassau.

It is fairly well known that the African Methodist Episcopal bishop Daniel Alexander Payne opposed the ring shout and tried to eliminate all forms of religious dance. One shocking spectacle that Payne observed at St. Paul's A.M.E. Church in Jacksonville (where Aunt Venie shouted) left such an impression upon him that he recorded his frustrations in his personal journal in 1892. His frustrations were intensified by the realization that even the parishioners of a Wilberforce-educated pastor (who should know better) danced at an A.M.E. "Love Feast."[65]

Another eyewitness account may serve as both a definitive example and a concluding reiteration of the persistence of this ritually induced and culturally patterned behavior known as shouting. Charles Edwardes, a white traveler, observed the event on a freezing January day some time in the early 1880s in an unspecified black church in Jacksonville. The building was filled with three to four hundred adults who initiated a "bread-and-water forgiveness festival" with the singing of this verse, repeated again and again:

> While Heaven's in my view,
> My journey I'll pursue;
> I never will turn back,
> While Heaven's in my view.

Then the spirit possession began:

> One woman—she was almost a girl—cried herself into what might have been a fit. But if a fit, it was of a kind well known to the other women, her neighbors, for two of these stood up by her side, and taking, each of them, an arm of her, they guided or supported her through all her contortions, with faces showing their amusement rather than concern. Even when she wrenched herself away from them, and threw herself backward, so that her head and the upper part of her body hung over into the next pew, they pulled her back and tightened their hold, while a third lady tried to put order into the dress and hair of the girl—and not one of the three was so absorbed by her task that she would devote her eyes and ears to it exclusively.[66]

The foregoing descriptions have in common the depiction of religious hysteria or possessionlike behavior, popularly known as "shouting," "getting happy," or "getting the spirit." Observed in certain black churches, it has been variously attributed to innate primitive emotionalism, residues of African culture, or just the simple emotionalism of the unwashed and uneducated masses. In 1930 Herskovits raised the question of the relation of "religious hysteria" among peoples of African origin in the United States, Haiti, the Guianas, and the West Indies to similar African phenomena. But, as Herskovits pointed out, few answers were forthcoming in 1930 because little systematic study of the religious practices of blacks in the United States had been conducted from the point of view of the ethnologist.[67]

Certainly not all black churchgoers exhibit the same degree or type of demonstrativeness in religious ceremonies. The amount of heat and emotional ecstasy generated seems to be closely related to social position. "It is of no little significance," wrote Louis Lomax, "that these mulatto Negroes of the 'genteel tradition' were Episcopalians, Presbyterians and Congregationalists while the black masses were members of the 'common' churches, such as the Baptist and Methodist congregations." The difference between the "genteel tradition" and the "common" tradition was to be found in the nature of the services. Those who claimed to be of the "genteel" group considered their services to be of a "higher order," which, according to Lomax, meant that their services were "a good deal less exciting." The association of the black masses with denominations having the more exciting brand of services led the Reverend Thomas Lomax, a black Georgia Baptist firebrand of the late nineteenth and early twentieth centuries and grandfather of Louis, to crack: "If you see a Negro who is not a Baptist or a Methodist, some white man has been tampering with his religion."[68]

The ritual known as the ring shout or simply the shout has been viewed by some writers as a phenomenon found only among the Gullah-speaking blacks of the Sea Islands off Georgia and South Carolina.[69] It is true that some of the most vivid eyewitness accounts of shouts originated in that region. Laura M. Towne, for example, described the shout as a religious ceremony representing possibly a modification of "the negro's regular dances; which may have had its origin in some native African dance."[70] Bernard Katz wrote that the antebellum and Civil War era shout usually came after the praise meeting was over, and no one but church members was expected to join.[71] The musicologist Eileen Southern considered the shout, held after the regularly scheduled service, to be "purely African in form and tradition" and argued that "it simply represented the survival of African tradition in the New World."[72] If this argument is accepted, there can be little doubt that the religious-musical-dance-drama form called the shout not only occurred in Florida during slavery times but exhibited a remarkable stability over time. The ring shout described by James Weldon Johnson probably happened in the late 1870s or early 1880s. In antebellum times, when most of the furnishings of the praise houses in which the shouts occurred were movable, the physical form of the shout was rather literally a ring. Wooden chairs or benches that were not nailed to the floor of these cabins were easily moved to the side, leaving empty floor space in the center of the building. After the Civil War the circular form of the shout probably persisted longest in churches with movable seats. With the appearance of heavy wooden pews, which were usually permanently riveted to the floor, the circular form of the shout had to be either modified or abandoned altogether.

Spirit possession pushes us toward direct confrontation with what has been called the Frazier-Herskovits debate over the extent and impact of African cultural influences in various parts of the Western Hemisphere. Two kinds of altered states of consciousness are pertinent here—drug trance and possession trance, both of which are widespread. In a survey of altered states in 488 societies, Erika Bourguignon found possession trance to be prevalent in (but of course not limited to) continental Africa. If, as Bourguignon and others influenced by Herskovits argued, "it is clear that possession trance in Haiti is historically related to what is essentially the same phenomenon in West Africa and in other West African-derived societies in the Americas,"[73] there is every reason to suspect, rather than to deny, that similar behaviors exhibited by Western and Central African–derived black populations in the United States are historically related to those parts of Africa. Possession behaviors are learned in both formal and informal ways, along with beliefs and associated ritual action. In human communities that view possession as a peak religious experience the behavior is widely interpreted as a communal event, an act that helps cement a spiritual and social community.

One universal aspect of spirit possession is the accompaniment of drum beats or drumlike rhythms. Although little systematic research has been conducted, Andrew Neher offered a tentative physiological explanation of the behavior found in ceremonies involving drums. "This behavior," he wrote, "is often described as a trance in which the individual experiences unusual perceptions or hallucinations. In the extreme case, twitching of the body and generalized convulsion are reported." Neher found support for the notion that "the behavior is the result primarily of the effects of rhythmic drumming on the central nervous system." Drum beats contain many frequencies that are transmitted along different nerve pathways in the brain. Since low-frequency receptors of the ear are more resistant to damage than high-frequency receptors, "it would be possible to transmit more energy to the brain with a drum than with a stimulus of a higher frequency." In a second part of his study Neher obtained responses to drumming that were similar to responses observed with rhythmic light stimulation of the brain. He argued that possession takes place when drum or drumlike pulses beat at the same rate as the alpha rhythm of the brain and that drum pulses are used deliberately in rituals to bring about a state of dissociation, or trance. Analyses of the drum rhythms of the beer dance of the Lala of Northern Rhodesia, the Sogo dance of the Ewe of Ghana, the beer dance of the Nsenga of Central Africa, and of Vodoun, Ifo, and Juba dances in recorded Haitian music found that the agitated possession behavior occurred with beats between seven and nine cycles per second. Polyrhythmic percussive techniques, such as the ones described for the Jacksonville ring shout by James Weldon Johnson, tend to heighten the intensity of the response.[74]

Death, Burial, and Funeral Rites

Numerous ethnographic accounts underscore the assertion of Fortes and Dieterlen that in many traditional African systems "death alone is not a sufficient condition for becoming an ancestor entitled to receive worship." A proper burial, they said, is "the *sine qua non* for becoming an ancestor deserving of veneration."[75] While the precise number of African-born individuals who arrived illegally in Florida after 1821 is not known, we do know from specific descriptions of "salt water" Negroes who did arrive in antebellum Florida that they did not have cultural amnesia the moment they stepped off the slavers. Accounts of the arrival of cargoes of Africans confiscated in midpassage on the seas and of their behavior upon landing in the United States clearly establish the carrying over of such cultural items as burial ceremonies. In May 1860, for example, the illegal slavers *Wildlife* and *Williams* were captured on the seas by two U.S. gunboats, the *Mohawk* and the *Wyandotte*, and taken to the port of Key West. Shortly after the arrival of the three hundred Africans aboard these two ships, one of the children died. Jefferson B. Browne described the burial ceremony:

> The interment took place some distance from the barracoon, and the Africans were allowed to be present at the services, where they performed their native ceremony. Weird chants were sung, mingled with wails of grief and mournful moanings from a hundred throats, until the coffin was lowered into the grave, when at once the chanting stopped and perfect silence reigned, and the Africans marched back to the barracoons without a sound.[76]

Some slaves in the lower South made a semantic distinction between "burying" and "preaching the funeral." James Bolton, a former slave in Oglethorpe County, Georgia, said: "When folkses on our plantation died, Marster always let many of us as wanted to go lay off work 'til after the burying. Sometimes it were two or three months after the burying before the funeral sermon was preached."[77] Among the African societies that traditionally practiced "second burial" was the Igbo:

> Greater complications arose when many children of many family heads became Christians, and were forbidden by the teaching of the missionaries to perform the second burial of their fathers. The Ibo practice was to bury an elderly person soon after death, with preliminary ceremonies. Then after a year or less, sometimes more, the second burial would take place with a lot more elaborate ceremonies than the first. It was believed that this second burial was

the one that helped the spirit of such departed elderly persons to rest comfortably with the ancestors in the land of ancestral bliss, from where they plead effectively with the gods for the well-being of their children on earth.[78]

In the traditional Igbo setting the matter of the inheritance of the father's property could not be properly settled until after the second burial. Being landless, the slave community was not likely to have found this consideration significant. One real-world element that reinforced the practice of second burial in its traditional Old World cultural setting was thus stripped away from the Igbos who were imported into the American colonies. A second consideration in the traditional context was the belief that without a proper second burial the extended family would be harassed and victimized by the hovering restless spirit of the dead person. This notion probably lost little weight in the transition from Africa to North America, and there is considerable evidence among late antebellum slaves, as recounted in W.P.A. narratives and published narratives and autobiographies, that belief in roaming restless spirits was still something to contend with long after the majority of the slaves was American-born.[79]

The possibility, conceptually available in many African societies from which slaves were extracted, of distinguishing between burial and "second burial" or "preaching the funeral" is important to an understanding of how Africans adapted to the restrictions on funeral attendance in the Old South. A deceased individual might be buried at night if the burial occurred during the work week (so as not to disrupt farm work) or at some other time separated by days, weeks, or even months from the time the public funeral ritual was performed. The funeral ritual, then, as distinguished from the physical act of burying the body, is a public phenomenon. Funeral rites in traditional African societies were often occasions for celebration, creating an intensely renewed sense of family and communal unity among the survivors. It was perhaps an analogous sense of celebration which, during the Reconstruction era, gave Ambrose B. Hart the mistaken impression that Negro services were held more for the recreation than the religion. Among the events reinforcing Hart's impression was an incident that bears a striking resemblance to the Igbo "second burial." Hart observed a group of Florida freed slaves gather to "repreach a funeral service for a child that had been 'buried prayed for and preached over two months ago.'"[80] It is conceivable that the immediate interment of the corpse was necessitated by the limitations of embalming techniques available at the time. Both blacks and whites in the antebellum period buried rather soon after death. Waiting until the nearest Sunday seems plausible, for it would not preempt a scheduled day of work and the maximum number of people in the neighborhood would be able to attend. But after slavery the patterns began to diverge between blacks and whites to the point where one Leon County informant in the 1970s perceived that "white people don't have no respect for their dead . . . they bury them so quick." With the advent of improved methods of embalming, the physical necessity of nearly immediate burial declined, but the possibility, perhaps even the preference, for delay remained among rural blacks. It is not unusual for more traditionally oriented and rural-based families to delay "preaching the funeral" for weeks, even now.

Richard Wright recognized in the 1930s that there was "a culture of the Negro which has been addressed to him and to him alone, a culture which has, for good or ill, helped to clarify his consciousness and create emotional attitudes which are conducive to action. This culture stemmed mainly from two sources: (1) the Negro church; and (2) the fluid folk-lore of the Negro people." According to Wright:

> It was through the portals of the church that the American Negro first entered the shrine of Western culture. Living under slave conditions of life, bereft of his African heritage, the Negro found that his struggle for religion on the plantation between 1820–60 was nothing short of a struggle for human rights. It remained a relatively progressive struggle until religion began to ameliorate and assuage suffering and denial. Even today there are millions of Negroes whose only sense of a whole universe, whose only relation to society and man, and whose only guide to personal dignity comes through the archaic morphology of Christian salvation.[81]

By focusing on blacks living within the confines of present-day Florida, this essay has depicted the entrance of African Americans "through the portals of the church" into what Wright called "the shrine of Western culture." In the process we have learned how, by this entry, these Africans not only transformed themselves into African Americans without totally losing their African past but also helped transform and enrich Western culture itself.

Notes

1. David E. Stannard, "Time and the Millennium: On the Religious Experience of the American Slave," in Jack Salzman, ed., *Prospects: An Annual of American Cultural Studies*, 2 (New York: Burt Franklin, 1976), 349.

2. William R. Bascom, "Acculturation among the Gullah Negroes," *American Anthropologist* (1941) 43:43–50; reprinted in *The Making of Black America,* 1, ed. August Meier and Elliott Rudwick (New York: Atheneum, 1969), 34–41.

3. Anthropologists and folklorists often call this blending *syncretism.* Two folklorists defined the term: "The merging of two or more concepts, beliefs, rituals, etc. so that apparent conflicts are rationalized away. Old beliefs and associated actions are not necessarily replaced or destroyed by new ones; they are rather, reinterpreted and absorbed. Syncretism may be seen in elements of early pagan rites modified to survive in later Christian rituals. Symbolism in Christmas (trees, etc.) and Easter (egg, etc.) celebrations are examples." Kenneth and Mary Clarke, *A Concise Dictionary of Folklore,* Kentucky Folklore Series no. 1 (June 1965), 32.

4. George P. Rawick, *From Sundown to Sunup: The Making of the Black Community* (Westport, Conn.: Greenwood, 1972), 14–29.

5. Robert Farris Thompson, "Black Ideographic Writing: Calabar to Cuba," *Yale Alumni Magazine,* Nov. 1978, 29. Also see Thompson's essay in this volume.

6. Bennetta Jules-Rosette, "Creative Spirituality from Africa to America: Cross-cultural Influences in Contemporary Religious Forms," *Western Journal of Black Studies* (Winter 1980) 4:275.

7. See, for example, Winifred Vass, *The Bantu Speaking Heritage of the United States* (Los Angeles: UCLA, Center for Afro-American Studies, 1979).

8. Melville J. Herskovits, *The Myth of the Negro Past* (Boston: Beacon Press, 1958), 111.

9. Mechal Sobel, *Trabelin' On: The Slave Journey to an Afro-Baptist Faith* (Westport, Conn.: Greenwood, 1979), 59.

10. Darold D. Wax, "Preferences for Slaves in Colonial America," *Journal of Negro History* (Oct. 1973) 58:371–401. Daniel C. Littlefield, *Rice and Slaves: Ethnicity and the Slave Trade in Colonial South Carolina* (Baton Rouge: Louisiana State University Press, 1981).

11. Ira Berlin, "Time, Space, and the Evolution of Afro-American Society on British Mainland North America," *American Historical Review* (Feb. 1980) 85:67. See also a recent treatment of the evolution of slave-naming practices: Cheryll Ann Cody, "There Was No 'Absolom' on the Ball Plantations: Slave-Naming Practices in the South Carolina Low Country, 1720–1865," *American Historical Review* (June 1987) 92:563–96.

12. Pensacola *Gazette,* Jan. 9, 1836.

13. *Florida Herald and Southern Democrat,* May 28, 1841.

14. Florida *Sentinel,* Apr. 27, 1852.

15. Sobel, *Trabelin' On,* 29–30.

16. *Georgia Gazette,* Apr. 2, 1764; quoted in Sobel, *Trabelin' On,* 26.

17. Sobel, *Trabelin' On,* 36.

18. Roderick Brambaugh, "Black Maroons in Florida, 1800–1830," paper read at the Annual Meeting of the Organization of American Historians, Boston, 1975.

19. Larry W. Kruger and Robert L. Hall, "Fort Mose: A Black Fort in Spanish Florida," *Griot* (Spring 1987) 6:39–48.

20. John D. Milligan, "Slave Rebelliousness and the Florida Maroons," *Prologue* (Spring 1974) 6:4–18.

21. Ibid., 9.

22. Robert W. Higgins, "South Carolina Merchants and Factors Dealing in the External Negro Trade, 1735–1775," *South Carolina Historical Magazine* (1964) 65:205–17.

23. Peter H. Wood, *Black Majority: Negroes in Colonial South Carolina from 1670 through the Stono Rebellion* (New York: Knopf, 1974), xiv.

24. Charles Loch Mowat, *East Florida as a British Province, 1763–1784* (Gainesville: University of Florida Press, 1964; reprint of 1943 ed.), 157.

25. James Grant to Lord Shelburne, Dec. 25, 1767, and Mar. 12, 1768, Colonial Office 5/549, 45–46.

26. Mowat, *East Florida*, 157.

27. *South Carolina and American General Gazette*, Dec. 24, 1773.

28. *Georgia Gazette*, Jan. 10, 1770; cited in *Journal of Negro History* (July 1939) 24:252.

29. The state reimbursed Qua's owner for the loss of a laborer resulting from this execution, General Account of Contingent Expenses, East Florida, June 25, 1777–June 24, 1778, Colonial Office 5/559; cited in J. Leitch Wright, Jr., "Blacks in British East Florida," *Florida Historical Quarterly* (Apr. 1976) 54:431. On specific traditional African language and naming patterns, see David Dalby, "Ashanti Survivals in the Language and Traditions of the Windward Maroons of Jamaica," *African Language Studies* (1971) 12:31–51; Roger W. Wescott, "Bini Names in Nigeria and Georgia," *Linguistics: An International Review* (1974) 124:22–32; and Frederick W. H. Megeod, "Personal Names amongst Some West African Tribes," *Journal of the African Society* (1917) 117. Other relevant articles and studies include F. Gaither, "Fanciful Are Negro Names," *New York Times Magazine*, Feb. 10, 1929, 19; U. T. Holmes, "A Study in Negro Onomastics," *American Speech* (1930) 5:463–67; Henning Cohen, "Slave Names in Colonial South Carolina," *American Speech* (1952) 28:102–107; N. C. Chappell, "Negro Names," *American Speech* (1929) 4:272–75; Newbell N. Puckett, "Names of American Negro Slaves," in *Studies in the Science of Society*, ed. G. P. Murdock (New Haven, Conn.: Yale University Press, 1937), 471–94; Puckett, *Black Names in America: Origins and Usage* (Boston: G. K. Hall, 1975); and John C. Inscoe, "Carolina Slave Names: An Index to Acculturation," *Journal of Southern History* (Nov. 1983) 49:527–54.

30. Pensacola *Gazette*, Dec. 12, 1840.

31. Patricia C. Griffin, "Mary Evans: Woman of Substance," *El Escribano* (1978) 14:71.

32. For a discussion of the concept of creolization by a linguist, see Robert A. Hall, Jr., *Pidgin and Creole Languages* (Ithaca, N.Y.: Cornell University Press, 1966), esp. xi–xv. Mechal Sobel suggests that the pidginization/creolization language process parallels, chronologically, analogous developments in the evolution of African Christianity, *Trabelin' On*, 36.

33. Peter H. Wood, "Jesus Christ Has Got Thee at Last," *Bulletin*, Center for the Study of Southern Culture and Religion (Nov. 1979) 3:1–7.

34. Zephaniah Kingsley, *A Treatise on the Patriarchal, or Co-Operative System of Society as It Exists in Some Governments under the Name of Slavery* (n.p., 1829), 14.

35. James Pope-Hennessy, *Sins of the Fathers: A Study of the Atlantic Slave Traders (1441–1807)* (New York: Knopf, 1968), 3.

36. *Niles Weekly Register*, Dec. 27, 1817, 296; Jan. 10, 1818, 324; and Jan. 17, 1818, 336–37. Cited in T. Frederick Davis, *Digest of the Florida Material in Niles' Register* (n.p., 1939), 27, 29.

37. Vass, *Bantu Speaking Heritage*, 48.

38. Reverend Simon Peter Richardson, *The Lights and Shadows of Itinerant Life: An Autobiography* (Nashville and Dallas: Publishing House of the Methodist Episcopal Church, South, 1900).

39. Jacksonville *Courier*, Apr. 16, 1835.

40. Dorothy Dodd, "The Schooner Emperor: An Incident of the Illegal Trade in Florida," *Florida Historical Quarterly* (Jan. 1935) 13:117–28.

41. Fredrika Bremer, *The Homes of the New World: Impressions of America*, trans. by Mary Howitt (London: Arthur Hall, Virtle, 1853), 289–90.

42. Charles J. Montgomery, "Survivors from the Cargo of the Negro Slave Yacht Wanderer," *American Anthropologist* (Oct. 1908) 10:611–23.

43. *The Ninth Census of the United States* (1870), Washington, D.C., 1872; see table 6, "Selected Nativity by Counties," 349.

44. Ellen Call Long, *Florida Breezes or Florida New and Old* (Gainesville: University of Florida Press, 1962; reprint of 1883 ed.), 181.

45. W. B. Cannon, "Voodoo Death," *American Anthropologist* (1942) 44:169–81.

46. Ellen Call Long, "Negro Witchcraft," typed manuscript fragment dated 1892, in the P. K. Yonge Library of Florida History, University of Florida, Gainesville, 1–3.

47. Tallahassee *Semi-Weekly Floridian*, Sept. 17, 1880.

48. Tallahassee *Weekly Floridian*, Feb. 12, 1878.

49. U.S. Department of Commerce, Bureau of the Census, *Thirteenth Census of the United States*, 1, *Population*, 1910 (Washington, D.C., 1913), 151.

50. Eli Boyd interview, W.P.A. Slave Narratives; reprinted in George P. Rawick, ed., *The American Slave: A Composite Autobiography*, 17, *Florida Narratives*

(Westport, Conn.: Greenwood, 1972), 39–40, hereinafter cited as Rawick, *Florida Narratives.*

51. Richard I. McKinney, interview with author, July 9, 1981. The link was consolidated and ritualized by George Patterson McKinney, a prominent Baptist minister during the late nineteenth and early twentieth centuries. George, the son of Ishmael (born into slavery around 1837), was the grandson of an Ashanti African known as Jacob. Jacob, who was born in West Africa around 1820 and illegally imported into the United States, repeatedly told his grandson that his tribe was Ashanti. Young George never forgot this and told all eight of his children, "You are Ashanti."

52. Shack Thomas interview, W.P.A. Slave Narratives; quoted in Lawrence W. Levine, *Black Culture and Black Consciousness: Afro-American Folk Thought from Slavery to Freedom* (New York: Oxford University Press, 1977), 87. Several African-born slaves who ran away between 1820 and 1850 had tribal marks or scars. Maria, "African by birth . . . face tatooed," ran away from her owner, Henry De Grandpre, in 1829, Pensacola *Gazette*, Dec. 16, 1829. And in 1842 Abraham, who had "worked in the employ of a corporation in the city of Tallahassee for two years," ran away bearing a "mark over the eyes on the forehead, as Africans are frequently marked," *Florida Sentinel*, Oct. 14, 1842.

53. Edith M. Dabbs, *Face of an Island* (Columbia, S.C.: R. L. Bryan, 1970), contains a photograph taken in 1909 of Alfred Graham, a former slave, who learned to weave baskets from his great-uncle, who brought the trade of basketry from Africa. Graham later taught George Brown, who became instructor of basketry at the Penn School on St. Helena Island. Joseph E. Holloway elicited this path of transmission in an unpublished interview with Leroy E. Brown, George's son.

54. Wood, *Black Majority*, 122.

55. James Dickerson, "Basket Weaving, Down-Home Style," Tallahassee *Democrat*, Nov. 23, 1978. For further discussion of African-inspired material culture in the low country, see Robert E. Perdue, Jr., "African Baskets in South Carolina," *Economic Botany* (1968) 22:289–92.

56. James Deetz, *Invitation to Anthropology* (Garden City, N.Y.: Anchor, 1967), 45.

57. Some writers have suggested that much of the emotionalism of southern evangelical religion derives from the contagious influence of blacks on revivalistic frontier religion. At least one prominent black scholar, however, argued that the emotionalism of the early evangelical faith of the whites influenced the nature of black religious worship rather than vice versa. As Harry V. Richardson, "The Negro in American Religious Life," in John P. Davis, ed., *The American Negro Reference Book* (Englewood Cliffs, N.J.: Prentice-Hall, 1966), 400, wrote:

> But if the simplicity of the evangelical faith did much to determine the number of Negroes who became Christians, the emotionalism of the early evangelical faith did much to determine the nature of

Negro worship. The religion that the Negro masses first received was characterized by such Phenomena as laughing, weeping, shouting, dancing, barking, jerking, prostration and speaking in tongues. These were regarded as evidence of the Spirit at work in the heart of man, and they were also taken as evidence of the depth and sincerity of the conversion. It was inevitable, therefore, that early Negro worship should be filled with these emotional elements. Although there is some tendency to regard high emotionalism as a phenomenon peculiar to the Negro church, in reality it is a hangover from the days of frontier religion.

58. Mrs. E. W. Warner to E. P. Smith, Sept. 3, 1868, American Missionary Association Papers.

59. G. W. Nichols, "Six Weeks in Florida," *Harper's New Monthly*, Oct. 1870, 663.

60. Jacksonville *Courier* as quoted in the Tallahassee *Weekly Floridian*, Oct. 3, 1871.

61. E. P. Eveleth to E. M. Cravath, Feb. 25, 1871, American Missionary Association Papers.

62. *Weekly Floridian*, Aug. 12, 1879.

63. Jonathan Gibbs, *Florida Agriculturist*, Jan. 17, 1874, 23.

64. James Weldon Johnson, *Along This Way: The Autobiography of James Weldon Johnson* (New York: Da Capo Press, 1973; reprint of 1933 ed.), 22.

65. Journal of Daniel Alexander Payne for 1891-93, entry of Dec. 12, 1892; cited in David W. Wills, "Womanhood and Domesticity in the A.M.E. Tradition: The Influence of Daniel Alexander Payne," in *Black Apostles at Home and Abroad*, ed. David W. Wills and Richard Newman (Boston: G. K. Hall, 1982), 144.

66. Charles Edwardes, "A Scene from Florida Life," *Living Age*, Sept. 13, 1884, 685; reprinted from *Macmillan's*.

67. Melville J. Herskovits, "The Negro in the New World: The Statement of a Problem," *American Anthropologist* (1930); reprinted in Herskovits, *The New World Negro: Selected Papers in Afroamerican Studies* (Bloomington: Indiana University Press, 1966), 10. One of the few studies published before 1966 was Alexander Alland, Jr., "'Possession' in a Revivalist Negro Church," *Journal of the Scientific Study of Religion* (April 1962) 1:204-13.

68. Louis Lomax, *The Negro Revolt* (New York: Harper, 1962), 58.

69. Wood, *Black Majority*, 172.

70. *Letters and Diary of Laura M. Towne, Written from the Sea Islands of South Carolina, 1862-1884*, ed. by Rupert Sargent Holland (New York: Negro Universities Press, 1969 reprint), 67.

71. Bernard Katz, *The Social Implications of Early Negro Music in the United States* (New York: Arno, 1969), 4-5.

72. Eileen Southern, *The Music of Black America* (New York: Norton, 1971), 162.

73. Erika Bourguignon, *Dance Perspectives* (Autumn 1968) 35:33–35. This special issue, written entirely by Bourguignon, was devoted to possession trance and ritual ecstatic dance.

74. Andrew Neher, "A Physiological Explanation of Unusual Behavior in Ceremonies Involving Drums," *Human Biology* (May 1962) 34:151–60.

75. M. Fortes and G. Dieterlen, eds., *African Systems of Thought* (London: Oxford University Press, 1965), 16.

76. Jefferson B. Browne, *Key West: The Old and the New* (Gainesville: University of Florida Press, 1973; facsimile reprint of 1912 ed.), 16–17.

77. Ronald Killion and Charles Waller, eds., *Slavery Times (When I Was Chillun down on Marster's Plantation)* (Savannah, Ga.: Beehive Press, 1975), 58.

78. Edmund Ilogu, *Christianity and Ibo Culture* (Leiden: E. J. Brill, 1974), 109. For another description of Igbo second burial, see Lorna McDaniel, "An Igbo Second Burial," *Black Perspective in Music* (Spring 1978) 6:49–55. McDaniel indicates that the ceremony could take place from one month to a year after death and could last several weeks.

79. Elliott J. Gorn, "Black Spirits: The Ghostlore of Afro-American Slaves," *American Quarterly* (Fall 1984) 36:549–65. See as an example *Florida Narratives*, 196–97.

80. Letter from Ambrose B. Hart to Father, June 15, 1869; quoted in Joe M. Richardson, *The Negro in the Reconstruction of Florida* (Tallahassee: Florida State University Press, 1965), 89.

81. Richard Wright, "Blueprint for Negro Literature," in *Amistad* 2, ed. by John A. Williams and Charles F. Harris (New York: Vintage, 1971), 6. A shorter version of Wright's paper was published in the fall 1937 issue of *New Challenge*.

Nine

Sacrificial Practices in Santeria, an African Cuban Religion in the United States

George Brandon

This essay examines sacrificial ritual as practiced in the United States in the African Cuban religion Santeria. Because Santeria was only recently transplanted from Cuba, it is neither well known nor well studied in the United States. I hope to provide a context in which Santeria, its sacrificial practices, and its place within the study of Africanisms in the United States become more comprehensible.

I will first describe the African origins and historical development of Santeria and suggest a perspective that places it within a variety of overlapping geographical and cultural contexts, thus clarifying its place within the study of Africanisms. The main body of the essay will give a detailed description of Santeria's sacrificial practices, along with references to cognate Yoruba practices where appropriate. Following this description I will comment on certain aspects of the meaning of these rites and the relation of the data presented to the observations of anthropologists and psychiatrists who take a psychological approach to the explanation of sacrificial rites. Then I will place Santeria's sacrificial practices, albeit sketchily, within the wider context of African sacrificial practices in the New World, with special emphasis on the United States. I will conclude with some suggestions of a general nature on the investigation of Africanisms in the United States for the present and future.

Sacrifice is a central ritual of Santeria, as it is of traditional African religions generally. It is also one of the most controversial and least understood aspects of this religion. Sacrifice is not, however, the whole of Santeria; nor is it the only aspect where African influence is clearly determinative. Almost any other domain within Santeria could serve equally well to demonstrate African influence. For, in its ritual and world view, etiquette and material symbols, liturgical music and dance, Santeria embodies a treasury of Africanisms in the New World.

Santeria

With the forced migration of millions of Africans to the Americas by the slave trade, large numbers of Yoruba, an African ethnic group now numbering some thirteen million people in southwestern Nigeria, were scattered across the vastness of the Atlantic world. The United States, the Caribbean, and Central and South America all received Yorubas through the slave trade, but it was in the Caribbean and northeastern Brazil that Yoruba culture remained most distinct and identifiable. That is especially true of the Yoruba's traditional religion, and African Cuban Santeria is an example of this fact.

Santeria is a New World African-based religion with a clear dual heritage. Imported into the United States from Cuba, its component traditions include European Christianity (in the form of Spanish folk Catholicism), traditional African religion (in the form of *orisha* worship as practiced by the Yoruba of Nigeria), and Kardecan spiritism, which originated in France in the nineteenth century and subsequently became fashionable in both the Caribbean and South America.

Origins

Cuba was a relative backwater of the Atlantic slave trade through the sixteenth, seventeenth, and most of the eighteenth centuries. The rejuvenation of Cuban agriculture in the 1760s changed that. When the plantation sector of the Cuban economy began to develop rapidly, leaving behind centuries of stagnation in response to the growing European and North American demand for sugar and tobacco, the need for labor was pressing. It was satisfied by the importation of African slave labor. Over the course of the entire slave trade Cuba imported between 702,000 and one million African slaves, with the greatest number (approximately 200,000) coming in during the nineteenth century.[1] The last African slaves to reach Cuba came in 1865, though rumors persist that a few were smuggled in as late as 1870.

In early periods Yorubas made up only a small portion of slave imports into Cuba, but in the peak years more Yorubas than any other ethnic group arrived in Cuba—34.52 percent of the total after 1850.[2]

In Cuba the *orisha*, the deities of the Yoruba pantheon, became identified with the saints of Roman Catholicism. There they are called *oricha* but also *santos*, hence the term *Santeria*, meaning "worship of the saints." Devotees use the terms *santos* and *oricha* interchangeably. The large influx of Yoruba slaves in the 1840s and the organization of black Catholic fraternities according to African ethnic affiliation provided the demographic and institutional bases for the persistence and growth of Santeria in the nineteenth century.[3]

With Catholicism the only legal religion in colonial Cuba, Kardecan spiritist literature arrived there in the company of other illegal literature in the 1850s. In the 1870s adherence to the teachings of the French engineer Kardec, who claimed his books were dictated to him by spirits, became a veritable rage throughout the Spanish and French Caribbean and Central and South America in the form of organized cult groups. Cuba was no exception.[4]

Many middle-class Cubans of the time embraced Espiritismo, the Hispanic version of Kardecan spiritism, as a scientistic, egalitarian, and potentially liberating ideology opposed to the Catholic Church, which they saw as an instrument of Spanish domination. When Espiritismo reached the lower classes and the rural areas it became mixed with the prevalent forms of folk Catholicism. Starting out as a non-Christian, European occult science, Espiritismo became much more Christianized in Cuba and assumed for many people the role of a noninstitutionalized form of Catholicism—including the cult of saints. The spirit guides of spiritist mediums frequently took the form of ethnic or professional stereotypes with which Cubans were familiar but which were not known to Kardec. Thus in Cuba both white and black spiritist mediums channeled the messages of spirit guides who were "Africanos de nacion"—Lucumi (Oyo Yoruba), Mandinga, Mina, and Congolese tribesmen who had been "disincarnated" during the slave trade.[5]

During the same period when Espiritismo was becoming widespread as a fashionable but illegal cult, the black Catholic fraternities that had been sanctuaries for Santeria were coming under severe repression from the Cuban government and the Catholic Church. It was inevitable that the two would meet in the occult underground that permeated Cuban society like a system of subterranean waterways.[6]

Despite the correspondences set up between Catholic saints and African deities and the influences derived from Espiritismo, the ritual system and cosmology of Santeria remain essentially African in character with a strong fidelity to Yoruba practices. Among the faithfully preserved aspects of Yoruba religion are the names and personalities of the African deities, divination procedures, ceremonial spirit possession and trance, liturgical music and musical instruments, Yoruba language, beliefs in ancestor veneration and reincarnation, dance as a vehicle of worship, and sacrificial practices. Santeria also contains a vast compendium of herbal medicine and healing ritual, much of which has African analogues.

Importation

The importation of Santeria into the United States seems to have begun in the mid-1940s with the immigration of individual priests, priestesses, and devotees. Information I have been able to obtain suggests that only a few Santeria priests were living in New York before the 1959 Cuban Revolution. Most of my informants agree that the first Santeria priest of the Ifa oracle to come to the United States, Pancho Mora, arrived in 1946. That was an especially noteworthy event because of the high esteem in which this oracle and its priests are held.

The overwhelming mass of emigrants left Cuba for the United States after 1959. The early period of immigration, 1959–62, was dominated by the upper and middle classes and did not accurately reflect the occupational distribution of urban Cubans. Subsequent waves brought persons of lower and lower social status. A lower-middle-class population of mainly clerical and sales people arrived in the mid-1960s; 1970 saw an overrepresentation of the Cuban urban working class; while the 1980 Mariel refugees had higher unemployment rates and lower skill levels than earlier immigrants.

In 1974 it was estimated that 100,000 to 200,000 Cuban families lived in U.S. territories.[7] Florida has the largest concentration of Cubans. Sixty percent of the Cuban American population lives there, with 20 percent in the New York–New Jersey area and the remainder in other states.[8] The vast majority of these Cuban Americans are considered white.[9] Most nonwhite Cubans live in the Northeast, especially the New York–New Jersey area.[10]

Santeros were being initiated in Puerto Rico in 1958 and in mainland United States as early as 1961. By the early 1960s some Santeria cult houses were already multiethnic, composed of both Cubans and Puerto Ricans. Other Hispanic groups and African Americans began coming into Santeria around that time. Devotees first traveled to Cuba or Puerto Rico for initiation into the priesthood, but eventually initiations were performed in the United States and other countries such as Colombia, Venezuela, Argentina, and Mexico.

Thus after the Cuban Revolution, as the number of Cuban residents in the United States increased dramatically, so did the number of Santeria devotees and priests. This was a population of exiles and refugees whose possibilities for returning permanently to Cuba dimmed with each passing year. Partly as a means of retaining ethnic identification and partly to cope with their estranged and ambivalent position, many of these immigrants turned to Santeria for support, fellowship, and a way of achieving their goals. Santeria probably has a larger number of Cuban adherents in the United States now than it had in Cuba at the time of the revolution.

Spread and Change

Santeria spread far beyond the confines of the Cuban American community to other Spanish-speaking groups (Puerto Ricans, Panamanians, Colombians, and Dominicans) and beyond them to African Americans, Jews, and European Americans, who became adherents in increasing numbers after 1960. Santeria has been affected in some of its details by its passage across ethnic boundaries. Already containing a wide range of variation, it has shaped and taken on the color of the receiving groups so that some Puerto Rican and black American versions of it are now indigenous to the United States.

The Puerto Rican variant might be called, for convenience, Santerismo, for in it Cuban Santeria has blended with Puerto Rican–style Espiritismo.[11] The overall context remains that of Puerto Rican spiritism, but some Santeria elements have crept in and others have been infused selectively. Adepts in this form of spiritism frequently have had previous contacts with Santeria, possibly having experienced some low-level Santeria initiations, but are not initiates into the priesthood. Spirit possession is the force that opened the way for the intrusion of Santeria traits among these spiritist mediums. The Yoruba gods now come down at spiritist *centros,* but under different circumstances from their appearances in Africa or Cuba. Drums may be replaced by phonograph recordings of cult music, and there is no collective dancing as in Santeria ritual. Meetings are essentially spiritist gatherings at which *oricha* put in an appearance. The saints behave differently and are treated differently than at Santeria ceremonies, but the spirits do come down. In these *centros* mediums may present bead necklaces as in Santeria and bring in herbal lore and even animal sacrifices. What they do not use are the specialized divination techniques; for these they substitute their own spirit guides. This Puerto Rican–style Santerismo is described inaccurately as Santeria by Alan Harwood in his study of Puerto Rican spiritists.[12]

Santeria has also experienced schism. A group of black American priests and priestesses split off to form a nationalistic religious sect called Orisha-Voodoo. Orisha-Voodoo retains the Yoruba framework encapsulated in Santeria but rejects the identification of *orisha* with Catholic saints and the symbolism that goes with it. Growing out of the black nationalist ferment of the 1960s, Orisha-Voodoo seeks a direct return to the sources of Yoruba religion as the kernel around which to rebuild a way of life on Yoruba traditions, including patterns of work, marriage, language, dress, and social organization. The spiritual center of this movement is now at Ọ̀yọ́túnjí Village, South Carolina, but for more than a decade the leader of the movement, Oba Oseijiman Adefunmi Efuntola I, was a significant figure in black cultural-nationalist circles in New York.[13] Oba Oseijiman was initiated into the Santeria priesthood in Cuba in 1959, established a public temple for *orisha* worship in Harlem, and later founded Ọ̀yọ́túnjí Village as a commune devoted to the practice and study of African religion. With input from visiting Nigerian priests and visits to Nigeria as well as the Caribbean, Orisha-Voodoo has incorporated influences from Dahomean and Haitian religious traditions as well as Bini traits. This conscious revitalization has been ongoing, especially since the founding of Ọ̀yọ́túnjí Village in 1972. Although Orisha-Voodoo has rejected the Catholic influence in Santeria, it has not rejected certain Cuban spiritist traits, which remain evident in some of its beliefs and its ritual.

Wider Contexts

To put Santeria into proper perspective we must consider it in several contexts simultaneously: global, New World, and local and national.

In global context Santeria belongs to the transatlantic Yoruba religious tradition, which has millions of adherents in Africa and the New World. It should be seen as a variant of this tradition, just as there are regional and doctrinal variants within the Christian, Buddhist, and Islamic religious traditions.

I noted earlier that Santeria is a neo-African religion having a dual heritage of European and African influences. In this respect Santeria is not unique. It is but one of a series of related Yoruba-based religious forms in the Caribbean, Central and South America, and now the United States. *Shango* in Trinidad and Grenada, *xango* and *candomblé* in Brazil, and *kélé* on St. Lucia are examples. Yoruba religion also entered into Haiti, to compose there, along with Kongo-Angolan and Dahomean practices, the religion of Vodun. Santeria should be viewed, then, in relation to its kindred New World forms.

In regard to the local and national context, Santeria was not the only African-based religious group I found during my field work in New York

City from August 1979 to October 1981. Several other African Cuban cult groups exist there (for example, Abakwa, Arara, and Palo Mayombe), along with a lively Haitian Vodun community and black American revitalization movements—black nationalist groups built around the intensive study and practice of African religious traditions. Furthermore, Santeria has begun to color the practices of many adepts of Espiritismo in New York's Latin communities, thus contributing further to this already complex syncretic mosaic. When placed within this context Santeria looks far less exotic and atypical. Far from being an isolated instance, Santeria is only one part—though possibly the largest—of an extensive African occult underground in New York, Philadelphia, Chicago, Los Angeles, Washington, Miami, and probably other U.S. cities.

In contrast with most other repositories of Africanisms, Santeria—and really the greater part of the African occult underground—involves not the retention of African traditions but rather their revitalization by African Americans and their reintroduction by immigrants from areas of greater African influence and fidelity. In this context the issue of Africanisms becomes not historical but contemporary, since it concerns processes of cultural change that can be observed in the present and the recent past.

Sacrificial Practices

The word *sacrifice* derives from the Latin *sacer* (sacred) and *facere* (to make) and so means "to make sacred" or "to make holy." The corresponding term in Santeria is *ebo* (also pronounced *egbo, embo, igbo,* and *erbo*), derived from Lucumi, literally "to do" or "the thing done." As a concept *ebo* includes offerings, sacrifices, and purification without distinction. The tendency to class offerings and sacrifices as different kinds of acts is entirely absent in both Yoruba religion and Santeria, though there is a usage in Santeria that sets animal sacrifices apart from others even though all are still classed *ebo*. This is seen in the use by the *santera* or *santero* of the Spanish *matanza* (meaning slaughter) in reference to sacrifices of animals.

Several subclasses of sacrifices exist. *Ebo guoni* ("reaching the Other World") is a sacrifice done during the initiation of a priest. It involves the slaughter of a four-legged animal and a series of rites extending over three days. *Ebo yure* is a sacrifice without a waiting period; everything gets done the same day. An example is the sacrifice of an animal, along with fruit and other things, that precedes a drum dance, or *bembe*. *Ebo itutu* is a propitiatory sacrifice in a sequence of mortuary rites. *Ebo lire* or *eleri* is a sacrifice to the head, a "strengthening" or "cleansing" of the head.

Diviners frequently make use of the term *ebo* while performing readings for clients who are in transit from one part of a sequence of rites to another. The diviner may say "*Ebo fi*" ("Do whatever needs to be done") as a vague reference to what is revealed in terms of rituals to be performed or as a confirmation that it is safe to go on to the next sequence of rituals. Sometimes a diviner will inquire about what a client has been told by other diviners, whether some ritual has been assigned to do. If some *ebo* has already been given and it accords with the diviner's perception of the situation, he may say "*Ebo da*" or "*Ebo keun*" ("Whatever is being done is all right"). *Orubbo* means that it is sufficient for the client to just pray and talk to the deity; that will constitute his sacrifice, his *ebo*. Small offerings (maybe a lighted candle or a little water or wine) and prayers are all the client need give to the deity, but the client does need to "talk to the *santo* a lot."

The tendency among many students of ritual has been to rigidly distinguish between offerings and other ritual acts or to subsume all sacrificial activities under a single type of sacrifice, whether it is an offering or a propitiatory sacrifice. This particular error evidently is so tempting that it has even affected native anthropologists, for J. O. Awolalu subsumes all Yoruba sacrifice under the rubric of offerings.

> In one sense one can say that sacrifice is an act of making an offering (of animal or vegetable life, of food, drink or of any objects) to a deity or spiritual being. In another sense, sacrifice can be seen as something consecrated and offered to God or a divinity. In other words, an offering of any kind laid upon an altar or otherwise presented to a deity or divinities for definite purposes is a sacrifice.[14]

This definition, however accurate it may be for the Nigerian Yoruba, of which Awolalu is one himself, is inadequate to describe *ebo* as practiced in New York and New Jersey. In many of the ritual acts called *ebo* nothing may be put before a shrine at all. In an *ebo* performed in the open air there may be no altar. In other ceremonies nothing may end up before the shrine but the fee paid by the devotee to the *santera* or *santero*. And, while the fee would be considered part of the *ebo*, the other things which may have been destroyed in whole or in part would also be classed as *ebo*. The detritus of a rite, the mess that results from successful purifications, is also *ebo*, even after it has been removed from the place of ritual and is being thrown away as a kind of sacred and defiling garbage. A man directed to put okra above his doorsill to ward off the attacks of witches is considered to have been given *ebo*. Neither an altar nor an offering is involved in this; the okra is not an offering but a shield.

For these reasons I think that a good perspective on Santeria sacrificial practices is one that centers on what happens to the objects and people involved and what the rites are supposed to accomplish. *Ebo* is best comprehended as a religious act consisting of ritual procedures for establishing communication with spiritual or superhuman beings in order to modify the condition of the persons on whose behalf it is performed or of objects with which they are concerned. These goals are accomplished through the mediation of a victim or victims—objects or beings that are necessarily consecrated and then destroyed (or considered destroyed) in the course of the rite.

Along with divination, *ebo* is a crucial underpinning for the ritual system. But its significance is not in fact narrowly ritual but is cosmological in scope, operating through all life as an ordering principle. In the words of a Santeria notebook:

> Nothing in the universe is attained by doing nothing. You must always give something to get something. It's extremely basic, you can't fill a cup without giving up its contents first. You can't even move to a new place in a room without giving up the space you now occupy. In other words sacrifice is a basic concept of our universe.[15]

In its starkest form, demonstrated over and over in stories of the diviners, the necessity of sacrifice is made clear by the refusal of the divinities to support people who do not make *ebo*. For persons plagued by illness, bad luck, poverty, or stress, *ebo* is the only way they can alter their fates. *Ebo* allows the fortunate ones to praise and reward the deities for watching over them. *Ebo* is the only reward the *orisha* ever get. When the divinities or ancestors are angry an *ebo* can make peace with them. With an *ebo* one can repair a defect in one's life, protect oneself from witches, and cure illness. *Ebo* fulfills a vow to spiritual beings or wards off the evil machinations of a personal enemy. When a taboo has been broken, whether by a person or an entire house, making an *ebo* purifies all. Making an *ebo* to strengthen worshippers against malign influences is common; so is the *ebo* whose main purpose is to establish contact between spiritual and human beings. Its purpose is to neutralize and oppose evils and to promote the vitality and ambitions of worshippers from wish into accomplishment.

It is in relation to this promise of magical efficacy that we should look at the litany of the Mojuba prayer to understand its position as the central prayer of the religion, one that accompanies almost all rituals. "Death is no more; sickness is no more; loss is no more; tragedy is no more;

obstacles are no more; unforeseen evils are no more; being overwhelmed is no more"—these are the direct goals of all *ebo*. In Nigerian Yoruba tradition, *iku* (death) and *arun* (sickness) were actually personified and appeared in Ifa divination poems in mythological combat with the *orisha* and ancestors. Such personifications were supplemented by other malevolent beings absent in the Santeria Mojuba: *egba* (paralysis), *epe* (curse), *ewon* (imprisonment), *ese* (generalized affliction)—surely no strangers to human beings anywhere. Santeria devotees do not now think of Iku, Arun, or Ofo as persons or as having personalities in the same way *orisha* do. Nevertheless, even as abstract names for concrete sufferings they remain the focus of sacrificial acts by the mediating spirits who have replaced the Yoruba *ajogun* (malevolent beings).

Thus *ebo* is Santeria's answer to the problem of suffering, a means to achieve harmony in a universe composed of teeming forces, both good and ill, whose relationships continually change and whose configurations are manipulable through sacrifice. Through the medium of *ebo* and communication with ancestors, deities, and malevolent spirits, the disordered universe is replaced by freshness, clarity, and peace.

The complementary aspect of *ebo* is its relation to the powers and sustenance of the ancestors and *orisha*. Sacrifices constitute their food. *Ebo* forges continuing links between the devotees and the spiritual beings they worship, links that are ritual enactments of the interdependence that exists between human and spiritual worlds. The metaphor of food and feeding is ubiquitous in Santeria sacrificial rites, especially in rites requiring animals as victims. For anything to have been "fed" in Orisha it must have been bathed in the blood of an animal sacrificed in a rite. The human head, stones, metal objects, bracelets, all become empowered by being "fed" with blood. Once dedicated to a deity in this fashion they can, by degrees, function as conduits for the deities themselves. Through this process they become *fundamentos* (foundations) in which the *orisha* resides and through which devotees influence, contact, praise, and care for the god. The *santos* are said to eat, to consume, the sacrifice. The entire procedure is embedded within a metaphor of gift exchange as an expression of reciprocity between the human and spiritual worlds rather than as a material exchange or as self-denial. Humans depend on the *orisha;* the *orisha* depend on human beings.

Halifax and Weidman, on the basis of studies of Santeria in Miami, came to a similar conclusion:

> It [sacrifice] represents an act of obeisance. But, because of Cuban patterns of gift-giving, it also puts the recipient, i.e., the orisha, in a position of indebtedness. The individual is, in effect, "buying"

power, a fact which may be reflected by greater confidence in subsequent relationships and activities.[16]

But it is only in a very remote sense that Halifax and Weidman's economic metaphor of "buying" power is correct. The values that underpin
these sacrifices are of a different order and turn upon reciprocity and
the attitude best expressed as "I give to you that you may give to me,"
or "If I give this thing to you I will always have it to give." The power,
aché, resides in the other world; *ebo* provides the bridge across which it
passes in and out of this world.

The ways in which victims are sacrificed are extremely varied. The
santera may nibble off little pieces of coconut and throw them at Elegba
and the saint being divined; this *ebo* establishes communication with the
deities. The pouring of a libation on the ground for the ancestors is a
form of *ebo*. When the *santera* takes a mouthful of rum, blows out her
cheeks, and sprays the rum on all sides or on objects or people, this is
the traditional African method of sacrificing an alcoholic beverage. *Ebo*
refers not only to animals used as sacrificial victims but also to plants,
food, and assorted objects, all of which are regarded as *ebo*.

A listing of typical sacrificial objects offered in Santeria should make
this matter clear, since the majority of the items used are not animals.
Prescriptions from priest-diviners for illness, atonement, personal problems, and initiations include such food plants and plant products as Cuban plantain, malanga, yams, okra, lompe sarguey tea, flour, gourds,
oils, grass wet with dawn's dew, and ground black-eyed peas wrapped in
plantain leaves and seasoned with salt. Among the animals and objects
used are hens, roosters, pigeons, goats, mice, turtles, woodchucks, guinea
birds, scrubbing pads, pieces of wood, dirt from the corners of a house,
money, a basket, a flag, drums made from cowhide or the skin of a sacrificed goat, and candles. A second category of sacrifices involves offerings made to the deities and the dead. These are almost always offered
in conjunction with communal feasts. Such offerings include bread, cigars, water, food cooked without salt, and candles.

Except when an animal victim's life is actually substituting for the
endangered life of the human being on whose behalf a sacrifice is being
made, animal sacrifice is only secondarily for the purpose of causing the
victim's death. The main purpose is to obtain the animal's blood for
application to ritual objects. The powerful but invisible fluid *aché* is created or increased by the application of blood still warm from the animal
victim. The saints drink the blood through the *fundamentos*, the sacrificial objects.[17] *Santeros* express this concept in different ways within the
metaphors of communication and eating: "Los animales son mensajeros

que van a reunirse con los ocha" (The animals are messengers that go
to reunite with the *orisha*); "Los santos no comen; son espíritus y solo
absorben el espíritu de la sangre" (The saints don't eat; they are spirits
and absorb the spirit of the blood).

Next in significance after the blood is the flesh. In most cases the
flesh is not considered destroyed as the blood is. After the blood has
been applied to the objects and the main rites have been concluded, the
person for whom the sacrifice was made washes off the blood with cold
water, and this blood cannot be used for anything else. Its vitality has
been transferred to the objects, and what remains is "strong," though
not deadly or harmful. The flesh, unless it is otherwise tainted in some
fashion, is not considered defiled and is consumed by those who participate in the rite. "La sangre para el Santo; la carne para el santero" (The
blood for the Saint; the meat for the *santero*).

The rules according to which sacrifices are prescribed and composed
are complex. There is an evident correspondence between specific deities and particular sacrificial victims. Each deity has its favorite animals,
plants, and foods; *ebo* takes these tastes into account. In some cases the
materials composing the *ebo* symbolize aspects of the person's problems
or desires. Although I will describe the sacrificial practices in as much
detail as my observations and information allow, as befits their significance within the context of the religion, I can do no more at this stage
of research than to confirm Zahan's statement of the matter:

> The "dosage" of these offerings, as well as the priority observed
> in their use, give evidence of a veritable "choelogy" of which Afri-
> cans are the incontestable masters. The fundamental principles of
> the science depend on a profound knowledge of the semantic value
> of the materials utilized and their adaptation to the different situa-
> tions in which man finds himself. Of course nowhere in Africa
> does this "science" exist in the form of a corpus of doctrines.
> Rather, it consists in the application of a mode of thought which
> constantly strives to grasp the relationships between beings and
> things, between beings and the conditions which determine them.[18]

Farrow gives a list of sacrificial victims and the corresponding problems for which they are sacrificed either singly or in combination (sheep
against death in sickness; ram, sheep, and old cock for victory in time
of war) and thus confirms Zahan's statement for the Nigerian Yoruba.[19]
It is true of Santeria as well and should be a focus for future researchers
investigating its ritual system.

Certain deities have to be "fed" by their priests at regular intervals.
Whether or not this must be done depends on the worshipper's position

within the social structure of the religion and on his or her possession of certain ritual objects. Any person possessing *guerreros* (warriors)—a special set of ritual objects—has to make *ebo* to them at regular intervals. This involves the sacrifice of a fowl and offerings such as candy, corn, gin, or honey. It is accompanied by prayer and consecration of the *ebo* to the deities represented by the *guerreros:* Eleggua, Ogun, Ochossi, and Osun. Both priests and non-priests who have *guerreros* perform this sacrifice. A priest, however, has to sacrifice to all the deities annually, a much more elaborate sacrifice that involves not only fowl but also goats or sheep and replicates the *matanza* of the priest's initiation. Another series of sacrifices may be offered on the feast days of the *orisha* with which the priest has a special relationship because he has been initiated into that deity's cult. As each of the *orisha* is identified with a Catholic saint, so does the saint's day fixed by the Catholic Church become a day on which the *orisha* is venerated. Not all Santeria cult houses do this. Nor is it absolutely required of them. The feasts may or may not involve sacrifices of animals. In either the annual sacrifices to a priest's *orisha* or sacrifices offered on saints' days, the sacrifice is followed by a communal feast in which the animal victims as well as the other food items are consumed by priests, invited guests, and visitors.

Other sacrifices are aperiodic. They are signaled by special events, such as personal, interpersonal, and spiritual problems requiring the advice of a diviner, or by initiations into the various ranks of the religion's membership. Sacrifices may be offered after consultation with a diviner for specific and serious problems of health, life crises, mental illness, and other problems, including the violation of taboos and ritual prescriptions. Sin, personal misfortune, and disease are all treated in much the same fashion. What the diviner gives the petitioner is a prescription for what ails him. An animal sacrifice is a frequent but by no means inevitable remedy. Other items listed earlier may be used. The specific animals, plants, or objects to be used will vary with the nature of the problem brought to the diviner and the petitioner's status within the religion.

The initiation of a priest is an elaborate rite extending over seven days, and sacrifice plays an important part in it. This is the first occasion on which the novice is actually able to witness the sacrifice of four-legged animals—or any sacrifice as it is carried out by priests. It is during the *asiento* (seat or seating) that the spiritual mechanism of sacrifice is explained to the novice. Henceforth the novice can be in the room where priests offer animal sacrifices and can assist in the rituals. Non-priests are barred from the room where these sacrifices are offered, and the room itself is screened off from the view of those who are not initiated priests. This sacrifice is among the most secret of the religion's practices. It involves animals in numbers appropriate to the deity regarded as ruling or protecting the initiate. The specific animals to be sacrificed also vary from deity to deity. After the *asiento* there are two other initiation periods, the end of each being marked by the making of an *ebo*. The second occurs three months after the *asiento* and the third a year and five days after the *asiento*. These *ebo* are on a much smaller scale than the first. They involve less time, fewer people, and far fewer animals, not usually including the four-legged animals that figure in the week-long *asiento*.

Other initiations may require the sacrifice of fowl in the process of acquiring the special ritual objects connected with the various Santeria deities. Their acquisition represents access to specific knowledge and powers within the religion and is the way in which adherents rise through the religion's social strata. These initiations do not occur with any predictable regularity. Their occurrence depends on the believer's religious knowledge, level of devotion, and personal ambition; the influence of the priest to whom the initiate is attached; and the initiate's ability to pay for the rite.

Aside from people who have *guerreros* and thus the right to sacrifice to them in their homes, only priests can sacrifice animals. And only those priests who have undergone a special initiation can sacrifice animals requiring the use of knives to cause their death. Such priests are said to "have knife" or *finaldo* (also pronounced *pinaldo*). *Finaldo* is the name of the ceremony by virtue of which a priest gains the ritual right to use the knife in sacrifices. In practical terms, it grants him the ritual right to sacrifice four-legged animals, since these are the only animals that must be killed with a knife. While women as well as men can undergo this initiation, women are not allowed to do the actual sacrificing of the animal. Women who "have knife" can learn the technique and pass it on to priests whom they instruct or initiate. The rite of *finaldo* involves animals sacrificed to the deity Ogun, who rules iron, warfare, and sacrifice. During the rite the initiate receives a set of knives that have been consecrated by prayer, incantation, herbs, and sacrificial offerings. From then on he uses these knives in carrying out his work.

The number of animals to be sacrificed is determined in several ways, all of which have currency throughout the Santeria community and are set by the rules of tradition for what is efficacious in ritual. If these rules are not obeyed the sacrifice will be ineffective. It is part of the priest's training to learn these rules, since they constitute his technique for dealing with sacred beings with whom he attempts to communicate through sacrifice.

I have observed the number of animals to be sacrificed determined in at least three ways, which are not mutually exclusive. In some cases the number is specified by a diviner in conformity with the directions derived from his set divination procedures. In other cases the number is specified by the symbolic correspondence between the specific deity being addressed and the number associated with that deity. These correspondences are fairly standard throughout the Santeria community. In still other cases the substitution method is used. Sometimes a set number of animals is considered equivalent to a much larger number of animals, usually based on some precedent in the copious mythology of the religion. The mythology serves as a guide and commentary on much of its ritual. At other times a certain number of one species of animal is considered ritually equivalent to either a larger or smaller number of animals of another species for the purposes of the specific sacrifice required.

Animals are sacrificed in one of four ways, depending on the type of animal involved. Three of these methods apply to fowl. In the first method the fowl, after being presented to the deity and enumerated among the items to be offered to it, is consecrated by prayer and incantation. The participants are cleansed by having the fowl brushed up and down their bodies. The fowl itself may be cleansed by having cigar smoke blown over its body. The bird's head is placed under the foot of the *santero* or *santera* and its head is wrung off. The *santero* simply bends over and forcefully yanks up the body of the bird. This is sufficient to sever the head. The animal dies instantly and its blood and feathers may then be used in ritual. In the second method presentations, prayer, and consecration occur as in the first, but from there the sacrifice proceeds in a different manner. Some *santeros* are strong enough to perform the sacrifice while holding the bird in their hands rather than underfoot. In this case the head and neck are wrung with the hands alone. This can be accomplished very quickly in a single motion, and the blood and feathers are then used in ritual. The third method also begins like the first, but in this case the bird's head is severed with a knife. The three methods are equally acceptable.

The sacrifice of four-legged animals is different, for they can only be sacrificed with a knife, requiring the service of a priest who has undergone the ritual of *finaldo*. The animal is held on a tether while being presented, enumerated, and consecrated. The animal may or may not be gagged with a piece of coconut and have its mouth tied shut to ease its way into the other world. The priest cuts the throat and severs the head in a single back-and-forth motion with the knife. This entire act can be accomplished in about twenty seconds depending on the size of the animal, the strength of the priest, and the sharpness of the knife. The blood is then drained from the body, collected into bowls, and used for ritual preparations.

I have given but a skeletal picture of the practice of *ebo*, the bare bones but not the flesh. This flesh, as religious conception and attitude, appears in the chants accompanying the sacrifice of animals and in a number of ceremonial gestures that punctuate formal sacrifices.

Before dedicating the animal victims to the warrior deities Eleggua, Ogun, and Ochossi, the officiating priest or priestess washes their heads and feet in cool water, enumerating each animal in this fashion: "Eleggua, Ogun, Ochossi mo fun o ni akuko kan" (Elegba, Ogun, Ochossi, I give you this rooster—or whatever the animal is). Following the dedication of the animals the priest and whoever else is present sing chants that parallel and comment upon the freeing of the victim's blood. The first chant announces the victim's ordeal.

Leader: Press, tearing and rending; press, tearing, rending; twisting.
Chorus: Elegba presses; tearing and rending. Elegba presses; tearing and separating.

As the chant evokes the rending of the victim's body, all those present show their sympathy and identification with the victim by pulling on the skin of their throats. In this way they imitate the victim, for it is at this site that the priest will sever the victim's head. Although the chant makes reference to Elegba blocking the victim's cry, generally the animals are surprisingly quiet throughout the sacrifice. *Santeros* sometimes remark on the apparent placidity with which many sacrificial animals endure even the moment of slaughter. Such animals are said to be *muy bravo*.

Although the first chant describes Elegba as "tearing and rending" the victim, this is partly misleading. Elegba is present at the rending of the victim and receives part of its blood but cannot take a life. Only Ogun among all the *santos* can do that. The sacrifice is not merely a life-taking but the preparation of a feast for the *orisha* in which Ogun carves the way for all the others so that the goal of the *ebo* can be achieved. At the same time Ogun assures and protects the sacrificers. In one chant the sacrificers allocate the responsibility for taking the victim's life to Ogun and not to themselves, for it is Ogun who rules the knife and governs the entire act of sacrifice. Ogun makes it possible for all the deities to feast.

Leader: Ogun makes a feast.
Chorus: Blood hit the mark; cover with drops in a circle.

The incantations continue with a call directly to the victim's blood and body to act as intermediaries. Together with Elegba the blood and flesh of the victim allay misfortune and death. The blood itself is considered hot. It is a solid thing melted by the knife in the act of sacrifice. It is, like rain or breath, full of potency. The imagery of the next chant suggests that under the sacrificial knife some of the flesh of the victim is transmuted to blood and becomes power, a repetition of a primordial act.

Leader: Blood is again melting and falling like rain.
Chorus: Indeed the life-breath, blood is again melting and falling like rain.
Leader: Blood going like rain; blood going like rain.
Chorus: Blood, blood, going like rain, blood.

It is at this point that the victim is killed and its blood and power become accessible. The officiating priest pours a little of the blood onto the floor as a libation to the ancestors, as a remembrance and a request for their approval of the sacrifice. A song taken up at this point indicates that the ancestors, too, are provoked and moved by offers of blood. Blood incites; blood is hot; blood "heats up" the room where the sacrifice is offered. Accordingly the bloodletting requires a great concentration of physical and mental energy on the part of the priest and participants and generates a heat only water can cool. So the priest then pours cool water for the ancestors on the victim's body, the emblems of the *orisha,* and the floor. Whereas blood provokes and excites, water brings gentleness and softness; for the intensity of blood, water is the refreshing antidote.

Leader: An antidote to gather and fasten together softness, behold!
An antidote to gather and fasten together softness, indeed!
An antidote, our father, so that we don't see death.
Chorus: Easiness, gentleness, gathered, tied together, softness.

Elegba and all the *orisha* being fed receive invocations to call them forth. The priest "feeds" them by pouring blood on their *fundamentos,* starting with Elegba. Honey, rum, and cigars are offered to Elegba as additional sacrifices. The reciprocal character of the offerings, their character as exchanges, is quite clear at this point. Each of the proffered objects has a meaning within the context indicated by the chants. Each object apparently symbolizes what it can be exchanged for with the *orisha*. Thus rum symbolizes comfort, honey sweetness, cigars satisfaction. The worshippers use palm oil and candles in the same way at later points; they represent wealth and knowledge, respectively. Candles also represent light in the sense of spiritual evolution.

> Leader: Elegba I give you honey, make my world sweet.
> Okra begs to be like honey, O!
> Okra begs to be like honey.
> Okra is very sweet and is like honey.
> Okra begs to be like honey.

The reference to okra is not clear to me. Sometimes devotees are told by diviners to put okra above their doorsills to prevent the entry of witchcraft into their homes. Perhaps a connection with fear and anxiety is being implied here, with the idea that okra represents security against these two mental plagues. While okra is humble, green, sweet, and protective, it does not have the golden sweetness of honey. Perhaps okra protects but does not invigorate, for security and pleasure in life can be light years apart.

When fowl are the animal victims the person offering the sacrifice tears feathers from the bodies of the dead birds and spreads them on the floor around the *orisha* emblems. If the *orisha* resides in an urn, the priest, when feeding the *orisha* by pouring blood into the urn, will allow some to drip onto the outer surface. Later when the priest spreads feathers around he smears some on the outside of the urn and the blood holds them on. When the process is over the *fundamentos* of the warrior deities are literally coated with feathers. In the chant that accompanies these acts the main goal of the sacrifices is expounded, that through the death and suffering of the animal victim and through the worshippers' incantation and praise of the *santos* these spirits will speak and make themselves known.

> Leader: They pluck the chicken's feathers little by little.
> With death, with suffering
> provoking the spirits, inciting them by naming their praise names
> to speak, to grunt.

Chorus: Incite the spirits by calling their praise names,
Incite the spirits by calling their praise names.

The worshippers mop the whole area around the *orisha* emblems with an improvised clump of feathers held in both hands. They get down on their knees to do this, and the mopping joins and mixes the spilled blood, the feathers, and the earth, which the floor of the room symbolically represents. They then lay this undifferentiated mass at the foot of the *orisha* altar for fortune and increase and to "see the dead."

Leader: Meat mixed for me, blood mixed for me.
Chorus: Meat, blood mixed for me.
Leader: Mixed so we see the Dead.
Chorus: Meat, blood mixed for me.
Leader: Mixed for a house.
Chorus: Meat, blood mixed for me.
Leader: Mixed for money.
Chorus: Meat, blood mixed for me.

Two acts close the ceremony. First is the removal of the bodies of the animal victims. Each victim is alternately raised and then touched to the ground three times. Once again those assembled acknowledge the crucial role of the victim as an intermediary between the spirits and themselves. When the body is touched to the earth they say "Wo ekun e nile" (Look at your sorrow on the ground). According to one priest the assembly says this to acknowledge that they have offered the animal in exchange for their own misfortunes and sufferings.[20] In the final act closing the ceremony the worshippers light a candle and offer a prayer to Elegba: "Elegba I give you a candle, give my world light and knowledge." Usually the candle burns until it consumes itself. The person on whose behalf the priest made the sacrifice remains until the candle finally flickers and expires.

In most cases the sacrificed animals are cooked and consumed by devotees. The animals may be butchered, cooked, and consumed all at the same site or divided among those present at the *ebo* and cooked and eaten later at their own homes. The animals may also be cooked immediately but served the next day.

After the immolation of the animal and its butchering, certain parts are set aside for priests involved in the rite and for the person on whose behalf the rite is being performed. The portions so divided are specified ritually. So are those portions that must be offered to the objects housing and representing the *santos*. These latter portions of the animals (their *aché*, the Lucumi word for power) are presented to the deities and placed in front of their shrines, where it is believed they consume the food's spiritual essence. Afterward the food is simply disposed of as garbage. But only a small amount is treated in this fashion. People consume most of it. In some instances, however, the victims of sacrifice may not be consumed. A divination ceremony may indicate that the *santo* wants the fowls as a burnt offering or that they should be taken to a hill, forest, or river and left there. If a fowl should die before the rites take place it cannot be used as a victim or consumed, and a diviner will have to determine what the *santo* wants done with it.

The other parts of the sacrificed animals remain to be accounted for. The blood, as we have seen, is poured by the priest on certain of the ritual objects, which are then empowered and further consecrated by contact with it. In some cases a few drops of the blood may be placed on the tongues or heads of those present by a priest. This act has the same effect on them as it does on the ritual objects. It consecrates, purifies, empowers, and brings about a union of the deity, the sacrificed animal, and all those present at the rite. The greater part of the blood is combined with an infusion of herbs, special waters, and assorted plants to make a ritual preparation called *omiero* (Yoruba meaning cool or cooling water), which will be used during the coming year in a number of major and minor rituals and as a medicine. The skins and hides are frequently used by drummers to make heads for their drums. I have also seen the skins of sheep used to make rugs, which are trotted out thereafter on important ritual occasions. Other parts are disposed of in the forest, the river, or another place dictated by divination or by the nature of the rite.

In Yorubaland priests made *ebo* at outdoor shrines. A priest working at a public Elegba shrine knew that once he had completed the *ebo*, scavengers would emerge from the bush and pick the shrine and emblems clean. While it is true that the Yoruba were and remain urbanites, it is also true that they are farmers who commute daily between town and farm areas that are surrounded by the bush, the forest, and its denizens. In a metropolis such as New York or any of the Cuban cities that are centers for Santeria, the sacrifices take place indoors and the devotees have to clean the emblems themselves by washing them in cold water, dry white wine, or white rum. A difference in ecology affects the disposal of the animals. While city parks may substitute for the forest in one sense, they lack predators. As a result a number of the victims of sacrifice end up in the hands of sanitation departments and the American Society for the Prevention of Cruelty to Animals (ASPCA), sometimes provoking public outrage. The symbiosis of town and bush which is such an important part of traditional Yoruba life was so strong that priests would even let the bush do sacrifices. On these occasions they would take the animal victim live to a public road and leave it there tied to a pole to be devoured by predatory birds and animals from the bush. The ecological symbiosis of bush and town is broken in the metropolis. Only a semblance remains.

After the ceremonies are over the room is ritually cleansed and then swept and scrubbed down. Not only does the cleansing restore the room to its former state for purely social reasons; it also allows people who are not priests to enter the room. It has now become safe for ordinary people.

In the spring of 1980 two priestesses of Santeria in New York had their houses raided by agents of the ASPCA. The priestesses were performing sacrificial rites, and the agents presented them with summonses and confiscated the animals. Such raids are not uncommon. They are one reason why *santeras* practice their religion in secret. But these *santeras* maintained that they were being subjected to harassment by the ASPCA and that the ASPCA's raids constituted interference with their constitutional right to freedom of religion. They organized a group of priests, circulated petitions, and obtained lawyers.

After I became aware of the raids I visited ASPCA headquarters in New York to find out what officials there knew about Santeria and to question inaccuracies I had seen in newspaper reports of the raid. I found that they were confusing Santeria with other religions. When I informed them that I was an anthropologist conducting research on Santeria, they were eager to have any information I could give them. I was eventually able to locate the two priestesses and assist them in their defense, in the process serving as a liaison between them and the ASPCA and American Civil Liberties Union.

The case and the trial wore on for about a year and a half. Eventually the ASPCA dropped its case; the priestesses, on advice of their lawyer, pleaded guilty to disorderly conduct charges, which bore no fine or sentence, and the organization of priests and priestesses entered into negotiation with the city. What the Santeria priests and priestesses wanted was legislation allowing them to purchase custom slaughter permits in conformance with New York state laws. That would allow them to carry out the sacrifices in their homes and would notify the ASPCA where the sacrifices were occurring and who was performing them.

Although the summonses were issued for violations of the agriculture and markets laws, the actual intent of the raids was to stop the sacrifices, which had been prejudged as cruel and whose religious basis was neither considered nor respected. That the case ever came up at all is testimony to the endurance and, in some places, the revitalization of Africanisms in the United States. Once the pivotal position sacrifice occupies in traditional African religion is recognized, it becomes clear that it was not two *santeras* but an African religion that was on trial.

The Meaning of the Rites

The full meaning of these sacrificial rites cannot be explained here, but some comments can be made in relation to the general context in which they occur and in relation to the observations of psychologists, psychiatrists, and anthropologists who have studied sacrifice in general or Yoruba-Santeria sacrifice in particular.

For the Cuban immigrants who brought Santeria with them to the United States the religion serves a purpose it did not serve in Cuba. It has become a system through which adjustments to exile in a foreign land and an alien culture may be mediated. Through divination and other rituals these immigrants attempt to put some order into the multitude of adjustments and changes in behavior and values they must make to survive. They use such rituals to help them cope with unemployment, illness, endangered personal relationships, disappointed expectations, isolation, discrimination, and the whole host of conflicts that arise. Sacrifice, as one element of the religion, should be seen within this overall context. That Santeria spread to segments of other ethnic groups that are also socially and culturally marginal suggests that it serves similar or related functions for African Americans, Puerto Ricans, and American Jews who have been entering the religion in slowly increasing numbers over the past twenty years.

The question of the psychological meaning of sacrificial ritual has been approached in a number of ways. Freud hypothesized that the rite expressed unconscious urges in which the death of an animal really represented the death of a human being whose murder was a desired but unthinkable act. Usually this act was a patricide and the sacrifice a symbolic enactment of oedipal wishes in which the slaying of the animal was the slaying of the father who was at once hated, feared, and loved.[21] That the sacrificial victim need not always represent the father was an idea put forward by Money-Kryle in the wake of Freud's work. While he agreed with the basic psychoanalytic idea that sacrifice satisfies a variety of unconscious fantasies, Money-Kryle thought that the sacrificial victim could represent a variety of human victims (father, mother, self) or even situations in which the sacrificer was not the slayer of the human victims (e.g., father murdering mother).[22]

Whether or not one agrees with either of these views, both take the position that animal sacrifice in religion is an expression of unconscious urges and that it is important to know who is being symbolically murdered. Raymond Prince, in a 1975 study of sacrifice among the Yoruba of Nigeria, was never able to come up with a clear determination on this point because informants gave him conflicting answers.[23] I will not be able to do much better. But material collected from Santeria practitioners may lend some new data, if not more clarity, to the issues.

A Santeria myth of Grillelu gives some answers. It refers to three main topics: how Olofi's plan for life on earth got derailed, how the spirit Grillelu got his name, and how the practice of sacrificing pigeons originated.

In the beginning when our present universe took shape Olofi [Jesus] summoned all men of knowledge to take part in the great scheme of life and all the races of men manifested on earth.

It was thus that each person living his own way presented Olofi with difficulties which in turn obstructed Olofi's master plan. At this point in time all knowledgeable men realized that under these circumstances no positive action could manifest. Olofi, considering his plan to be failing, felt vanquished.

A spirit appeared to him which said, "Sacrifice as an ebo one hundred and one pigeons to purify with their blood the different maladies that affect the good will of the positive spirits."

Olofi, upon hearing this from the spirit, started to shake because the life of the pigeons was connected to his own and to that of Olodumare [God]. Within all this his sentence says: "For the good of all my children there is no other alternative."

And for the first time pigeons were sacrificed.

The spirit who suggested this to Olofi guided him to all the places where a drop of blood would be placed to purify everything. This way all of Olofi's wishes were done and he, in turn, represented Olodumare.

And when everything Olofi wanted was completed he summoned this great spirit and called him Grillelu and said to him: "You have helped me and I bless you unto eternity and your name shall be Grillelu."[24]

The lives of both Olofi and Olodumare are seen as connected to the lives of the pigeons being sacrificed, so that in sacrificing the fowl they are sacrificing part of themselves also. That is why Olofi was afraid and had to be convinced that no other act would suffice to purify the world of its sicknesses and problems. According to this myth, then, at this first sacrifice both Olodumare and Olofi were present in the sacrificial victims and, even more important, were powerless to order earthly life without the bodies and blood of these animals. This bespeaks a conception of the continuity and interdependence of all life forms (spiritual, human, animal) that is characteristic of African religions and of all forms of animism.

The believer is also asked to behave as the *orisha* did; in a case of grave difficulty the believer is to imitate the deities by offering a similar sacrifice. Although the data are not entirely clear on this point, it may well be that Olofi and Olodumare are present not just in the primordial sacrificial victims described in the Grillelu myth but in all sacrificial victims. To the degree that a sacrifice reenacts this first one, the persons on whose behalf it is conducted is also identified with the sacrificial victim.

The sacrifice, then, is a meeting place, a nexus, where the animal's, Olofi's, Olodumare's, and the sacrificer's lives all combine without distinction. At this meeting place new power becomes available to humans and deities alike. At several points in the rituals the sacrificers make gestures or speak in ways that identify them with the victim. It will be recalled that when a rooster is offered for sacrifice each person present commiserates with the victim's plight by pulling at the skin of his or her own throat. Mason informs us that before the bodies of the slain fowl are taken away, they are touched to the ground, at which point the priest says in Yoruba, "Wo ekun e nile" (Look at your sorrow on the ground). This is intended to remind the person that the life of the blood sacrifice was offered in exchange for the person's own misfortunes and sorrows.[25] Either of these behaviors may be tentatively interpreted as identification of self with the sacrificial victim.

Another approach to the psychological meaning of sacrifice sees a connection between sacrificial ritual and personal guilt, conscious or unconscious. Anthropologist A. F. C. Wallace clearly stated this point of view:

> Now these sacrifices and offerings have in common a quality similar to that of taboo: the giving up of something of value in order to avoid injury by supernatural forces. It is not difficult to infer that such actions are motivated, consciously or unconsciously, by the wish to appease a being toward whom the person making the sacrifice feels guilty.[26]

While both Santeria and Yoruba traditional religion contain such propitiatory or penitential sacrifices, they are not the only kind found, and a conception of sacrifice that reduces it entirely to propitiation is a narrow one indeed. The liturgy of Santeria-Yoruba emphasizes not propitiation of the deity but acquisition of power and benefits through relationships of exchange with the deities, as is clear from chants used in sacrificial rites. It becomes a kind of barter in which what is obtained is not a forestalling of divine vengeance or even forgiveness of transgression but assistance in realizing personal desires and aspirations.[27] The goal of atonement is replaced by the goal of personal achievement and the granting of forgiveness by the acquisition of power. Prince asked whether the healing power of ritual lay in the catharsis through symbolic expression of unconscious conflicts or in the generation of hope and conviction. Ultimately, despite his psychoanalytic orientation, he came to favor the latter option in relation to Yoruba sacrifices because "the verbal, symbolic and motor activities all represent expressions of consciously desired ends in varying degrees of concreteness."[28] I believe that Prince's statement is as true for *orisha* devotees in the northeastern United States as it is for their West African counterparts.

The New World Context

Caribbean and South America

Metraux gives a description of sacrificial practices in Haitian voodoo that can be compared to Santeria practices. In the Haitian religion "the blood sacrifice is the climax of the series of Catholic or pagan rites which make up what is called a 'service.'"[29] In Santeria, animal sacrifice is set off quite clearly from Catholic rites and cannot be seen as a climax to them. This is not true of offerings, however. A Catholic church may be the place where certain remains from sacrificial offerings are deposited. In this case the church comes in at the end of the rite instead of at a point leading up to it. In both cases sacrifice maintains its central position in the two systems of ritual.

G. E. Simpson described the sacrificial rites of the Shango cult of Trinidad, a group of Yoruba origin that retains a number of Yoruba linguistic and ritual traits, among them the names of the *orisha* and spirit possession. Forms of this cult also exist on St. Lucia, where it is called *kele*, and on Grenada and Carriacou.

> The African cult on the Caribbean that most closely resembles kele is a type of ancestor ritual called the Big Drum Dance (the Nation Dance, or simply saraca [sacrifice]) in Grenada and Carriacou. . . . In Grenada, Shango was originally the ritual of Africans who arrived from Ijesha, Nigeria in 1849 after the abolition of slavery.

After completing their indentures, these Yoruba people settled at Munich, Concorde, and La Mode. Years later, when they and their descendants began to move away from these closed communities, their religious cult attracted many followers.[30]

M. G. Smith noted that as the cult spread "it was marked by syncretisms of form and content, numerous traits being taken over from the Nation Dance as well as from Catholicism, until Shango is now the representative form of African ritual among Grenadians."[31] That should make us consider the question of Africanisms in terms other than retention under the regime of slavery. Grenadian Shango originated after slavery. Like Santeria, it seems to have changed its complexion as it spread beyond its original closed confines and to have grown rather than diminished in the postslavery period.

Brazil has several Yoruba-based as well as Yoruba-derived religious groups that have been copiously described. Some of these groups have also been greatly influenced by spiritism, which penetrated deeply into Brazilian society.[32] Simpson noted several differences between sacrificial practices in Yoruba and the Yoruba-derived groups in Brazil and practices in Haiti and Trinidad.[33] Eduardo and Carneiro also give descriptions of sacrificial practices in neo-African cults in Brazil.[34]

United States

References to sacrifice in the literature of black religion in the United States are rare. Most accounts I found date from the 1930s and refer back to even earlier periods. They show that certain aspects of the rites were either hidden from the informants, were beyond their knowledge or comprehension, or were not thought safe to divulge to outsiders.

There were at least four contexts in which sacrifices and sacrificial offerings occurred among blacks in the United States: funeral rites, whether in wakes ("settin-ups") or en route to the burial site; healing rituals, especially for victims of sorcery or conjure; initiation into hoodoo practice; and magical rites for the acquisition of malign occult power. Examples cited, while mainly southern, are not exclusively so. While not attempting any close analysis or comparison of these examples with Santeria practice, I will append a few comments.[35]

FUNERAL RITES
Sacrifice of a fowl as part of funeral ceremonies. Sarah Washington, Pine Barrens, near Eulonia, Georgia, 1939: "Aunt Sarah said that they went

to set-ups and that in the old days, after the mourners had arrived, a chicken was killed. Neither Aunt Sarah nor Uncle Ben, however, knew the reason for this."

Sacrifice of a fowl at the entrance to a house as part of funeral rites. Jane Lewis, Darien, Georgia, 1939: "Yes'm, dey sho did hab regluh feasts in dem days, but tuhday, at mos settin-ups, yuh dohn git nuttn but coffee and bread. Den dey would cook a regluh meal an dey would kill a chicken in front uh duh doe, wring he neck an cook um fuh duh feas. Den wen we all finish, we take wut victual lef an put it in a dish by duh chimley an das fuh duh sperrit tuh hab a las good meal." *Comment:* This looks like an entrance *ebo* and a communal feast followed by an ancestral offering inside the house.

Sacrifice of a hog in funeral rites. Katie Brown, Sapelo Island, Georgia, 1939: "Yes'm, we hab set-ups wid duh dead, bit I ain know bout killin chicken. At duh fewnul, dey kills hawg and hab plenty tuh eat. Duh reason fuh dis is so dat sperrit had plenty at duh las."

Sacrifice of a fowl as part of a funeral wake and as protection from spirits of the recent dead. Shad Hill, Sapelo Island, Georgia, 1939: "Yes'm, Gran Hestuh tell me uh set-ups. Dey kill a wite chicken wen dey hab set-up to keep duh spirits way. She say a wite chicken is duh only ting dat will keep duh spirits way an she alluz keep wite chicken fuh dat in duh yahd. Lak dis. Hestuh she hab frien and frien die. Ebry ebenin friens spirit come back an call tuh Hestuh. Hestuh knowed ef she keep it up, she die too. Hestuh den kills wite chicken, tro it out uh doze, an shut doe quick. Wen she tro it out she say, 'Heah, spirit, moob away—dohn come back no mo.' I dunno wut she do wid duh blood an fedduhs."

Sacrifice of a white chicken as part of a night funeral. Jim Myers, Mush Bluff Island, Georgia, 1939: We asked him to tell us more of his African great grandmother. . . . We asked again about night funerals. "She just say they have em at night but she didn say wy. She did say they alluz kill a wite chicken at the time they go to bury em an they take the blood an feathuhs an they do sumpm special with em but I ain unduhstood how it is."

HEALING

Sacrifice of fowl as part of a ritual treatment for conjuration. Bessie Royal, White Bluff, Georgia, 1939: "I dohn known how it wuz done but muh faduh wuz cunjuhed by a suttn uhmun dat wuz said to be a hag. He go crazy sometimes lak he was sked by sumpm chasin im. He get wus and dey take im tuh a root doctuh. Duh root doctuh say he wuz conjuhed. He hab us ketch a white chicken wich he split open wile duh chicken

wuz still libe. He place dis chicken, blood an all wile it wuz still wome, on top uh muh faduh head an boun it deah. Well, muh faduh git bettuh fuh a wile. Den all at once he hab anudduh attack an he die befo duh doctuh could git tuh im. Attuh dis I belieb in conjuh mo dan ebuh."
Comment: This use of the sacrificed fowl in healing resembles both Yoruba and Santeria healing rites, e.g., "sacrifice for the head." Of course, use of sacrificed fowl like this is not limited to the Yoruba and is probably found in many other African traditional healing systems.

INITIATION
From New Orleans in the 1930s comes Zora Neale Hurston's description of a sacrifice that was part of her initiation into hoodoo practice under Luke Turner, who claimed to be the nephew of the nineteenth-century queen of New Orleans voodoo Marie Laveau. Hurston's initiation under Turner was the most elaborate of those she described.

> The crate containing the black sheep was opened and the sheep led forward into the center of the circle. He stood there dazedly while the chant of strange syllables rose. . . . The head and withers of the sheep were stroked as the chanting went on. Turner became more and more voluble. At last he seized the straw and stuffed some into the sheep's nostrils. The animal struggled. A knife flashed and the sheep dropped to its knees, then fell prone with its mouth open in a weak cry. My petition was thrust into his throat that he might cry it to the Great One. The broom was seized and dipped in the blood from the slit throat and the group swept vigorously—back and forth, back and forth—the length of the dying sheep. It was swept from the four winds towards the center. The sweeping went on for as along as the blood gushed. Earth, the mother of the Great One and us all, has been appeased. With a sharp stick Turner traced the outline of the sheep and the digging commenced. The sheep was never touched. The ground was dug under him so that his body dropped down into the hole. He was covered with nine sheets of paper bearing the petition and the earth heaped upon him. A white candle was set upon the grave. . . . [36]

Comment: This description has striking resemblances to sacrificial practices in Santeria. Choice of a black sheep would usually be prohibited in Santeria, however, because of the associations attributed to black in Santeria color symbolism. It is notable that this victim was not consumed. Particularly striking is the placing of the petition in the throat of the animal, similar to placing a piece of coconut in the mouth to gag a four-legged sacrificial victim.

OCCULT POWER

An account of sacrifice in pursuit of evil power (i.e., the sorcerer's power) from Adams County, Illinois, concerns acquisition of the famous and terrible black cat bone. The collector, Hyatt, noted that before 1935 this belief was "strictly Negro" in Adams County.

> If you want to be a evil fortune teller, take and kill a black cat, and take the bones out of the top of the cat's head, and a teaspoon of brains, and a bone out of the cat's neck, and a chicken wishbone; then go out to the four corners of the road on a very dark night—if it is raining that would make it still better—holding all these things in your left hand. Then turn your back first on the east, swearing, using the Lord's Name in vain; then turn your back on the north, swearing, using the Lord's Name in vain; then the west, and the south last. Then kneel down and pray, using the Lord's Name in vain again. Now you have turned your back on the world. Go home and you can do any evil you want to, for you have the devil on your side.[37]

Comment: This description leaves out some of the more lurid details of the rite, such as boiling the cat alive, and sees the power as deriving from different bones in the cat than many other accounts.[38] What it does include, however, and what does not appear in many other accounts, is the use of prayer (in addition to curse) as part of the rite. Despite the verbal communication against God, the real communication going on here is with the Devil.

CONTINUING METAPHOR

Even when the sacrificial act does not occur it can still serve as the metaphor through which other rites gain a deeper meaning. This was brought to my attention during research on black folk healers in Newark. A rootworker and owner of a religious store remarked that candle burning was just another version of sacrifice, because candles were made from animal fat and burning a candle was simply another means of sacrificing an animal. It retained that association, he said, even if candles were now made of different materials.

In Search of Africanisms

In the study of the contributions of Africa to the cultures and societies of the New World (and the United States, in particular) it has been common to speak in terms of African survivals or retentions rather than of adaptation to account for the persisting cultural distinctiveness of

African American culture. But to speak of Africanisms solely in terms of survivals is, in a quite literal sense, to speak of them as a kind of superstition, for superstitions are isolated traits or cultural forms left "standing over" after their original institutional supports and the whole system of ideas and values that gave them coherence have collapsed around them. True survival demands plasticity, not petrification.

Adaptation, on the other hand, is not necessarily a rupture with the past but an accommodation within the context of change. A tradition that does not accommodate itself to changed circumstances in ways that will allow it to persist will be unable to reproduce itself and will be extinguished. If the ancestral institutional forms or support have been cut off, that does not mean that new ones have not been found, filled with African content, or molded in line with African patterns of social interaction, worldview, or aesthetic valuation.

The choice between survival and adaptation as approaches to the persisting distinctiveness of African American cultures is a false one. Survival and adaptation are neither complementary nor inherently opposed. Even if the two approaches could be merged the result would still smack of incompleteness because attention to the internal dynamics of the cultures involved would be absent. Adaptation itself is a process.

In searching out the contributions of African immigrants to the United States the tendency to concentrate on individual traits that are traceable to African origins often leads to ambiguous or tendentious results. In many cases such a strategy proves impossible given the present state of knowledge, the specific interests of past investigators, and the momentous changes occurring in Africa itself. Over against this is the proposition that, even when found and traced back to specific African ethnic groups, such individual items do not constitute the only, or perhaps even the most important, contribution of Africans to American culture. Indeed, such items, even when they occur in abundance, may be seen as equivalent to a list of separate individual words from a language. Their presentation and continued existence are important data, but as a simple list of words they are not nearly so important as the patterns and structures that organize them. Dillard, from the point of view of the creolist, has insisted on this point for language, and it may well be true for other domains as well: "If a lot of British occult beliefs—even an overwhelming majority of the items—are shaped in an 'African' pattern, then 'Africanism' is a very prominent factor in such beliefs. In fact, it could properly be said to dominate the belief system."[39]

Once the idea that such deeper-level organizational principles exist is seriously entertained, a further possibility comes into view: not only might such principles be preserved in New World contexts; they might also be generative, shaping adaptations and new cultural production whether from African, European, or African American materials. These new productions and adaptations would be buried beneath the surface of disparate African and non-African traits or items. If that is so, we can retain much that has been learned but we should also begin to reorient our approaches to complement survivals with structures, adaptations with processes, and retentions with principles of generativity. It also means that we must study Africanisms not only as historical phenomena, as persisting remains of American slavery, but also in relation to events of the postslavery era, especially black migration out of the South; Caribbean, South American, and African emigration to the United States; ongoing and historical relationships between Africans and African Americans; and black revitalization movements. Then we can go on to document, study, and better understand the complex and multidimensional culture history of African American communities. From this perspective the search for Africanisms becomes not only historical but also contemporary and can illuminate ongoing processes of preservation and change. I intend this essay as a modest contribution toward that end.

Notes

Research used in this essay was supported by U.S. Public Health Grant no. 5 R01 MH28467, "Inner-City Support Systems Project," from the National Institute of Mental Health to the University of Medicine and Dentistry of New Jersey, Department of Psychiatry and Mental Health Science, Dr. Vivian Garrison, principal investigator; and by a dissertation fellowship from the National Fellowships Fund. Special acknowledgment is due John Mason, through whose kind permission I was able to use the fine translations of sacrificial chants.

1. Philip Curtin, *The Atlantic Slave Trade: A Census* (Madison: University of Wisconsin Press, 1969), 46 table 11. Hugh Thomas, *Cuba: The Pursuit of Freedom* (New York: Harper and Row, 1971), 170, 183. Manuel Moreno Fraginals, "Africans in Cuba: A Quantitative Analysis of the African Population of the Island of Cuba," *Annals of the New York Academy of Sciences* (1977) 292:188–89.

2. Moreno Fraginals, "Africans in Cuba," 190–91 tables 2–4.

3. Ibid., passim. Fernando Ortiz, "Los cabildos afro-cubana," *Revista Bimestre Cubana* (1921) 16:5–39.

4. Allan Kardec, *El libro de los espíritus* and *El libro de los mediums* (Tlacoquemecatl, Mexico: Editorial Diana, 9th ed., 1963). Roger Bastide, *African Civilizations in the New World* (New York: Harper and Row, 1971), 107. For descriptions of Mexican American and Brazilian variants of Kardecan spiritism, see June Macklin, "Belief, Ritual and Healing: New England

Spiritualism and Mexican-American Spiritualism Compared," in *Religious Movements in Contemporary America*, ed. I. Zaretsky and M. Leone (Princeton: Princeton University Press, 1974), and Esther Pressel, "Umbanda in Sao Paulo: Religious Innovation in a Developing Society," in *Religions, Altered States of Consciousness and Social Change*, ed. Erika Bourguignon (Columbus: Ohio State University Press), 264–318. For descriptions of early Cuban Espiritismo, see Fernando Ortiz, "La filosofía penal de las espiritistas," *Revista Bimestre Cubana* (1914) 9:30–39, 122–35, and Armando Andres Bermudez, "Notas para la historia del espiritismo en Cuba," *Etnología y Folklore* (1967) 4:5–22, and "La expansion del 'espiritismo del cordon,'" *Etnología y Folklore* (1968) 5:5–32. For Puerto Rican Espiritismo in the United States, see Vivian Garrison, "Doctor, Espiritista or Psychiatrist? Health-Seeking Behavior in a Puerto Rican Neighborhood of New York City," *Medical Anthropology* (1977) 1(2):65–180, and Alan Harwood, *RX: Spiritist as Needed, a Study of a Puerto Rican Community Mental Health Resource* (New York: Wiley, 1977).

5. Lydia Cabrera, *El Monte* (Miami: Colección Chichereku, 1971), 64–65.

6. Ortiz, "Los cabildos," and *Hampa afro-cubano: Los negros brujos* (Miami: Ediciones Universal, 1973; first published in 1906).

7. R. D. Rumbaut and R. G. Rumbaut, "The Family in Exile: Cuban Expatriates in the U.S.," *American Journal of Psychiatry* (1976) 133(4):395.

8. Thomas Boswell and James R. Curtis, *The Cuban-American Experience: Culture, Images and Perspectives* (Totowa, N.J.: Rowman and Allenheld, 1984), 108.

9. Benigno E. Aguirre, "Differential Migration of Cuban Social Races," *Latin American Research Review* (1976) 11:115. This is true of the senior Santeria priesthood as well but not of the general population of Cuba, which in 1953 was 27 percent mulatto; see ibid., 104, and Boswell and Curtis, *Cuban-American Experience*, 103. Over the course of their development the secret religious practices ceased to be the exclusive property of persons of African descent. For the practice of Santeria in Regla, Cuba, primarily by Hispanics, see Romulous Lachatanere, *Manual de Santeria* (Havana: Editorial Caribe, 1942), 33.

10. Aguirre, "Differential Migration," 115.

11. I borrowed the coinage *Santerismo* from Vivian Garrison, personal communication.

12. Harwood, *RX: Spiritist as Needed*. For a more accurate description of Santeria among Puerto Ricans that distinguishes it from Espiritismo, see Garrison, "Doctor, Espiritista or Psychiatrist?"

13. Amiri Baraka, *The Autobiography of LeRoi Jones/Amiri Baraka* (New York: Freundlich Books, 1984), 205, 215–17, 236. Carl M. Hunt, *Oyotunji Village: The Yoruba Movement in America* (Washington, D.C.: University Press of America, 1979). George Brandon, "Santeria, Black Nationalism and Orisha-Voodoo," paper given at Rutgers University Latin American Insti-

tute Conference on Intrahemispheric Migration, Eagleton Institute, New Brunswick, N.J., Oct. 1980.

14. J. O. Awolalu, *Yoruba Beliefs and Sacrificial Rites* (London: Longmans, 1979).

15. Santeria notebook, personal document no. 2, author's files, 1980.

16. Joan Halifax and Hazel Weidman, "Religion as a Mediatory Institution in Acculturation," in *Religion and Psychotherapy*, ed. R. H. Cox (Springfield, Ill.: Charles C. Thomas, 1973), 327.

17. William Bascom, "The Focus of Cuban Santeria," *Southwestern Journal of Anthropology* (1950) 6(1):64–68.

18. Dominique Zahan, *The Religion, Spirituality and Thought of Traditional Africa*, trans. by Kate and Lawrence Martin (Chicago: University of Chicago Press, 1979), 33.

19. Stephen Farrow, *Faith, Fancies and Fetish, or Yoruba Paganism* (New York: Negro Universities Press, 1969 reprint), 96–97.

20. John Mason, *Ebo Eje (Blood Sacrifice)* (New York: Yoruba Theological Archministry, 1981), 10.

21. Sigmund Freud, "Totem and Taboo," in *Basic Writings of Sigmund Freud* (New York: Modern Library, 1938; first published in 1920).

22. R. Money-Kryle, *The Meaning of Sacrifice* (London: Hogarth Press, 1929).

23. Raymond Price, "Symbols and Psychotherapy: The Example of Yoruba Sacrificial Ritual," *Journal of the American Academy of Psychoanalysis* (1975), 3(3):321–38.

24. Nicolas Anagarica, *Manual de orihate, religion lucumi* (n.p., n.d. [1955?]), 89.

25. Mason, *Ebo Eje*, 1, 4.

26. A. F. C. Wallace, *Religion: An Anthropological View* (New York: Random House, 1966), 65.

27. Awolalu, *Yoruba Beliefs*. Mercedes Sandoval, "Santeria: Afro-Cuban Concepts of Disease and Its Treatment in Miami," *Journal of Operational Psychiatry* (1977), 3(2):137–52.

28. Prince, "Symbols and Psychotherapy," 334.

29. Alfred Metraux, *Voodoo in Haiti* (London: Andre Deutsch, 1959), 168–77.

30. G. E. Simpson, *Religious Cults of the Caribbean: Trinidad, Jamaica and Haiti* (Rio Piedras: Institute of Caribbean Studies, University of Puerto Rico, Monograph Series no. 15, 3d ed., 1980), 318. See also Simpson, *The Shango Cult of Trinidad* (Rio Piedras: Institute of Caribbean Studies, University of Puerto Rico, 1965), 46, 52–53n.5.

31. M. G. Smith, "A Note on Truth, Fact and Tradition in Carriacou," *Caribbean Quarterly* (1971) 17:134–35.

32. See Roger Bastide, *The African Religions of Brazil* (Baltimore: Johns Hopkins University Press, 1978), and Pressel, "Umbanda in Sao Paulo."

33. G. E. Simpson, *Black Religions in the New World* (New York: Columbia University Press, 1978), 182, 351n.25.

34. Octavia da Costa Eduardo, *The Negro in Northern Brazil: A Study in Acculturation* (New York: J. J. Augustin, 1948). Edison Carneiro, *Candombles da Bahia* (Rio de Janeiro: Conquista, 3rd ed., 1961).

35. Examples are from Works Progress Administration, Georgia Writers' Project, *Drum and Shadows: Survival Studies* (Garden City, N.Y.: Anchor Books, 1972; reprint of 1939 ed.), 136, 147, 160, 167, 192, 79–80.

36. Zora Neale Hurston, *Mules and Men* (Bloomington: Indiana University Press, 1970), 211–12.

37. Harry M. Hyatt, *Folklore from Adams County, Illinois* (Hannibal, Mo.: Western Publishing, 2nd ed., 1959), 794 item 15864.

38. Cf. Hurston, *Mules and Men*, 228–29.

39. J. L. Dillard, *Black Names* (The Hague: Mouton, 1973), 9–10. See also Dillard, *Black English: Its History and Usage in the United States* (New York: Random House, 1972).

Ten

Kongo Influences on African American Artistic Culture

Robert Farris Thompson

The centuries-old Kongo culture expanded not just hundreds of miles through the territory of the Bakongo and their neighbors but also into the New World. The Kongo influence contributed to the rise of the national music of Brazil, the samba; to the fundamental dance of Cuba, the rumba; and to the most sophisticated and important popular North American music, jazz. All three words derive from Ki-Kongo, an immediate indication of the prominence of the Kongo influence in the formation of these important cultural achievements of blacks in the Western Hemisphere.[1] But the influence goes still deeper, into fundamental beliefs and practices concerning life and death, as I intend to show in this survey of Kongo cosmograms, gestures, bottle branches, and grave adornments as they reappear in the black Atlantic world.

The Rise of Kongo American Culture

A leading scholar of the slave trade, Philip Curtin, prepares us for complexities we face in tracing influences from Central Africa to the Western Hemisphere:

South of Cape López, "nationalities" are . . . loosely used. "Congo" which really meant Bakongo in the early sixteenth century had now [during the French trade of the eighteenth century] become generalized to a Bantu-speaking people from western Central Africa. Nor is the "Mondongue" of the lists equivalent to present day Mondonga. At best, it meant the man in question came from the interior, roughly to the north and east of the Congo mouth, just as "Angola" referred equally vaguely to the region south and east of the Congo.[2]

In the nineteenth century another terminological shift arose in Kongo and Angola slaving:

> The "Angola" of earlier tables can now be divided into two— "Congo North" taking in coastal points from Cape López southward to and including the mouth of the Congo River, and "Angola" now taken as Angola proper, the region from Ambriz southward to Benguela.[3]

Curtin also demonstrates a shift toward "Congo North" in Brazilian slaving during the nineteenth century. There is good reason to believe, on the evidence of North Congo names found among the self-help black societies that emerged in Cuba in the nineteenth century, that this same shift occurred in Cuba.

Against the background of such evidence it is essential that we examine slave origins from the Kongo area, lest we assume that the impact of Kongo came from just one society—the Mboma, for instance, or the Yombe. The truth is problematic. What seems to have happened is that a mixture of Kongo and Kongo-related cultures was brought to the New World and reinforced the more salient and important of shared general Bantu cultural traits. In this fusion, memory and grandeur and the name of Kongo itself were maintained.

Degrandpré's *Voyage to the Western Coast of Africa in the Years 1786 and 1787* includes a précis of Kongo slaving as it existed just before the French Revolution. Here the slave trade was essentially concentrated on the coasts of Loango, Kongo, and Angola, with the northern ports of Loango, Malembe, and Cabinda especially active. "Congue" (Bakongo) slaves passed through Malembe; Loango drew on Yombe, Teke, and "Quibangue" (Mbamba Kongo?) sources; and "Congue," "Mondongue," and "Sogne" (Bakongo, persons upriver from Kongo, and Sogno Kongo persons?) passed through Cabinda. Degrandpré remarks that "these are the names of the people who furnish the slaves or through which they pass, and thus retain the denomination."[4]

Now we may compare a partially mirroring list of slave origins for Haiti in the eighteenth century: Mayombe, Mousombes, Mondongue, Congos.[5] Commenting on the great number of persons from Kongo, Jean Price-Mars, the late doyen of African-Haitian studies, remarked: "Saint-Mery, historian of Saint Domingue, has borne formal witness to the fact that the most numerous slaves of the colony [which became Haiti] came from Kongo."[6]

We may also compare George W. Cable's "The Dance in Place Congo," from New Orleans:

> a public square just beyond draws a graceful canopy of oak and sycamore boughs. That is the place . . . that is Congo square. See them come! . . . men and women from all that great Congo coast— Angola, Malimbe [Malemba?], Ambrice [Ambriz] . . . *these are they for whom the dance and the place are named, the most numerous sort of Negro in the colonies, the Congoes and the Franc-Congoes.*[7]

New Orleans, city of the birth of jazz, had a strong and predominant Kongo element arising from the slave trade. It is no accident that one of our few documented North American attestations of the Kongo *funda nkata* seated position comes from Congo Square. In that culturally fabled place, where young New Orleans athletes once played a cognate form of early lacrosse (*raquette*) with Amerinds, Kongo *ndungu*, extremely long and sonorous drums, were played.[8] The tremendous creative energies released when Kongo-derived traditions combined in New Orleans with those from the equally sophisticated Malian, Nigerian, and Cameroonian traditional civilizations must have been amazing. That does not even take into account the final fillip: the blending of it all with the equally complex mix of musics—French, Spanish, English —in that culturally strategic city.

Robert Goffin, a Belgian scholar of jazz, compared descriptions of Congo Square dance and music with the structure of early jazz and came up with some interesting statements about the latter's origins. Cable had noted that the great, or bass, drum was beaten in Congo Square with "slow vehemence," whereas the smaller drum was played "fiercely and rapidly." The full complement of instrumentation included a four-string banjo, and for a spell all the other instruments would drop out while the banjoist expounded; then there would come a cry of "yeaaaaaah!" and then the crash of drums, horns, and rattles. Goffin reacts to Cable's account by suggesting that

> the presence of jazz can already be sensed from this description. The two-to-the-bar rhythm of the bass drum and the faster beat of the traps, the added melody of the banjo and the pipes of Pan . . . the sudden stopping of the instruments for a break, their re-entry, the shouts of satisfaction punctuating the music—all these are present.[9]

These traits are also present in some forms of African-Haitian music and in some cases were probably reinforced by similar structures in overheard European-derived folk music. But the long drums at the center of all this energy almost certainly were *ndungu*, remembered from Kongo.[10]

So Bakongo and their neighbors formed the majority population in New Orleans—the people who named Congo Square, who gave that place its Kongo dance and lent their minds to the formation of the new creole styles that eventually reverberated through the entire world.

But Charleston, too, was a portal of cultural entry for Kongo slaves, hence Kongo influences. During the five-year period between 1735 and 1740, 70 percent of all incoming slaves appear to have been drawn from Africa's Angola region.[11] They would have included Kongo groups and Kongo-related persons from north and south of the Kongo. And it all added up to a powerful sum of "Kongoisms" in South Carolina, of which the most famous may be the Charleston, a dance which, in its angulations, kicking patterns, and timing, is strikingly similar to the "one-legged" (*sémbuka*) style of kicking and hand-clapping dance common in parts of northern Kongo.[12]

Intensive slaving from Kongo and Angola had an even more significant effect on Cuban popular culture. The richness of Kongo culture in the formation of black artistic culture in Cuba is attested by the presence of certain *cabildos*, or self-help confraternities, in nineteenth-century Cuba: "*cabildos* called Kongo Real, Ntótila, or Nsombo, Kongo Banguela, Kongo Mumbala, Kongo Mumboma, Kongo Mundamba, Kongo Motembo, Kongo Musuni, Kongo Masinga, Kongo Mondongo, Kongo Musoso, Kongo Mayombe, Kongo Munyaca, Kongo Musalela, Kongo Mumbaque, Kongo Cabenda, Kongo Loango."[13] The names of these brotherhoods reflect a mixture of actual Kongo clans, such as the Mboma, Nsundi, Yombe, and Bazombo ("Nsombo"); extra-Kongo groupings, such as Mondongo, corresponding to Degrandpré's Mondonque; and ports of slaving, such as Benguela, Cabinda, and Loango. In Havana each *cabildo* was supposed to have been made up of persons descended from these separate groups. But the case was probably nearer to that described for the country where "a single *cabildo* Kongo would comprise all Bantu people from that portion of Central Africa, without distinguishing them by Ntótila (Mbanza Kongo) and other heritages." In the welter of specialized references to geography and subethnicities we sense the tremendous richness of the Kongo and Kongo-related impact on Cuban culture. Without that impact, the rise of rumba, conga, mambo, and mozambique in African Cuban music would have been unthinkable. Moreover, the instrumentation of Latin American popular music, which frequently incorporates the conga drums and patterns of pulsation associated with African Cuban music, would have been critically impoverished.

In Brazil the strength of Kongo cultural influence in music and dance is equally dramatic and deep-rooted. Gerhard Kubik, in *Angolan Traits in Black Music, Games and Dances of Brazil*, confronts materials similar to those observed in Cuba:

> What were called "nations" in Brazil were defined by a curious assortment of African names which were not always ethnic. "Benguela," for instance, is the name of a port in Angola from which many people were shipped to Brazil. One of the groups was mostly composed of Kirenge, Humbi, Handa, Mwila, Chipongo, Ambo, Kwisi, and other ethnic divisions from the wide area of southwestern Angola. *The Bantu had a similar culture and were able to communicate among themselves.*[14]

I have emphasized the last point because it applies especially to the similar merger of Yombe, Nsundi, and other Kongo groups on Brazilian soil in terms of a synthesis of principal ideas and beliefs. Fusion through multiple reinforcement would appear, on the face of it, to result in well-nigh indelible cultural continuity. But it is an ethnic current that gradually transforms itself into a cultural resource, without a specific ethnic badge. Thus the Kongo *samba* dance became a national Brazilian mode of art. Baumann, a German ethnologist, long ago illustrated the similar sharing in many Central African civilizations of the concept of *Kalunga*.[15] *Kalunga* is "the sea," in the sense of God's perfection and completion (*lunga*) of all being. Out of the merger of Kongo and Angola strands emerged African-Brazilian instances of the concept *Kalunga*. Brazilian folktales link the word to the sea, and a carnival dance, *maracatu*, has a main protagonist who brandishes a doll called *Kalunga*, "representing the goddess of the sea and death."[16]

In *The Bantu Speaking Heritage of the United States*, Winifred Vass makes an observation that in effect symbolizes the entire process throughout the Western Hemisphere where Kongo and Angola persons came together, attracted by similarities of thought and culture, and in the process imparted indelibly reinforced elements of culture to world history:

> Bantu speech has a proven ability to move into a culture, to absorb it, and to change its language. It has adopted and adapted each new culture group as it has spread from its original nucleus area, probably in the Nok region of Nigeria, down over almost the entire African subcontinent south of the Sahara. The outstanding linguistic

homogeneity of this entire region is due to this central body of inherited Proto-Bantu vocabulary that still ties all Bantu languages together and proves their once common source. Bantu-speaking slaves from Central Africa enjoyed a linguistic unity and ability to communicate with their fellow-captives that slaves of West Africa did not share.[17]

Cosmograms

In northern Kongo, specialized ritual experts called *nganga nkodi* and *nganga nsibi* cut designs on the bodies of living fish, or turtles, and then release these creatures in their element. *Banganga nkodi* and *nsibi* are specialists in using words, sending intense messages to the dead. They cut their signs (*bidimbu*) into the shell of a tortoise so that the reptile, diving back into the water, will carry them across the *Kalunga* line into the world beyond. There the ancestors will receive the encoded messages and act upon them on behalf of their descendants.[18]

Now compare Harry Stillwell Edwards's nineteenth-century account of an African-born slave on a plantation in the United States:

> The things in connection with Minc that puzzled me . . . were his superstitions. Doubtless they were taught him by his mother, and the first intimation of them I had was when he caught a gopher [a burrowing terrapin] and with a bit of wire ground to an exceedingly fine point cut on its shell a number of curious signs or hieroglyphics, different from anything I had ever seen, except that there was a pretty fair representation of the sun. He then took this gopher back to where he had found it and turned him loose at the entrance to his burrow, making gestures indicating that the gopher was going far down into the earth. He did something of this kind for every gopher he caught. One day he succeeded in snaring a green-head duck and upon its broad bill he carved some hieroglyphics. This done . . . he tossed the bird high in the air and laughed as it sped away. As the years went by I saw him treat many birds after the same fashion. If there was room for only one or two figures he would put them on, and let the bird go.[19]

In sending a "signed" turtle into the earth and a "signed" feathered being into the sky, an African captive in America was apparently trying to communicate with his ancestors. Perhaps he was trying to tell them where he was or ask them for spiritual sustenance. By sending messages "far down into the earth," to the ancestors, and high into the sky, to

God, he had in effect written in living characters, reptile and fowl, the Kongo cosmogram.

Bakongo trace this basic symbol today with their right hands, the index fingers indicating God above, the ancestors below, the *Kalunga* line, and then, in a reverse direction, their throats. In other words, they implicate their very lives in the truthfulness of what they have just sworn, by the sign of cosmos. This gesture is called *leva Nzambi*, "swearing on God," or *zenga Nzambi*, "tracing God."[20]

Bakongo traditionally stood upon this sign, traced on the ground, to swear a vow in the name of God and the ancestors. They also stood important charms upon this sign, securing its powers on the certitude and truth of the Almighty and the immortal dead. It was also a sign that persons initiated into the mighty Lemba Society of northern Kongo stood upon. They did this upon initiation to demonstrate that they understood the meaning of life and death. With this sign Bakongo miniaturized not only the structure of the universe but also the eternal sources of moral sanction, God above and the dead below. This sign was thus a seal and witness of sacred equity, justice, truth. "On the Coast," Lievin van de Velde noted in 1886 of the Bakongo, "I have frequently seen blacks trace a cross on the earth when they wanted to swear with all their force the taking of a vow."[21]

Bounded by the unblinking gaze of God and the dead, the Kongo cosmogram pervades myriad provinces of Kongo visual culture. In addition, among neighboring civilizations, persons were sworn into traditional societies in the presence of cognate signs written on the earth, as exemplified by Bapende, Ndembu, and Tu-Chokwe rituals.[22]

Crossroads or forks in a path are viewed in many Bantu cultures of the Kongo-Angola region as virtual cosmograms *trouvés*. These points of literal intersection were where one might go to offer sacrifice or prayer to the ancestors. A forked stick further miniaturized the concept, providing a scale model of the line that divides the living from the ancestral realm. For example, among the Basuku people east of Kongo, a father might make a hunting charm (*mokongu*) for the luck of his son from a bifurcated piece of branch and thereby indicate the invocation of "forces on the other side." Such charms were sometimes placed at an actual crossroads.[23]

Protean manifestations of the basic cosmogram, in earth drawings, gestures, and actual crossroads and forked sticks, constitute a time-resistant vision of certitude and truth in Kongo and Angola. This cosmogram provided New World Bakongo with an unshakable ground for cultural continuity. Written on the earth, these cosmograms reemerged precisely where persons influenced by the life and lore of Kongo lived and thought.

A main institutional channel through which Kongo ways were kept alive in North America was black folk healing.[24] Men and women in black communities who practiced ancient cures compounded of leaves and roots also tended to know the cosmogram or its visual equivalents, such as the crossroads, or to use forked branches as mediatory emblems.

In the second volume of his study of traditional healing and rootwork among black North Americans, Harry M. Hyatt speaks of his most voluble informant, a man from Waycross, Georgia, whose interview filled "26 Telediphone cylinders." Waycross is near the tidewater region where veritable founts of Kongo and Angola influence were established. This healer told Hyatt how to tie a person mystically, by means of a formula that included the sign of the four moments of the sun (figure 1):

> Take a clean sheet of paper and you draw you a circle on that clean sheet of paper and put a cross in there just like that, you understand. That's the four corners of the earth . . . you put that seal on the ground. You put [an] envelope [with] graveyard dirt [inside] and [a] photograph in there—you put that down on top of that seal . . . you put your right foot on it and you turn your face to the west, you see, which is the sun going down, you see. Well, you take, well, you can speak the words if you ain't got it wrote out, you say O. L. Youngs, L. L. Young, you come to me and do as I say to you. . . .[25]

A healer from Memphis, Tennessee, used the same drawn sign for treasure hunting and for remedies. He called this emblem "the four corners of the world" and the "four winds of heaven."[26] These descriptions suggest a dual provenance, for they are found in Revelations 7:1. And this Memphis healer, too, drew the cosmogram.

Newbell Niles Puckett, in an early classic of African American scholarship, observed that the sign of the cross was used "far too often to allow us to assume a Christian origin." He suggested that "its original effectiveness" could probably be attributed "to the fact that it pointed towards all four cardinal points, hence allowing nothing to get by it."[27] That ancient surrogate for the cosmogram, the crossroads, also functioned as a powerful symbol in African American folklore. It was where one went, as in Central Africa, to get in touch with one's ancestors. It was where one went to ask favors of the cosmos. One North Carolina black sacrificed a chicken at the fork of the road, begging relief from an epidemic that had caused the animals of his region to die off rapidly.[28] And there are legends of black musicians going to crossroads and trad-

FIGURE 1. Cosmogram, four moments of the sun.

ing their guitars with spirits to confirm or enhance their talents. In Kongo, persons kneel before tombs at the threshold between worlds. In the United States the same image is created anew in that occasional narrative of Kongo and Angola influences upon America, the blues:

I went down to the crossroads, fell down on my knees
I went down to the crossroads, fell down on my knees
Ask the lord above for mercy, say boy, if you please.[29]

We catch sight of similar imagery in certain of the black barrios of the cities of western Cuba. Fernando Ortiz, the African-Cubanist, published a drawing copied from a rendering by a Kongo Cuban priest in chalk on the ground, a seal upon which to situate in power the important *mbumba* charm (figure 2).[30] Moreover, blacks in Cuba remembered the precise Ki-Kongo terms for the cardinal points emphasized by the drawing: heaven (*nsulu*) at the top, the land of the dead (*nsi a fwa*) below, and the *Kalungu* line dividing the realm of the living, earth (*ntoto*), from the dead. Lydia Cabrera, Cuba's foremost folklorist, records testimony that to members of Kongo Cuban groups the circle signified "certainty," while the cross within the circle stood for all the powers activated or concentrated upon this point.[31]

In Brazil and Haiti, similar figures of imaginative experience blossomed into virtual national expressions. Haitian and Brazilian men and women influenced by Kongo ground-painting and visual-invocation traditions attained a different order of social and historical significance. Their ground drawings and cruciforms of initiation and swearing-in overlapped the originating functions of the form in ancient Kongo. Apparently because of the special intensity and complexity of African-influenced religious life in Rio and Port-au-Prince, however, Kongo charms (*minkisi*), Roman Catholic saints, deities (*orisha*) of the Nigerian Yoruba, spirits (*vodun*) of the Fon and Ewe of Benin Republic, even elements of Masonry and European spiritualism fused. The result was *macumba* in Rio de Janeiro and *vodun* in western Saint Domingue. The fusions were different, for *macumba* and *vodun* are independent and distinguishable expressions of New World black religiosity. But both stimulated the blossoming of Kongo-derived cruciform ground signs into full-fledged New World aesthetic blazons that directly reflect the complexity of the particular black folk religions from which they emerged.

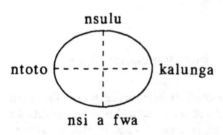

FIGURE 2. Seal with the four cardinal points.

The result in Rio was an explosion of Kongo-influenced ground signs called *pontos riscados* (points drawn). The main purpose of tracing the cosmogram on the earth in Kongo was to immerse oneself in larger spiritual dimensions. In some cases one anointed one's forehead with the spirit-drenched clay of the grave or took moistened earth from a cruciform trench or incision cut into the earth above a tomb. Comparably, we find that in Brazil, from the beginning, the *ponto* tradition reflected an identical concern with the invocation of spirit upon a visually drawn and indicated point.

It is said that the earliest cruciform patterns drawn on the earth in Rio were simple crosses or, as in Kongo, a cross in a circle. These patterns also must have served to center charms, invoking the spirit by using its visual name. In *Lemba 1615-1930: A Drum of Affliction in Africa and the New World*, Janzen makes an important observation: the list of Kongo personified medicines in Brazil resembles a list of *minkisi* in Kongo given in Dapper's text of 1668. Thus certain seventeenth-century *minkisi* of Kongo retain their existence in Brazil, especially in the ecstatic songs of the *macumba* cult in Rio that are peppered with Ki-Kongo healing terms and phrases. In these songs the *minkisi* are called Zambi, Bumba, Lemba, and other terms.[32] Both the songs, which invoke these creolized Kongo medicines—conceptually mixed with Roman Catholic saints and Yoruba-Fon deities, deepened sometimes by allusion to Amerindian spirits—and the drawings, which call the spirits, are "points." The precise date of the earliest Kongo cosmograms in Rio remains to be established, however, as Bastide notes:

> We do not at present have evidence on the precise moment when these designs first emerged in Rio *macumba* [rites]. Nevertheless, the latter are, above all, of Kongo and Angola origin. The traditional religions of these Bantu areas use initiatory designs written on the earth. . . . the *pontos*, as an artistic movement, are Kongo and Angola in concept, but embody local invention and contact with other African-descended forces in their final form. In the

FIGURE 3. Early Kongo-derived cosmograms in Rio (informants' reconstruction).

characterization of their emergence we must also add the influence of Masonry and books of European esoteric magic.[33]

The influence of the sign of the four moments of the sun in the rise of the myriad signs and blazons in Rio may be shown by examining a rather complex series of modern *pontos*. Janzen notes that the Rio fusion of Kongo *minkisi*, Dahomean *vodun*, Yoruba *orisha*, and Roman Catholic saints has not been haphazard. On the contrary, it has followed a logic of correspondences, and the *pontos riscados* are the quintessence of this ongoing art of classification. In Rio the cross within a circle, the Kongo concept of the crossroads (figure 3), has fused with the Yoruba spirit of the crossroads, Eshu-Elegba.

Because of the believed unpredictability of Eshu-Elegba, this West Coast spirit comes to be associated with the biblical Devil. This quality is present also in his Rio *ponto*. Thus the basic symbolism of intersecting worlds is read to a double power of cultural interpretation, Kongo-Yoruba and Western. The cardinal points in one *ponto* become Satan's pitchforks, and the points between them are sometimes similarly rendered. The unpredictability of Eshu suggests itself in a swirling pinwheel pattern at the center of one of his designs (figure 4). And in another example the original intersecting axes of the cosmogram yield to greater emphases of visual improvisation and repetition (figure 5).

Pontos, outwardly straightforward blazons of the spirits and the gods, thus are palimpsests of multiple allusions. Western pitchforks are written over the crossroads of the ancient cosmogram. The fusion of far-flung impulses is mirrored by elements of the cultic nomenclature in force today in Rio. The name of a female Eshu, Pomba Gira, represents a Brazilian creolization of the Kongo term for crossroads (*mpamba nzila*).[34] There is also a reference to *Kalunga*, God's ocean, in the name of this *ponto*. Novel experiences and contact with different cultural influences evidently were decisive for the patterning of such blazons.

It seems to be a tradition with unlimited potential for increase. As Bastide points out, "interest in *pontos riscados* precisely lies in the fact that each priest is constantly inventing new ideographic formulations within the ancient shapes and forms."[35] In 1951, 132 visual *pontos* had been noted, classified, and published; by 1975 the number had multiplied to fifteen hundred.[36] The spread of art and concept was accompanied by the appropriation of new media—embroidery on silk, paint on

FIGURE 4. Modern *ponto riscado* for Eshu Change-the-World.

FIGURE 5. Modern *ponto riscado* for Eshu Pomba Gira de Kalunga.

glass—and novel patternings made in sand on the beach at Ipanema and Copacabana and lit by candles. In 1969 Wesley R. Hurt collected a *ponto* for Eshu the king in Curitiba, capital of Paraná state, some four hundred miles south of Rio. And once again the imaginary pitchforks of Eshu form the intersecting lines of cosmos, there painted on a square of styrofoam and covered carefully with red transparent plastic, like a wrapped offering to the spirit.[37] From the most amazing appropriations of the modern world the signs of cosmos stare back at us, as through three depths of cultural experience, creole black, Latin Catholic, and modern technological.

Gestures

The important kinds of gestures symbolized by Kongo funerary art live beyond the individual persons who originally embodied them. Their re-instatement in the black Americas is obvious and overwhelmingly re-peated. William Stewart, an American linguist, is preparing a definitive dictionary of African American speech, having already compiled more than ten thousand entries. He finds that many English words also have their black meanings.[38] As part of this monumental work he will include a dictionary of gestures, particularly Gullah ones. Such a dictionary will be invaluable to historians of Kongo art in Atlantic perspective.

Funda Nkata

Let us begin our examination of Kongo gestures with the cross-legged seated position, *funda nkata*. Provisionally, it would appear that this courtly gesture lacked the staying power of attitudes more widely dis-seminated through Kongo culture. Nevertheless, *funda nkata* appears early in the nineteenth century in New Orleans' Congo Square, where "the performer, sitting crosslegged, held the [*mbira*] in both hands and plucked the ends of the reeds with his thumb-nails."[39] This scene recalls a common theme of Kongo sculpture.[40] A scholar of black life in Trini-dad, Jacob Elder, recalls that on that island, too, in this century, "there was an old Kongo man who shaved his head and sat cross-legged . . . thinking of his ancestors."[41]

Tuluwa Lwa Luumbu

A second gesture, *tuluwa lwa luumbu,* arms crossed on the chest to symbolize self-encirclement in silence, retains its strong symbolic wordlessness in some North American black communities. In 1980 I saw a black man on the New Haven city green cross his arms before his chest to end a conversation. This sign signaled that he had no more to say. Stewart has seen the same emblem of negation among the Gullah of South Carolina, "used in slightly combative situations, where a person, crossing arms on chest, is not arguing, per se, but wishes to communicate that he definitely does not like what is being laid on him."[42] The *luumbu* gesture survives, clearly and distinctly, among certain African Cuban populations in the Caribbean. Lydia Cabrera has seen a Kongo ritual expert (*nganga*) in Havana cross his arms thus, signaling hauteur and reserve.[43] The same gesture, with contrasting Yoruba and Kongo meanings, appears in a strongly Kongo-flavored folk dance, *rumba yambu.*[44] Once again, an aspect of the sculpture of the Bakongo is echoed by patterns of dance and music in the black New World.

Nunsa

The related standing or seated pose with head averted, *nunsa,* is also present in black America. As a point of departure, we may consider a fine rendering of *nunsa* in classical Kongo ivory sculpture. Here a woman is depicted in a state of ritual nakedness. She kneels and places her hands on her thighs (*fukuma, ye mooko va bunda*). This is an ancient pose of assuagement, asking forgiveness. Yet she contradicts this grace with a second resolutely rendered sign: head averted, she signals denial and negation. My informant Fu-Kiau's translation of this fusion of two coded attitudes, one negative and one positive, placed together on a single royal scepter, is "Be warned, the attention of the king favors those who know how to make authority feel not only their grievances but also their respect."[45]

A flowering of this Kongo gesture appears in the Western Hemisphere. But it is invisible to those who do not live among or do not closely observe black people. In African Cuban ceremonies in which certain persons become possessed by the spirit of a dead person (*mfumbi*), they dance with their heads turned to one side. The spirit thus distances itself from the world in which it finds itself in fleeting visitation. This stance recaptures some of the inherent hauteur of the *nunsa* gesture.[46] In 1977 I saw a black man from New Orleans counter accusations by turning his head to one side, with lips firmly pursed. He thus became an icon of denial. There are countless mirrors of this pose in Gullah country, especially when a black mother sharply rebukes her child. Stewart writes that "the child purses the lips, turns his head to one side, and it stays there."[47] A cognate expression was observed in colonial times by Charles William Day: "when Negroes quarrel they seldom look each other in the face."[48] A marvelous Kongo rendering of the *nunsa* pose in the Berlin Museum distinctly records both the turning of the head and the determined pursing of the lips as if the subject were pointing with the lips to the grounds for her denial. In "Dynamics of a Black Audience," Annette Powell Williams summarizes an extension of this fundamental gesture in black United States: "an indication of total rejection is shown by turning one's head away from the speaker with eyes closed."[49]

Kébuka

The related *kébuka* pose, in the context of *ngoma* playing, logically unites with the gestural procedures of black players of conga drums in Cuba and Hispanic North America. Earl Leaf photographed the African Cuban percussionist Chori in the 1940s in this characteristic pose, head turned to the side, concentrating on his music, canceling out all distractions from the flow and pacing of his rhythms. So long as there are conga drums (*tumbadoras*) and *timbales* to be played traditionally and well, this ancient sign of creative withdrawal into a zone of concentration and reflection will live on in America.

Pakalala

The arms akimbo pose with both hands on the hips, *pakalala*, is a challenge stance. The word itself is a verb of attitude, referring to pricking up one's ears, unfurling an umbrella, and images of readiness and sharpness.[50] To stand with hands on the hips in Kongo proclaims the person ready to accept the challenges of a situation.

In the United States, standing with both hands on the hips has become the black woman's classic challenge pose. Ambrose E. Gonzales, in *Laguerre: A Gascon of the Black Border*, has two descriptions of black women in combative poses, with arms akimbo, in legal situations.[51] When works such as Gonzales's have been sifted and compared, it may be possible to show that such poses constitute reconstellations of the

FIGURE 6. Haitian woman, *deu me sou koté* (arms akimbo).

poses of a *mambu*, recollected and enacted by black people in the United States. In Haiti, women sometimes adopt such a challenge pose, *deu men sou koté*, often while dancing with a man, as in an Earl Leaf photograph from the 1940s (figure 6). With this stance they test or counter the thrust of the male dancer with grace and humor. It is a light-hearted use of an attitude with a generally stern and forbidding appearance in the world of *minkisi n'kondi* in Kongo itself.[52]

Crossroads

The crossroads pose, with right hand up to heaven and left hand parallel to the horizon line, characterizes the *niombo* figure. Interestingly, a painted representation of the Haitian graveyard spirit Baron Samedi shows his body in this pose. The graveyard spirit, surrounded by implements of death (a headstone and a pick and shovel for digging graves) is pointing with his upraised right hand while, with his left hand, he bears down with a cane. But the outline of the gesture remains intact.[53]

Another rendering of this gesture is overwhelmingly present in Haiti: decoration of the summit of the staffs of *vodun* flags. Such flags are unfurled to announce the coming of the gods. They are often processed in a cosmogrammatic way, saluting the cardinal points of a given sanctuary. Thus they indicate the boundary between worlds. Significantly, many of them bear, at the summit of the shaft, an added S-curved element carved in wood and nailed or pinned to the shaft. The result is a cryptic gesture with right hand up and left hand down, recalling the anthropomorphic reading of the hand-guards of the *mbele a lulendo*, the royal swords of execution in ancient Kongo. It ought to be considered a possible creole reformulation of a Bakongo mode of phrasing. In Kongo this gesture, on swords and *niombo*, marked the boundaries between two worlds, and that is precisely the function of the *vodun* flag.

Télama and Fútika Nkome

Perhaps the most dramatic incursion of a Kongo gesture in Haiti is the reemergent *biika mambu* stance. This pose, with left hand on hip and right hand forward, is frequently called *télama lwimbanganga* in northern Kongo. The ethnic origin of this attitude was known and identified as such in the 1930s. Courlander wrote that "women sometimes use a Congo pose, with the left hand on hip and the right arm held outward, a gesture which lends a good deal of grace to what might otherwise be rather violent aesthetics."[54] In Kongo, placing the left hand on the hip is believed to press down all evil, while the extended right hand acts to "vibrate" the future in a positive manner. Important women used this pose at dawn to "vibrate positively" the future of town warriors. Advocates used its power to block or end a lawsuit.

Biika mambu is said to be a very common gesture in African-Haitian ritual dancing. It was also adopted by the baton-twirling *major joncs* of pre-Lenten street parade groups called *rara*. *Rara* instrumentation is strongly influenced by Kongo music. The famous *rara* one-note bamboo trumpets (*vaccines*) almost certainly derive from one-note Kongo bamboo trumpets (*disoso*), as I noticed in comparing the *vaccine* players in a modern Haitian painting and an actual *disoso* player at Luangu Nzambi on the north bank of the Zaire during summer 1980. The hooting resonance of the single *disoso* note or the pair of notes is echoed closely by the sounds of the *vaccines*. Both derive from pygmy hocketing, where only one or two notes are played by each musician.[55] In this tradition, melodic line emerges from the fusion of these miniature multiple parts. *Rara* bands observed in the winters of 1975 and 1976 in western Port-au-Prince included a long metal instrument resembling a tin ear. It suggested a translation into metal of the equally long transverse flute used in Kongo, made of *carica papaya*.[56] Thus there is a significant clustering of these influences, especially the hocketing technique. Presumably this technique traveled to Haiti from the known and continuing pockets of pygmy culture just north of the Bakongo. Therefore it is certain that the originators of *rara* included or were strongly influenced by the music of persons of Kongo heritage.

Today, however, *rara* has become a Haitian cultural strategy, not a badge of African ethnicity. Knowledge of conscious links to Kongo practice have been erased by thoroughgoing improvisation and change. Yet the "Kongo pose" remains an integral part of the percussive structuring of certain leaders marching to the *rara* beat. In Kongo it was a pose correlated with authority. In Haiti it is a prerogative of the important *major jonc*, "who juggles with a metal baton."[57] When one *rara* group meets a rival group, the respective *major joncs* twirl their batons and strike the Kongo pose, as if attempting to ward off their rivals' virtuoso powers. R. Duvivier, a Haitian painter, brilliantly captured the *rara* spirit in a work apparently dating from the early 1970s. Duvivier's group is led by a mounted person and another person bearing the group's standard. Women dance in front in the challenge pose, *vaccines* are played, and Kongo-derived drums are sounded. In the middle of this joyous scene, one *major jonc* bends to the earth twirling his metal baton while a second, in a gleaming spangled jacket, spins his baton with his right hand, keeping his left hand on his hip. Thus he prepares the way with vitality and power.

We know that the so-called shotgun shacks of black New Orleans actually derive from Haitian prototypes, brought by black migrations from Saint Domingue to the Mississippi port in the early nineteenth century.[58] There can also be little doubt that the beaded, spangled, sequined, and feathered glory of the street costumes of the "Wild Indian" black groups in New Orleans derive, in concept and detail, from similar costumes in African-Haitian *rara*—the same type of costume worn by persons making the *biika mambu*-like gesture in the Duvivier painting.

The Kongo pose can thus be traced through these various streams of documented influence. *Tëlama lwimbanganga* became *pose Kongo* in Haiti, then *pose Kongo* became the drum majorette pose in the United States. Almost all the early baton twirlers in and around New Orleans were black, or so it has been asserted by informants in New Orleans.[59] But the commanding, strictly chiseled, crisp quality of the pose was too powerful, evidently, for whites to resist. Today the world center of baton twirling is said to be Mississippi—just east of Louisiana and not far removed from the influence of New Orleans. Constance Atwater's *Baton Twirling: The Fundamentals of an Art and Skill* was kindly shared with me by John Szwed. In this text teaching people how to strike poses, Atwater observes that the proper mode of presentation involves placing

FIGURE 7. Hip/arm stance (left) and hip/hand stance as rendered by Elizabeth Fine.

the left hand on one's hip and twirling the baton with the right hand. Szwed, arguing as early as 1971 that baton twirling—now considered all-American and even Anglo-American—might conceal deep African roots, inspired a reinvestigation of this important cultural phenomenon.[60]

From urging warriors on to victory in Kongo to urging sports players on to victory in Mississippi, the function of this gesture has changed very little. This complicated gesture also lives on in other contexts. It is an icon of black American performance. In the mid-1960s, the Supremes were famous for a song in which they shouted "Stop! in the Name of Love!" while striking the very pose Kongo elders use to stop misbehavior at a traditional dance: left hand on hip, right hand or palm before the body. And this gesture is only one facet of a reality that probably involves the whole of African American verbal art.

In "Aesthetic Patterning of Verbal Art and the Performance-Centered Text," Elizabeth Fine examined the stylistic means of the black verbal performer James Hutchinson in action, retelling the saga of Stagolee, a classic of the black verbal arts. Fine observed that Hutchinson "accomplishes his graceful, fluid character changes through an extremely economical, highly patterned system of stances." His most common stance had two variations.

> He frequently stands with his left hand on his hip and his weight on his left foot, either with his right hand held up about shoulder level to emphasize points, or with his right arm held across his chest, with his hand closed. These two closely related stances occur so often that I began to abbreviate them as either the hip/hand or hip/arm stances.[61]

Fine rendered these basic gestures schematically (figure 7).

Both gestures are Kongo-related icons, lived as fundamental African American expressions. The hip/hand stance is the *télama* gesture, instantly recognizable as deriving from the lexicon of ancient Kongo gestures, especially those famous contexts of declamation and high oratory, the courts of law. But the hip/arm stance, left hand on hip, right hand against the heart—called in Kongo *fútika nkome*—we have not yet met

in our discussion of the gestures of the Bakongo. It, too, carries significant semantic weight, as my informant Fu-Kiau told me:

> In Kongo *fútika nkome* ("tie the thumb") or *kanga mooko* ("tie the
> hand"), holding closed right hand over the heart, with left hand on
> hip, is very common. It is a way of trying to escape a negative
> situation. You press down the evil side with your left hand on hip
> and, with your fist over heart, a sign of power, you are trying to
> communicate, without words, a feeling that you have to your heart
> (*ntima*), reaching what is deep inside of you. You start, like a mo-
> tor, your heart with this gesture and then you fly, free of oppress-
> ing, evil power.[62]

The *télama* and the *fútika nkome* gestures thus have to do with power
and mediating force. The black performer in Texas used these icons,
which originally symbolized power grasped and evil contained, as culturally aesthetic stratagems rather than as strictly applied weapons in
a lawsuit or some other important sacred moment. But we constantly
come back to their recurring power and force, so rhythmic as to almost
stop the flow of time itself. As Fine states:

> These basic stances also form part of the rhythmic structure. They
> provide a basic "rhythmic grid," to use Harold Scheub's term,
> from which all of the other non-verbal images emerge. One way in
> which the non-verbal grid functions aesthetically is to build antici-
> pation in the audience. As the non-verbal patterns begin to emerge,
> the audience's attention is captivated by the attractiveness of the
> patterned repetitions. It is an anticipation that is felt. . . . Part of the
> power behind [Hutchinson's] movements of imitating Stagolee's
> run and his "giving skin" to the brothers and sisters in Hell seems
> to lie in their difference from so many of the icons that are built
> out of the hip/arm and hip/hand stances.[63]

Fine's description of these stances as icons is historically appropriate.
That was precisely the impact and reality they had in the worlds of
Kongo jurisprudence and funerary art. It was certainly the impact of
the hip/hand stance in the realm of law-imparting, morally intimidating images par excellence, *minkisi n'kondi*.[64]

Bottle Branches

From eastern Texas to the coast of South Carolina there extends an
amazing African American visual tradition: bottle trees.[65] Eudora Welty
mentions them in one of her Mississippi short stories:

... a clear dirt yard, with every vestige of grass patiently uprooted and the ground scarred in deep whorls from the strike of Livvie's broom. . . . coming around up the path from the deep cut of the Natchez Trace below was a line of bare crape myrtle trees, with every branch of them ending in a colored bottle, green or blue.[66]

Bare-swept earth around compound habitations is a commonplace in traditional West and Central Africa. The bottle tree itself is a creole invention, deriving from subtly blended sources. But let us return to Welty's narration:

Livvie [a black woman] knew that there could be a spell put in trees and she was familiar from the time she was born with the way bottle trees kept evil spirits from coming into the house—by luring them inside the colored bottles, where they cannot get out again. Solomon had made the bottle trees with his own hands over the nine years, in labor amounting to about a tree a year, and without a sign that he had any uneasiness in his heart, for he took as much pride in his precautions against spirits coming in the house as he took in the house, and sometimes in the sun the bottle trees looked prettier than the house did.[67]

Mississippi bottle trees are not only ritual objects. They are carefully executed works of art. The sun in the bottle, seen against the bare sky, is dazzling indeed. In fact, the effect is so dazzling that white neighbors borrowed the custom and made it their own, blending the Kongo-derived bottle branch with the image of the Christmas tree. The difference in the two traditions is marked by phrasing, with the black version more in tune with the organic skeletal outline of the tree, producing a kind of gestural dancing of the cobalt blue, green, and other colored bottles at the ends of the branches. Welty illustrated the black mode at Simpson County, south of Jackson, in the 1930s. The Anglo–American rendering differs from her example, which was executed on crape myrtle and other species in a style we might designate bottle-and-branch, and James D. Martin, a Mississippian who has written a careful study of these forms, tells why.

Whites prize cedar trees, as frames for bottle-trees, because of the shape: they like the fact that it has upward-reaching branches, and lots of them, for placing bottles on display. Cedars are Mississippi Christmas trees, for the same reason, and the wood is hard and durable and relatively rot-resistant.[68]

Anglo-American bottle trees in Mississippi often show the trimmed and tightly clustered effect of a Yuletide fir, decked with colored spheres and baubles. An Anglo-American in the village of Sarepta in the northern portion of Mississippi just south of Oxford blended African American "flash" (the brilliant blues, browns, and greens of his selected bottles) with accents from the industrial West and Christianity, placing at the top of his tree an automobile headlight part and, over it, a tin star of Bethlehem.

While Christmas comes only once a year, the bottle tree stands the whole year long, and white mimesis cannot hide the origins of this tradition. There can be little doubt that the custom of guarding yards and households from all evil with branches decked with glass vessels came from Kongo and culturally related territory in Central Africa. The custom arrived in the memories of blacks from Kongo via New Orleans, Charleston, and the West Indies. In some parts of the West Indies there have been bottle trees since the late eighteenth century.

L'Abbé Proyart's *History of Loango*, published in 1776, mentions the original custom of combining tree branches with vessels, as seen on the coast of northern Kongo:

All, after having cultivated their field, take care, in order to drive away sterility and the evil spells, to fix in the earth, in a certain manner, certain branches of certain trees, with some pieces of broken pots. They do more or less the same thing before their houses, when they must absent themselves during a considerable time. The most determined thief would not dare to cross their threshold, when he sees it thus protected by these mysterious signs.[69]

Nowadays in North Kongo owners of fruit trees place medicated containers (calabashes, bottles, and so forth) called *nkisi lusoli* in the branches to ward off thieves. This practice seems quite similar to the African American bottle tree tradition. In addition, a 1909–10 photograph by R. R. Gérard of a traditional cemetery near what is now the town of Mbanza Ngungu, between Kinshasa and Matadi, illustrates the deliberate display of pierced Western plates and bottles, either nailed on the trunk of a tree or carefully fixed on the ends of specially sharpened branches (figure 8).[70] This plate-branch sculpture is akin to the bottle-branch sculpture reported by Proyart.

Fu-Kiau explained why these constellations of glass and faience, circles and cylinders are lifted above the grave:

You can see bottles raised on poles above a grave almost anywhere in traditionally minded villages in Kongo. The bottles may have knives or nails inside them. The lifted bottles (*manika bwaata*) are placed on high like a flag (*tedimisa bwaata*). . . . The bottles may contain palm wine, through which the living ask the dead person

FIGURE 8.   Plate-branch sculptures for the dead, Mbanza Ngungu, Zaire, 1909–10.

[in this case, a noted palm wine tapster] not to take all his skills to
the other world with him. Or the bottles may be filled with palm
oil, meaning that a dead healer is being asked not to take all his
soothing cures and insights with him into the grave, so that the
living are not forced to relearn his lore by themselves.[71]

In the case of the grave near Mbanza Ngungu, the power and bless-
ing of the spirit of the person who owned these forcefully pierced and
elevated tokens is invoked to stay, to continue to inspire and enhance the
fortune of the living. Elevation breaks contact with the ground. It arrests the departure of the treasured insights, accumulated like mystic
microdots, upon these plates, bottles, and utensils. Bringing these ele-
vating and encapsulating gestures from the graveyard to the front yard
is indeed intimidating.

James D. Martin recalled that the bottle trees of his Delta childhood
were especially beautiful: "I remember an azure edifice along the Yazoo
River . . . mostly, if not entirely, blue and casting a blue shadow across
the yard. I remember the owner's statement, firm and positive, that it
kept away the river spooks." He was also told by a black maker of bottle

trees near Oxford that the main purpose of building these gleaming structures was the catching of "haunts." That informant even revealed to Martin the formula for making bottle trees: "Pour paint into the selected bottle to cover the inside entirely, using bright colors to attract hesitant spirits: grease the mouth of the bottle with a touch of fat so that the haunts will slip right in: and arrange the bottles on a tree in a sunny location so that the morning light will destroy the trapped evil spirits." On a road to the town of Bruce, south of Oxford in Calhoun County, a most elaborate bottle tree was found, bearing 225 bottles in different shapes and sizes. But most of these structures include far fewer receptacles.[72]

The custom is related to improvisational forms of outdoor art in black America and the West Indies. Roger Abrahams told me in summer 1972 that blacks on the island of Nevis tie metal plates and objects in trees for "flash." A black man who lives by himself near Killen, Alabama, has, for reasons of his own, nailed slippers and other objects onto the trunk and branches of a tree in front of his house. These are private sparks, struck by the collision of Kongo and Angola culture with the creative perceptions of black Americans.

Grave Adornments

The tombs of Kongo and the graves of North American blacks who inherited a set of Kongo and Angola formal influences take their power beyond the things that adorn the mounds. An *mbota* tree, planted on an elder's grave, provides an eternal signpost to a world beneath its roots. Lengths of iron or ceramic plumber's pipe similarly suggest travel through water underground. A white conch shell renders time and cosmos in exquisite spatial miniature but also indicates "the white," the world of the ancestors beneath or beyond the sea.

Thus caparisoned, Kongo tombs become ritual earthworks, conceptual doors to another universe, an intricate field of mediatory signs (figures 9 and 10). The function of these signs, sometimes materially simple but conceptually very rich, anticipated certain aims of modern Western art. Powerful analogies exist, for example, between the "readymades" of Marcel Duchamp and objects placed on Kongo and African American graves—stopped clocks, telephones with receivers off the hook, shorn handlebars, anchors. Like Duchamp, Bakongo seek to impose a fourth dimension upon the three-dimensionality of ordinary things. But the placement of a sewing machine or an umbrella on a Kongo grave establishes more than aesthetic surprise and expressive potentiality through unusual juxtapositions. When such objects were the last things used by the dead, they are believed to be impregnated with traces of the spirit, traces that may be used to persuade the dead to release their talents in dreams and inspiration to the benefit of their descendants.

Kongo art for the dead imposes the wisdom and the glitter of the world of the fourth moment of the sun—the noon of the dead, when it is midnight in our world—upon objects lit by the first three moments of the sun, the span of time defining the arc of a person's life. In fact, Kongo tomb decorations impose multiple dimensions upon outwardly simple shapes and gestures. These dimensions in Kongo include medicine, law, urbanity, ideographic power of expression, and mediation. Incising lozenges upon the side of a terra cotta grave marker cuts through the materiality of the objects so treated. It links them to their spiritual doubles, where all the holes are filled in the completion of the circle of the sun within the kingdom of the dead.

Since the perdurance and importance of a tradition is defined in terms of the richness of the associative values clustering about its most appropriate expressions, it is clear how and why Kongo art for the dead always changes and yet remains the same. It may incorporate any number of new expressions to complete the ancient gestures of spiritual accomplishment and power. No matter that the technique of making *niombo* figures apparently was lost in the Atlantic trade to the Americas. The same point of spiritual return that might be summarized by painting an emblematic conch shell spiral on the chest of a large red cloth figure in northern Kongo was rendered by placing an actual conch shell on the surfaces of graves in black cemeteries in Texas, Missouri, Georgia, South Carolina, Delaware, and elsewhere in the South. And no matter that the custom of carving *bitumba* or *mintadi* was restricted to a particular time and space in Kongo. The same felicity of spiritual presence and surveillance, exquisitely miniaturized, could be summoned in Kongo or in South Carolina by placing on the surface of the tomb china figurines associated with the departed persons. China figurines become *mintadi* surrogates in the Kongo Atlantic world.

The disappearance of the social structure and the sets of institutions that gave rise to elegant *moboondo* terra cotta markers was unimportant in terms of Kongo time. In Kongo the eternal association of the lawsuit with death could be symbolized by calling lawsuits *bulu*—holes torn in things. Conversely, the same image of death and the end of things within this world could be indicated by piercing the bottom of an ordinary porcelain mug deposited on a grave. Identical symbols of breaking the shell of life, reinforced by similar conceptions, beliefs, and practices among other West and Central Africa civilizations, give rise to breaking the bottoms of glasses, mugs, pitchers, and cups laid on top of African

FIGURE 9. Kongo tomb with stone, bottles, vessels, and china doll figures, early twentieth century.

FIGURE 10. Grave of a Kongo chief, with bottle-marked *luumbo* enclosing kettle (*kinzu*).

American graves. And the enclosing (*luumbu*-making) and embedding (*nkondi*-recalling) gestures that are closely interwoven in the making of these charmed precincts of the dead acquire a logic of creative traversal of time and space. Embedded bottles in Kongo thus become a single embedded pottery form on a grave in western South Carolina, or a *luumbu* of bottles, midway between the palisades of ancient Kongo and the concrete walls and screens of modern Kongo tombs, gives way to neat quadratic curbs of poured concrete in western South Carolina. Nonetheless, enclosing walls of inverted bottles still marked graves in nearby Georgia as late as 1950 and equivalents of the *kinzu* (iron kettles) and *nsusu mpembe* (white chicken images) of Kongo tomb decoration continue to be used in late twentieth-century South Carolina (figures 11 and 12).

Kongo and Kongo-influenced grave art, linked to abiding ideologies of mediation and legitimacy, displays its own logic of perdurance, transcending time, place, and class. Its remarkable power of self-abstraction, compacting and reshaping cherished insights, has risen above the shocks of slavery, imperialism, independence, and the special challenges and alarums of our own century.

The twentieth-century transformation of concrete architecture into new expressions of timeless certainties in the burials of important Bakongo is matched by the amazing spread of similar influences from the original slaving ports of Annapolis, Charleston, New Orleans, and elsewhere to vast portions of North America along the rivers, trails, and railroads of the old Deep South. The result of this influence was the rise of a fundamental form of African-influenced North American art. The memories of *Mbanza* Kongo and the tribunals of lords and people were lost as Kongo ethnicity blurred into generalized African American cultural assertions. Nevertheless, a belief in the grave as an animate charm for mediation of the spirit remained intact. So did the belief that the mound of earth above the grave was at one with the spirit within the grave. There were also vague echoes of the concept of the tomb as courtyard or enclosure in the circumscribing of many African American tombs with a line of shells or glass. Most impressive was the continuity of a field of signs that admonished the spirit within the enclosure and beneath the mound with emphases of ancient currency.

The sources of my preliminary assessment of Kongo artistic influence on New World black burials should be made explicit. The links between Kongo and North America are discernible not only in the literature of travel in the Deep South during the nineteenth century and sometimes earlier but also in the corresponding literature of the Caribbean—Haiti in particular—where massive numbers of blacks arrived

FIGURE 11.   Grave with enclosure of stones and pottery, South Carolina, 1975.

FIGURE 12.   Grave, South Carolina, dated 1967, photographed in 1976.

from Kongo and Angola during the eighteenth century. Haitians use some of the same symbols Bakongo used in the decoration of their graves: trees, shells, miniature houses. Moreover, sometimes they regard these elements in ways exactly congruent with Kongo arguments. This point is crucial, considering the well-documented contacts between the artistic cultures of Haitian and New Orleans blacks by way of migrations in the early nineteenth century.[73]

In all of this the master symbol of inclusive consciousness concerns the definition of the tomb as an *nkisi* (charm) for moral intimidation and spiritual transcendence. The gist of an *nkisi* in Kongo is the enclosure of spirit within an appropriate container amid spirit-embedding earths, along with spirit-admonishing elements that tell the spirit, through shapes, puns, and gestures, what to do or not do for the owner of the charm. Kongo and Kongoizing tombs literally enclose spirit in earth. That earth is believed to be charged with mystical powers. Witness the rise in black North America of myriad charms, a primary ingredient of which is "goofer dust," earth from the surface of a grave. This term derives from the Ki-Kongo word for a dead person, *Kufwa*. Thus the grave functions as an unseen court of last appeal, where a person who has suffered humiliation may go to his ancestors and ask them to wreak vengeance, mystically, upon his tormentors. Similarly, in North America it is said that a black woman worried about her husband's alcoholism may go to the graveyard and mark off his grave by the length of one of his garments. At the end of that axis she may hammer in a stake as a headboard and, by so doing, awaken spirit in the graveyard earth, like the soul of an *nkondi* awakened by the hammering in of blades and nails. The spirit then takes the literal measure of the errant spouse, who would do well to mend his ways immediately. Bringing spirit (symbolized by the graveyard ground) in contact with a person (in the measurement of his garment) exemplifies spirit-directing in the making of a charm. By concentrating on these organizing principles, spirit-embeddedness and spirit-admonishment, we can understand the flow of other elements in the Kongo Atlantic tradition.

We will examine just three elements of spirit-admonishment in Kongo Atlantic graves: the planted tree and related usages, such as shells and lamps placed on graves; arrest of the spirit in the last-used object (*kanga mfunyu*); and the theme of the white chicken (*nsusu mpembe*).

The Planted Tree

Trees are planted directly on the grave in both Kongo and black America to express the idea of immortality and perdurance. There is, in fact, a whole collection of trees in Kongo, each with its special symbolic nuance that comes forward dramatically in the mortuary context. *Mbota* trees, famous for their extremely hard wood, suggest the hardiness of the elders' spirit and resistance to the force of time. This suggestion may have reinforced the similar use of cedar in black America as a preferred wood for stakes and headboards. *Mfuma* trees are planted on royal graves in Kongo, using word play to command the king (*mfumu*) to seek originating (*fuma*) power, according to the saying "He who is in touch with origin remains alive" (*mu kala kintwadi ya tubu i mu zinga*).[74] For ordinary persons, a tree may be planted to command the spirit to follow the roots, which indicate the direction of the kingdom of the dead: "This tree is a sign of the spirit on its way to the land of the ancestors" (*nti wau sinsu kya mooyo ku mpemba*).[75]

The persistence of this vision in black America was noted in the nineteenth century. In *Letters of a Traveller* (1850), William Cullen Bryant recorded that a white burial in South Carolina was sited just outside the town, whereas blacks buried their kin "near a forest . . . [where] a few trees trailing with long moss, rise above hundreds of nameless graves."[76] To this day the more spectacularly traditional graves in black Georgia and South Carolina often are sited by and, in a few cases, even hidden within woods or clumps of forest. Eugene Aubin illustrated a *mapou* tree standing dramatically upon a tomb on the Léogane Plain in southern Haiti at the beginning of this century. On the south peninsula, where Kongo influences are strong, nineteenth- and early-twentieth-century cemeteries have tombs under commanding trees, some deliberately nestled in their roots. The trees are said to provide honor and shade to the dead. More important, they represent, as in Kongo, the persistence of the spirit: "Trees on graves in Haiti symbolized the fact that trees live after us, that death is not the end."[77] Rigaud Benoit's fascinating 1973 painting *The Recall of the Dead* is a powerful document of the role of trees in relation to the dead in Haiti. And in a catalogue of Haitian painting, Pierre Apraxine glosses some meanings of this ritual shown unfolding near the roots of a tree by the water that, in Haitian consciousness, divides this world from the next: "Souls, responding to the invocation of the *hougan* [ritual expert] and using water as a gateway, pass from the abyss to the *govis* or earthen vessels in which they will be kept and worshipped on the family altar."[78]

There are myriad examples of such plantings in the United States. In a cemetery near the South Carolina coast the grave of Lenard Johnson (1836–1923) is presided over by a wind-slanted pine tree that has long since burst the metal pot in which it was planted; it soars from the middle of the grave. The same burial ground has a pine tree planted at the head of a grave in November 1975. These traditions have diffused across the southeastern portion of the United States and extended into Texas and other southwestern states. In Dallas, where the first slaves reportedly arrived in 1847 with the Miller family of Tennessee, the L. Butler Nelson Memorial Park, an all-black cemetery, has numerous trees planted within a few inches of headstones. There is no mistaking the correlation tree = immortal spirit, so frequently are the headstones accompanied by towering living presences.

SHELLS

In Haiti one finds beautiful and impressive conch shells adorning the surfaces of tombs and graves. André Pierre, a priest in the national folk religion of Haiti and one of the nation's most distinguished painters, glossed the meaning of this element when he told me that

> shells symbolize the existence of spirit in the sea: the body is dead but the spirit continues on its way. The shell encloses elements of water, earth, and wind. It is a world in miniature. It symbolizes the animation of succeeding generations by the spirit of the ancestors. It indicates the island in the sea to which we all shall journey.[79]

While doing research into the meanings of black graves at White Bluff, Georgia, in the summer of 1950, Simon Ottenberg discovered that, for one informant, shaping the mound was a sensitive act of communication with the dead. "Some people built up piles of dirt on top of graves again," Ottenberg wrote. "He [the informant] did not think that this was right. It was not respectful. It was like touching the dead."[80] But in many burials a "rule" is broken. Reestablishing a mound and pressing a fence of shells into its mass admonishes the spirit with a complex message of concern, protection, arrest, and immortality (figure 13).

In Kongo, shells intuit immortality through a fundamental pun, linking *zinga* ("spiral-form shell") with *zinga* ("to live long"), and give rise to a remarkable concept with its associated prayer:

> *Mbamba* is a large sea-shell. Finding many of these shells, the people in the old days consecrated them [to] their *bisimbi*. They hid their souls in the shells and dug them down in the woods with only the tips showing above ground, addressing them as follows: "As strong as your house you shall keep my life for me. When you leave for the sea, take me along, that I may live forever with you."[81]

Compare an African American recapitulation of the essence of these patterns of belief in this example from St. Simons Island, Georgia:

FIGURE 13. African American burial enclosed in shells, tidewater South Carolina, November 1975.

The shells stand for the sea. The sea brought us, the sea shall take us back. So the shells upon our graves stand for water, the means of glory and the land of demise.[82]

MIRRORS AND LAMPS

Bakongo ritual experts used to embed the glittering, iridescent wing case of a particular kind of beetle into their charms as "something full of light, like water, that you can see through, to the other world." Later, when imported Western mirrors (*tala-tala*) exactly duplicated this powerful effect, the concept deepened in material extension and retranslation. But in the original wing-case charms the idea of the glitter of the spirit fused with the notion of second sight through symbolized flight, miniaturized neatly by the insertion of the beetle's wings. The meaning of the flight was "to expand the beyond" (*vila mu bángula bweno a ku mpemba*).[83]

The intimation of glory in glittering objects and the embedding of spirit therein become a spiritual fundament in the making of African American charms. Charmed walking sticks include a rhinestone or some other flashing element.[84] Puckett reported from black Missouri that "a

FIGURE 14.   Grave with embedded lamp chimney, western South Carolina, 1975.

more complicated luck ball was one made for Charley Leland. . . . into it was put tinfoil (representing the brightness of the little spirit who was going to be in the ball)."[85] In coastal Georgia as in modern Kongo, mirrors or glass are taken from the dead man's house and embedded on his mound or sometimes fitted within his headstone. This practice holds the spirit at a safe distance from the living. Remarkable mirror equivalents have also appeared, such as the automobile headlights set in headstones in Oldham County, Kentucky, and tidewater Georgia. Such a monument, like the charmed wings of a beetle inserted in a Kongo charm, at once arrests the spirit with its light and hints of movement to the other world. Similar beliefs impel the embellishing of tombs with shining aluminum paint in tidewater Virginia and probably explain a practice witnessed in many Southern black burials, including those at the Mount Zion Methodist Church burial ground in Jacksonville, Florida: "On all of the new graves the flower-pot wrappings, a green foil, had been turned onto its reverse side which was a shining, silvery white. The foil sparkled brilliantly and drew attention to the graves."[86]

Consciousness of spirit in brilliance and illumination gave rise to another Kongo custom: the lighting of bonfires on certain graves to guide the souls of leaders into the other world. That custom may be compared with the creole black custom in the Deep South of planting lamp chimneys on burial mounds. Texas blacks say this practice leads the deceased on into glory. In the fullness of this lore, impressive grave sites have emerged, with fragmentary lamp chimneys exuding spiritual brilliance, as in a western South Carolina instance, where the lamp is placed together with flower vessels wrapped in gleaming tinfoil (figure 14).[87]

Arrest of the Spirit

Some objects that decorate graves—cups, weatherbeaten hats, rusting scissors—lack the flash that embeds the spirit. Often these things arrest the being of the departed person in other ways. Because of their intimate relation to the deceased, the things last used by the dead person become especially important. As Fu-Kiau told me, "The last strength of a dead person is present within the objects." To touch them is to receive powerful messages from the dead, communicated in dreams. "By touching these objects automatically," Fu-Kiau said, "I comprehend the *mambu* my mother was willing to transmit to me."[88] Placing such objects on the grave safely grounds their awesome potentiality, keeping the dead from coming to the house to claim them back. This process is called "arresting the emanations of a person" (*kanga mfunyu*). The phrase also means "tying effluvia" and, by a pun, "tying the anger of the dead."

Kanga mfunyu came intact from Kongo to black America. A witness to that is in a remark dating from the period 1845–65 at Colerain plantation near Savannah: "Negro graves were always decorated with the last article used by the departed."[89] This remark may be compared to beliefs held by residents of St. Helena Island, South Carolina, in 1919, that the last drops of medicine remaining from a sick person should be allowed to drain into the earth above the grave. This practice assures the healing of the dead person in the other world and avoids displacement of the spirit.[90]

The White Chicken

In 1887 R. E. Dennett recounted the burial of a Kongo lord in a great eight-wheeled coffin, the top of which was ornamented with a stuffed leopard, an open umbrella, various vessels, and two wooden boxes, one carved in the shape of a duck, the other in the form of a hen. When the great wheeled structure—a kind of quadratic *niombo* (Kongo mummy) —was finally laid to rest, the hen and the other ornaments were placed on the surface of the grave.[91] Images of hens, painted white, are placed on graves in parts of Kongo to this day. These *nsusu mpembe* (white chicken) images symbolize, first, "the ancestors, the dead."[92] In addition, they symbolize the mediation of great power, often healing power, from the dead:

> Then she took up a white chicken, held it up toward the sky and addressed God in heaven. "If this child dies, it will be 'the white chicken,'" thereby adjuring help to save his life. Initiation released powers from the "white" beyond the water. These powers were mediated by a white chicken and two plants, endowing Nzoamambu with purity and sight.[93]

No later than 1816 we find this custom also in the black English-speaking Caribbean: "The whitewashing of tombs is repeated carefully every Christmas morning and formerly it was customary on these occasions to kill a white cock and sprinkle his blood over the graves of the family."[94] The invocation of healing power from beyond by means of a white fowl appears in black Mississippi in the first quarter of this century: "The strangest cure I think I ever heard of in Mississippi was when Overlea, a seventh son and born double-sighter, loosed five white pigeons that had never known freedom, for a sick child. When the pigeons crossed water the child was cured."[95] Peter Alston, an old black worker from the tidewater areas east of Charleston, told me in fall 1975 that he remembered "lots of china chickens" on the graves of his region in the first quarter of this century.

Now let us look closer at the grave of a male black child who died in 1967 in western South Carolina (figure 15; also see figure 12). An enormous white rooster guards the tomb, itself sparkling with a careful covering of white driveway gravel and enlivened with further loving touches: a pair of miniature shoes in metal and small lamps for mystic illumination, like a night light for the bedroom of a child who will wake in glory and walk to God in silver-colored shoes, feet crunching on glittering white gravel.

Modern Emblems of Mediation

When modern means of voyaging came to Kongo they were gathered into all that has concerned us here—the concentration upon a sacred point of spirit mediation. Wyatt MacGaffey photographed, at Ndemba in 1965, a modern Kongo tomb set within a screened-off area (figure 16). The tomb rises in four tiers, the levels of which signify that "this person lived positively vis-à-vis the people and now they expect him to come back." His followers caused his grave to be specially surmounted by the image of an airplane "to call him quickly back" from beyond the

FIGURE 15. Grave of African-American child, dated 1967, photographed in December 1978.

four doors of cosmos, here indicated by representations of four bottles at the cardinal points.[96]

Similarly, a tomb near Lombe in Ingembe territory, Bas-Zaire, was photographed about 1949 by L. Cahen (figure 17). A concrete sculptural rendering of an automobile, it is first and foremost a structure preoccupied with the ancient vision of return and only secondarily with the aspect of modernity. To see this tomb as merely an emblem of "acculturation" is to miss a rich implied rephrasing of ancient idioms of transcendence. This tomb's symbols indicate that here we have the grave of a man who was a noted driver. Such tombs sometimes honor men who died in automobile accidents, but whether or not this man died in a violent crash, spiritually he left this world by car. For a Kongo person in the 1930s or 1940s to say "I am a driver" conveyed to the elders a very powerful message of strangeness and potentiality.[97] So there is potency in the shaping of this vehicle-tomb, adding force to the communal

FIGURE 16. Kongo tomb with airplane marker, Ndemba, Bas-Zaire, photographed in 1965.

prayer that the departed person continue to work on behalf of his descendants in that modern mode of motion. Like a heroic piece of *maboondo* pottery, the car is strongly pierced, with a deliberately doorless opening and further slits suggesting architectural openings. Anchored in the earth yet traveling magically across vast time and space, its headlights blazing invisibly, the ghost-car moves with an assonance of fourth dimensionality.

In the traditional graveyards of black America, modern vehicles have been similarly transformed. A headstone engraved with the outline of a ship is found at Newport News. A handlebar shorn from a bicycle adorns a grave in Georgia. And on the grave of a dead boy in western South Carolina a toy jet airplane lay rusting in the sun of a November afternoon in 1975 (figure 18). The late sheriff of Beaufort, South Carolina, J. E. McTeer, an author of numerous works on aspects of traditional African American religion, saw the jet as a means of "getting to heaven fast."[98]

Notes

1. I discussed these etymologies in *Flash of the Spirit* (New York: Random House, 1982).

FIGURE 17. Kongo tomb with concrete automobile, Lombe, Bas-Zaire, 1940s.

FIGURE 18. Grave of a
child, with toy airplane
on the mound, South
Carolina, 1975.

2. Philip Curtin, *The Atlantic Slave Trade: A Census* (Madison: University of Wisconsin Press, 1969), 188.

3. Ibid., 241.

4. Degrandpré, xxiii. He said that what was commonly understood under the generic name "coast of Angola" was the "whole country situated between Cape López and Benguela," 1.

5. Harold Courlander, *Haiti Singing* (Chapel Hill: University of North Carolina Press, 1939), 3.

6. Jean Price-Mars, "Les survivances africaines dans la communauté haitienne," *Études Dahomeennes* 6 (Porto Novo: Institut Français de l'Afrique Noire, 1951), 7.

7. George W. Cable, *The Dance in Place Congo* (Carrollton: Faruk van Turk, 1972), 1–2, 6; reprint of 1886 article in *The Century*. Dena Epstein's *Sinful Tunes and Spirituals* (Chicago: University of Chicago Press, 1977) includes many references that suggest the continuous presence of Kongo dances in early-nineteenth-century New Orleans (95, 96, 133).

8. Edward Larocque Tinker, *Toucoutou* (New York: Dodd, Mead, 1930), 93. *Raquette* was played with two small racquets instead of one as in modern lacrosse.

9. Robert Goffin, *Jazz: From Congo to Swing* (London: Musician Press, 1946), 25.

10. Cf. Bertil Söderberg, *Les instruments de musique au bas Congo et dans les regions avoisinantes* (Stockholm: Statens Ethnografiska Museum, 1956), pl. 19, man playing *ndungu* drum, Kimpongi village, Bembe territory, 1.

11. Peter H. Wood, *Black Majority: Negroes in Colonial South Carolina from 1670 through the Stono Rebellion* (New York: Knopf, 1974), 335.

12. Witnessed by the author in Zaire, March and June 1973.

13. Fernando Ortiz, *Los instrumentos de la música afrocubana* 3 (Havana: Ministerio de Educación, 1952), 390.

14. Gerhard Kubik, *Angolan Traits in Black Music, Games and Dances of Brazil* (Lisbon: Junta de Investigaçóties Científicas do Ultramar, 1979), 10.

15. H. Baumann, *Schopfung und Urzeit des Menschen im Mythus der Afrikanischen Völker* (Berlin, 1936), 89.

16. Roger Bastide, *The African Religions of Brazil* (Baltimore: Johns Hopkins University Press, 1978), 347.

17. Winifred Vass, *The Bantu Speaking Heritage of the United States* (Los Angeles: UCLA, Center for Afro-American Studies, 1979), 3.

18. Fu-Kiau, interview with author, Feb. 1, 1981.

19. Harry Stillwell Edwards, *The Two Runaways and Other Stories* (New York: Century, 1889), 202–203, 205.

20. Balu Balila, Muanda village (Bawoyo), Collectivité de la Mer, interview in Kinshasa, June 26, 1980.

21. Lievin van de Velde, "La région de bas-Congo," *Bulletin Société Royale Belge de Geographie* 10:383.

22. Bapende: Tervüren Museum photo archive, no. 117556, Kiwila initiation (for women), Pende people, Kandale region, Kinzunda village. Ndembu: Victor Turner, *Chihamba: The White Spirit* (Manchester: Manchester University Press, 2nd ed., 1969), pl. 8b, "image of Kavula." Tu-Chokwe: Eduardo dos Santos, *Sobre a religatiô dos quicos* (Lisbon: Junta de Investigaçôtíes do Ultramar, 1962), fig. 1, "the ideogram called Kalunga."

23. Igor Kopytoff, personal communication, Mar. 1968.

24. W. E. B. Du Bois, "The Religion of the American Negro," *New World,* December 1900, 618; quoted in John W. Blassingame, *The Slave Community: Plantation Life in the Antebellum South* (New York: Oxford University Press, 1972), 33: "the chief remaining institution was the priest [ritual expert]. . . . He early appeared on the plantation and found his function as the healer of the sick, the interpreter of the unknown, the comforter of the sorrowing, the supernatural avenger of wrong. . . . "

25. Harry Middleton Hyatt, *Hoodoo-Conjuration-Witchcraft-Rootwork*, 2 (Hannibal: Western Publishing, 1970), 1173. I have standardized Hyatt's picturesque orthography.

26. Ibid., 1266.

27. Newbell Niles Puckett, *Folk Beliefs of the Southern Negro* (New York: Dover, 1969), 319.

28. Ibid.

29. *Robert Johnson: King of the Delta Blues Singers* (Columbia LP CL1654, side 1, band 1), recorded Nov. 1936.

30. Ortiz, *Los instrumentos,* fig. 168, 168–69.

31. Lydia Cabrera, *Reglas de Congo: Palo Monte, Palo Mayombé* (Miami: Peninsular Printing, 1979), 146.

32. I am grateful to Professor John Janzen for allowing me to read and cite from his forthcoming work.

33. Roger Bastide, personal communication, May 8, 1968.

34. John Janzen, personal communication, summer 1979.

35. Roger Bastide, personal communication, May 8, 1968.

36. *Pontos cantados e riscados da Umbanda,* 9th ed. (Rio de Janeiro: Editora Espiritualista, 1951), and 3000 *pontos riscados e cantados da Umbanda e Candomblé* (Rio de Janeiro: Editora Eco, 1975).

37. Wesley R. Hunt, personal communications, winter 1975 and spring 1981.

38. William Stewart, personal communications, Dec. 1980.

39. Cable, *Dance in Place Congo,* 3. Also in George W. Cable, *Creoles and Cajuns* (Garden City: Doubleday Anchor, 1959), 370.

40. See Warren Robbins, *African Art in American Collections* (New York: Praeger,

1966), pl. 247, a musician seated cross-legged playing the thumb-piano; Sundi, from Ward Collection, Smithsonian Institution, Washington, D.C.

41. Jacob Elder, personal communication, Oct. 18, 1970.

42. William Stewart, personal communication, Dec. 1980.

43. Lydia Cabrera, personal communication, Jan. 1981.

44. Raul Martinez Rodríguez and Pedro de la Hoz Gonzáles, "De la Colombia al Guaguancó," *Bohemia*, June 4, 1976, 13.

45. Fu-Kiau, interview with author, Dec. 15, 1980.

46. Lydia Cabrera, personal communication, Nov. 1980.

47. William Stewart, personal communication, Oct. 1980.

48. Charles William Day, *Five Years Residence in the West Indies*, 2 (London: Colbourn, 1852), 61–64. It is cognate but not identical because they "generally turn back to back."

49. Annette Powell Williams, "Dynamics of a Black Audience," in *Rappin' and Stylin' Out: Communication in Urban Black America*, ed. Thomas Kochman (Urbana: University of Illinois Press, 1972), 103.

50. K. E. Laman, *Dictionnaire Kikongo* (Brussels: Librairie Falk, 1936), 2:842.

51. Ambrose E. Gonzales, *Laguerre: A Gascon of the Black Border* (Columbia, S.C.: The State Company, 1924), 79: "Alice put her arms akimbo and regarded him contemptuously, as one who would presently, under the mandate of the Court, usurp her precious privilege of speech!"; 265: "Daphne, arms akimbo, tense as a coiled steel spring, stood invitingly before him, and the invitation was pressing for she was determined to goad him into hitting."

52. In the *n'kondi* context, the *pakalala* gesture symbolized readiness to take on the difficulties and responsibilities of a lawsuit. André Pierre maintains (interview with author, Mar. 22, 1981) that the arms akimbo, or *deu men sou koté*, gesture is associated with the deity the Queen of Kongo because it "demonstrates that she is queen of the earth, the right and the left. And her pacquet is also like that, standing, to represent divine force in four parts, high, low, left and right." In other words, he reads the gesture cosmographically.

53. In Haiti the upward-pointing gesture of the right hand is tinged with Christian interpretations: "the resurrection of Jesus," the "triumph of God's power over death."

54. Courlander, *Haiti Singing*, 131.

55. "Pygmy . . . music is characterized . . . particularly by the hocketing or *durchbrokene Arbeit* technique in which each individual in a group of singers contributes, with precise timing, one, two, or three notes to a longer melodic line," Alan P. Merriam, "African Music," in William Bascom and Melville J. Herskovits, *Continuity and Change in African Cultures* (Chicago: University of Chicago Press, 1959), 77.

56. Söderberg, *Instruments*, pl. 23, "player of transverse flute made of carica papaya, Bembe, Mouyondzi," 6.

57. Harold Courlander, *The Drum and the Hoe* (Berkeley: University of California Press, 1960), 107–108.

58. John Vlach, *Sources of the Shotgun House: African and Caribbean Antecedents for Afro-American Architecture*, 1 (Ann Arbor: University Microfilms, 1975), 69–73.

59. Although baton-twirling cheerleaders are more or less restricted to football games in the United States at large, in the black South they accompany, or used to accompany, basketball, baseball, and other sports events. This popular art is firmly rooted among blacks in the South, where its origin— or, at the very least, its most intensive development—appears to have taken place. This phenomenon parallels and is reinforced by the rise of baton twirling, with left hand on hip, in the black Caribbean, notably Haiti.

60. John Szwed, introduction to Arthur Huff Fauset, *Black Gods of the Metropolis* (Philadephia: University of Pennsylvania Press, 1971), vii: "Most commentators on possession in North America have in the past noted that some Euro-American people, especially in the American South, also practice spirit possession in their services, and thus have argued that the practice must have spread from white to black. The same arrogant logic would presumably attribute Afro-American contributions to American culture, such as jazz, baton twirling, black dialects, and black cuisine, to Europe, simply because a large number of whites also practice them."
    The definitive history of baton twirling in the United States remains to be written. Atwater's *Baton Twirling* is useful mainly for the Anglo-American dimensions. Sampling the available evidence, I have the impression that the main baton-twirling pose, with left hand on hip, was incorporated from black sources in the South after the rise of football and half-time ceremonies. In 1939 it was noted that "some of the most versatile cheerleaders" were at southern colleges, notably Alabama and Tennessee; see "All-America," *Time*, Dec. 11, 1939, 42. A host of European and African American influences swept in together, merged, or were independently performed. In the process, jazz steps and strutting routines reinforced the black component and, through the tumult and creativity, the *télama* pose maintained itself intact; see *American* magazine, Nov. 1940 and May 1941, where photographs without comment record the continuity of the mode. Probably not until Terry Southern's article on baton twirling in *Esquire*, February 1963, did the veil of white imitation begin to part: "the best Strutting is done at the colored schools of the South, and of these the greatest of all is to be seen at Alabama State Teachers College," 103. For nineteenth-century documentation of blacks twirling batons, left hand on hip, see Middleton Harris, *The Black Book* (New York: Random House, 1974), 42, 43, 45.

61. Elizabeth Fine, "Aesthetic Patterning of Verbal Art and the Performance-

Centered Text," *Working Papers in Sociolinguistics* 74–80 (Austin, Tex.: Southwest Educational Development Laboratory, Nov. 1980), 31.

62. Fu-Kiau, interview, Nov. 26, 1980.

63. Fine, "Aesthetic Patterning," 32.

64. For example, among exemplars of the Tervüren Museum study collection of *minkisi n'kondi:* nos. 19845, 22480, 22433, 59.48.1, and so on.

65. The distribution of bottle trees across the face of the South is impressive, but a full discussion cannot be undertaken here. The more important clusters are in East Texas (personal communication, Mrs. C. E. Hilton, San Augustine Library, Dec. 8, 1978), southeastern Arkansas (personal communication, James D. Martin, Oct. 1980), and southern Alabama (personal communication, James Poteet, fall 1979).

66. Eudora Welty, *The Wide Net and Other Stories* (New York: Harcourt Brace Jovanovich, 1971), 156.

67. Ibid. The passage is interesting not only for its estimate of time expended by a black craftsman on his trees (nine years, roughly one tree per year) but also for the remark on the care devoted to this spiritual structure, matching or even surpassing that devoted to the actual house.

68. James D. Martin, personal communication, Jan. 1981.

69. L'Abbé Proyart, *Histoire de Loango, Kakongo, et autres royaumes d'Afrique* (Paris: Berton and Crapart, 1776), 192–93.

70. Tervüren photo archive, no. 21124.

71. Fu-Kiau, personal communication, November 1980. Fu-Kiau adds that "to lift up plates on trees symbolizes not the end. Death will not end our fight. Dishes left, not on the ground, but in the air mean we are not yet finished." This statement is consistent with the idea of continuity of the talents of the dead person.

72. "Mississippi Bottle Trees Ward Off 'Evil Spirits,'" *Evening Post*, Vicksburg, Mississippi, Feb. 20, 1974, 22; James Martin, personal communication, Feb. 1981.

73. For sources in the search for Kongo influence in the West Indies during colonial times, see John F. Szwed and Roger D. Abrahams, *Afro-American Folk Culture: An Annotated Bibliography* (Philadelphia: Institute for the Study of Human Issues, 1978).

74. Fu-Kiau, interview, Apr. 17, 1981.

75. Fu-Kiau, interview, Oct. 9, 1977.

76. William Cullen Bryant, *Letters of a Traveller, or Notes of Things Seen in Europe and America* (New York: Putnam, 1980), 94.

77. Eugene Aubin, *En Haiti* (Paris: Librairie Armand Colin, 1910), 212.

78. Pierre Apraxine, *Haitian Painting* (New York: American Federation of Arts, 1973), 27.

79. André Pierre, interview, Mar. 22, 1981.

80. Simon Ottenberg, typewritten segment of a field notebook, summer 1950, 3. See also Simon Ottenberg, "Leadership and Change in a Coastal Georgia Negro Community," *Phylon*, Spring 1959, 2018.

81. K. E. Laman, *The Kongo* (Uppsala: Studia Ethnographica Upsalienia, 1953), 3:37.

82. Bessie Jones, interview, fall 1975.

83. Fu-Kiau, interview, Apr. 22, 1981.

84. For example, the Patton family cane, circa 1916, Cherry Valley, Arkansas. This African American–made scepter is decorated with the standing figure of a man at the summit, an implied serpent, and the flash of inserted rhinestones.

85. Puckett, *Folk Beliefs*, 233.

86. Jeremiah Bentley, "Kongo Influences on an Old Black Cemetery," unpublished paper, May 1977.

87. James Agee, *Let Us Now Praise Famous Men* (New York: Ballantine Books, 1966), has a haunting photograph of this tradition among poor whites in Alabama.

88. Fu-Kiau, interview, Sept. 30, 1980.

89. Sarah Hodgson Torian, "Notes and Documents: Ante-Bellum and War Memories of Mrs. Telfair Hodgson," *Georgia Historical Quarterly*, Dec. 1943, 352.

90. Elsie Clews Parsons, *Folk-Lore of the Sea Islands of South Carolina* (Cambridge, Mass.: American Folklore Society, 1923), 214.

91. R. E. Dennett, *Seven Years among the Fjort* (London: Sampson Low, 1887), 177–79 and illustration facing 104.

92. Fu-Kiau, interview, Oct. 25, 1980.

93. John M. Janzen, *The Quest for Therapy in Lower Zaire* (Berkeley: University of California Press, 1978), 162–63.

94. Alexander Barclay, *A Practical View of the Present State of Slavery* . . . (London: Smith, Elder & Co., 1828), 131–33.

95. Ruth Bass, "Mojo," in *Mother Wit from the Laughing Barrel*, ed. Alan Dundes (Englewood Cliffs: Prentice-Hall, 1973), 382.

96. Fu-Kiau, interview, Apr. 18, 1981.

97. Ibid.

98. Sheriff J. E. McTeer, interview with author, Nov. 13, 1975.

Eleven

Africanisms in African American Music

Portia K. Maultsby

Since the first quarter of the twentieth century scholars have examined African American history and culture in the context of an African past.[1] Their studies support the premise that the institution of slavery did not destroy the cultural legacy of slaves nor erase the memories of an African past. The survival of slaves in the New World depended on their ability to retain the ideals fundamental to African cultures. Although slaves were exposed to various European-derived traditions, they resisted cultural imprisonment by the larger society. Slaves adapted to life in the Americas by retaining a perspective on the past. They survived an oppressive existence by creating new expressive forms out of African traditions, and they brought relevance to European American customs by reshaping them to conform to African aesthetic ideals.

The transformation of African traditions in the New World supports the position of Lawrence Levine that culture is a process rather than a fixed condition. Levine argues that culture is

> the product of interaction between the past and present. Its toughness and resiliency are determined not by a culture's ability to withstand change, which indeed may be a sign of stagnation not life, but by its ability to react creatively and responsively to the realities of a new situation.[2]

The continuum of an African consciousness in America manifests itself in the evolution of an African American culture. The music, dance, folklore, religion, language, and other expressive forms associated with the culture of slaves were transmitted orally to subsequent generations of

The Evolution of African American Music

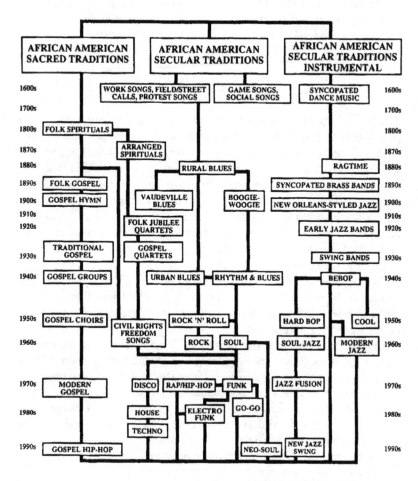

© 1992 Portia K. Maultsby, Ph.D.
Revised 1995, 2004
All Rights Reserved

American blacks. Consequently, Levine adds, many aspects of African culture continue "to exist not as mere vestiges but as dynamic, living, creative parts of group life in the United States." This position contradicts that of earlier scholars who interpreted the fundamentals of African American culture as distorted imitations of European American culture.[3]

The music tradition established by slaves evolved over centuries in response to varying circumstances and environmental factors. Each generation of slaves and freeborn blacks created new musical genres and performance styles (see figure). These forms are unique by-products of specific contexts and historical periods. The purpose of this essay is to show that an identifiable conceptual framework links these traditions to each other and to African music traditions.

The African Musical Dimension

The first scholars to examine customs and practices among blacks in the New World described the existence of African retentions in quantitative terms.[4] Although this practice of trait listing is valid, it does not account for changes that took place within the American context. Over the centuries specific African elements either have been altered or have disappeared from the cultures of New World blacks altogether. Yet the concepts that embody and identify the cultural heritage of black Americans have never been lost. The African dimension of African American music is far-reaching and can be understood best when examined within this conceptual framework.

Early accounts of African performance in the New World, for example, document the existence of instruments clearly of African origin.[5] Eventually Western European musical instruments began to infiltrate and dominate African American musical practice. Because the tempered tuning of these Western instruments differed from that of African instruments, black musicians were forced to deviate from certain African principles of melodic structure. Challenged to explore new means of melodic expression, blacks unconsciously created new ideas founded on existing African musical concepts. The result was the emergence of "blue notes" (flatted third and seventh degrees) and the production of pitches uncommon to Western scale structures.

Africanisms in African American music extend beyond trait lists and, as African ethnomusicologist J. H. Kwabena Nketia observes, "must be viewed in terms of creative processes which allow for continuity and change."[6] This point of view is shared by Olly Wilson, who concludes that African retentions in African American music are defined by the sharing of conceptual approaches to the music-making process and hence are "not basically quantitative but qualitative." Moreover, Wilson argues that the African dimension of African American music does not exist as

a static body of something which can be depleted, but rather [as] a conceptual approach, the manifestations of which are infinite.

The common core of this Africanness consists of the way of doing something, not simply something that is done.[7]

Music is integral to all aspects of black community life.[8] It serves many functions and is performed by individuals and groups in both formal and informal settings. The fundamental concept that governs music performance in African and African-derived cultures is that music-making is a participatory group activity that serves to unite black people into a cohesive group for a common purpose. This use of music in African American communities continues a tradition found in African societies where, as Nketia observes,

> music making is generally organized as a social event. Public performances, therefore, take place on social occasions—that is, on occasions when members of a group or a community come together for the enjoyment of leisure, for recreational activities, or for the performance of a rite, ceremony, festival, or any kind of collective activity.[9]

The conceptualization of music-making as a participatory group activity is evident in the processes by which black Americans prepare for a performance. Since the 1950s, for example, black music promoters have advertised concerts as social gatherings where active audience involvement is expected. Promotional materials encourage potential concertgoers to "Come and be moved by" a gospel music concert or to "Come and jam with," "Come and get down with," or "Come and party with" a secular music concert. As Nketia notes, regardless of context—church, club, dance hall, or concert hall—public performance of black music serves

> a multiple role in relation to the community: it provides at once an opportunity for sharing in creative experience, for participating in music as a form of community experience, and for using music as an avenue for the expression of group sentiments.[10]

This communal approach to music-making is further demonstrated in the way contemporary performers adapt recorded versions of their songs for performance on the concert stage. Many begin their songs with ad lib "rapping" (secular) or "sermonettes" (sacred) to establish rapport with the audience. When the singing actually begins, the style of the performance complements the "we are here to jam" or "we are here to be moved" attitude of the audience/congregation. The audience/congregation is encouraged to participate in any way, sometimes even to join performers on stage. Soul singer Sam Moore of the duo Sam and Dave recalls how he "would stop the band and get hand-clapping going in the audience [and] make them stand up."[11] Many black performers use this technique to ensure the active participation of audience members in the music event.

Music-making in Africa requires the active involvement of all present at the musical event. This approach to performance generates many of the cultural and aesthetic components that uniquely characterize music-making throughout the African diaspora. In a study of gospel music, ethnomusicologist Mellonee Burnim defines three areas of aesthetic significance in the black music tradition: delivery style, sound quality, and mechanics of delivery.[12] These categories are useful in examining qualities common to both African and African-derived music.

Style of Delivery

Style of delivery refers to the physical mode of presentation—how performers employ body movements, facial expressions, and clothing within the performance context. Burnim accurately asserts that music-making "in Black culture symbolizes vitality, a sense of aliveness."[13] This "aliveness" is expressed through visual, physical, and musical modes, all of which are interrelated in African musical performances. Olly Wilson defines the African musical experience as a

> multi-media one in which many kinds of collective human output are inextricably linked. Hence, a typical traditional [African] ceremony will include music, dance, the plastic arts (in the form of elaborate masks and/or costumes) and perhaps ritualistic drama.[14]

In African American culture, the element of dress in musical performance is as important as the musical sound itself. When performers appear on stage, even before a musical sound is heard, audience members verbally and physically respond if costumes meet their aesthetic expectations. Performers establish an image, communicate a philosophy, and create an atmosphere of "aliveness" through the colorful and flamboyant costumes they wear. In the gospel tradition, Burnim observed that performers dress in "robes of bold, vivid colors and design." She also noted:

> At the 1979 James Cleveland Gospel Music Workshop of America in New Orleans, Louisiana, one evening's activities included a competition to select the best dressed male and female in gospel

choir attire. The fashions ranged from brightly colored gowns and tuxedos to matching hooded capes lined in red.[15]

Ethnomusicologist Joyce Jackson, in her study of black gospel quartets, also observed that costumes are judged as part of the overall performance in gospel quartet competitions.[16]

The importance of dress in black music performances is demonstrated further in the popular tradition. In the film *That Rhythm . . . Those Blues*, vocalist Ruth Brown recalled how audiences expected performers to dress in the latest fashions. Responding to this expectation, Brown labeled herself as one of the first female singers

> that became known for the crinoline and multi-petticoats and the shoes that matched the dresses. All of the singing groups [of the 1950s and 1960s] were impeccably dressed [in coordinated outfits] when they went on stage. If they wore white shoes . . . they were *white* shoes. Griffin shoe polish made all the money in the world.

The array of colors and fashions seen in concert halls, black churches, and other black performance sites is a vital part of the total visual experience. It is such a fundamental part of black cultural expression that these same principles of dress are observed by the audience. For example, audiences at Harlem's Apollo theater always wore the latest fashions. During the 1930s, the men "appeared in tight-belted, high-waisted coats" and the women "gracefully glided throuh the lobby in tight slinky dresses, high heels, and veils."[17]

The visual dimension of performance, according to Burnim's model, extends beyond dress to the physical behavior of musicians and their audiences. In communicating with their audiences, musicians display an intensity of emotion and total physical involvement through use of the entire body. Nketia points out that physical expression is part and parcel of music-making in African cultures:

> The values of African societies do not inhibit this. . . . it is encouraged, for through it, individuals relate to musical events or performing groups, and interact socially with others in a musical situation. Moreover, motor response intensifies one's enjoyment of music through the feelings of increased involvement and the propulsion that articulating the beat by physical movement generates.[18]

Accounts of religious services conducted by slaves illustrate the retention of these cultural values and attitudes in the New World. During the worship, slaves became active participants, freely responding verbally and physically to the sermon, the prayer, the music, and each other. This behavior prompted missionary Charles Colcock Jones to describe a revival meeting of slaves as a "confusion of sights and sounds!"

> Some were standing, others sitting, others moving from one seat to another, several exhorting along the aisles. The whole congregation kept up one loud monotonous strain, interrupted by various sounds: groans and screams and clapping hands. One woman specially under the influence of the excitement went across the church in a quick succession of leaps; now down on her knees with a sharp crack that smote upon my ear the full length of the church, then up again; now with her arms about some brother or sister, and again tossing them wildly in the air and clapping her hands together and accompanying the whole by a series of short, sharp shrieks. . . . Considering the mere excitement manifested in these disorderly ways, I could but ask: What religion is there in this?[19]

Observers of other religious gatherings of slaves noted that "there is much melody in their voices; and when they enjoy a hymn, there is a raised expression of the face. . . . " And "they sang so that it was a pleasure to hear, with all their souls and with all their bodies in unison; for their bodies wagged, their heads nodded, their feet stamped, their knees shook, their elbows and their hands beat time to the tunes and the words which they sing. . . . "[20]

The style of delivery that characterized musical performance during the seventeenth, eighteenth, and nineteenth centuries continues to be operative in both sacred and secular spheres of contemporary black America: black people consciously use their entire bodies in musical expression, and music and movement are conceived as a single unit. These concepts clearly are demonstrated in the presentation style of performers of popular music. Soul singer Al Braggs, for example, concluded his shows

> by pulling out all the vocal and choreographic stops . . . in the general manner of James Brown or Little Richard. He screams; he groans; he crawls rhythmically across the stage on his stomach dragging the microphone behind him; he leaps over, under, and around the microphone behind him; he lies on his back and kicks his feet in the air; he does some syncopated push-ups; he falls halfway over the edge of the stage and grabs the nearest hands; initiating a few unfinished dance steps, he does the limbo; he bumps and grinds; and gradually maneuvers himself off stage with a flying split or two, still twitching and shouting.[21]

This "unification of song and dance," as Burnim describes it, characterizes contemporary performances of black music. In the gospel tradition, choirs "march" in synchronized movements through the church during the processional and "step," "clap," and "shout" (religious dance) to the music performed during the worship.[22] This intrinsic relationship between music and movement is also seen during performances by popular music groups. Sam Moore commented that he and his partner, Dave Prater, "danced and moved around so much" during their performances that they lost "at least four or five pounds a night in sweat."[23] The accompanying musicians also danced in synchronized steps while playing their instruments, a concept patterned after black marching bands.

Sound Quality

The participatory dimension of music performance is only one aspect of the conceptual approach to music-making. Descriptions of black music performances over several centuries reveal that timbre is a primary feature that distinguishes this tradition from all others. The concept of sound that governs African American music is unmistakably grounded in the African past. As Francis Bebey suggests,

> The objective of African music is not necessarily to produce sounds agreeable to the ear, but to translate everyday experiences into living sound. In a musical environment whose constant purpose is to depict life, nature, or the supernatural, the musician wisely avoids using beauty as his criterion because no criterion could be more arbitrary.
>
> Consequently, African voices adapt themselves to their musical contexts—a mellow tone to welcome a new bride; a husky voice to recount an indiscreet adventure; a satirical inflection for a teasing tone, with laughter bubbling up to compensate for the mockery—they may be soft or harsh as circumstances demand.[24]

In Africa and throughout the diaspora, black musicians produce an array of unique sounds, many of which imitate those of nature, animals, spirits, and speech. They reproduce these sounds using a variety of techniques, including striking the chest and maneuvering the tongue, mouth, cheek, and throat.[25] When arranged in an order and bound together by continuity of time, these sounds form the basis for musical composition.

The unique sound associated with black music results from the manipulation of timbre, texture, and shading in ways uncommon to Western practice. Musicians bring intensity to their performance by alternating lyrical, percussive, and raspy timbres; juxtaposing vocal and instrumental textures; changing pitch and dynamic levels; alternating straight with vibrato tones; and weaving moans, shouts, grunts, hollers, and screams into the melody. The arbitrary notion of beauty has resulted in descriptions of black music as "weird," "strange," "noise," "yelling," "hollering," "hooting," "screaming." The use of these words clearly indicates that the black music tradition does not adhere to European American aesthetic values.

Instrumental sounds in African and African-derived music imitate timbres produced by the voice. Bebey observes that

> Western distinctions between instrumental and vocal music are evidently unthinkable in Africa where the human voice and musical instruments "speak" the same language, express the same feelings, and unanimously recreate the universe each time that thought is transformed into sound.[26]

Black instrumentalists produce a wide range of vocally derived sounds —"hollers," "cries," "grunts," "screams," "moans," and "whines," among others—by varying timbre, range, texture, and shading. They create these sounds by altering traditional embouchures, playing techniques, and fingerings and by adding distorting devices.[27] The vocal dimension of instrumental sounds is reflected in such phrases as "make it talk," "talk to me," and "I hear ya talkin'" used by black people to communicate that their aesthetic expectations have been met.

Mechanics of Delivery

The distinct sounds produced by black performers are combined with other aesthetic components to generate a pool of resources for song interpretation. Black audiences demand variety in music performances, and they expect musicians to bring a unique interpretation to each performance and to each song. Black performers meet these expectations in demonstrating their knowledge about technical aspects of performance. Within the African context, Bebey observes that "there is always plenty of scope for improvisation and ornamentation so that individual musicians can reveal their own particular talents and aptitudes. Thus, no two performances of any one piece will be exactly alike."[28] Improvisation is central to the category mechanics of delivery, which forms the third part of Burnim's aesthetic model.

Burnim convincingly argues that time, text, and pitch are the three basic components that form the structural network for song interpretation in black music. The element of time in black music is manipulated in both structural and rhythmic aspects of the performance. Time can be expanded by extending the length of notes at climactic points, by repeating words, phrases, and entire sections of songs, and by adding vocal or instrumental cadenzas. The density of textures can be increased "by gradually adding layers of hand-claps, instrumental accompaniment, and/or solo voices."[29] This latter device, referred to as staggered entrances, characterized the improvised singing of slaves:

> With the first note of the hymn, began a tapping of feet by the whole congregation, gradually increasing to a stamp as the exercises proceeded, until the noise was deafening. . . . Then in strange contrast to this came the most beautiful melody the negroes have —a chant, carried by full bass voices; the liquid soprano of the melody wandering through and above it, now rising in triumphant swell, now falling in softened cadence. . . . [30]

The call-response structure is the key mechanism that allows for the manipulation of time, text, and pitch. The response or repetitive chorus provides a stable foundation for the improvised lines of the soloist. The use of call-response structures to generate musical change has been described many times in black music literature.

> These ditties [work songs sung by slaves], though nearly meaningless, have much music in them, and as all join in the perpetually recurring chorus, a rough harmony is produced. . . . I think the leader improvises the words . . . he singing one line alone, and the whole then giving the chorus, which is repeated without change at every line, till the general chorus concludes the stanza. . . . [31]

The call-response structure also is used by jazz musicians to establish a base for musical change and rhythmic tension.

> [Count] Basie's men played short, fierce riffs. Their riff patterns were not even melodic elements, they were just repetitive rhythmic figures set against each other in the sections of the band. Against this sharp, pulsing background, Basie set his soloists, and they had free rein.[32]

Perhaps the most noticeable African feature in African American music is its rhythmic complexity. Early descriptions of this tradition reveal that

> Syncopations . . . are characteristic of negro music. I have heard negroes change a well-known melody by adroitly syncopating it. . . .

nothing illustrates the negro's natural gifts in the way of keeping a difficult tempo more clearly than his perfect execution of airs thus transformed from simple to complex accentuations.[33]

In both African and African American music, rhythm is organized in multilinear forms. Different patterns, which are repeated with slight, if any, variation, are assigned to various instruments. The combination of these patterns produces polyrhythms.[34] Polyrhythmic structures increase the overall intensity of musical performances because each repetition produces added rhythmic tension. At the same time the repetition of patterns in one part allows for textual and melodic variation in another.

Many accounts of black music have described its repetitious form while noting the creative ways in which performers achieve variety. An example is this 1862 notice:

Each stanza [of a song sung by slaves] contains but a single thought, set in perhaps two or three bars of music; and yet as they sing it, in alternate recitatives and choruses, with varying inflections and dramatic effect . . .[35]

Under the mechanics of delivery category, the element of pitch is manipulated by "juxtaposing voices of different ranges or by highlighting the polar extremes of a single voice." Pitch is also varied through the use of "bends, slides, melismas, and passing tones" and other forms of melodic embellishment "in order to achieve the continuous changes, extreme latitude, and personalization"—an identifying trait of black musical expression.[36] "Playing" with pitch—or "worrying the line," as Stephen Henderson calls it[37]—is a technique integral to the solo style of many black performers, including blues singer Bobby Blue Bland.

All the distinctive features of Bland's vocal style are in evidence, notably the hoarse cry and his use of melisma on key words. Bland's cry usually consists of a twisted vowel at the beginning of a phrase —going from a given note, reaching up to another higher one, and coming back to the starting point. . . . Almost without exception Bobby uses more than one note per syllable on the concluding word of each phrase. . . . In slower tempos he will stretch out syllables with even more melisma, using as many as ten or eleven notes over a two-syllable word.[38]

Time, text, and pitch are manipulated by black performers to display their creative abilities and technical skills and to generate an overall intensity within their performance.

When performers create and interpret songs within the aesthetic boundaries framed by black people, audiences respond immediately. Their verbal comments and physical gestures express approval of both the song being performed and the way it is performed. For example, performances by musicians in the popular idiom often are based on principles that govern black worship services. These principles are recognized and valued by black audiences who respond in the same manner as they do to the presentations of black preachers and church choirs. Sam Moore recalled:

> When we performed, we had church. On Sundays the minister would preach and the people in the pews would holler and talk back to him. This is what we started doing. I arranged the parts between Dave and me so that one of us became the preacher and would say "Come on Dave" or "Come on Sam." The audience would automatically shout "Come on Sam" or "Sing Dave" or "Yes Sir." That was our style.[39]

Vocalist Deniece Williams believes that an audience actively participates in her performances because they identify with the gospel roots of her delivery style:

> You hear that [Church of God in Christ] in my music even though it is not the same deliverance of Aretha Franklin. But you feel it. A lot of people say to me "when you sing I feel it." I think that feeling comes from those experiences of church, gospel music and spirituality, which play a big part in my life.[40]

Audiences of Bobby Bland also respond in the character of the Sunday morning service:

> women sprinkled throughout the audience yell back at him, shaking their heads and waving their hands [in response to Bland's melisma]. . . . Suddenly the guitarist doubles the tempo and repeats a particularly funky phrase a few times accompanied by "oohs," "aahs," and "yeahs" from the audience.[41]

When performers demonstrate their knowledge of the black musical aesthetic, the responses of audiences can become so audible that they momentarily drown out the performer. The verbal responses of audiences are accompanied by hand-clapping; foot-stomping; head, shoulder, hand, and arm movement; and spontaneous dance. This type of audience participation is important to performers; it encourages them to explore the full range of aesthetic possibilities, and it is the single criterion by which black artists determine whether they are meeting the aesthetic expectations of the audience. Songwriter-vocalist Smokey Robin-son judges his concerts as unsuccessful if the audience is "not involved in what's happening on the stage."[42]

The concept of "performer-audience" as a single unit is even appar-ent in the way black people respond to music in nonpublic settings. Twentieth-century technological advances make music accessible twenty-four hours a day, every day. African Americans often use recorded music as a substitute for live performances. While listening to recordings they become involved as active participants, singing along on familiar refrain lines and choruses, snapping their fingers, clapping their hands, moving to the beat, and verbally responding to especially meaningful words or phrases and sounds with "sing it baby," "tell the truth," "play your horn," "tickle them keys," and "get on down." This level of involve-ment, which replicates interaction at live performances, preserves an Af-rican approach to music-making in contemporary society.

Music-making throughout the African diaspora is an expression of life where verbal and physical expression is intrinsic to the process. This conceptual framework links all black music traditions together in the African diaspora while distinguishing these traditions from those of Western and Western-derived cultures. A salient feature of black music is the conceptualization of music-making as a communal/participatory activity. In addition, variation in timbre, song interpretation, and pre-sentation style mirrors the aesthetic priorities of black people.

An African approach to music-making has been translated from one genre to the next throughout African American musical history. Al-though these genres (see figure) are by-products of specific contexts and time frames, each genre is distinctly African American because it is gov-erned by the conceptual framework already discussed. The remainder of this essay provides a chronology of African American musical forms from slavery to the present.[43] The discussion presents evidence of how this conceptual unity has been transmitted from one African American genre to the next since the first musics were created in the New World.

Music in the Slave Community

For more than 150 years slave traders and slaveholders unwittingly helped preserve an African identity in the African American music tra-dition. Slave traders brought African instruments on board ships and encouraged slaves to sing and dance for exercise during the long voyage to the New World. These artifacts and creative expressions were among the cultural baggage slaves brought with them to the Americas.[44]

Studies of the institution of slavery point out that slave systems varied throughout the Americas and among colonies in the United States.[45] In situations where slaves had some measure of personal freedom they engaged in leisure activities that clearly reflected their African heritage.[46] In the United States, for example, slaves celebrated holidays for more than two centuries in African style. Two of the most spectacular and festive holidays, 'Lection Day and Pinkster Day celebrations, were observed from the mid-eighteenth through the mid-nineteenth centuries. On 'Lection Day slaves in the New England colonies elected a black governor or king and staged a big parade. Dressed in elaborate outfits, slaves celebrated by playing African games, singing, dancing, and playing African and European instruments in a distinctly African style. Pinkster Day was of Dutch origin, but slaves and free blacks in the North and South transformed it into an African-style festival.[47]

The unique character of the Pinkster Day celebration prompted James Fenimore Cooper to record his impressions:

> Nine tenths of the blacks of the city [New York], and of the whole country within thirty or forty miles, indeed, were collected in thousands in those fields, beating banjos [and African drums], singing African songs [accompanied by dancing]. The features that distinguish a Pinkster frolic from the usual scenes at fairs . . . however, were of African origin. It is true, there are not now [1845], nor were there then [1757], many blacks among us of African birth; but the traditions and usages of their original country were so far preserved as to produce a marked difference between the festival, and one of European origin.[48]

The diaries of missionaries, travelers, and slaveholders and the accounts of slaves themselves further document that slaves continued to keep African traditions alive in the United States. In 1680 a missionary observed that slaves spent Sundays singing and dancing "as a means to procure Rain." An army general heard his slaves sing a war song in an African language during a visit to his plantation after the Revolutionary War. In another instance, a slave born in 1849 reported that African-born slaves sang their own songs and told stories about African customs during Christmas celebrations. And many observers noted the African flavor of the songs slaves sang while working.[49]

Slaveholders generally did not object to these and other African-derived activities provided they did not interfere with the work routine of slaves. Missionaries, on the other hand, objected to the singing and dancing, which they described as pagan and contrary to the teachings of Christianity. Committed to eliminating these activities, they mounted a campaign to proselytize slaves. Missionaries experienced success in the

New England colonies but met resistance among slaveholders in the South, who feared that a change in religious status would alter the social status of slaves as chattel property.[50]

By the nineteenth century southern slaveholders had begun to support the activities of missionaries. Faced with the growing number of slaves who ran away, sabotaged plantation operations, and organized revolts, they believed that tighter control over slaves could be exercised through religion. Many slaveholders allowed their slaves to receive religious instruction, and some even facilitated the process by building "praise houses" on the farms and plantations.[51] Despite these and other efforts, the slaves' acceptance of Christianity was at best superficial. They interpreted Christian concepts and practices through the filter of an African past, transforming the liturgy into an African ritual.

When slaves were allowed to conduct their own religious services, they defied all rules, standards, and structures established by the various denominations and sects. Their services were characterized by an unorthodox sermonizing style, unconventional behavior, and spontaneous musical expressions.[52] Missionaries frequently expressed disapproval of these services:

> The public worship of God should be conducted *with reverence and stillness on the part of the congregation;* nor should the minister— whatever may have been the previous habits and training of the people—encourage demonstrations of approbation or disapprobation, or exclamations, or response, or noises, or outcries of any kind during the progress of divine worship; nor boisterous singing immediately at its close. These practices prevail over large portions of the southern country, and are not confined to one denomination, but appear to some extent in all. I cannot think them beneficial.[53]

Missionaries were especially critical of the music they described as "short scraps of disjointed affirmations . . . lengthened out with long repetitious choruses."[54] The call-response structure and improvisatory style unique to musical performances of slaves did not adhere to European American aesthetic values. These aesthetic differences prompted missionaries to include psalm and hymn singing in the religious instruction of slaves so that they would

> lay aside the extravagant and nonsensical chants, and catches and hallelujah songs of their own composing; and when they sing, which is very often while about their business of an evening in their houses [and in church], they will have something profitable to sing.[55]

In spite of these efforts, slaves continued to sing "songs of their own composing" while adapting psalms and hymns to conform to African aesthetic principles. Henry Russell, an English musician who toured the United States from 1833 to 1841, described this process:

> When the minister gave out his own version of the Psalm, the choir commenced singing so rapidly that the original tune absolutely ceased to exist—in fact, the fine old psalm tune became thoroughly transformed into a kind of negro melody; and so sudden was the transformation, by accelerating the time, that, for a moment, I fancied that not only the choir but the little congregation intended to get up a dance as part of the service.[56]

One observer who witnessed the changing of a hymn into a "Negro song" commented that "Watts and Newton would never recognize their productions through the transformation they have undergone at the hands of their colored admirers."[57]

Other descriptions of religious services conducted by slaves confirm that they frequently fashioned Protestant psalms, hymns, and spiritual songs into new compositions by altering the structure, text, melody, and rhythm. They transformed the verse structure of the original song into a call-response or repetitive chorus structure; replaced the original English verse with an improvised text of African and English words and phrases; wove shouts, moans, groans, and cries into the melody of the improvised solo; substituted a faster tempo for the original one; and produced polyrhythmic structures by adding syncopated foot-stomped and hand-clapped patterns.[58] The body of religious music created or adapted by slaves and performed in a distinctly African style became known as "folk spirituals."

The religious tradition of slaves dominated the eighteenth- and nineteenth-century literature on African American music. The scarcity of information on the secular tradition results in part from the reluctance of slaves to sing secular songs in the presence of whites. Missionaries discouraged slaves from singing secular songs, and slaves responded by going underground with these songs. The few accounts of secular music performances nevertheless confirm that this tradition shares the aesthetic qualities characteristic of folk spirituals:

> The negroes [a dozen stout rowers] struck up a song to which they kept time with their oars; and our speed increased as they went on, and become warmed with their singing. . . . A line was sung by a leader, then all joined in a short chorus; then came another [improvised] solo line, and another short chorus, followed by a longer

chorus. . . . Little regard was paid to rhyme, and hardly any to the number of syllables in a line; they condensed four or five into one foot, or stretched out one to occupy the space that should have been filled with four or five; yet they never spoiled the tune.[59]

As in the folk spiritual tradition, the call-response structure allowed for improvised solos and recurring refrain lines.

Music in the Free Community

The northern states began to abolish slavery during the first half of the nineteenth century. Yet freed slaves were faced with discriminatory state legislation that once again placed restrictions on their mobility. The small percentage of freed slaves who lived in the South were in precarious positions because their "color suggested servitude, but [their] status secured a portion of freedom." Only a "portion of freedom" was theirs because legislation barred southern free blacks from participating in mainstream society.[60] Determined to create a meaningful life, freed blacks in the North and South established communities and institutions where they defined their own mode of existence and cultural frame of reference.[61] The black church became the center of community life, serving an array of functions—religious, cultural, social, educational, and political. Within this context, many blacks kept alive the cultural traditions and musical practices associated with the praise houses of the South.[62]

The abolition of slavery in the South temporarily disrupted the communal solidarity of the slave community. Individually and in small groups, African Americans attempted to establish new lives within the larger society. Some migrated from rural areas to cities and from South to North in search of social, political, and economic viability. Discriminatory practices, however, restricted their employment possibilities to such menial roles as domestic servants, janitors, chauffeurs, and delivery boys. Many could not find even menial jobs and, as a last resort, worked as sharecroppers on the land they had farmed as slaves. Others attempted to take advantage of educational opportunities to upgrade their social status. Despite these efforts toward "self-improvement," the broader society continued to control the mobility of blacks, forcing the masses to remain economically dependent on whites.[63]

The Fourteenth Amendment to the U.S. Constitution, ratified in 1868, guaranteed citizenship to freed slaves, and the Fifteenth Amendment of 1870 gave black men voting rights. Yet African Americans became victims of discriminatory state legislation.[64] Many blacks survived as free persons in America because they relied on their traditional past for direction. They created a meaningful existence by preserving old values, fashioning new ones when necessary, and reestablishing the group solidarity they had known as slaves.

For many decades following the Civil War, blacks continued to make music from an African frame of reference. White northerners who migrated south to assist blacks in their transition into mainstream society were especially critical of this practice among children at school:

> In the infant schoolroom, the benches were first put aside, and the children ranged along the wall. Then began a wild droning chant in a minor key, marked with clapping of hands and stamping of feet. A dozen or twenty rose, formed a ring in the centre of the room, and began an odd shuffling dance. Keeping time to this weird chant they circled round, one following the other, changing their step to quicker and wilder motion, with louder clapping of the hands as the fervor of the singers reached a climax. The words of their hymns are simple and touching. The verses consist of two lines, the first being repeated twice. . . . As I looked upon the faces of these little barbarians and watched them circling round in this fetish dance, doubtless the relic of some African rite, I felt discouraged. . . . However, the recollection of the mental arithmetic seemed a more cheerful view of the matter.[65]

Another observer concluded that common aesthetic features link the secular and religious traditions:

> Whatever they sing is of a religious character, and in both cases [performances of secular and religious music] they have a leader . . . who starts a line, the rest answering antiphonally as a sort of chorus. They always keep exquisite time and tune, and no words seem too hard for them to adapt to their tunes. . . . Their voices have a peculiar quality, and their intonations and delicate variations cannot be reproduced on paper.[66]

These descriptions confirm that African aesthetic concepts—of music and movement as a single unit, the varying timbres, the shadings, and the use of call-response structures to manipulate time, text, and pitch —remained vital to black musical expression in postbellum African American culture.

Other accounts of postbellum black music reveal that both children and adults continued to sing songs from the past while creating new musical forms out of existing traditions.[67] As I wrote in an earlier essay,

"The old form persisted alongside the new and remained a vital form of expression within specific contexts."[68] The new idioms, including blues, jazz, gospel, and popular music, became a unifying and sustaining force in the free black community. These and the older forms reaffirmed the values of an African past and simultaneously expressed a sense of inner strength and optimism about the future.

The secular music tradition became increasingly important. Even though missionaries had attempted to discourage slaves from singing secular songs, many free blacks asserted their independence by responding to the daily events in their lives through secular song. The secular form that became and remains particularly important to African American culture is the blues.

The blues form shares general features and aesthetic qualities with past music traditions. It combines the musical structure and poetic forms of spirituals, work songs, and field cries with new musical and textual ideas. The improvisatory performance style emphasizes call-response (between the voice and accompanying instruments). Integral to the melody are slides, slurs, bends, and dips, and the timbres vary from moans, groans, and shouts to song-speech utterances.[69] The accompanying instruments—guitar, fiddle, piano, harmonica, and sometimes tub basses, washboards, jugs, a wire nailed to the side of a house, and other ad hoc instruments—are played in an African-derived percussive style.[70]

For more than a hundred years the essence of the blues tradition has remained the same. Amplified instruments added in the 1940s, rhythm sections in the 1950s, and horns in the 1960s are perhaps the only significant—yet in a sense only superficial—changes that have taken place in this tradition. In the twentieth century the "blues sound" crossed into the sacred world, giving life to an original body of sacred music called gospel.

Gospel music is a by-product of the late nineteenth- and early-twentieth-century black "folk church." This church, associated with the Holiness and Pentecostal sects, is a contemporary version of plantation praise houses. Its character, as Pearl Williams-Jones has stated, "reflects the traditional cultural values of Black folk life as it has evolved since slave days, and is a cumulative expression of the Black experience."[71] The black folk church is distinguished from black denominational churches by the structure and nature of its service, religious practices, and philosophical concepts and the socioeconomic background of its members. The official doctrine of the folk church encourages spontaneous expressions through improvised song, testimonies, prayers, and praises from individuals.[72] Unlike other black churches, the folk church did not evolve from white Protestant denominations. Its musical repertoire, therefore, is distinctly different from that of mainline Protestant churches.

The music of the folk church, known as "church songs," has as its basic repertoire the folk spirituals and modified hymns sung by slaves in plantation praise houses. The new songs that became standards in the folk church were created spontaneously during the service by the preacher and congregation members, and they were performed in the style of folk spirituals. The only substantive change made in this tradition was the addition of musical instruments to the established accompaniment of hand-clapping and foot-stomping.[73] These instruments included tambourines, drums, piano, guitar, various horns and ad hoc instruments, and later the organ. The "bluesy," "jazzy," and "rockin'" sounds from these instruments brought a secular dimension to black religious music. The instrumental accompaniment, which became an integral part of religious music in the folk church, defined new directions for black religious music in the twentieth century.

During the first two decades of this century, the prototype for gospel music was established in the folk church. Horace Boyer noted, however, that members of this church "were not the first to receive recognition as gospel singers. Until the forties, Holiness churches did not allow their members to sing their songs before non-Holiness persons."[74] This policy did not confine the emerging gospel sound to the Holiness church. Members of the black community whose homes surrounded these churches were well aware of their existence.

Gospel music first reached the black masses as a "composed" form through the compositions of ministers and members of black Methodist and Baptist churches. Charles Albert Tindley, a Methodist minister in Philadelphia, created the prototype for a composed body of black religious music between 1900 and 1906. Some of these songs were hymnlike verses set to the melodies and rhythms of folk church songs; others were adaptations of spirituals and revival hymns.[75]

In the 1920s the Baptist songwriter Thomas Dorsey used Tindley's model to compose an identifiable and distinct body of black religious music called gospel. The former blues-jazz pianist organized his compositions around the verse-chorus form in which is embedded the call-response structure. Drawing from his blues background, he fashioned his melodies and harmonies using blues scale structures and developed a "rockin'" piano accompaniment in the boogie-woogie and ragtime traditions.

Unlike other black music genres, gospel songs often are disseminated as printed music. Yet the score provides only a framework from which performers interpret and improvise. Gospel music performances are governed by the same aesthetic concepts associated with the folk spiritual tradition. In interpreting the score, performers must demonstrate their knowledge of the improvisatory devices that characterize black music performances.

For more than eighty years the gospel tradition has preserved and transmitted the aesthetic concepts fundamental to music-making in Africa and African-derived cultures. Since its birth in the Holiness and Pentecostal churches it has found a home in storefront churches of various denominations and in many black middle-class Baptist, Methodist, Episcopal, and Catholic churches. The impact of gospel has been so great that its colorful African-derived kaleidoscope of oratory, poetry, drama, and dance and its musical style established a reservoir of cultural resources that contributed to the development of black popular music.

New secular forms of black musical expression were created in response to changes in society following World War II. The war years stimulated growth in the American economy, which in turn led to changes in the lives of black Americans. As I recounted in an earlier monograph, almost two million southern rural blacks abandoned "their low-paying domestic, sharecropping and tenant-farming jobs for work in factories located throughout the country. In cities, both Blacks and whites earned the highest wages in American history. So Americans, especially Black Americans, had much to celebrate during the postwar years."[76] The music to which they celebrated was termed rhythm and blues—a hybrid form rooted in the blues, gospel, and swing band traditions.

Blacks left the rural South with expectations of improving their economic, social, and political status. They soon discovered that opportunities for advancement in society were limited and that the segregated structure of cities restricted their mobility. Discriminatory housing laws, for example, forced many blacks to live and socialize in designated sections of cities—ghettos. These and other patterns of discrimination led to the reestablishment of familiar institutions, thereby continuing southern traditions and practices in the urban metropolis.

The ambiance of southern jukejoints was transferred to blues bars, lounges, and clubs, which became the center of social gatherings in urban cities. Southern music traditions—blues and jazz—were central to the activity in these establishments. The segregated environment, the faster pace, the factory sounds, the street noises, and the technology of the metropolis gave a different type of luster, cadence, and sophistication to existing black musical forms. In response to new surroundings, the familiar sounds of the past soon were transformed into an urban black music tradition.

Blues, jazz, and gospel performers were among the millions of blacks who moved to the cities. They joined forces to create an urban-sounding dance music, rhythm and blues. This music is characterized by a boogie bass line, "riffing" jazz-derived horn arrangements, blues-gospel piano, "honking" and "screaming" tenor sax, "whining" blues guitar, and syncopated drum patterns. The intensity of this sound was increased by the addition of blues and former gospel singers who "moaned" and "shouted" about life in the city. The rhythmic complexity and the performance style of rhythm and blues music preserved traditional values in the music of the city dwellers.

The spirit that captured the excitement of postwar city living began to fade in the mid-1950s. Conditions deteriorated, and life continued to be harsh for many African Americans, especially the inner-city dwellers. They responded by organizing a series of grass-roots protest activities that quickly gained momentum and attracted national attention. The spread of these political activities throughout the country was the impetus behind the civil rights and black power movements of the 1950s and 1960s. "Soul music" was a byproduct of the 1960s movements.[77]

Leaders of the black power movement encouraged the rejection of standards and values of the broader society and a return to values of an African past. Many soul music performers became ambassadors for this movement. Through song they communicated its philosophy, advocating an awareness of an African heritage, encouraging the practice of African traditions, and promoting the concept of black pride. Their "soul message" was communicated in a style that captured the climate of the times and the spirit of a people. This style embraces all the aesthetic qualities that define the essence of the gospel tradition.[78]

The interrelatedness of soul and gospel music is illustrated through the interchangeability of the genres. For example, many gospel songs have been recorded under the label "soul" and vice versa. In some instances the text is the only feature that distinguishes one style from another. In others, genre identification may be determined only by the musical identity of the artist who first recorded the song. Performances of soul and gospel music further illustrate that an aesthetic conceptual framework links the secular and sacred traditions to each other.

The era of soul music reawakened the consciousness of an African past. It sanctioned the new thrust for African exploration and simultaneously gave credence to an obscured heritage. This profound era also established new directions in black popular music that would continue to merge African expressions into new forms. The decade of the 1970s heralded this new music.

The 1960s ended with the anticipation of new opportunities for economic independence and full participation in mainstream life. Affirmative action, school desegregation, and other legislation was passed, and the early 1970s implied future changes in the structure of society. Such legislation cultivated a renewed sense of optimism among blacks, and many began to explore new economic, political, and social opportunities outside the black community.

By the mid-1970s this optimism had begun to fade with increased opposition to affirmative action legislation. The economic recession and the "reverse discrimination" concept of the 1970s led to a retrenchment of civil rights and economic opportunities designed to effect equality for blacks. Whites protested against busing and affirmative action policies. In response, the federal government retreated on earlier commitments to rights for blacks. The "gains" made in the early 1970s gave way to fiscal and social conservatism in the late 1970s and the 1980s. The general opposition to any social advantages for blacks fostered a return to the status quo where racism shaped the American ethos.[79]

Blacks responded to the realities of the 1970s and 1980s in diverse ways and with mixed feelings. Many assessed progress toward social, economic, and political equality as illusory at best. Some felt conditions had worsened, though a few privileged blacks believed the situation had improved.[80] The ambivalent feelings about social progress for blacks found its expression in new and diverse forms of black popular music—funk, disco, rap music, and personalized or trademark forms.

The song lyrics and music styles of funk, disco, and rap music epitomize the changing and sometimes conflicting viewpoints about progress. Although many performers continued to express optimism about the future, some introduced lyric themes of frustration, disillusionment, and distress. The "soul sound" dominated during the first half of the 1970s, but by the mid-1970s it had been transformed. Whereas soul carries the trademark of "message music," funk, disco, and rap music bore the stamp of "party" music.[81] It injected a new spirit of life into black communities and became a major unifying force for a core of African Americans. This spirit is reflected in the lyric themes: "party," "have a good time," "let yourself go," and "dance, dance, dance." These themes suggest that the music had a therapeutic function. Rather than communicate political or intellectual messages, it encouraged blacks to release tension by simply being themselves. At the same time, the infectious beat of this music created an atmosphere that allowed for self-expression and unrestricted social interactions.

Funk, disco, and rap music are grounded in the same aesthetic concepts that define the soul music tradition. Yet the sound is distinguished from soul because emphasis is given to different musical components.

These forms of the late 1970s are conceived primarily as dance music where melody plays a secondary role to rhythm. The African-derived polyrhythmic structures, the call-response patterns, and the quasi-spoken group vocals generate audience participation. The percussive sounds and timbral qualities of synthesizers and other electronic devices add another dimension to the black sound. The musical and cultural features in 1970s and 1980s popular traditions continue to give credence to the vitality of an African past in contemporary forms of black music.

Conclusions

A study of African American music from the seventeenth through the twentieth centuries reveals that African retentions in African American music can be defined as a core of conceptual approaches. Fundamental to these approaches is the axiom that music-making is conceived as a communal/participatory group activity. Black people create, interpret, and experience music out of an African frame of reference—one that shapes musical sound, interpretation, and behavior and makes black music traditions throughout the world a unified whole.

The New World experiences of black people encouraged them to maintain ties to their African past. This unspoken association enabled them to survive and create a meaningful existence in a world where they were not welcomed. They adapted to environmental changes and social upheavals by relying on familiar traditions and practices. Music played an important role in this process. Although specific African songs and genres eventually disappeared from the culture of African Americans, Nketia points out that new ones were "created in the style of the tradition, using its vocabulary and idiom, or in an alternative style which combined African and non-African resources."[82] In essence, new ideas were recycled through age-old concepts to produce new music styles. The fundamentals of culture established by slaves persist in the twentieth century; they are reinterpreted as social times demand. African retentions in African American culture, therefore, exist as conceptual approaches—as unique ways of doing things and making things happen—rather than as specific cultural elements.

Notes

1. Historical studies include Ira Berlin, *Slaves without Masters: The Free Negro in the Antebellum South* (New York: Vintage, 1974); Eugene D. Genovese, *Roll Jordan Roll: The World the Slaves Made* (New York: Pantheon,

1974); John Blassingame, *The Slave Community* (New York: Oxford University Press, rev. ed., 1979); Gerald W. Mullin, *Flight and Rebellion* (New York: Oxford University Press, 1972); and Robert Haynes, *Blacks in White America before 1865* (New York: David McKay, 1972).

For cultural studies, see John W. Work, *Folk Song of the American Negro* (Nashville, Tenn.: Fisk University Press, 1915; reprinted by Negro University Press, New York, 1969); James Weldon and J. Rosamond Johnson, *American Negro Spirituals*, 2 vols. (New York: Viking Press, 1925 and 1926; reprinted in one volume by Da Capo Press, New York, 1969); Zora Neale Hurston, "Spirituals and Neo-Spirituals" [1935], in *Voices from the Harlem Renaissance*, Nathan Huggins, ed. (New York: Oxford University Press, 1976), 344–47; Hall Johnson, "Notes on the Negro Spiritual" [1965], in *Readings in Black American Music*, Eileen Southern, ed. (New York: Norton, 2d ed., 1983), 273–80; Henry Krehbiel, *Afro-American Folksongs* (New York: Ungar, 1914); Melville J. Herskovits, *The Myth of the Negro Past* (Boston: Beacon Press, 1958); Lawrence Levine, *Black Culture and Black Consciousness* (New York: Oxford University Press, 1977); Dena Epstein, *Sinful Tunes and Spirituals* (Chicago: University of Chicago Press, 1977); Alan Dundes, ed., *Mother Wit from the Laughing Barrel* (Englewood Cliffs, N.J.: Prentice-Hall, 1973); Norman E. Whitten and John F. Szwed, eds., *Afro-American Anthropology* (New York: Free Press, 1970); Paul Oliver, *Savannah Syncopators: African Retentions in the Blues* (New York: Stein and Day, 1970); Albert J. Raboteau, *Slave Religion* (New York: Oxford University Press, 1978); Frederick Kaufman and John Guckin, *The African Roots of Jazz* (Sherman Oaks, Calif.: Alfred Publishing Co., 1979); Olly Wilson, "The Significance of the Relationship between Afro-American Music and West African Music," *Black Perspective in Music* (Spring 1974) 2:3–22; and J. H. Kwabena Nketia, "African Roots of Music in the Americas: An African View," 82–88, Olly Wilson, "The Association of Movement and Music as a Manifestation of a Black Conceptual Approach to Music," 98–105, and David Evans, "African Elements in Twentieth-Century United States Black Folk Music," 54–66, in Report of the 12th Congress, London, American Musicological Society, 1981.

2. Levine, *Black Culture*, 5.

3. For a summary of theories advanced by these writers, see Herskovits, *Myth*, 262–69; Guy B. Johnson, *Folk Culture in St. Helena Island* (Chapel Hill: University of North Carolina Press, 1930); Lawrence Levine, "Slave Songs and Slave Consciousness," in *American Negro Slavery*, Allen Weinstein and Frank Otto Catell, eds. (New York: Oxford University Press, 2nd ed., 1973), 153–82; and Dena Epstein, "A White Origin for the Black Spiritual? An Invalid Theory and How It Grew," *American Music* (Summer 1983) 1:53–59.

4. Richard Waterman, "African Patterns in Trinidad Negro Music," Ph.D. dissertation, Northwestern University, 1943, 26, 41–42; "Hot Rhythm in Negro Music," *Journal of the American Musicological Society* (1948) 1:24–37; and "On Flogging a Dead Horse: Lessons Learned from the African-

isms Controversy," *Ethnomusicology* (1963) 7:83–87. Alan Lomax, *Folk Song Style and Culture* (Washington, D.C.: American Association for the Advancement of Science, 1968). Herskovits, *Myth*, 261–69. Krehbiel, *Afro-American Folksong*.

5. For a summary of these accounts, see Epstein, *Sinful Tunes*, 19–99.

6. Nketia, "African Roots," 88.

7. Wilson, "Significance," 20.

8. For a discussion of the way music functions in African societies, see J. H. Kwabena Nketia, *The Music of Africa* (New York: Norton, 1974), 21–50, and Francis Bebey, *African Music: A People's Art*, Josephine Bennett, trans. (New York: Lawrence Hill, 1975), 1–38.

9. Nketia, *Music of Africa*, 21.

10. Ibid., 22.

11. Sam Moore, interview with author, Feb. 25, 1983.

12. Mellonee Burnim, "The Black Gospel Music Tradition: A Complex of Ideology, Aesthetic, and Behavior," in *More than Dancing*, Irene V. Jackson, ed. (Westport, Conn.: Greenwood Press, 1985), 154.

13. Ibid., 159.

14. Wilson, "Association of Movement," 99.

15. Mellonee Burnim, "Functional Dimensions of Gospel Music Performance," *Western Journal of Black Studies* (Summer 1988) 12:115.

16. Joyce Jackson, "The Performing Black Sacred Quartet: An Expression of Cultural Values and Aesthetics," Ph.D. dissertation, Indiana University, 1988, 161–90.

17. Ted Fox, *Showtime at the Apollo* (New York: Holt, Rinehart and Winston, 1983), 69.

18. Nketia, *Music of Africa*, 206–207.

19. Letter from Rev. R. Q. Mallard to Mrs. Mary S. Mallard, Chattanooga, May 18, 1859, in *The Children of Pride*, Robert Manson Myers, ed. (New Haven, Conn.: Yale University Press, 1972), 483.

20. Andrew Reed and James Matheson, *A Narrative of the Visit to the American Churches* (London: Jackson and Walford, 1835), 219. Frederika Bremer, *Homes of the New World*, 1, trans. Mary Howitt (New York: Harper, 1854), 393.

21. Charles Kell, *Urban Blues* (Chicago: University of Chicago Press, 1966), 122.

22. Burnim, "Black Gospel Music Tradition," 160.

23. Sam Moore, interview with author, Feb. 25, 1983.

24. Bebey, *African Music*, 115.

25. See Ruth M. Stone, "African Music Performed," in *Africa*, Phyllis M. Martin and Patrick O'Meara, eds. (Bloomington: Indiana University Press, 2nd ed., 1986), 236–39, and Bebey, *African Music*, 119–24, for more in-depth discussions of musical sound in African cultures.

26. Bebey, *African Music*, 122.

27. Instrumental playing techniques of black musicians are discussed in Thomas J. Anderson et al., "Black Composers and the Avant-Garde," in *Black Music in Our Culture*, Dominique-Rene de Lerma, ed. (Kent, Ohio: Kent State University Press, 1970), 66, 68; David Evans, "African Elements," 61; Oliver, *Savannah Syncopators;* and Wilson, "Significance of the Relationship," 15-21.

28. Bebey, *African Music,* 30.

29. Burnim, "Black Gospel," 163.

30. [Elizabeth Kilham], "Sketches in Color," *Putnam's,* Mar. 1870, 306.

31. Philip Henry Goose, *Letters from Alabama* (London: Morgan and Chase, 1859), 305.

32. Samuel B. Charters and Leonard Kunstadt, *Jazz: A History of the New York Scene* (New York: Da Capo Press, 1981), 288.

33. Quoted in Epstein, *Sinful Tunes,* 294-95.

34. For discussions of rhythmic structures in black music, see Wilson, "Significance of the Relationship," 3-15; Nketia, *Music of Africa,* 111-38; Evans, "African Elements," 17-18; Portia K. Maultsby, "Contemporary Pop: A Healthy Diversity Evolves from Creative Freedom," *Billboard,* June 9, 1979, BM-22; and Pearl Williams-Jones, "Afro-American Gospel Music in Development of Materials for a One Year Course," in *African Music for the General Undergraduate Student,* Vada Butcher, ed. (Washington, D.C.: Howard University Press, 1970), 211.

35. J[ames Miller] McKim, "Negro Songs," *Dwight's Journal of Music,* Aug. 9, 1862, 148-49.

36. Burnim, "Black Gospel Music Tradition," 165.

37. Stephen Henderson, *Understanding the New Black Poetry* (New York: Morrow, 1973), 41.

38. Keil, *Urban Blues,* 124.

39. Sam Moore, interview with author, Feb. 25, 1983.

40. Deniece Williams, interview with author, Apr. 22, 1983.

41. Keil, *Urban Blues,* 124, 139.

42. Smokey Robinson, radio interview, WBLS, New York City, Jan. 16, 1983.

43. My discussion in this limited space necessarily centers on selected genres, but a review of black music literature will show that the principles discussed are applicable to all genres of African American music.

44. See Epstein, *Sinful Tunes,* 8-17.

45. See Laura Foner and Eugene D. Genovese, eds., *Slavery in the New World* (Englewood Cliffs, N.J.: Prentice-Hall, 1969), and Blassingame, *Slave Community.*

46. See Epstein, *Sinful Tunes.*

47. See Eileen Southern, *The Music of Black Americans* (New York: Norton, 2nd ed., 1983), 53-59, and Epstein, *Sinful Tunes,* 66-68.

48. J[ames] Fenimore Cooper, *Satanstoe*, 1 (London: S.&L. Bentley, Wilson, and Fley, 1845), 122–23.

49. Descriptions are found in Morgan Godwyn, *The Negro's and Indian's Advocate, Suing for Their Admission into the Church* (London: F.D., 1680), 33; Jeanette Robinson Murphy, "The Survival of African Music in America," *Popular Science* (1899) 55:660–72; Epstein, *Sinful Tunes*, 41, 127–38, 161–83; and Southern, ed., *Readings*, 71–121.

50. See Epstein, *Sinful Tunes*, 63–76, and Charles C. Jones, *Religious Instruction of the Negroes in the United States* (New York: Negro Universities Press, 1969; reprint of 1842 ed.), 21, for information on the proselytizing activities of missionaries.

51. Praise houses were places designated for the slaves' worship. For detailed information about the conversion of slaves, see Raboteau, *Slave Religion;* Milton Sernett, *Black Religion and American Evangelicalism* (Metuchen, N.J.: Scarecrow Press, 1975); John Lovell, *Black Song: The Forge and the Flame* (New York: Macmillan, 1972), 71–374; and Epstein, *Sinful Tunes*, 100–11, 191–216.

52. See Raboteau, *Slave Religion;* Sernett, *Black Religion;* Epstein, *Sinful Tunes*, 191–237; and Levine, *Black Culture*, 3–80.

53. Quoted in Epstein, *Sinful Tunes*, 201.

54. Southern, *Readings*, 63.

55. Jones, *Religious Instruction*, 266.

56. Henry Russell, *Cheer! Boys, Cheer!: Memories of Men and Music* (London: John Macqueen, Hastings House, 1895), 85.

57. [Kilham], "Sketches," 309.

58. See Portia K. Maultsby, "Afro-American Religious Music 1619–1861," Ph.D. dissertation, University of Wisconsin-Madison, 1974, 182; Epstein, *Sinful Tunes*, 217–358; and Murphy, "Survival of African Music," 660–62. These aesthetic concepts may be heard on recordings: *Been in the Storm So Long*, recorded by Guy Carawan on Johns Island, South Carolina (Folkways Records FS 3842); *Afro-American Spirituals, Work Songs, and Ballads*, ed. Alan Lomax, Library of Congress Music Division (AAPS L3); *Negro Religious Songs and Services*, ed. B. A. Botkin, Library of Congress Music Division (AAFS L10).

59. Epstein, *Sinful Tunes*, 169–70. The secular musical tradition of slaves is discussed in Levine, *Black Culture*, 15; Harold Courlander, *Negro Folk Music U.S.A.* (New York: Columbia University Press, 1963), 80–88, 89–122, 146–61; and Epstein, 161–90.

60. Richard C. Wade, *Slavery in the Cities: The South 1820–1860* (New York: Oxford University Press, 1964), 249.

61. Leon F. Litwack, *North of Slavery* (Chicago: University of Chicago Press, 1961), 14, 64.

62. For descriptions of services associated with independent black churches,

see Berlin, *Slaves without Masters*, 284–303; Wade, *Slavery in the Cities*, 160–76; Epstein, *Sinful Tunes*, 197, 223; Portia K. Maultsby, "Music of Northern Independent Black Churches during the Ante-Bellum Period," *Ethnomusicology*, Sept. 1975, 407–18; Avrahm Yarmolinsky, ed., *Picturesque United States of America: 1811, 1812, 1813* (New York: William Edwin Rudge, 1930), 20; and Southern, *Readings*, 52–70.

63. Information about the status of blacks after the Civil War may be found in E. Franklin Frazier, *The Negro in the United States* (New York: Macmillan, 1949), 171–272; Levine, *Black Culture*, 136–70; C. Vann Woodward, *The Strange Career of Jim Crow* (New York: Oxford University Press, 2nd rev. ed., 1966), 11–65; and Jeff Todd Titon, *Early Downhome Blues: A Musical and Cultural Analysis* (Urbana: University of Illinois Press, 1977), 3–15.

64. See Frazier, *Negro in the United States*, 123–68; Woodward, *Strange Career*, 11–65; and Michael Haralambos, *Right On: From Blues to Soul in Black America* (New York: Drake, 1975), 50–51.

65. Quoted in Epstein, *Sinful Tunes*, 281–82.

66. J[ames] W[entworth] Leigh, *Other Days* (New York: Macmillan, 1921), 156.

67. Ibid., 274–81, and Levine, *Black Culture*, 191–217, 239–70.

68. Portia K. Maultsby, "The Role of Scholars in Creating Space and Validity for Ongoing Changes in Black American Culture," in *Black American Culture and Scholarship* (Washington, D.C.: Smithsonian Institution, 1985), 11.

69. See Samuel Charters, *The Bluesmen* (New York: Oak Publications, 1967); Haralambos, *Right On*, 76–82; Titon, *Early Downhome Blues;* Levine, *Black Culture*, 217–24; Keil, *Urban Blues*, 50–68; Oliver, *Savannah Syncopators*, 36–66; and Evans, "African Elements," 57–62.

70. See William Ferris, *Blues from the Delta* (New York: Anchor Press, 1978), 37–38; David Evans, "Afro-American One-Stringed Instruments," *Western Folklore* (Oct. 1970) 29:229–45; Oliver, *Savannah Syncopators*, 37–38; and Evans, "African Elements," 59–60.

71. Pearl Williams-Jones, "The Musical Quality of Black Religious Folk Ritual," *Spirit* (1977) 1:21.

72. See ibid., 23, 25, and Melvin D. Williams, *Community in a Black Pentecostal Church* (Pittsburgh: University of Pittsburgh Press, 1974), for religious practices associated with this church.

73. See Pearl Williams-Jones, "Afro-American Gospel Music: A Crystallization of the Black Aesthetic," *Ethnomusicology* (Sept. 1975) 19:374, 381, 383; Levine, *Black Culture*, 179–80; and Mellonee Burnim, "The Black Gospel Music Tradition: A Symbol of Ethnicity," Ph.D. dissertation, Indiana University, 1980. A variety of instruments used to accompany early gospel music may be heard on *An Introduction to Gospel Song*, compiled and edited by Samuel B. Charters (RBF Records RF5).

74. Horace Boyer, "Gospel Music," *Music Education Journal* (May 1978) 64:37.

75. Arna Bontemps, "Rock, Church, Rock!" *Ground* (Autumn 1942) 3:35–39. Bontemps gives the years 1901–1906 as the period when Tindley wrote his first songs, whereas Boyer believes the period to be between 1900 and 1905.

76. Portia K. Maultsby, *Rhythm and Blues (1945–1955): A Survey of Styles* (Washington, D.C.: Smithsonian Institution, 1986), 6.

77. For a history of these movements, see Martin Luther King, Jr., *Why We Can't Wait* (New York: Signet, 1964), and Stokely Carmichael and Charles V. Hamilton, *Black Power: The Politics of Liberation in America* (New York: Vintage, 1967).

78. Portia K. Maultsby, "Soul Music: Its Sociological and Political Significance in American Popular Culture," *Journal of Popular Culture* (Fall 1983) 17: 51–52. Many James Brown recordings released between 1969 and 1974 illustrated the black pride concept in soul music; also see Cliff White, "After 21 Years, Still Refusing to Lose," *Black World*, Apr. 1977, 36. Other performers whose music reflected the social climate of the 1960s and early 1970s include the Impressions, "We're a Winner" and "This Is My Country"; Marvin Gaye, "Inner City Blues"; Staple Singers, "Respect Yourself" and "Be What You Are"; Gladys Knight and the Pips, "Friendship Train"; O'Jays, "Back Stabbers" and "Love Train"; Sly and the Family Stone, "Thank You for Talkin' to Me Africa," "Africa Talks to You," and "The Asphalt Jungle"; Temptations, "Cloud Nine"; and Diana Ross and the Supremes, "Love Child."

79. See Gerald R. Gill, *Meanness Mania: The Changed Mood* (Washington, D.C.: Howard University Press, 1980); Faustine Childress Jones, *The Changing Mood: Eroding Commitment?* (Washington, D.C.: Howard University Press, 1977); Harry C. Triandis, *Variations in Black and White Perceptions of the Social Environment* (Urbana: University of Illinois Press, 1976); Angus Campbell, *White Attitudes toward Black People* (Ann Arbor: Institute for Social Research, University of Michigan, 1971); Charles Murray, *Losing Ground: American Social Policy 1950–1980* (New York: Basic Books, 1984); George Davis and Glenn Watson, *Black Life in Corporate America* (New York: Anchor, 1982); William Moore, Jr., and Lonnie H. Wagstaff, *Black Educators in White Colleges* (San Francisco: Jossey-Bass, 1974); Marvin W. Peterson, Robert T. Blackburn et al., *Black Students on White Campuses: The Impact of Increased Black Enrollments* (Ann Arbor: Institute for Social Research, University of Michigan, 1978); and Janet Dewart, ed., *State of Black America* (New York: National Urban League, 1987).

80. See Gill, *Meanness Mania;* Jones, *Changing Mood;* and Dewart, ed., *State of Black America.*

81. Maultsby, "Role of Scholars," 19–21.

82. Nketia, "African Roots," 83–84.

Twelve

Africanisms and the Study
of Folklore

Beverly J. Robinson

The word *folklore* has passed many lips, yet few people understand it. Even those scholars who are dedicated to the field of folklore have only begun to agree on an acceptable and useful definition of the term. *Folklore* has been used to describe what a storyteller relates or, more broadly, to describe art forms that are unique to a particular group of people. Complications arise, however, when one seriously attempts to identify what comprises folkloric behavior and artifacts among various cultural communities, and particularly when one is attempting to identify the historical origins of collected data.

The study of African American art and artifacts especially requires careful definition of the term *folklore* for two important reasons. First, the people who produced the unique treasure of black folklore rarely documented their traditions themselves. Second, historical commentaries and debates—mostly from non-African voices—about the roots of black traditions often confuse rather than clarify its sources. That being the case, can we hope to identify African roots that survive in America, or did the historical experience of slavery produce a potpourri that reflects a dominant European colonial influence with only scant vestiges of African traditions? Owing to the impact of slavery, some scholars believe that any cultural luggage enslaved Africans may have carried during the transatlantic movement was systematically repacked after the New World arrival to reflect a non-African culture. But folklorists, by the way they have looked at African American materials, may themselves have excluded any allusions to Africanisms, since the approach to the material traditionally has determined the results or the findings.

The Meaning of Folklore

At least twenty-one definitions of *folklore* are found in the *Dictionary of Folklore, Mythology, and Legend.*[1] Although there is no apparent consensus on the term's definition, every scholar of folklore as a cultural discipline has been taught that the word *folklore* was coined by William J. Thoms, an Englishman, in 1846. He introduced it to replace the term *popular antiquities.* Eventually *folklore* came into popular usage. Then, as now, no one was quite certain exactly what folklore consisted of. Agreement is overwhelming, however, that folklore has the quality of being important and is something folklorists study.[2] In this essay I use the term to refer to the folk culture of black Americans, including traditions and characteristics originating in Africa.

In the early years the study of folklore was restricted essentially to verbal texts. Ballads, epics, folk songs, legend, myths, and sayings (including jokes, proverbs, and superstitions) were the foci of collective research. Most of these documented items were drawn from the uneducated masses—the peasants or folk in Europe, the poor, illiterate, immigrant, and enslaved classes of America. The researchers harbored an underlying belief that it was necessary to capture verbal texts representing oral traditions that might someday become extinct. An additional stimulus in the United States has been to assert a sense of national culture and pride. American nationalism does not rely on European sanction; it is a distinct result of capturing the relics of generations of immigrant cultures and items that distinctly developed in America—for example, the narratives and songs of such real or mythological characters as Coyote, Daniel Boone, Stagolee, Paul Bunyan, and John Henry. Both John Henry and Stagolee have been extensively recorded among African Americans, but not because of the Africanisms they may reveal. Researchers have placed Stagolee into folkloric prominence primarily because, as a narrative poem, it supposedly exemplifies the black man's hypervirility, anxieties, and need to achieve self-respect. John Henry has suffered the same fate, albeit with the added nobility of being an epic hero struggling to survive in a modern society.[3]

Little research has been devoted to comparing epic hero traditions recorded throughout Africa with those that have survived in America. It is indeed possible that narrative heroes such as John Henry and Stagolee have functioned to reify a black verbal in-group art form, with only minor interest in whether these narrative heroes indeed existed. Or perhaps their narrative existence among African Americans has been mainly instructional, with philosophical implications much akin to traditional African narratives. The key to exploring such possibilities is understanding the context in which these verbal texts normally function. But texts are only one part of folklore. The field has grown to include art, architecture, costume, dance, drama, food, and various other expressive categories.

The word *folklore* is of course a composite of *folk,* now meaning "people" regardless of its earlier class connotation, and *lore,* meaning "knowledge." Thus it is the knowledge of the people—not just any knowledge but a particular knowledge that has proved to be valuable within a community because it has passed the test of time, a lore that people have found to contain important representations of themselves as a group. The folklore of specific groups of people, moreover, helps explain how people come into unity; again, it is a way of looking at their community. In examining African American folklore one finds that the expressive knowledge based in the traditions of African Americans discloses their sense of community and heritage.

Tales Out of Africa

The tale is a major folkloric category documented among African Americans, and much debate ensued over the origin of the folk tales recorded by Joel Chandler Harris in 1880 in *Uncle Remus: His Songs and His Sayings.* Harris, in the introduction to this first publication of the African American tales, discussed Creek Indian and African parallels in the collection. He was convinced that if one were to deny the African origins of the tales "the proof to that effect should be accompanied with a good deal of persuasive eloquence." Harris swore that "not one tale nor any part of one is an invention of mine. . . . It may be said that each legend comes fresh and direct from the Negroes."[4]

The tale Harris titled "Why the Negro Is Black" states that a pond of water said to turn people white existed at the beginning of time when everyone was black. Those who were soapless and arrived first were cleansed first, obviously leaving the water dirty. When the next soapless crowd arrived, they did not get as clean and left as mulattoes, having used up most of the water. By the time the last group of blacks arrived there was only enough water to wash their palms and the bottoms of their feet. When the seven-year-old boy who has been listening to the tale questions Uncle Remus about the Indians and the Chinese, he is told that they were among the mulattoes. The child points out to Uncle Remus that he was taught by his mother that the Chinese have straight hair. To which Uncle Remus replies that for those who arrived at the pond in time to put their head in the water "de water hit onkink der ha'r," concluding that the Chinese are blessed to be that way.

People who have used this tale to point out the subjugation of blacks overlook the strongest aspect of Africanism found here: pride. After all, the tale begins by saying that the first people were all black. The end of the tale is most revealing of this sense of pride: "en downter dis day dey ain't no w'ite 'bout a nigger 'ceppin' de palms er der han's en de soles er der foot." This conclusion certainly reflects an attitude that is not derogatory.

On the other side of the debate, Stith Thompson's 1919 landmark dissertation, *European Tales among the North American Indians,* supported what Alan Dundes calls "the European-centered orientation of American folklorists coupled with their tendency to neglect African folklore."[5] Thompson believed that the native American tales he had collected were of undoubted European origin, and any similar tales recorded among blacks were consequently classified as belonging to a European heritage. Looking at the narrative elements in tales, he concluded that "the animal tales here treated are usually of Negro and Spanish origin—all of them ultimately belonging to European tradition."[6] His conclusions may have influenced the work of Franz Boas, who believed that the Africans had learned their tales from Spanish and Portuguese sailors. Boas theorized that Africans transported to Portugal in the fifteenth century as agricultural workers might have taken their tales with them, and "this way the Portuguese and Spaniards were instrumental in disseminating tales of Negro origin."[7] But he concluded that better evidence was needed to support an African genesis theory and that the origins were essentially European.

There are at least two reasons why such a debate raged. First, early recorders of African American expressive traditions seemed content to acknowledge that the song and music styles of Africans initially brought to America were undoubtedly rooted in Africa. Songs, unlike languages (including those produced by drums), were allowable rhythms on ships carrying cargoes of slaves, and the plantations would later bear their chants. The indigenous languages used by enslaved Africans to sing aboard ships or during their introduction to the New World went undocumented as of little import. The recording of these transatlantic and New World songs came primarily as a result of non-Africans' documenting of the familiar, the understandable. Such familiarity was recorded in journal and diary entries attesting to the Africans' love for singing and dancing and the apparent childlike behavior and illiteracy of blacks.

A second reason for the debate stems from the fact that the Western world has historically revered language (specifically a written one) as a key to tracing and ultimately acknowledging a people's cultural ancestry. This type of thinking has been used to support the belief that slavery, as a system, obliterated any cultural identities with the African motherland. The languages enslaved Africans transported to their new environment were rarely considered examples of civilized communication. Ivan Vansertima, in summarizing these early misconceptions regarding African languages and intellect, noted that

> It has been said that the slaves who came here from Africa came here speaking a savage gibberish. Slowly they began to acquire a civilized form of communication, but because of their intellectual inferiority or physiological differences they failed to acquire the language properly. Their thick lips and oversized tongues got into the way of the English and murdered it. . . . These myths are rooted not only in a profound prejudice against black people, but in a profound ignorance about Africa.[8]

When people are already viewed as inferior or illiterate, the next step is to suggest that these people had no language or that at best language was not a key factor in understanding their folklore. It is not surprising, then, that tales collected from early generations of Africans in the New World were seldom examined for their Africanisms but as products borrowed or learned from various groups of native Americans or Europeans.

The Case of *Juba*

When folklorists began examining tales in the context of other expressive genres such as games, more insight into African culture in America emerged. Many games, songs, and tales were identified among African Americans, and especially among the Georgia Sea Islanders. Unlike the single-genre approach and accompanying analyses of earlier tale collections, expressive cultural documentation among the islanders proved to be an interweaving of several genres with the added impact of double entendre. A word could bear several contextual meanings. That is true in the case of *juba*.

One of the earliest records of the term *juba* dates back to American minstrelsy. Both Juba and Jube consistently appeared as names of enslaved Africans who were skilled musicians and dancers. The father of a celebrated black artist who was popular outside the minstrelsy circuit, Horace or Howard Weston, was named Jube. He was a music and dance teacher in Connecticut.[9] William Henry Lane, a performer with white minstrels who was compared to Terpsichore, the Greek muse of dance, was known as Master Juba.

The term *juba* can be traced to one of the largest African language families, Bantu, in which *juba* or *diuba* means to pat, beat time, the sun, the hour. The term, linguistically simplified from the African *giouba*, has been used to describe an African step dance recorded particularly in

South Carolina and the West Indies. *Juba* is also the Akan female day name for a child born on Monday.

Moreover, the term embraces folk knowledge attesting to early dietary conditions of enslaved Africans. *Juba* recalled a time when enslaved Africans working in plantation houses gathered leftover food to share with those working in the fields. The leftovers were called juba, jibba, or jiba. On Saturday or Sunday the leftovers were thrown together and no one could distinguish the meats from the bread and vegetables. The juba was placed in a huge trough where pigs and other animals were fed, and children, field hands, and others not working in the "big house" shared it. Bessie Jones, a traditional African American folk performer, noted in recounting this history:

> They would have all the slaves down there to eat that stuff. Not just to eat, [but] they had them there to play games, sing songs—do things they did in Africa. My grandfather said many, many days they had to eat that stuff. They would make up things because they didn't like what they was doing, but they couldn't tell them they didn't want to do it.[10]

If the enslaved Africans were fortunate, they would mix the juba with milk; otherwise water sufficed. To prepare psychologically to eat what was usually labeled slop, they made up a song that sounded like merriment but carried a double message. The words of the song are in the left column, Bessie Jones's explication in the right column.

Juba this and Juba that	Means giblet this [a little of this] and giblet that [a little of that]
Juba killed a yella' cat	Because they couldn't say mixed-up food might kill the white folks. They was afraid to say that because white folks'd kill them.
Get over double trouble, Juba.	Means, some day they would get over double trouble . . . cook my own food. I don't have to wait until the bread get cold and been done et off of, and the cake is et up and down to the crumbs and give it to me. But I'll eat mine fresh some day.

You sift the meal,
You give me the husk.
You cook the bread,
You give me the crust
You fry your meat,
You give me the skin.
And that's where mama's
trouble begin.

The mother would always be
talking to them about she wished
she could give them some of that
good hot cornbread, hot pies or
hot whatnot. But she couldn't.
She had to wait and give that
old stuff that was left over. And
then they began to sing it and
play it. . . .

Juba up, Juba down,
Juba all around the town.
Juba for ma, Juba for pa,
Juba for your brother-in-law.

That means everywhere, all
around the whole country . . .
everybody had juba. And they
made a play out of it. So that's
where this song come from; they
would get all this kind of thing
off their brains and minds.[11]

Bessie Jones was one of the original Georgia Sea Islander Singers. She learned the song and its meaning from her grandfather, who was born in slavery and left her with a rich repertoire of traditional songs, games, and tales, along with their meanings. The text is innately African, belonging to what Paul Carter Harrison called a derivative of drum languages. Such languages express a "communalism of objectives . . . through authentication of symbolic rhythmic effects common to the tonal style of Black language . . . but also in symbolic content so as to secure the unity necessary for nation-building." A variant of this text was recorded by Frederick Douglass.[12]

Juba and its variants were sung with such gaiety and vitality that it was not uncommon for a plantation owner to have the song performed for visitors or just as a plantation pastime. Of course, the owner was unaware of the double meanings. Older blacks would rhythmically pat juba on their thighs, while younger ones performed the juba dance. Everyone would sing. The dance portion became so popular that whites gave it the name of Charleston, the southern city and major slave port. The dance was later introduced to the American stage in an all-black production by F. E. Miller and Aubrey Lyles entitled *Runnin' Wild* in 1926, and the Charleston became the dance craze of the 1920s.

Dr. Wyeth, who assisted Dorothy Scarborough with her 1925 publication, *On the Trail of Negro Folk Songs,* stated that *juba* was an old African melody (*Juba* in this case defined as the name of an old African ghost). Still other references suggest that the word derived from the

African *nguba*, which means groundnut (or *gingooba* for goober, a pea-nut).[13] Both explanations point to African origins. More important are the contexts (situations) and variations (text) wherein *juba* has survived. On one hand, it documents the treatment of enslaved Africans in a game Bessie Jones learned and taught, in a song by a group called Jubilee-Beaters, in the retention of an African naming practice, and in a black dance of renown. On the other hand, *juba* records the borrowings of early white minstrel artists who depended on black games and dances for their repertoire.

The cakewalk, too, has a history in African American folklore. Of African American origin, the dance was a stylized caricature of whites minueting or waltzing.[14] Eliza Diggs Johnson, a former slave and mother of performer Charles Johnson, "told of the cakewalk held on the Missouri plantation where she was born." *Ebony* reported that

> in the old days, his mother had told him, white folks from the big house carriaged down to the clearing in back of the piney woods to watch their slaves couple off and do a dance-walk that was as elegant and poised as a Mozart minuet but yet was flavored with an exaggerated grace that was sometimes comical. Music for the cadenced walking and high stepping was supplied usually by a violin, a drum and horn of some kind. Prize for the winning couple would usually be a towering, extra sweet coconut cake.[15]

Charles Johnson, dubbed the Cakewalk King, with his wife, Dora Dean, and the team of Williams and Walker took the cakewalk to Broadway as early as 1895. What started as a parody of whites became a financial success for Johnson and Dean. The cakewalk inspired theatrical productions, including *Clorindy* by Will Marion Cook and Paul Lawrence Dunbar, was adapted by Debussy in his "Petite Suite," and was used in the works of Sousa and Stravinsky. The exclamation "Doesn't that take the cake!" denoting an element of surprise or something that is not to be outdone is uttered today with little knowledge of its origin.

The Evidence of Folk Beliefs

A rather large body of African American folklore that has been investigated for items pertaining to magic and superstition is folk beliefs. One of the few early African American collectors of folk beliefs (including superstitions and customs) was Zora Neale Hurston. For Hurston, these beliefs belonged to a worldview that was an integral part of her life beginning with her childhood, her data collections, and resultant writings; they were not to be mocked and sensationalized.[16] Though this genre of folklore also encompasses folk healing and medicine, many researchers (excluding Hurston) tend to separate folk belief from folk medicine.[17] Folk beliefs have traditionally consisted of the religiomagical practices of African Americans, including superstitions. Many of these practices were African in origin.

Albeit superstitions can be identified among all peoples, the term often carries a pejorative connotation when used to describe black behavior. That may account for the lack of interest among African American scholars in conducting major research in the area of traditional beliefs. African American beliefs are metaphysical traditions belonging to an African worldview adapted to an American milieu. They include forms of conjuration, healing, and attendant styles and methods (prayers and incantations) of activating these traditions. There are also words and phrases that cannot readily be traced to European origins. Robert Farris Thompson noted that one of the "most important words in black United States conjure-work, 'goofer,' refers to grave dirt. . . . In the Kongo territory, including Zaire, earth from a grave is considered at one with the spirit of the buried person. 'Goofer dust' harks back to the Ki-Kongo verb *kufwa* ('to die')."[18]

The resurgence in midwifery studies in the past decade and the growth of holistic health programs have stimulated a rethinking of the nomenclature used to describe the belief systems of African Americans who possess health practices that do not conform with a standardized Western concept. Out of this thinking has arisen a concern for the healing practices blacks brought across the Atlantic. These practices are primarily rooted in traditions nurtured in the southern United States and inherent in an African cultural base. The training ground was evident in the days of slavery, and America's early pioneering health practices were greatly influenced by the enslaved Africans' concern for health, well-being, and preventive medicine. In fact, this concern is a result of the institutionalized system of slavery, which mandated that enslaved Africans rely on a holistic form of survival as a consequence of their economic, political, and social status.

Africans in America, like European colonial settlers, possessed their own materia medica, which proved to be of value not only for their own health but for the health of all of early America. One instance is the "buying of the smallpox—a method of inoculation designed to prevent the onset of this dread disease by the use of a serum from human patients having the infection in a mild form." In Igboland of West Africa this method was used to control local outbreaks of smallpox. Knowledge of birth by cesarian section and snake-bite cures are among the other medical contributions Africans brought to America.[19]

Folklorists and other cultural scientists recently uncovered evidence that enslaved Africans had a worldview encompassing the balance of nature and did not separate mind and body. Psychologists described this worldview as

> involved in the decisions and judgements we make, the values we adopt, the cultural practices and the aesthetic forms by which we are motivated to express ourselves, all of which are under the control of the human brain. . . . The African world view, in comparison with the Western world view, allows the individual a greater opportunity to acquire and maintain optimal mental health. . . . [20]

The more common healers in the United States are known as spiritual healers or advisers, folk doctors, grannies, and midwives. Some practitioners, more fearsome, are known as root workers, hoodoo, juju, and voodoo doctors, hainsters, and conjurers. In traditional African culture preventive medicine was practiced by the traditional root doctors. They controlled the major diseases and epidemics. But whatever their names and titles, they are all concerned with relieving and curing illness, and they have occupied a respected position in many black communities since the days of slavery. Many of the skills of these black practitioners, such as midwifery, were direct carryovers from Africa.

African American healing is rooted in belief and thus is a religious act, which places folk practitioners and their art in the world of the spiritual. In some instances the healer is likened to a preacher or to what W. E. B. Du Bois called the priest and medicine man, a major support system enslaved Africans transported to the West. Beliefs that were sacred within the worldview of enslaved Africans could be validated and amalgamated with their Christian religious worship. The priest, medicine man, or preacher-type figure became an important catalyst in reinforcing this worldview. According to Du Bois, "he early appeared on the plantation and found his function as a healer of the sick, the interpreter of the Unknown, the comforter of the sorrowing, the supernatural avenger of wrong. . . . "[21]

John S. Mbiti, in *Concepts of God in Africa* (1969), studied nearly three hundred groups of people throughout Africa that were unrelated to Christian and Muslim communities to ascertain their concepts of God. He noted that without exception God was minimally and fundamentally understood to be a Supreme Being in Africa. The oral tradition —a process of passing a verbal language from one generation to the next —has been a major communication system throughout Africa wherein knowledge of God is expressed through such verbal modes as prayers, songs, narratives, names, and proverbs. Mbiti offered innumerable examples of omniscient, omnipresent, and omnipotent attributes of God, or the Supreme Being. Among the Akan, for example, God is known as "He who knows or sees all." The Banum refer to God as "He who is everywhere," while a traditional Pygmy hymn states: "In the beginning was God, today is God, tomorrow will be God."

Prayer is important as an expression of dependence on a power superior to that of the officiant (the person offering the prayer) and the participants. Kofi Asare Opaku found that traditional prayers among the Akan are

> usually made up of petitions and requests for material blessings—health . . . protection from enemies and death . . . prosperity and blessings on all well-wishers, and condemnation to all who wish others ill. As the officiant prays, the onlookers express aloud their concurrence with, or approach of, the contents of the prayer, after each pause by saying "Ampa ara" (It is just the truth) or "Yonn" (Yes indeed!).
>
> The petitions may be an expression of the will of man who asks favor for himself and those who wish him well and damnation for his enemies. But the true nature of the Akan prayers will be appreciated if it is borne in mind that the petitioner addresses his requests to the Determiner of Destiny upon whose will alone depends the answer to his requests. So that the ultimate outcome of the prayers does not depend on the will of the petitioner but rather on the will of the One to whom the petition is addressed.[22]

In addition to a Supreme Being there are intermediaries—divinities and ancestors (whom Mbiti refers to as the "living dead"). Their powers are derived from God, and they can serve as mediums between those praying and the Supreme Being.

In America this African worldview through prayer is contextually recognizable. Jesus as a prophet or divinity of the Supreme Being has been figuratively adopted as an ancestor based on his deeds, sufferings, and transcendence. The prayers of African Americans thereby reflect an African continuum of an oral tradition and pattern of thought evoking the same definable purposes as those Mbiti and Apaku found throughout Africa. Excerpts from prayers collected in Los Angeles in 1978 demonstrate this continuum:

> This is God of yesterday, the same God we're calling upon today. We thank you because we know you're still a prayer-answering God. You haven't lost a case neither have you lost a battle. We thank you Lord because you're so good to us. You woke us up early this morning. You put running in our feet. You put clapping in our

hands. Lord, somebody is calling upon you. . . . Somebody had
heart condition. Somebody had blood condition. Somebody is waiting on prayer. There's power in prayer. There's deliverance in
prayer for it is a direct contact with you. We're praying. We're asking for you to have mercy upon us. You've been better to us than
we've been to ourselves. We need you. . . . You can give deliverance
to the body. . . . Jesus have mercy right now.

Because African American healing defines its roots in religion, a common bond of belief and shared religion enhances the power of the folk
healer. The healer is a recognized member of the African American
community, which separates the folk healer from the Western health
practitioner. Rather than isolating and labeling the behavior of patients,
the folk healer approaches problems and cures relative to the physical,
social, economic, and emotional stresses placed on the individual by the
cultural milieu. Folk healers have no need for such labels as paranoia
and Oedipus complex, since problems result from not living according
to God's plan or from falling under the influence of an other than ordinary source.

Cures are administered through rituals, charms, herbs, concoctions,
and religious means. Apotropaic instruments include objects made of
iron, stones, pieces of earth (e.g., goofer or goober dust), and sticks of
wood that are believed to have magical qualities. Herbs and concoctions
may include plants with local names, such as blackroot, kidney weed,
and the life-everlasting plant, to "prolong life and act as a charm against
illness." According to Faith Mitchell, the use of these herbs was recorded among African Americans in the Sea Islands, an area known for
African retentions, and only the life-everlasting has been found to be
used among native and European Americans.[23] The religious approach
to healing almost always includes prayer, and it is not uncommon to
combine cures as opposed to compartmentalizing their use.

Just how one becomes a healer varies. The role may be inherited, one
may be trained by a skilled practitioner (the apprenticeship type of association), or one may be led to it through the medium of dreams. Phyllis
Carter of Tifton, Georgia, learned to cure a baby of the disease thrash,
or thrush, through a dream.

Before her initial healing practice, [Aunt Phyllis] had never seen a
baby with thrash and her first patient . . . had been taken to several
doctors for help, but to no avail. . . . That evening the Lord showed
her how to blow in a baby's mouth "about three times" and pray.
The next day the [father] brought his daughter and Aunt Phyllis
carried out her dream successfully. Afterwards, she began curing
thrash suffered by local babies as well as by babies whom she never

saw but was given their names. "I don't care if they way yonder somewhere. If I don't never see it [the baby], I'll cure it. The Lord show me such as that."[24]

Mrs. Carter was part of a southern midwife tradition that was a direct derivation from an African health practice. In Africa the female healers were also known as midwives.[25] Midwifery was common from the Senegambia to the Kongo region, and in America it was one of the few caring roles permitted and reinforced during slavery. Many of the early midwives gained some legitimacy from physicians who used them to assist them with childbirths. As a way of earning their stay on plantations, enslaved women who could no longer bear children became nurses or midwives.

Because folk healers are members of the African American community, they know how to analyze both verbal and nonverbal cues. With this knowledge they are able to provide environments that elicit the trust of their patients. It is much easier to explain one's condition using shared linguistic and cultural cues. African American English is often misunderstood when it is used to express the condition of one's health. A doctor who asked a patient how she was feeling was told: "The pain gone." The doctor thought the patient was on the road to recovery until a visitor of the patient who overheard the conversation and understood the use of tenses told him that "The pain gone" meant that it had left temporarily. The patient spoke Ebonics, a black language that, as Vansertima noted, utilizes English to describe "an action along a continuum of time"—an element common to many African languages. "It gone," "It done gone," "It done been gone," and "It gone gone" communicate time variances.[26]

The folk healer provides a service to people of limited income and accepts only donations, not fixed fees. An exception may be found with the more fearsome healers (hoodoo, juju, conjure doctors, and so forth), who may have fixed fees or require more money. None of the fees, however, is in the high-priced range of allopathic practitioners. Thus the folk healer's services are accessible to people of limited income. Whether these fees can be equated to an African tradition is presently unknown. But the belief in folk healers and the accessibility of these people accompanied by cultural traditions (verbal and nonverbal cues, prayers, amulets) is a bonded trust found among African peoples of both continents.

There is an active tradition among African Americans to have allopathic or other medical services complemented by the services of a folk healer or adviser. If a healer or adviser is not requested by the patient, a family member will commonly seek this service to ensure the entire well-being of the sufferer. The extent to which the folk healers succeed can be measured best by the importance of the tradition. But the holistic concept, derived from an African worldview of healing the mind and spirit along with the body, remains the basis of this practice.

Conclusion

Folklore and Africanisms among African Americans is still an open area of research for cultural scientists. The earlier preoccupation with the question of origins is a circumvolutory one, at best creating myopic results. The overlapping of genres related to language, tales, performance, beliefs, and other expressive modes within the context of African American cultural usage will unlock the traditions of Africa surviving in America. Context evokes meaning, and the key to understanding a large part of the meaning will always lie with the people. Artistically, as the musician and writer Hall Johnson aptly stated,

> Afro-Americans . . . are in a most peculiar situation with regard to what we have to give the world. In our several hundred years of enforced isolation in this country we have had plenty of time and plenty of reason to sing each other songs and tell each other tales. These songs and stories have a hidden depth of meaning as well as a simple and sincere external beauty. But the same wall which forced them into existence has closed in tight upon their meaning and allows only their beauty to escape through the chink. So that our folk culture is like the growth of some hardy yet exotic shrub whose fragrance never fails to delight discriminating nostrils even when there is no interest in the depth of its roots. But when the leaves are gathered by strange hands they soon wither and when cuttings are transplanted into strange soil they have but a short and sickly life. Only those who sowed may know the secret of the root.[27]

Perhaps the fundamental essence of Africanisms rests within a worldview, a view not founded on the color of one's skin but on an inner color, permeated by shapes of thought, that enables Africans to congregate and "know" each other in spite of varying historical circumstances. Africanisms in this century have been tangible factors rooted in an African heritage, surfacing and surviving among non-African traditions. The deep structure of this survival has been euphemistically called soul, an entelechy that binds people culturally regardless of skin hues, hair textures, and overt physical variables. Soul is an inner rhythm outwardly expressed and recognizable most often in nonverbal language. It is particularly understood by way of rhythms found in the walks, nods, drumming, poses, phrasing, phonology, and grimaces of Africa's people. Ironically, these expressions, rooted so deeply in a people's history, are transmitted by the people often without knowing the heritage from which they arose, and are taken for granted as an individual shape of thought rather than a community style.

Notes

The initial research for this essay was inspired by Hazel J. Bryant of New York City and Gladys Little of Los Angeles, both of whom left very strong legacies supporting the importance of African American culture.

1. *Dictionary of Folklore, Mythology, and Legend,* Maria Leach and Jerome Fried, eds. (New York: Funk and Wagnalls, 2 vols., 1949–50).

2. See Francis Lee Utley, "A Definition of Folklore," and Alan Dundes, "Ways of Studying Folklore," in *American Folklore,* Tristram Coffin III, ed. (Washington, D.C.: U.S. Information Service, 1968), 3–16, 41–50, and Dan Ben-Amos, "Toward a Definition of Folklore in Context," in *Readings in American Folklore,* Jan Brunvand, ed. (New York: Norton, 1979), 427–43.

3. Lawrence W. Levine, *Black Culture and Black Consciousness* (New York: Oxford University Press, 1977), 418–29.

4. Joel Chandler Harris, *Uncle Remus: His Songs and Sayings* (New York: Penguin, 1982; originally published by D. Appleton, 1880), 45, 17.

5. Alan Dundes, "African Tales among the North American Indians," *Southern Folklore Quarterly* (1965) 29:207.

6. Stith Thompson, *European Tales among the North American Indians* (Colorado Springs: Colorado College, 1919), 449–57.

7. Franz Boas, *Race, Language and Culture* (New York: Free Press, 1966; reprint of 1940 ed.), 521.

8. Ivan Vansertima, "African Linguistics and Mythological Structure in the New World," in *Black Life and Culture in the United States*, Rhoda L. Goldstein, ed. (New York: Crowell, 1971), 13–14.

9. Marian Hannah Winter, "Juba and American Minstrelsy," *Dance Index* (Feb. 1947) 6(2):28–49.

10. B. J. Robinson and Kate Rinzler, "All Things in My Remembrance," unpublished monograph, Smithsonian Folklife Program, Smithsonian Institution, Washington, D.C.

11. Bessie Jones and Bess Lomax Hawes, *Step It Down* (New York: Harper and Row, 1972), 38.

12. Paul Carter Harrison, *The Drama of Nommo* (New York: Grove Press, 1972), 52. Frederick Douglass, *My Bondage and My Freedom* (New York: Dover, 1969; reprint of 1844 ed.), 252–53.

13. Newman Ivey White, *American Negro Folk-songs* (Cambridge, Mass.: Har-

vard University Press, 1928), 4–6, and Guy B. Johnson, *Folk Culture on St. Helena Island, South Carolina* (Chapel Hill: University of North Carolina Press, 1930), 60.

14. In the 1940s ninety-year-old Shep Edmonds noted that the cakewalk's origins stemmed from blacks mocking plantation owners: "They did a take-off on the high manners of the white folks in the 'big house,' but their masters, who gathered around to watch the fun, missed the point." Marshall and Jean Stearns, *Jazz Dance* (New York: Schirmer, 1979), 22, 122–23.

15. "The King of the Cakewalk," *Ebony*, Feb. 28, 1953.

16. Robert E. Hemenway, *Zora Neale Hurston: A Literary Biography* (Urbana: University of Illinois Press, 1977), 66–69, 118–23.

17. Loudell F. Snow, "Mail Order Magic: The Commercial Exploitation of Folk Belief," *Journal of the Folklore Institute* (Jan.–Aug. 1979) 16(12):58n.4.

18. Robert Farris Thompson, *Flash of the Spirit* (New York: Random House, 1983), 105.

19. Herbert M. Morais, *The History of the Negro in Medicine* (New York: Association for the Study of Negro Life and History, 1967), 8–20.

20. Alfred B. Pasteur and Ivory L. Toldson, *Roots of Soul* (Garden City, N.Y.: Anchor Press, 1981), 24.

21. W. E. B. Du Bois, *The Souls of Black Folk* (New York: Signet, 1969; originally published in 1903), 144.

22. Mbiti's and Opaku's essays appear in C. Eric Lincoln, *The Black Experience in Religion* (Garden City, N.Y.: Anchor Press, 1974), 275–82, 292–94.

23. Faith Mitchell, *Hoodoo Medicine: Sea Islands Herbal Remedies* (Berkeley, Calif.: Reed and Cannon, 1978), 36, 56, 59.

24. Beverly J. Robinson, *Aunt [Ant] Phyllis* (Oakland, Calif.: Regent Press, 2nd ed., 1988), 18–19.

25. Ira E. Harrison, "Health Status and Healing Practices: Continuation from an African Past," *Journal of African Studies* (Winter 1975) 2(43):558.

26. Vansertima, "African Linguistics," 20. Also see John A. Rickford and Angela E. Rickford, "Cut-Eye and Suckteeth: African Words and Gestures in New World Guise," in *Readings in American Folklore*, Jan Brunvand, ed. (New York: Norton, 1979), 355–73, and Edward Twun-Akwaboah, "From Pidginization to Creolization of Africanisms in Black American English," monograph, University of California, Los Angeles, fall 1973. The term *Ebonics* (ebony + phonics, or "black sounds") was introduced at a conference on Cognitive and Language Development of the Black Child in St. Louis in 1973. Ernie A. Smith of California State University, Fullerton, defined *Ebonics* as "verbal and non-verbal sounds, cues and gestures which are systematically and predictably utilized in the process of communication by Afro-Americans"; see his "Ebonics," *Western Journal of Black Studies* (1978) 2(3):202–207.

27. Hall Johnson, *Opportunity* (Jan. 1936) 14(5):28.

Thirteen

The African Heritage of White America

John Edward Philips

The study of Africanisms in the United States today has the same two general tendencies it did at the time the first edition of this book was published: the documentation of specific Africanisms, often traced to a particular area in Africa, in an attempt to show the distinctively African nature of African American society, and the increasing acknowledgment of the influence of Africanisms not just on African Americans but also on the culture of whites in the New World. These two tendencies have increasingly merged since the original edition of this book, and indeed this entire book, not the final chapter alone, represented a new synthesis of these approaches. Every chapter of the original edition of this volume dealt, to some extent or other, with the adoption of African culture by whites. Increasing acceptance of the idea that much white American culture comes from Africa is thus a triumph for the perspective of this book. Indeed, researchers have found far more instances of "White Africanisms" in the decade since this book was first published.

For example, in 1994 *Roy Blount's Book of Southern Humor* not only mingled humor by black and white southerners indiscriminately, it boldly proclaimed that "One thing we need to get straight about Southern humor—Southern culture generally—is that it is Africo-Celtic, or Celtico-African."[1] He pointed to the orality of Irish and African cultures contributing to the convergence, and spoke of "leprechauns and Yoruba tricksters, Brother Dave Gardner and Little Richard, George Wallace and Stokely Carmichael together" in ways that few anthologists had before.[2] Southern, indeed American, culture is now being better understood as being to a large extent African.

Thus the perspective of this chapter is no longer unique, but it is still worth considering again the accumulated evidence for African culture among whites in the United States, especially since so much research has been added in the past decade. This increasing evidence has implications not only for our understanding of the nature of European American society but also for such issues as the study of culture interaction and change over time, and the nature of American society in general, as well as practical implications for coming to terms with the continuing American dilemma of ongoing racial friction.

The documentation of specific Africanisms by such scholars as Winifred Vass, Dana Epstein, and others was intended to prove the specifically African nature of African American society and culture by specifying aspects of African culture that had survived through slavery and segregation among late-twentieth-century African Americans. The conscious attempt of this perspective was to refute the deculturation hypothesis associated with E. Franklin Frazier and others by proving that there is in fact a demonstrably African content that distinguishes African American culture from European American culture in the United States. Vass made her arguments by suggesting survivals of Bantu vocabulary in place names, folklore, and other aspects of American lexicon and literature, especially in the deep south. Epstein presented a particularly detailed documentary history of the banjo, demonstrating conclusively its African origin in order to demolish assertions that whites had invented it in the southern United States, or even that it had been introduced from Europe.[3]

This line of argument, especially in the instances cited, presented certain difficulties almost amounting to internal contradictions. Although the intent was to document Africanisms to support the contention of a uniquely African basis for the culture of blacks in the United States, the evidence advanced touched equally if not more on the culture of whites at the time it was published. Epstein's banjo is today far more characteristic of whites than of blacks. Although folklorists occasionally discover a few aging black banjo players, there is not a city in the United States where tuning the radio dial until the sound of a banjo is heard is a good way to find black-oriented radio stations. The place names used by Vass as one of her most important sources of evidence for Bantu influence are in use as much among whites as among blacks. Even folk songs such as "Polly-Wolly Doodle," and specific words such as *tote* (meaning to carry) are as common among whites as among blacks, and indeed are sometimes documented from white sources.

Another problem, perhaps related, has to do with the time and space of the Africanisms documented. Some of those that come specifically from blacks, such as African choruses in work songs, were documented from slave times when there were significant numbers of first-generation African Americans. It is questionable how many such songs survived slavery and the end of African-style gang labor outside the southern prison system. Other African survivals were recorded from the Georgia or South Carolina Sea Islands, isolated areas of unusually strong African culture.

Thus it is questionable whether Vass, Epstein, and others have been able to document much that is specifically African about the way black culture in the United States differs from white culture. It seems that they have instead demonstrated how African influences are one important way in which American culture differs from European. Although their approach has contributed much to the documentation of the survival of African culture in the United States, it has ultimately documented as much African culture among whites as among blacks, and has thus failed in its announced intention of explaining the differences in black culture as African retentions.

The second tendency, exemplified by Peter Wood and others, did not shy away from arguing that African cultural survivals among whites in the United States were specific and pervasive. It looked for Africanisms as a means of proving points about white society in the United States. Like the foregoing, this perspective was conceived as an ultimate triumph for the Herskovits thesis, and indeed was foreshadowed by Melville J. Herskovits himself.[4]

This perspective has created its own problems and contradictions, too. If the influence of African culture on whites in the United States is really as pervasive and long lasting as argued by Wood and others, one must look to something other than African cultural heritage to explain the obvious and extensive differences between black and white cultures in the United States today. This conclusion thus turned back toward the Frazier perspective, which looked at the experiences of slavery and the color caste system of segregation to explain the peculiar customs and society of black Americans. Blacks are not just another immigrant ethnic group contributing part of their culture to the American stew; they are the traditional subordinate caste whose culture could profitably be compared with that of other casted groups around the world.

The Wood perspective also brought us back to Frazier in another sense. By highlighting the close personal ties and mutual influences between slaves and their owners in the early United States, Wood and his followers resurrected the acculturation theme of Frazier, with its emphasis on demographics and the dispersal of the black population among whites.[5]

A New Synthesis

The synthesis of the Herskovits and Frazier perspectives proposed in the first edition of this work was suggested not only by the latest research on Africanisms but by the nature of the disciplinary backgrounds of the giants of the debate. While partisans of the positions of Herskovits and Frazier abound in every discipline, their own disciplines tell us the most about the debate they began. Sociology (Frazier) and cultural anthropology (Herskovits) are quite similar disciplines. They differ most notably in the types of societies they usually study, and in their methods. Looking at this difference helps to explain how these two scholars, and their followers, could look at the same African American society from different perspectives and interpret it so differently.

Anthropology has traditionally concerned itself with "primitive" societies and obscure corners of Western civilization, such as southern Appalachia and the Georgia and South Carolina Sea Islands. Its traditional methods shun quantified data for oral data gathered from informants, many of them non-literate. Sociology, for its part, has a bias toward the urban, the average, and the quantifiable behavior patterns of modern, urban society. That which is traditional, personal, individual, or otherwise distinctive it has often ignored. It focuses on the current, even the transient, and is more concerned with where people are going than with where they came from. The behavior and attitudes that Herskovits and his followers discussed—hard to quantify, often from out-of-the-way areas—are ignored by many sociologists. Both disciplines have sometimes been accused of neglecting history and the historical development of the societies they study, but this is no more true of one than the other. What is true is that sociology has often been more future oriented to the point of neglecting tradition, and that anthropology has often been more past oriented, to the point of often speaking in an "ethnographic present" tense that actually describes the past.

Both Herskovits and Frazier worked in both African and American societies, but their research interests, their methods, and therefore their conclusions were strikingly different. The perspectives of the disciplines they represent are equally valid, and the persons they concentrated on studying are equally real. Yet their contrasting foci and methods often left them talking past each other, making seemingly contradictory but equally valid points.[6]

That sociologists have a tendency to side with their colleague Frazier was recognized by the anthropologists Roger Abrahams and John Szwed in their analysis of the Herskovits-Frazier debate. They specifically identified the Herskovits position with anthroplogy as a discipline and the Frazier position with sociology, while admitting that some anthropologists had come to share the Frazier perspective, a position they attributed to the allegedly overwhelming dominance of the Frazier position.[7]

The synthesis presented here was intended to lead to a diminishing of interdisciplinary wrangling and to lead instead to a more holistic, interdisciplinary, and comprehensive understanding of American society. It was and still is the contention of this author that the disagreement between Herskovits and Frazier is more apparent than real, and that as social scientists and historians investigate systematically the survival of African culture among whites in the United States, especially in the South, they will discover as much as they have previously found among blacks in the United States. Thus, while Herskovits was right in asserting that much African culture survived in the United States, Frazier was equally correct in asserting that such African cultural survivals were not the distinguishing characteristics of African American culture. Moreover, as will be noted below, while some Africanisms survive most characteristically among whites, there are aspects of European culture that survive just as characteristically among blacks. The implications of such findings for our understandings of American culture (black, white, other and common) have yet to be fully apprehended. Future researchers must not shy away from considering these implications.

The investigation of African cultural influences among whites in the United States has long faced obstacles that the investigation of African, or even European, cultural influences among blacks has not faced. For too long in this country whites have denied learning from blacks. That black intellectual contributions have been slighted is only too obvious from the life stories of black intellectual giants such as W. E. B. Du Bois. Many blacks have had to hide their intelligence just to survive. The study of the legacy of African culture has an even greater obstacle to overcome in that many blacks who were most adamant about being recognized for their contributions were most reluctant to claim African culture and most anxious to assimilate European norms. To label something African was often a sure way to have it avoided by both blacks and whites. An absurd example is the white southern claim to have invented the banjo.

This essay is not considering such panhuman traits of African origin as upright posture, tool making or the control of fire. Nor is it considering such African contributions to world civilization as coffee (of Ethiopian origin). It will not even concern itself with recent influences of African culture on jazz musicians, Peace Corps volunteers, and others. Rather it considers aspects of African culture that were transported across the Atlantic by Africans during the slave trade and which still survive today among white Americans, especially in the South.

For the second edition of this chapter, new findings will be added from the secondary literature, to the findings which were summarized for the first edition. More and more of these findings are concerned with explaining the nature of American society in general, or southern society in particular, rather than African American society specifically. Nevertheless, we have still not yet reached a stage where we can come to definitive conclusions about the nature of African cultural survivals in the United States, based on a comparison of survivals among both whites and blacks. Too much work still needs to be done to document African culture among whites, which is still a relatively neglected area of research.

This chapter will make suggestions for further research and consider the ways in which African culture could have come to influence whites. This question is still important not only for explaining the source of the now well-documented "white Africanisms" but also for larger theoretical issues of culture contact and transmittal. Anthropologists in the United States, under the influence of Franz Boas, have long recognized that culture is not transmitted genetically, but they have not always been willing to recognize the implications of this fact, especially in considering the nature and extent of African cultural survivals in the United States. Herskovits himself, in the heat of his debate with Frazier, reverted to descent as an explanation of the parallels between African and African American culture, even if the trait in question was equally typical of European American culture.

Perhaps more important than the necessarily limited impact these findings will have among academics is the implications they have for wider understanding of the nature of American society and American civilization. Is the United States, as Samuel Huntington and others have argued, an extension of Western European civilization, or is it, as others have argued, a unique civilization unto itself? Has the twentieth-century United States been uniquely influential culturally because its military power has projected American culture outward in a form of cultural Imperialism? Or has American culture spread around the globe because people all over the world find some aspects of American culture that seem familiar to them? What will be the result of more cultures, especially from Asia and Latin America, becoming more prominent in the United States? Investigating the past influence of African culture among white Americans can thus help us understand not only the past of American culture, and its present nature, but even the future directions in which it is likely to develop and spread.

White Africanisms

In the vast literature of African cultural survivals, it is still true that very few articles deal with the impact of African culture on whites in any systematic way. One of the few that does is by Melville Herskovits himself. In "What Has Africa Given America?" he discussed five areas in which African culture had had an influence on whites in the United States.[8] This short article, only six and a half pages, was for far too long the only one which attempted to discuss in any detail the various forms of African culture found among whites, rather than mentioning them briefly in discussions and analysis of African cultural survivals found among blacks. Even this article was primarily concerned with African culture among blacks. Only recently has what should have been a call to further research been followed up.

The first area of African cultural influence which Herskovits discussed was music. He dealt with only two forms of American music, those perhaps most associated with blacks in the public's mind: spirituals and jazz. Herskovits mentioned specific African elements in these genres, and how jazz in particular had come to influence American popular music, a field in which black Americans had achieved some of their most notable early successes. Neither in this essay nor in his book *The Myth of the Negro Past,* however, did Herskovits mention the banjo or consider how Africa might have influenced white folk or country music. The emphasis was still on African culture among blacks, on black music and the role of blacks as entertainers in American society.

The second of Herskovits's points was that American, especially southern, dialect speech had been influenced by Africa. Here he dealt forthrightly with whites and their culture, briefly asserting that the distinctive pronunciation of southerners, together with the musical quality of southern speech, derived from Africa. Unfortunately, he did not give many details about specific instances and examples.

The elaborate etiquette of the South, with its respect for elders, its use of terms of endearment and kinship in speaking to neighbors, and its general emphasis on politeness, was another aspect of southern life that Herskovits discussed. He acknowledged that the forms were European, indeed feudal, but argued that the spirit was African.

Southern cuisine was the next aspect of American culture which

Herskovits discussed, and here he spoke in considerably more detail. Fried chicken, gumbo, okra, and other dishes common in the South showed obvious African influence. The word *gumbo* was itself of African origin, and the seasoning of southern dishes, often heavier than in the north, was another influence from Africa.

Finally Herskovits discussed religious behavior, arguing that European possession cults practiced a very personal form of autohypnosis, whereas American churches engaged in a more social form of group excitation induced by the rhythms of the liturgy and the droning of the preacher. Such a trance form was African but was characteristically found among whites who belonged to churches with large numbers of black members and in the Pentecostal sects.

Almost thirty years later, John A. Davis offered another assessment of the influence of African culture on America. Like most other investigators he was concerned primarily with the influence of Africa on blacks in the United States and mentioned the formal politeness and courtesy of the South almost in passing.[9]

Then in 1969 C. Vann Woodward, in a plea for the continued presence of whites in the field of African American studies, asserted that many whites had more African culture in their background than many blacks. He did not, however, go into detail about what sorts of African culture were involved; nor did he explain how whites had come to possess that culture.[10] In 1984, Joel Williamson stated that "a significant amount of the African heritage that survived in the slave South survived outside the black world in the white." Like Van Woodward, though, he did little to detail the kinds of survivals involved.[11]

Let us here begin our own account of African culture among whites with the most obvious example, the one Herskovits ignored most surprisingly: the banjo. Thanks to the work of Dena Epstein, the banjo has now been shown to be of indisputably African origin, though its use at present is far more characteristic of whites than of blacks. Little research has been done as to why this should be the case or on what other aspects of white folk music in the United States might be African in origin. It has been asserted, for instance, that the African earth-bow became the washtub bass.[12]

Other facts about white Appalachian music immediately become apparent when we start considering the music as partly African in origin. Banjos are commonly struck on the head while being played, a technique characteristic of Senegambian music. Improvisation and the solo-chorus response style of singing—both so characteristic of Africa—are notable features of bluegrass music. Syncopation is built into American traditional music, at least in the South, in a way alien to British music of the eighteenth century, giving it a rhythmic complexity that Alan Jabbour believes could not have come from Europe.[13]

Samuel Charters, who went to West Africa a few years ago looking for the roots of the blues, found that traditional mountain banjo music was "certainly closer in style to African sources" than was the blues. "Sadly the era of recording began after the banjo had largely been taken over by white performers" he noted.[14] But why sadly? Had white musicians not taken up the instrument it might not have survived at all, and the musical heritage of the United States might be poorer for it, since most of the few black banjo players who survived into the late twentieth century lived in white majority areas and performed in a largely white milieu. Surviving styles of Appalachian banjo music are likely the most authentically African music in the United States, but there are still few musicologists who have ever considered, much less investigated, the question of African elements in white Appalachian folk music. One of the few who have considered the question concluded that the structural characteristics of camp meeting songs showed strong black influence, presumably including African characteristics.[15]

The banjo is not the only African instrument found primarily among whites. As part of his research on African influences in the Blues, Gerhard Kubik found that mouth bows of a type probably from Angola or Mozambique were "now sold to tourists as authentic 'hillbilly' artifacts" but that no memory of that African origin survived.[16]

Yodeling is known to be common in many areas of Africa in addition to being similar to the "field hollers" of African American folk tradition. Thus we can postulate a partially African origin for Jimmie Rodgers's distinctive "blue yodel" style of singing, so important in the development of Country Music. Rodgers grew up where blacks were in the majority, and his music shows profound black influences in other respects than his yodeling in particular or even his singing in general. Some ethnomusicologists try to draw a distinction between the "true" yodel (found among whites and of European origin) and the falsetto leap (found only among blacks and from Africa), but the use of falsetto leaps by such white country musicians as Jimmy Martin and the presence of true yodels in Africa and among African American musicians such as Pharoah Sanders shows that the distinction, if valid at all, is not relevant to race.[17]

Outsiders are often struck by the importance music has in both American and African societies. In both, music is a constant accompaniment to work, rest, and play. It is an aspect of popular culture that takes up enormous time and energy. It is, in fact, a major industry in both cultures. The musical cultures of Africa and the United States are both quite strong and have had a strong influence on the music of other areas, as has the musical culture of Brazil, another area of strong African influence. Could this very importance of music for Americans be yet another African influence on the culture of the United States?

In religious belief, too, the possibility of African influences among whites has never been adequately considered. Much that is often considered peculiarly black about black Pentecostal and Holiness churches is often equally characteristic of white churches, so that those seeking to differentiate the churches on the basis of race must resort to fine points of emphasis rather than substantive matters of doctrine or ritual.[18] Many features of Pentecostal churches are demonstrably African in origin, including possession trances, ritual dancing, drumming, and ecstatic speech (thought to be the language of angels or spirits).[19] Yet few if any historians, ethnographers, or sociologists of religion in the United States have sought to look for the African origins of white religious belief and behavior. Connections between snake-handling churches of the American South and West African snake cults come to mind immediately as one possibility. The style and rhythms of southern preachers, not to mention the music and behavior of their congregations, are also quite different form those of northerners, and undoubtedly owe much to African antecedents.[20]

Non-Christian belief systems, such as voodoo, are also a common feature of both white and black culture in the United States. Although the European cultural impact on voodoo cannot be ignored, the many whites who believe in voodoo must be considered to share an African cultural heritage with their black compatriots. Investigators of white supernatural beliefs in the West Indies have been surprised by evidence of the profound influence which black belief systems there have had on whites. Whites have even been shown to practice Obeah, the distinctly African witchcraft system found in many areas of the Caribbean.[21] Those studying religion and supernatural beliefs in the United States should also be aware that there may be beliefs and practices found among whites that have African antecedents, whether or not such beliefs and practices still survive among blacks—as is the case with musical instruments such as the banjo.

Nor are white Africanisms confined to such stereotypically "black" areas of culture as music and religion. Traditions of generosity and hospitality are another aspect of culture that is as characteristic of whites as of blacks in the southern United States. Even though southern society was traditionally segregated, it was pervaded by an ethic of hospitality of which southerners of all races are justifiably proud. A formal but sincere courtesy is characteristic of both the southern United States and Africa. Those who have experienced both can testify to their mutual resemblance. It cannot logically be argued that black southern hospitality is from Africa but white southern hospitality is not, unless one is prepared to argue either that culture is hereditarily transmitted or that blacks in the early south were incapable of influencing whites. It is more likely, as astute observers have noted since slave times, that those slave owners and overseers whose behavior most accorded with traditional African concepts of leadership and aristocracy were most successful in controlling their slaves. Thus, traditions of good manners, honor, and hospitality passed from black to white throughout slavery times and helped make the south more of a shame culture than the guilt-ridden puritanical society of the north. Even the characteristically southern "good ole boy" probably owes his epithet "ole" not to his age but to African traditions of respect for seniority.[22] Who knows, perhaps even the U.S. Congress's traditional reliance on seniority in appointments, so strange to many observers from the North, is also an influence of such African traditions.

Okra is a crop native to West and Central Africa, yet members of all races eat it in the southern United States. Peter Wood argued that sorghum, too, was also introduced into the United States from Africa.[23] Blackeyed peas and other crops commonly grown and eaten in the United States are African in origin, and so are the fish stews and gumbos for which Louisiana is famous. Deep fat frying, so common in homes and restaurants all over the United States, has been called "a cooking technique which Africans introduced to America." These African elements are as common among whites as among blacks, but there is at least one major African culinary survival which even the staunchest partisans of a separate African heritage for blacks must admit is more characteristic of whites than of blacks: "Nut soups, which are of African origin, are made and enjoyed by the epicureans of America, but not by the descendants of the people who created the dishes."[24]

Most people are now aware that many cowboys of the American West were black, contrary to their usual portrayal in the movies and on television. Only recently have we begun to recognize the extent to which cowboy culture had African routes. The annual north-south migratory pattern followed by the old-time cowboys was unlike the cattle-keeping patterns in Europe but analogous to the migratory patterns of the Fulani cattle herders who lived scattered from the Senegambia through Niger and Nigeria to the Sudan. Early descriptions of Senegambian patterns strikingly resemble later descriptions of cattle herding in the South Carolina hinterland.[25] The cattle egrets found all over the American South are from Africa, and the famous Texas longhorns are of at least partly African origin.[26] Many details of cowboy life, work, and even material culture can be traced to Fulani antecedents, but there has been little work on this question by historians of the American West.

In the area of language, many have long acknowledged black influence on whites, including influences of African origin. Linguists are far from agreement about the extent of African influence on African American speech or of differences between the speech of blacks and whites of the same social class and region in the southern United States. David Dalby has documented many Americanisms of African origin, very few of which are any longer peculiar to blacks. Most are from either Mande or Wolof and were important words in black slang before the jazz and beat cultures of the twentieth century popularized them.[27] As whites became familiar with and began to regularly use black slang, blacks invented new terminology to they could communicate without whites understanding them.[28] Therefore, as Africanisms entered the speech of whites they tended to leave black speech. It is now difficult to decide whose speech is more African.

Many southern whites, especially those in close contact with or raised by blacks, have exhibited diglossia, or fluency in two dialects used in different situations. In the case of those raised by blacks, which was typical of upper-class Southerners, the "black" dialect would have to be considered their native speech, since formal English was usually acquired later, often at school.[29] Thus, region and class are at least as important as race in determining who speaks what kind of English in the United States, regardless of the controversy surrounding the extent of African influence on both the southern dialects of American English and their black variants. One of the few rigorous comparative studies found middle-class blacks speaking Standard English but southern white dialects "in which copula deletion does operate quantitatively" much as in vernacular black English, and "from this point there is a continuum of white varieties which continuously diverge." The same findings held for other grammatical features as well.[30] This suggests that class is a more important factor than race but that blacks are more likely to speak black English because a higher proportion of blacks are in the lower classes.

Even recognizing black influences on white speech patterns in the south would not result in classification of southern speech into class varieties the way British or New England speech is so easily classified. The English actress Fanny Kemble noted that in coastal Georgia the speech of the black majority was becoming the speech of the whites as well as of the blacks.[31] As an actress, she could be expected to be particularly aware of nuances in speech pronunciation, and thus her observations in this matter are particularly likely to be accurate.

J. L. Dillard has recently tied the argument that there was massive black influence on southern white dialects to his hypothesis of a plantation Creole language in early colonial days.[32] This would also tie African influence on southern U.S. English to his argument that Creole languages are based on African languages. It is not necessary to go this far, however. Individual African words, and other African influences, could have seeped into the English of the southern United States through slaves from Africa or even the Caribbean without having to postulate the presence of a Creole language throughout the southern plantation areas. Black English can easily be classified as one variety of southern, which itself is more diverse than many from outside the region realize. Black English thus is not necessarily more, or less, African than any other variety of southern. It should also be remembered that blacks from different parts of the United States speak as differently as whites do.

One aspect of American culture that has been largely ignored in the debate over African cultural survivals in the United States is the development of feminism. It should be remembered that one of the first feminist demands in the United States was for the right to own property and engage in trade—a right unquestioned in West Africa, where the power of the market women is considerable. Two facts suggest the possibility of African influence. First, the feminist movement grew out of the abolitionist movement, with black women abolitionists such as Sojourner Truth taking leading roles. Second, the demand for equal property rights was first met in South Carolina, a black majority area where the retention of African culture was high. One history text states that "South Carolina was one of the few places in the Western World where women had full legal rights of property ownership."[33] It has been suggested that the dominance of women in the markets of the West Indies, another black majority area, resulted from African conceptions of women's roles, which departed from the European norm whereby a women's property is subsumed into family property under the control of the husband. Yet despite their insistence that early African Americans influenced white culture in profound ways, Mintz and Price, who make the suggestion, never seem to have considered the extent to which this same factor differentiates North American and European cultures.[34]

Peter Wood mentioned a few other Africanisms, such as leaving gourds on poles as birdhouses and techniques of alligator wrestling, which are also aspects of white culture in the South.[35] Gourd birdhouses and funerary pottery used by whites in a manner identical with their use by blacks appear in the 1930s photographs by Walker Evans. Other foods, mechanical skills, and similarly useful aspects of culture were introduced or taught to whites by blacks during the early years of North American colonization.

Among types of white Africanisms discovered since the original edition of this chapter are medical practices. The use of weakened smallpox virus for inoculation was the only preventive treatment available before Edward Jenner's discovery that the relatively innocuous disease cowpox also conferred immunity from smallpox in 1796. Cotton Mather recommended use of the weakened smallpox virus after a slave of his from the Gold Coast informed him of its effectiveness. Whites also borrowed other African medical treatments. It is even likely the discovery of the effectiveness of quinine bark in treating malaria was a direct result of the African tradition of interest in herbs as medicines.[36] George Washington later used the inoculation methods introduced from Africa to protect his troops at Valley Forge from smallpox. His continuing inoculation of new recruits gave him an army that was less disabled by smallpox, and which therefore feared disease less, than did his opponents in the British army. Thus this early African influence may have been important or even decisive in the military struggle for American independence.[37]

New Orleans's famous Mardi Gras celebration is another aspect of American culture, white and black, which owes much to Africa. While the movable date of the holiday is determined each year by the beginning of Lent in the ecclesiastical calendar of the Catholic Church, the nature of the celebration in Louisiana more closely resembles that of African-influenced festivals in the Caribbean than it does the celebrations found in France. Indeed, the Mardi Gras celebration in New Orleans, although perhaps most of its participants are white, is part of a complex of pre-Lenten celebrations in the African diaspora that spreads from South America to the United States, most famously in Rio de Janeiro and Trinidad as well as in New Orleans.[38]

Perhaps the most surprising white Africanism yet uncovered is the African cultural heritage of the racist, white supremacist Ku Klux Klan. In retrospect, it is perhaps not so surprising that an organization designed for the social control of blacks should have made use of cultural forms associated with blacks. There is in fact much resemblance in the nature of the activities carried out by the early Klan, especially in immediate post–Civil War days, and the activities of secret societies in West Africa. Local white traditions collected in Pulaski, Tennessee, where the Klan originated, are ignorant of the resemblance, and credit the use of Klan ritual to the accidental discovery that it was effective in awing local blacks. Suggestive of African influence, though, is the fact that the original Klan robes were not the white robes most of us are familiar with from the 1920s Klan, which was heavily influenced by the Hollywood movie, *Birth of a Nation*. The original Klan robes were primarily red, not white, and resembled those of African and Caribbean maskers far more than they did those of European tradition. In 1876 Fanny Kemble recorded a rumor that whites were taking advantage of African superstitions to frighten blacks away from the polls. Clearly, white supremacists after the Civil War were aware of black traditions and exploited them in the regalia of their secret society.[39]

Folklore has been a field where the Herskovits-Frazier debate has been especially loud. Richard Dorson took a pro-Frazier position, arguing that the folktales he collected from blacks in Michigan were more European than African. William Bascom, on the other hand, argued for the Herskovits position, that African diaspora folktales were largely of African origin, and heavily African influenced. Of course they were both right, but they were arguing from different data sets, so, as is so often the case in this Herskovits-Frazier debate, their differences were more apparent than real. Dorson was talking about the African Americans he studied in Michigan while Bascom was talking about the New World as a whole.

More important for this chapter is the question of African folktales among whites. Here Bascom noted that "these African folktales in the United States are not confined to blacks. They are found in collections of Anglo-American, Hispanic-American, Franco-American, and American Indian tales as well." He stated "I believe that it is important, not only for folklorists and Afro-Americans, but for all Americans and for Africans to recognize the African contribution to American folklore."[40]

Literature and popular culture are closely allied to folklore and have been important avenues by means of which African influences have reached out beyond the South to the wider American culture in the North and the West as well. Joel Chandler Harris's retellings of slave folktales familiarized the nation at large with the trickster rabbits of Africa and even specific African motifs, such as the tar baby.[41] Harris's (or more accurately his slave and ex-slave informants') character Brer Rabbit is the direct ancestor of the world-famous cartoon character Bugs Bunny, whose given name "Bugs" also betrays his African ancestry. Mark Twain is probably the single most important American author, and the strong black and therefore indirectly African influence on his techniques has been well documented by Shelley Fisher Fishkin.[42] Another important nineteenth-century American author with recognizable African influences is Herman Melville. *Moby Dick* includes "numerous references to the Yoruba god Legba" and the short story "Benito Cereno" made use of Ashanti drumming and ritual that has been called "evidence of Melville's insight into Ashanti rituals and the shrewd political use his characters made of those traditions." T. S. Elliot was likewise influenced by black and African culture.[43]

Conclusion

Nearly all the African aspects of white culture documented in the first edition of this book were uncovered incidentally during the search for Africanisms among black Americans. With the possible exception of Peter Wood, no scholar seems to have begun his or her investigations with the intention of finding African culture among whites in the United States, at least before this chapter was published. The emphasis was not on the growth of a distinctly American, or perhaps Southern, culture common to both blacks and whites, but on trying to explain the peculiarities of African American culture by means of African retentions, thereby stressing the "otherness" of African American culture, as well as, perhaps incidentally, minimizing the disorganizing effects of slavery on that culture. Had the study of African culture in the United States not been subject to this distortion, an essay such as this one, concerned solely with redressing the balance, would have been unnecessary.

Why these aspects of white American culture had been largely ignored has still not been adequately answered. How they became part of white culture in the first place and then survived should also be a subject of inquiry. Others will undoubtedly suggest other research areas, as some already have, as more and more scholars investigate the subject of "white Africanisms." With the limited knowledge available now I can only suggest possible avenues for early black influence on white American culture, some of the significances that a greater appreciation of the African roots of their culture could hold for white Americans, and some theoretical implications that this aspect of New World Africanisms has for the study of acculturation.

The most obvious situation favoring the transmission of African culture from black to white Americans would be when a light-skinned black crossed the color line and "passed" for white. Many blacks have used this avenue out of the black community, but the fear of exposure often meant that such persons were more careful than many whites to avoid obviously black behavior patterns. Thus, although "passing" has had profound effects on the white population, it is unlikely to have been a major vehicle for the transmission of African culture from blacks to whites.

The next most obvious situation leading to the adoption of African culture by white Americans is one in which blacks are a majority of the population. In such a situation blacks can better retain their own culture and be seen often enough by whites to exercise a discernable influence over their behavior. Such was the case in South Carolina and in Mississippi, where Jimmie Rodgers developed his characteristic "blue yodel" style of singing. This hypothesis would lead one to expect that black majority areas of the West Indies and Latin America would also be good places to look for African cultural survivals among whites.

As Wood pointed out, the frontier situation of early colonial days, when the relationship between master and slave was closer and more personal than it was later, encouraged mutual interchange between blacks and whites.[44] What we now know as American culture was still in the process of formation, and later immigrants, both black and white, were assimilated into a culture that had its origins in the early colonial period. Blacks certainly had opportunities then to contribute African influences to the general speech and cultural patterns of the southern states, and it is to those blacks who were first imported that we must look for the source of the majority of African cultural survivals among both blacks and whites.

For the early years of the intensive slave trade in Virginia, 1710–1769, Curtin recorded that the highest percentage of slaves (37.7 percent) were imported from the Bight of Biafra region of West Africa. In second place was the Gold Coast (16.0 percent) followed closely by Angola (15.7 percent), and Senegambia (14.9 percent). But these data disguise the change of flow with time, since the Senegambian imports seem to have peaked early, in the 1710s. In South Carolina Senegambian slaves were strongly preferred by planters, and accounted for almost one fifth of all imports. These slaves were mostly Malinke and Bambara from the interior who spoke different dialects of the same language and could easily communicate with each other. This language, also spoken by some slaves from Sierra Leone and even the Gold Coast, was often referred to as "Mandingo" in the accounts of the time.[45] The high status and early arrival of these West African slaves, who were often of the Muslim faith, would have combined to help elements of their culture survive, especially in the upper South, which was settled early and which did not have the overwhelming Bantu influence studied by Vass and Holloway.

The important role blacks played in raising the children of the slave owners constitutes another possible avenue for the introduction of African culture to whites. Racist abolitionists attacked what they saw as the strong influence of blacks on the behavior of their masters.[46] Mintz and Price suggested that whites were strongly influenced in their speech patterns, food preferences, and other characteristics by the blacks who raised them,[47] but these authors decided not to follow up their own suggestion. There is no reason for future researchers to ignore the possibilities. Here is an area where the recent emphasis on unconscious, attitudinal, and cosmological retentions might be especially valuable. Attitudes transmitted in this way would be particularly influential, since they would affect members of the ruling class more strongly than others.

The presence of the banjo in Appalachia, a region where few whites owned slaves and where blacks were therefore a small minority, presents special problems, although Gerhard Kubik has recently argued that African influences would find greater general acceptance among whites in areas where blacks were a small minority and therefore would be seen as less of a threat.[48] Robert B. Winans suggested routes the banjo could have taken in reaching the southern Appalachians. He mentioned the role of blacks in building the first railroads in the mountains. The minstrel show craze swept the nation between 1840 and about 1870, Winans also noted, introducing the music of the slaves to the nation at large. He even quoted sources suggesting that the famous minstrel entertainer Dan Emmet learned to play the banjo in western Virginia in 1840 from "a banjo player by the name of Ferguson, who was a very ignorant person, and 'nigger all over' except in color," indicating that at least some whites in the mountains were learning from blacks at an early date.[49]

For the creation of a strong tradition affecting the whole of Appalachian society, though, Winans suggested that the upheaval of the Civil War must have played a decisive role. Rural life was disrupted all over the mountains, throwing formerly isolated people into contact with new influences, including blacks. Soldiers on both sides of the war played banjos, and Winans felt that Appalachian volunteers and refugees took banjos home after the war. Blacks escaping slavery via the underground railway, which largely ran up the western side of the Appalachians, also could have been the contact through which mountain farmers, many of them abolitionists, picked up banjo music.

Finally, the possibility that some blacks had higher status than some whites during an early period of American history cannot be ignored. It is often forgotten that the first blacks came to on America on an equal footing with most whites, as indentured servants rather than as slaves. The house slave of a prominent plantation owner could have been in a much more favored position than a poor, back-country white, and in any case probably lived on a higher material level than the white. Carter G. Woodson, the "father of African American history" and a West Virginian, long ago pointed out that slavery in Appalachia was most often domestic slavery and that there, far from the large plantations of the fertile lowlands, the institution maintained a patriarchal character, marked by greater contact between the races than in other areas.[50]

Daniel Littlefield, in *Rice and Slaves,* showed that Senegambian Africans had the highest status of any black group, largely owing to their rice-growing experience in Africa.[51] More recently Keith Cartwright claimed that "Senegalese were valued as the most intelligent, the most attractive, and the most dependable slaves."[52] Senegambia was not only a rice growing area but more conspicuously a Muslim area long before the eighteenth century, and there may be a tradition of special respect for Muslim blacks among white Americans. Essien-Udom, in his study of the Nation of Islam (the Black Muslims) in the United States, mentioned that an important reason given by many of them for converting to Islam was that whites tended to accord Muslims a greater degree of respect.[53] Research by Douglas Grant showed that the Royal African Company instructed its agents on the Gambia River in 1734 to allow all Muslim captives to be ransomed.[54]

Cecelia Conway has finally made a thorough investigation of the ways in which the banjo spread from blacks to whites in the United States.[55] She noticed the "overlapping regional repertories of blacks and whites"[56] and that black and white banjo playing tends to "overlap in surprising ways" not only in terms of repertories but also in terms of playing techniques.[57] She used detailed comparisons of playing styles and their developments to argue that rather than being transmitted from blacks to minstrels to Appalachian whites, that banjos and the techniques of their playing were transmitted from blacks to southern poor whites directly, separately from the minstrel adoption of the instrument. Her extremely important study is entirely in the spirit of reconciling Herskovits and Frazier that this article argued for. She blends the African survivals of Herskovits with the demographics and cultural interactions of Frazier to show how African culture came to influence whites at least as much as blacks in the south, and gave rise to a distinctively southern culture in the United States.

More recently many other aspects of black American culture that may or may not be of African origin have been eagerly adopted by white Americans: hand-slapping, hair styles, clothing fashions, clothing fashions, handshakes, and much of contemporary black music. A fuller appreciation by whites of their own African cultural backgrounds would probably make them more willing to accept blacks as equals. Some white Americans may oppose racial integration because they think it is something they should do for blacks, that blacks would benefit from the experience of being with whites. The possibility that whites could benefit culturally, indeed have already benefited culturally, from interaction with blacks has never been seriously presented. Pride in their African heritage is something that white children should be taught along with blacks. It could help improve not only black self-images but also white images of blacks, black images of whites, and perhaps even some whites' images of themselves. A new insistence on the African origin of the banjo might even make "hillbilly" music more respectable among whites and blacks alike. Tours of Africa for country and western fans might even become common. And the widespread popularity of country and western music in Africa might no longer seem strange to African Americans.

We are already beginning to develop more complex paradigms to explain African cultural retentions than the old, inadequate formula "African culture plus imperfect adoption of European norms equals African American culture" which never even tried to explain the adoption of African culture by whites. The consequences of culture being transmitted along non-biological routes also needs to be better thought out. In conditions of culture contact in the New World, common aspects of European and African culture tend to reinforce each other. Previously, when the same cultural traits were found among both whites and blacks, scholars often considered them to be European cultural traits among whites but African traits among blacks. It would be better to assume a dual origin for these cultural traits in both cases, and in any case not to make unwarranted assumptions that blacks and whites were necessarily different in culture when empirically they obviously were not.

Scholars trained in European studies have tended to regard many aspects of African American culture as of European origin, while scholars trained in African studies have considered the same traits to be of African origin. Those trained only as Americanists seem to have accepted uncritically whatever they read, or whatever fit their prejudices. A scholar wishing to write the definitive history of African cultural survivals must acquire a triple expertise: as an Americanist, an Africanist, and a Europeanist. Folklorists, who commonly discuss the ways in which European American songs, tales, superstitions, and so on have diverged from those of Europe must take into account the impact of African culture in explaining this divergence. African culture among whites should not be treated as just an addendum to studies of blacks but must be included in the general curriculum of American studies. Black studies must not be allowed to remain segregated from American studies but must be integrated into our understanding of American society, for our understanding of white American society is incomplete without an understanding of the black and African impact on white America.

This means not just considering the implications of the African cultural heritage of white America, it means equally considering the implications of the European cultural heritage of black America. The cultural gap between Africans and African Americans is obvious to anyone who has dealt much with members of both groups. When I was first in Lomé, Togo, I spoke about African Americans to someone who seemed to recognize no personal connection to them, and who asked me what part of Africa these African Americans had come from. When I told him that it was from right here and that the area was once called the "Slave Coast," he was stunned. It was in fact my realization that the behavior of the people in the area was more like that of white southerners than of blacks that led to the writing of this essay.

When I read an earlier version of this chapter at a university in Nigeria, I was taken to task for not realizing that the "real story" was the overwhelming adoption of European culture by blacks in the United States, who are in fact sometimes referred to in Hausa as "black Europeans." The real story, to my mind, is neither the adoption of African culture by whites nor the adoption of African culture by whites, but the creation of a common American culture by both, a culture which has many regional and racial variants and subvariants, all influenced to some extent by Africa as well as by Europe. Just as the African banjo survives most prominently among whites today, so the Welsh custom of jumping the broom survives most prominently among blacks.[38] Just as Herskovits was right that much African culture survives in the United States, so Frazier was right that such cultural survivals are not what distinguishes black from white culture in the United States. We Americans are not so much overseas Europeans or diaspora Africans, or even Asians overseas, or Native Americans, as we are Americans. What we really need to do is not so much to define ourselves as to understand ourselves, which really means understanding each other.

Notes

1. Roy Blount, Jr., *Roy Blount's Book of Southern Humor* (New York: W. W. Norton, 1994), 27.

2. Blount, *Southern Humor*, 29.

3. Winifred Vass, *The Bantu Speaking Heritage of the United States* (Los Angeles: UCLA Center for Afro-American Studies, 1979); see esp. 27–29, 76, 82–86. Dena J. Epstein, "The Folk Banjo: A Documentary History," *Ethnomusicology*, Sept. 1975, reprint 33 (Los Angeles: John Edwards Memorial Foundation, Folklore and Mythology Center, University of Califor-

nia, Los Angeles), and *Sinful Tunes and Spirituals* (Urbana: University of Illinois Press, 1977), 120–22, 147. Epstein suggests that the term *banjo* derived from the Kimbundu term *mbanza*. Her noting of such terms as *bangelo* and *banjil* from farther north in Africa, as well as the term *banjar* noted by Jefferson and others in eighteenth-century America suggests that the common Appalachian pronunciation *banjar* is the result of an /l/ to /r/ sound shift rather than the intrusive /r/ sound of southern Appalachian dialect.

4. Peter H. Wood, *Black Majority* (New York: Knopf, 1974). Melville J. Herskovits, "What Has Africa Given America?" *New Republic* (1935) 84 (1083): 92–94; reprinted in *The New World Negro*, ed. Frances S. Herskovits (Bloomington: Indiana University Press, 1966), 168–74.

5. William D. Piersen, *Black Legacy: America's Hidden Heritage* (Amherst: University of Massachusetts Press, 1993), 156–57, has once again brought the dispersal of the black population among whites to the attention of scholars, thus following the lead of the first edition of this book in reconciling the perspectives of Herskovits and Frazier.

6. Alan Dundes also made this point in discussing the Dorson-Bascom debate over African influence in African American folklore (*vide infra*). "In some ways the argument resulted from the two protagonists talking past one another." In his foreword to William Bascom, *African Folktales in the New World* (Bloomington: Indiana University Press, 1992), xi–xii.

7. Roger D. Abrahams and John F. Szwed, introduction to *After Africa* (New Haven, Conn.: Yale University Press, 1983), 4–6.

8. Melville J. Herskovits, "What Has Africa Given America?"

9. John A. Davis, "The Influence of Africans on American Culture," *Annals of the American Academy of Political and Social Science* no. 354 (July 1964), 79.

10. C. Vann Woodward, "Clio with Soul," *Journal of American History* 56(1) (June 1969):17.

11. Joel Williamson, *The Crucible of Race* (New York, Oxford: Oxford University Press, 1984), 38.

12. D. K. Wilgus, Professor of Folklore and Mythology, and J. K. Nketia, Professor of Music, University of California, Los Angeles, personal communications.

13. Alan Jabbour, liner notes, *The Hammons Family* record album (Washington, D.C.: Library of Congress, 1973), 25.

14. Samuel Charters, *The Roots of the Blues: An African Search* (Boston: Marion Boyars, 1981), 122, 126.

15. W. H. Tallmadge, "The Black in Jackson's White Spirituals," *Black Perspectives in Music* 9(2) (Fall 1981):139–60.

16. Gerhard Kubik, *Africa and the Blues* (Jackson: University Press of Mississippi, 1999), 12–16.

17. Nolan Porterfield, *Jimmie Rodgers* (Urbana: University of Illinois Press, 1979), mentions that many Swiss yodelers toured the United States but fails to consider whether the popularity of European yodeling in the United States had been influenced by earlier exposure to black yodeling. For falsetto leaps by Jimmie Martin listen to, among other songs, "The Sunny Side of the Mountain" on the album *Will the Circle Be Unbroken?*

18. J. R. Washington, *Black Sects and Cults* (Garden City, N.Y.: Anchor, 1973), pp. 61, 65, 67, 71–72.

19. James S. Tinney, "William Joseph Seymour: 'Father' of 60 Million Pentecostals," paper presented to the Annual Convention of the Association for the Study of Afro-American Life and History, Philadelphia, 1981.

20. Piersen, *Black Legacy*, 172–76.

21. Jane C. Beck, "The West Indian Supernatural World: Belief Integration in a Pluralistic Society," *Journal of American Folklore* 88(349) (July–Sept. 1975):235–44.

22. Piersen, *Black Legacy*, 162–70, 178–79.

23. Wood, *Black Majority*, 119–24.

24. The comments on deep fat frying and nut soups are by Helen Mendes, *The African Heritage Cookbook* (New York: Macmillan, 1971), pp. 74, 78. For further information on African cooking traditions found among both blacks and whites, see also pp. 35–36, 79, and 83–84.

25. Wood, *Black Majority*, 29–31.

26. The problem of the origins of Texas longhorns is complicated by several facts. Among these is the fact that the feral cattle of the Great Plains from which they descended were a considerably mixed breed. Even cattle from the Canary Islands found their way into Mexico and Texas. See J. Frank Dobie, "Longhorn," *Encyclopedia Brittanica* 14 (1970), pp. 299–300.

   Furthermore, the modern breed known as "Texas Longhorns" have only a tenuous relation to the original feral cattle of the plains. In addition, African cattle are genetically quite closer to European cattle than to Asian, and Spanish cattle are closer to North and West African cattle than they are to French. For genetic studies of cattle, see R. T. Loftus et al., "Mitochondrial genetic variation in European, African and Indian cattle populations," *Animal Genetics* 25 (1994), pp. 265–71, and Ruedi Fries et al., "The bovine genome map," *Mammalian Genome* 4 (1993), pp. 405–28. For a brief introduction to the history of Texas Longhorns, see the International Texas Longhorn Association website at http://www.itla.com/LonghornHistory.htm.

27. David Dalby, "The African Element in Black American English," in Thomas Kochman, ed. *Rappin' and Stylin' Out* (Urbana: University of Illinois Press, 1972), pp. 170–86. As with so much research in the field of Africanisms, although Dalby's essay is addressed to the question of African cultural survivals in African American culture, most of the data are as relevant to whites as to blacks.

28. Roger D. Abrahams, "Rapping and Capping: Black Talk as Art," in John F. Szwed, ed., *Black America* (New York: Basic Books, 1970).

29. William A. Stewart, "More on Black-White Speech Relationships," *Florida FL Reporter* (Spring–Fall 1973), p. 38. J. L. Dillard, *Black English: Its History and Usage in the United States* (New York: Vintage, 1973), is still the best study of African American speech patterns. Dillard maintains that "it has long been recognized that certain forms of Southern White speech have been influenced by the Negro" and that "unreasonable conditions have been placed upon . . . investigators who have wanted seriously to evaluate the African (or Black American) contribution to American English," pp. 217–18. For further information on the relations between black and white speech in the southern United States, see Ernest F. Dunn, "The Black-Southern White Dialect Controversy: Who Did What to Whom?" in *Black English: A Seminar*, D. T. Harris and T. Trabasso, eds. (Hillsdale, N.J.: Lawrence Earlbaum Associates, 1976); Joy L. Miller, "Be Finite and Absence: Features of Speech—Black and White?" *Orbis* 21(1) (1972):22–27; and R. I. McDavid and V. G. McDavid, "The Relationship of the Speech of American Negroes to the Speech of Whites," *American Speech* 26(1) (Feb. 1951):3–17.

30. Walt Wolfram, "The Relationship of White Southern Speech to Vernacular Black English," *Language* (Sept. 1974), pp. 498–527.

31. Keith Cartwright, *Reading Africa into American Literature* (Lexington; University Press of Kentucky, 2002), p. 135.

32. J. L. Dillard, *A History of American English (Longman Linguistics Library)* (London, New York: Longman, 1993), p. 94.

33. Forrest McDonald, Leslie E. Decker, and Thomas P. Govan, *The Last Best Hope: A History of the United States* (Reading, Mass.: Addison-Wesley, 1972), p. 89.

34. Sidney W. Mintz and Richard Price, *An Anthropological Approach to the Afro-American Past: A Caribbean Perspective*, Occasional Papers in Social Change, no. 2, Institute for the Study of Human Issues, Philadelphia, 1976, 16.

35. Wood, *Black Majority*, pp. 119–24.

36. Piersen, *Black Legacy*, pp. 101–104.

37. Garance Franke-Ruta, "George Washington's Bioterrorism Strategy: How we handled it last time," *The Washington Monthly Online* (Dec. 2001), http://www.washingtonmonthly.com/features/2001/0112.franke-ruta.html.

38. Piersen, *Black Legacy*, chap. 6, "The Hidden Heritage of Mardi Gras."

39. Piersen, *Black Legacy*, chap. 7, "The Mixed Bloodlines of the Ku Klux Klan."

40. "Preface" to *African Folktales in the New World*, pp. xxiv, xxv.

41. Cartwright, *Reading Africa into American Literature*, p. 129.

42. *Was Huck Black? Mark Twain and African American Voices* (Oxford: Oxford University Press, 1999).

43. Shelley Fisher Fishkin, "Reclaiming the Black Presence in Mainstream Culture," in Sheila S. Walker, ed., *American Roots / American Cultures* (Oxford: Rowman & Littlefield, 2001), p. 82.

44. Wood, *Black Majority*, pp. 53–55.

45. Philip D. Curtin, *The Atlantic Slave Trade: A Census* (Madison: University of Wisconsin Press, 1969), pp. 157 table 45, 223, 156–57, 184–85.

46. Hinton Rowan Helper, *The Impending Crisis of the South: How to Meet It* (New York: Burdick Brothers, 1857).

47. Mintz and Price, *Anthropological Approach*, p. 1.

48. Kubik, *African and the Blues*, pp. 15–16.

49. Robert B. Winans, "The Folk, the Stage, and the Five-String Banjo in the Nineteenth Century," *Journal of American Folklore* 34(354) (1976):407–37.

50. Carter G. Woodson, "Freedom and Slavery in Appalachian America," *Journal of Negro History* 1(2) (1916).

51. Daniel Littlefield, *Rice and Slaves: Ethnicity and the Slave Trade in the Colonial South Carolina* (Baton Rouge: Louisiana State University Press, 1981).

52. *Reading Africa into American Literature*, p. 205.

53. E. U. Essien-Udom, *Black Nationalism* (Chicago: University of Chicago Press, 1962), pp. 116–18.

54. Douglas Grant, *The Fortunate Slave* (London: Oxford University Press, 1968), pp. 110, 144.

55. *African Banjo Echoes in Appalachia* (Knoxville: University of Tennessee Press, 1995).

56. *African Banjo Echoes*, p. 23.

57. *African Banjo Echoes*, p. 120.

58. Alan Dundes, "'Jumping the Broom': On the Origin and Meaning of an African-American Wedding Custom," *Journal of American Folklore* 109(433) (Summer 1996).

Fourteen

The African Character of African American Language
Insights from the Creole Connection

Selase W. Williams

Introduction

The language of the African American community is an enigma to most Americans, regardless of their ethnic or racial background. Is it a dialect of English? Is it a collection of slang terms created by black adolescents? Or, is it something else? Those who come in frequent contact with the language know that it differs significantly from what is referred to as Standard American English (SAE); yet, there are many English elements in it. Where does African American Language (AAL), often called Ebonics,[1] fit in the history of human languages?

This chapter will present convincing evidence that AAL has a form and structure like any other language. It will be demonstrated that those features and structures that make AAL different from SAE closely resemble or are identical to features found in African languages and are typically not found in European languages.

Languages are rule-governed, meaning that the speakers of a given language have agreed to use a particular inventory of sounds, a particular set of pronunciation patterns, a particular set of rules for making words out of sounds, and another set of rules for combining words and other meaning-bearing units of sounds to create sentences. The rules of the French language are different from the rules of the Hausa language, even though many similarities may be found between both systems of rules. It is the collective set of rules, sounds, and features that constitute a language. Only through the sharing of a commonly agreed upon set of "rules" can individuals communicate with each other.

397

The large majority of the vocabulary items found in AAL are of English origin, leading most people to conclude that AAL is just an aberrant or distorted dialect of English. What many people do not realize is that a language is comprised of much more than its vocabulary. In view of the fact that the unique characteristics of AAL are immediately associated with African Americans, one should logically conclude that AAL is an "African" language rather than a European language. Instead, AAL is usually thought of as bastardized English.

The history of the people who speak AAL and the general attitude of European peoples toward them are informative. For centuries, from 1518 to 1880, individuals, families, and, in some cases, whole villages of African people were taken captive by slave marauders, in service of an expanding European capitalist enterprise. In spite of the fact that these African languages were used to build the great civilizations of the continent, allowing the people to conceptualize in highly abstract and scientific terms, once the villages had been plundered, hundreds, thousands, and then millions enslaved, and the local authorities overthrown, the languages of the African peoples were denigrated and characterized as "mumbo-jumbo." How African languages spoken by the people who developed the most highly developed civilizations in the world went from being revered to being reviled is the topic for another book.

The efforts of the enslaved Africans to communicate with their captors was described by writers of the time as bastardized forms of the colonial language. It was generally thought by the colonists that the lips of the Africans were too thick, the noses too broad, and the brains too small to articulate well the King's English or the prestige forms of French, Spanish, Portuguese, or Dutch. Characterizations of this kind, along with the determination that Africans were uncivilized heathens, placed on the earth only for a more superior race of people to make use of them, were necessary for the colonists to justify their cruel, inhumane, maniacal treatment of other human beings. These views prevailed for so long that it became a part of the European psyche.

Given the psychological posture of Europeans in relation to their black brothers and sisters, along with the vicious and brutal methods used to strip the enslaved Africans of everything they possessed and valued, it is not surprising that many writers since that time, including well-respected scholars, have denied the "African character" of the language of the black community in America. In fact, many scholars and educators,[2] even today, believe that most, if not all vestiges of African cultural heritage were destroyed by slavery. While there is little doubt about the brutal physical treatment of enslaved Africans or the dehumanizing effects rendered by the enslavers, the impact of this on the culture of the enslaved Africans has been grossly overstated. One's culture is more than the material artifacts and exact replications of traditional practices. One's culture is also the set of learned behaviors, beliefs, values, and worldview that express a particular humanity and group identity. These, often invisible, cultural components are passed on from generation to generation. It is also important to realize that all humans have the capacity to modify their culture to adapt to changes in their physical and/or social environment. One need only review the historical record of any group to come to this conclusion.

Similarly, it has been assumed that, by refusing to allow the enslaved Africans in America to use their African languages in the presence of whites and black overseers, the languages would simply disappear. Language, however, is that set of internalized, subconscious rules and muscle habits that can not easily be eradicated. Try as one might to speak a different language, especially if no formal training is provided to teach the rules of that language, the pronunciation patterns and grammatical structures of one's first language will prevail. It will be argued in this chapter that some of the most characteristic features of West African languages have been preserved in AAL.

African Languages and Their Relationship to History and Other Languages

On the continent of Africa there are over one thousand languages, some of which are as different from each other as Spanish is from German. However, as is the case in Europe and elsewhere in the world, there exist language families in Africa. Languages which belong to the same family have historical connections with each other, all having developed from a common ancestral language and all having a number of characteristics that have systematic correspondences with each other. These systematic correspondences can be found in the vocabulary, in the pronunciation rules, or in the grammatical structure of the languages. Some examples of systematic linguistic correspondences reveal the kind of evidence that supports membership in the same language family and, by extension, a historical connection.

The following examples demonstrate the German t/d correspondence with the voiced th [ð] in English; the German ch [velar fricative] correspondence with English [k]; the German [b] correspondence with the English [v]; and the Germanic ablaut, the rule that requires a change in the quality of the vowel in the verb to reflect a change in tense/aspect:

German	English
Muter	mother
Vater	father
Bruder	brother
Das	that
Diese	these
Buch	book
Bach	Bach [pronounced with a k sound]
Kuchen	cook
Haben	have
Geben	give
Singen, sangen, gesungen	sing, sang, sung
Bringen, brangen, gebracht	bring, brang, brought

Primary membership in one language family does not necessarily preclude membership in another language family. For instance, although English is clearly in the Germanic Language Family, it is also a more distant relative in the Romance Language Family, cousins, if you will, of the larger Indo-European Family, as the systematic similiarities in the following examples show:

Spanish	French	English
uno	un	one
dos	deux	two
tres	trois	three
ses	sise	six
nueve	neuf	nine

Americans in general know little about the multiplicity of African languages and the composition of African language families. Nor is it commonly known that, in spite of the substantial linguistic diversity found among African languages, there exist numerous commonalities within African language families. One of the most important language families in Africa is the Niger-Congo Family.[3] It is comprised of languages that span much of West and Central Africa, the areas from which the overwhelming majority of enslaved Africans in America came. Subira Kifano and Ernie Smith (2000)[4] identified some of the most prominent characteristics of Niger-Congo that have been described by prominent scholars of African languages (e.g., Peter Ladefoged,[5] William Welmers,[6] Victoria Fromkin[7]). Below are listed a number of these characteristics:

Some General Characteristics of Niger-Congo Languages

1. Consonant-Vowel—Consonant-Vowel Shape of Niger-Congo Words

One of the most pervasive characteristics of the phonological system of languages that belong to the Niger-Congo Family is the restriction on the canonical shape of words resulting in a (consonant) vowel . . . consonant-vowel (C)V . . . CV pattern. While there are, of course, exceptions within the family and while almost every language finds some words that end in a consonant, the undeniable majority of the words in all of these languages follow this general pattern and end in a vowel. This can easily be observed, as seen in the examples below:

Personal Names[8]
Ayodele, Joko, Selase, Modupe, Ama, Kwaku, Fumika, Isa, Kofi

Commonly Used Verbs

Wolof	Twi	Hausa	Swahili	
sEtsi	Ba	zo	ja	"come"
lEka	Di	chi	la	"eat"
dafa	kO	tafi	enda	"go"
tEda	da	kwana	usingizi	"sleep"

Even the names of the languages themselves demonstrate this characteristic:

Bambara, Igbo, Fante, Bantu, Ewe, Kikongo, Kpelle, Mende, Twi, Hausa, Swahili

2. Restrictions on Consonant Clusters, Especially in Word-Final Position

Consistent with the ideal word form being (C)V . . . CV is the restriction against consonant clusters (a sequence of two or more consonants) at the end of words. Consonant clusters may be found in word-medial position, but typically only as a sequence of a nasal consonant [n, m, ŋ] followed by a voiced or voiceless stop consonant. Consequently, while we may find words in Niger-Congo languages, like <u>kamfo</u> (Twi) "pray" and <u>kuenda</u> (Swahili) "to go," we do not find words like *kamf or *kuend.

It should be noted that even Wolof, a language of the Senegambia, and one which contains a large number of words that end in consonantal sounds, does not countenance word-final consonant clusters. Some Wolof examples follow:

<u>lal</u> "bed"	<u>lak</u> "to burn"	<u>xarit</u> "friend"	<u>fas</u> "horse"	<u>wax</u> "to talk"
<u>gor</u> "noble man"	<u>dof</u> "mad"	<u>xalis</u> "money"	<u>dEk</u> "city"	<u>kEr</u> "house"

3. Absence of Particular Sounds in the Phonetic Inventory of Niger-Congo Languages

Fromkin and Rodman (1975)[9] point out that while English and Twi have many vowels and consonants in common (as do many languages across language families), absent from the Twi inventory are $\underline{z}$, $\underline{v}$, $\underline{l}$, and the voiced and voiceless <u>th-sounds</u> ([ð] and [θ], respectively) found in English. While English contains voiced and voiceless pairs of the over-whelming majority of its non-nasal consonants, we find that Hausa has [f], but not [v] and [sh], but not [zh] and Yoruba has [f], but not [v] and [j], but not [ch] and neither [sh] nor [zh]. The absence of the voiced and voiceless th-sounds is not exclusively a feature of Twi. In fact, it is a general feature of Niger-Congo languages. The th-sounds are also absent from Wolof, Hausa, and Yoruba.

4. Pre-Verbal Tense/Aspect Markers with Constant Verb Form

One prominent morpho-syntactic feature of many Niger-Congo languages is the occurrence of tense and/or aspect markers that appear immediately in front of an unchanging verb. This phenomena is observed in Swahili as a legitimate representative of the Bantu language group of East and Central Africa. Some might argue that the markers are affixes in a larger verbal complex. The author of this chapter is not aware of any research that has demonstrated the psychological reality of a verbal complex, as opposed to separate word status for the tense/aspect markers. Look at the following examples from Swahili:

Swahili Examples

Ni	<u>na</u>	kwenda	nyumbani.
(I	Pres.	go	to-house)
"I	am	going	home."

Ni	li	kwenda	nyumbani
(I	Past	go	to-house)
"I	went		home."

Ni	ta	kwenda	nyumbani
(I	Future	go	to-house)
"I	am going	to go	home."

Ni	me	kwenda	nyumbani
(I	Completed	go	to-house)
"I	have gone		home."

Turning to a language spoken in Ghana, in West Africa, across the continent from the Swahili speaking area, we find even clearer demonstration of this pervasive characteristic in Niger-Congo. Twi[10] is the language of the Ashanti people and a member of the Kwa languages, a genetic language family that is represented by numerous languages from Nigeria to Sierra Leone. Notice how productive the Tense/Aspect Marker + Verb pattern is.

Twi Examples

Present Continuous—re

Mo	re	kO	he?
(you	Pres. Contin.	Go	where)
"Where are you going?"			

Yε	re	kO	kurom
(We	Pres. Contin.	Go	town)
"We are going to town."			

Me	adamfo	no	re	sua	Twi	wO	Legon.
(My	friend	he/she	Pres. Contin.	study	Twi	Location	Legon)
"My friend is studying Twi at Legon."							

Simple Future—bε

Mo	bε	kO	kurom.
(You-pl.	Simple Future	go	town)
"You (pl) are going to go to town."			

WO	bε	kO	kurom.
(You-Sg.	Simple Future	go	town)
"You are going to go to town."			

Me   b&   kO   kurom.
(I   Simple Future   go   town)
"I am going to go to town."

Me   na   b&   tO   ntama   ame   me.
(My   mother   Simple Future   buy   clothes   for   me)
"My mother is going to buy clothes for me."

Immediate Future—reb&

Me   reb&   tO   aduan.
(I   Immed. Future   buy   food.)
"I am getting ready to buy some food (right now)."

YE   reb&   kO   kurom   seesei
(We   Immed. Future   go   town   right now)
"We are going to go to town right now.)

Perfect—a

Abofra   no   a   kO   sukuu.
(Child   he/she   Perfect   go   school)
"The child has gone to school."

Me   a   di.
(I   Perfect   eat)
"I have already eaten."

Present/Habitual—#

Mmofra   no   #   to   dwuom   wO   fie
(Children   they   Pres.   sing   song   Location   home)
"The children sing songs at home."

Me   #   to   dwuom   wO   fie
(I   Pres.   sing   song   Location   home)
"I sing songs at home."

Me   yere   #   horo   ntaade   wO   aguaree
(My   wife   Pres.   wash   clothes   Location   bathroom)
"My wife washes clothes in the bathroom."

5. Existence of Adjective Verbs

Many African languages express "adjectival" concepts through words that behave like stative verbs in the language. For instance, Twi language possesses words like brE "get tired," ntam "be friendly," and yare "to be sick/ill/." When they appear in a sentence, they function like other verbs in the language:

Me	a	brɛ. [In normal pronunciation becomes <u>ma brɛ</u>.]
(I	Perfect	get-tired)

"I am tired."

Yen	#	ntam	wo
(We	Hab.	Be-friendly	to-you)

"We are friendly."

Similarly, Wolof[11] possesses adjectival verbs like <u>sonn</u> "be tired," <u>xiif</u> "be hungry," and <u>rɛy</u> "be big." When the subject of the sentence is a pronoun, it comes at the end of the sentence and the verb is followed by a marker of completion. Alternatively, the verb may simply be followed by the emphatic form of the pronoun. Observe the following examples:

Sonn	na	nu
(tired	Compl.	we)

"We are tired."

Sonn	nga.
(tired	Emph. you)

"*You* are tired."

If the subject is a noun, rather than a pronoun, then, the noun appears first, followed by the verb, which, in turn, is followed by the completion marker, as is the case below:

Sama	jɛkkɛr	xiif	na.
(My	husband	hungry	Compl.)

"My husband is hungry."

Xale	rɛy	na.
(Child	big	Compl.)

"The child is big."

6. Absence of a Copula Verb

Consistent with the sentence type that arises from the presence of adjectival verbs are sentences which require a copula verb in English ("to be"), but which depend merely on word collocation in languages like Wolof. What follows are examples of predicate locative and predicate nominal sentences in Wolof:

Maa   ngi
(I   here)
"I am here." or "Here I am."

Nu   ngi
(We   here)
"We are here." or "Here we are."

Man   Wolof   la
(I-Emph. Wolof   Emph. Pred.)
"I am Wolof."

Man   la
(I-Emph. Emph. Pred.)
"It is me."

Moom   la
(He-Emph. Emph. Pred.)
"It is him."

African American Language Features

Until one demonstrates the systematic nature of AAL features and reveals the systematic relationships between AAL and Niger-Congo, the majority of Americans will continue to think of AAL as an erratic set of slang expressions and ungrammatical utterances, disconnected from the historical development of African global communication. Fortunately, however, the evidence is bountiful and can be found in the major linguistic components, the Vocabulary and Semantic System, the Sound System, and the Grammar or Syntactic Structure.

Vocabulary / Lexicon of AAL

The study of the lexicon of African American Language began formally in 1949 with the publication of Lorenzo Dow Turner's Africanisms in the Gullah Dialect.[12] Gullah, or Geechee, has been considered to be one of the most conservative forms of AAL, due largely to the isolation of those who spoke it on the islands off the coast of Georgia and South Carolina, as well as on the mainland adjacent to them. Turner found thousands of words of direct African origin still being used by the Gullah speakers. The name of the language itself probably refers to a language spoken in modern day Liberia, the Gola Language, or to the country, Angola. Geechee is thought to be a derivative of Kisi, a language also spoken in Sierra Leone and Liberia, but some sources suggests a Bantu origin.

Turner's investigation revealed words in common use in Gullah from more than two dozen African languages. Prominent among those languages were Wolof, Malinke, Mandinka, Bambara, Fula, Mende, Vai, Twi, Fante, Ga, Ewe, Fon, Yoruba, Bini, Yoruba, Hausa, Igbo, Ibibio, Efik, Kongo, Umbundu, and Kimbundu. The native homes of these languages are the African countries running from Senegal to Angola, the very places, from which there is clear documentation that Africans were stolen into slavery.

Over three thousand of the words recorded in Turner's research are personal names. As he observes, most African names carry particular meanings. For instance, in the Akan languages, everyone is given a day-name. Among the Twi, a boy-child born on Friday is called "Kofi." A girl-child born on Tuesday is called "Abena." Other names characterize the conditions under which a child was born or the season of the year, the clan name, the name of a protective deity, or a name that indicates the order in which a child was born in relation to other siblings. And, of course, some names are given as nicknames to describe a person's temperament, physical attributes, or particular interests.

An exemplary, but clearly not an exhaustive list of African names found in Gullah that have persisted into contemporary AAL are the following:

Ada	<	Adekunle or Adebisi (Yoruba) "The crown fills the house" or "My coming causes an increase"
Addy	<	
Anika	<	Anyika (Vai) "She is very beautiful."
Nikki	<	
Bebe	<	Bibi (Yoruba) "Begotten"
Bibi	<	
Cece	<	SEsi (Ewe) "Well, strong"
Coffee	<	Kofi (Twi/Ewe/Ga/Fante) "Boy born on Friday"
Cuffee	<	
Ola	<	Olabisi (Yoruba) "Honors increase"
Nana	<	Nyanya (Yoruba) "Female deity"
	<	Nyanya (Twi) "Grandparent"

Nina	<	Nina (Mende) "New"
	<	Nina (Bambara) "A gift"
Puki	<	Mpuku (Konge/Tsiluba) "Field mouse"
Sambo	<	Sambo (Mende/Vai) "To disgrace or be ashamed"

It is common knowledge to students of the African American experience that the enslaved Africans were forced to give up their indigenous names over time. However, names continue to be very important to African Americans.

One of the outcomes of the black cultural revolution which began in the 1960s was a revival of traditional African naming practices among some African Americans. In many cases, the parents did extensive research before assigning such names to make sure that the names assigned to their children were appropriate for them. In other cases the name was selected solely because it was clearly "African." Common among these names are the following:

Female	Male
Aisha	Akili
Karimu	Kwaku
Nubia	Kamau
Kenya	Kwame
Imani	Jamal

While most of the readily identifiable "black," or African American, names do not carry meaning, like those found in indigenous African names, they continue to carry a potent message. It is an act of conscious or unconscious pride, and sometimes defiance, that African Americans give their children unusual names to distinguish them from their Anglo-American counterparts, as if to announce, "I am still an African person with an African identity." Examples of these names are listed below:

Female	Male
Lakisha	Tremaine
Shamika	Sheron
Shanita	Jermaine
LaShandra	Fabion
Quishana	DuWayne

Talamika	Larron
Shanikwa	Mizell
Keisha	Kendrae
Latoya	Davion
Latanya	Trevon
Keniqua	Tyrone
Rashandra	Darnell

The reader should notice that the female names conform to the ideal canonical shape of Niger-Congo words (CV . . . CV). Male names, on the other hand, tend to end in a nasal or liquid consonant (n or l). Thus, the African American naming system is one which, phonologically, distinguishes individuals based on gender. Further study of this phenomena is clearly warranted. Proof of the almost universal recognition of these names as "black" or "African American" comes from research conducted by Marianne Bertrand and Sendhil Mullainathan, University of Chicago and MIT economists. Their research, which attempted to uncover discrimination in the workplace, found that "resumes with 'White-sounding' names—like Jay, Brad, Carrie and Kristen—were 50 percent more likely than those with 'Black-sounding' names [like Aisha, Latonya, Rasheed, and Jermaine] to receive a callback."[13]

Those resumes submitted by women with "black" names were rejected at a higher rate than those submitted by men with "black" names. This was the case, regardless of the strength of the women's resumes or the zip codes of the neighborhoods in which they lived. To what degree does the greater conformity of African American women's names to traditional African phonological principals contribute to the higher level of discrimination found against African American women in this study? Whatever the answer to this question might be, the research findings are independent verification of the fact that Americans recognize African American naming practices as different from those of White Americans.

The fact that AAL possesses a vocabulary that is unique to it is well documented. As John and Russell Rickford point out in their book, *Spoken Soul* (2002),[14] a number of dictionaries and lexicons of AAL have been produced in the last few decades to complement the work of Lorenzo Turner and other earlier writers. J. L. Dillard's *Lexicon of Black English* (1977)[15] is now a classic work in the field, and Joseph E. Holloway and Winifred K. Vass, *The African Heritage of American English* (1993) is an important contribution that builds on Lorenzo Dow Turner's and Vass's previous scholarship joined by Geneva Smitherman's *Black Talk: Words and Phrases from the Hood to the Amen Corner* (1994).[16] In the same year that *Black Talk* was published, Clarence Major published a revision of his earlier work which now appears as *Juba to Jive: A Dictionary of African American Slang* (1994).[17] While these sources document the rich and creative word variety in the African American community, only a few of these words are attributed to African source languages. David Dalby (1969)[18] was one of the few scholars to boldly argue for the African origins of many unique vocabulary items in AAL, some of which have been absorbed into mainstream American English.

Dalby provides evidence that a number of words emanated from a specific West African language, Wolof. Rather than one or two isolated words, here we are presented with a cluster of words which can all, fairly neatly, be traced back to Wolof words with similar pronunciations and consistent meanings. It is highly unlikely that these are mere coincidences. Additional support for these etymologies comes from the fact that Wolof is one of the major languages spoken in the Senegambia, one of the geographical regions of Africa closest to North America. While these words may have entered into African American language at different times, Dalby proposes that several of them became popularized during the "jazz era." However, only a subset of these words have a direct connection with music. Observe these words and their African antecedents:

Wolof Form	*African American / American Form*
dega "to understand"	dig (as in "Can you dig it?")
gay "fellows, guys"	guy(s)
jev "to talk disparagingly"	jive (misleading talk)
hipi "to open one's eyes"	hip or hep (to know what is going on)
kat "a person who . . . "	cat (as in "hip cat"—Wolof hipi-kat "person who knows what's going on")
hong "red, pink"	honkie (whites are commonly referred to as "red" men in African languages. Note the AAL term "red-neck.")
fass/fuss "range horse"	fuzz (in reference to the police. Note that the runaways were chased down by "police" on horseback.)
waw "yes" + kay "emphatic"	okay (alright/certainly)
jam "slave"	jam (as in "jam session")

The discovery of a set of words originating from one African language does not suggest that this language was the sole contributor of African vocabulary to AAL, only that we can expect to find clusters of words from other languages with equally clear connections.

The African Character of African American Language

411

Winifred Vass points out in her book, *The Bantu Speaking Heritage of the United States* (1979),[19] that roughly 59 percent of all enslaved Africans in North America had their provenience in West Africa, while 41 percent came from Central and Southern Africa. Therefore, in addition to AAL vocabulary which can be traced to West African languages, we should expect to find a substantial number of terms that have their origins in the languages of Central and Southern Africa. Vass identifies a number of Bantu place names and a variety of words of Bantu origin largely found in songs, folktales, and narratives.

In Lorenzo Dow Turner's trailblazing research, we find words of African origin in Gullah that come from Central and Southern Africa, as well as from West Africa. Notice that the words selected below also found their way into the mainstream of American English:

Source Language	Gullah Form	American English Form
Kimbundu—nguba "peanut"	guba	goobers
Mandingo—yambi "wild yam"	yam "sweet potato"	yam
Kikongo—tota "pick up"	tot "carry"	tote
Mende—sasi "treat w/contempt"	sasi "ridicule"	sassy
Bambara—kunu "boat"	kunu "boat"	canoe
Fon/Ewe—vodu "spirit/demon"	wudu "witchcraft"	voodoo
Umbundu—ochingɔmbo "okra"	gumbo "okra"	gumbo "okra stew"
Wolof—jiga "insect"	jiga "insect/flea"	jigger

Examples of words that made their way from African sources into Gullah and, then, into AAL, without becoming adopted more broadly are the following:

Source Language	Gullah Form	American English Form
Arabic—shaut "move around the Kaaba until exhausted"	shout "ring dance"	shout "get the holy spirit"
Efik—mbakara "White man"	buckra	buckra

This brief introduction to the vocabulary of AAL barely scratches the surface. More extensive research in this area would be fruitful for those researchers who are willing to commit themselves to the study of the relevant African languages as well as the regional variants of American English.

Pronunciation Patterns/Phonological Rules in AAL

In earlier pages of this paper it was pointed out that one of the most pervasive characteristics of Niger-Congo words is the Consonant-Vowel (. . . Consonant-Vowel) pattern. While AAL does not possess the same phonological constraints that exist for words and morphemes in Niger-Congo, it does possess a set of rules that conspire to get closer to the ideal African word form than the typical English (or Germanic) word forms. One rule restricts the pronunciation of the retroflex liquid consonant [r] after a vowel, especially at the end of a word. The following examples demonstrate the operation of this constraint in word-medial position:

Word	In SAE		In AAL
Paris	[pɛrIs]	>	[pɛIs] or [pɑs] (pronounced like "pass")
furnace	[fʌrnIs]	>	[fʌnIs] (pronounced like "funess")
garbage	[garbIj]	>	[gabIj] (pronounced like "gobbidge")
fork	[fork]	>	[fok] (pronounced like "folk")
pork	[pork]	>	[pok] (pronounced like "poke")

Although this AAL restriction is highly stigmatized by speakers of SAE, it has not prevented the rule from continuing to operate when African Americans are gathered together for social or ceremonial purposes. It is heard more frequently in rural and southern regions of the country, but is not a stranger to the urban north.

When the restriction operates on a Vowel + [r] sequence at the end of a word, the result is a word that ends in a vowel sound, leaving the word with the more ideal African word form of CVCV. Not only is this phonological feature pervasive across black America, it has been adopted by many white pop vocalists who are trying to give their music a "soulful" sound. Observe the examples of the restriction against post-vocalic [r] at the end of a word:

mother	[mʌðʌr]	>	[mʌðʌ] (pronounced like "mutha")
brother	[brʌðʌr]	>	[brʌðʌ] (pronounced like "brutha")
player	[pleyʌr]	>	[pleyʌ] (pronounced like "playa")
sister	[sIstʌr]	>	[sIst ʌ] (pronounced like "sista")
after	[ɑftʌr]	>	[ɑftʌ] (pronounced like "afta")
together	[tʌgeðʌr]	>	[tʌgeðʌ] (pronounced like "tagetha")

This phonological principle that restricts the occurrence of post-vocalic [r] in AAL is very powerful, or generalizable, meaning that it applies

wherever those conditions are met. In other words, the "African" character of AAL is strongly preserved.

Another phonological rule, with very much the same intention as
the Post-Vocalic R Rule, that being to maintain a pattern as close to
CVCVCV as possible, is the Word-Final Consonant Cluster Rule. This
rule prevents the occurrence of more than one consonant at the end of
a word. SAE, by contrast, does not possess such a rule. SAE easily accepts clusters of two or three consonants at the end of words. In fact,
some such clusters are created when a suffix indicating "past tense" is
added to a verb which already possesses one or more word-final consonants. Look, first, at a set of basic words and, then, at some which are
inflected for past tense:

Word	In SAE		In AAL
soft	[sɔft]	>	[sɔf] (pronounced like "soff")
left	[lɛft]	>	[lɛf] (pronounced like "leff")
past	[paest]	>	[paes] (pronounced like "pass")
find	[faynd]	>	[fayn] (pronounced like "fine")
miss + ed	[mɪst]	>	[mɪs] (as in "I miss my train this morning.")
staff + ed	[staeft]	>	[staef] (as in "Who staff the desk last night?")
move + ed	[muvd]	>	[muv] (as in "They move there last week.")

Again, this is a very productive phonological principle or rule in AAL.
Note how similar it is to the restriction against consonant clusters found
in Niger-Congo.

A third phonological feature of AAL that differs from SAE is the
absence of the th-sounds (theta and thorn). These sounds are found
only very rarely in African languages. "Theta," represented phoneti-
cally as [θ], is the voiceless member of this pair of sounds, "thorn" being its voiced counterpart, represented by the symbol [ð]. As foreign
sounds in African languages, the th-sounds have limited appearance in
AAL.

"Theta" appears at the beginning of words in AAL, such as think,
thin, thimble, and thumb, but does not appear at the end of words.
There, it is transformed into the sound that is most similar to this consonant in the African source language(s). As a consequence, we find the
following pronunciations of theta at the end of words in AAL:

with	[wɪθ]	>	[wɪf] ~ [wɪt] ~ [wɪd]
teeth	[ti θ]	>	[tif]

| both | [boθ] | > | [bof] |
| south | [sawθ] | > | [sawf] |

The labio-dental fricative [f] seems to be, by far, the replacement of choice in AAL, although [t] and [d] appear to be regional or ethnic variants.[20]

Thorn, by contrast, occurs in very few words in word-final position in SAE. In those rare words, the pronunciation of choice in AAL appears to be [v], as follows:

| breathe | [briδ] | > | [briv] |
| bathe | [beδ] | > | [bev] |

However, "thorn," the *voiced* interdental fricative, at the beginning of a word is replaced in AAL by [d], the voiced alveolar stop, consistently. The most commonly used words following this pattern are pronominal forms.

they	[δe]	>	[de]
them	[δem]	>	[dɛm]
this	[δIs]	>	[dIs]
that	[δat]	>	[dɑt]
those	[δoz]	>	[doz]

Notice that these patterns are not haphazard or random but very systematic, sensitive to positioning within a given word, and sensitive to the voiced or voiceless quality of the model sound. This is truly rule-governed behavior that differs significantly from SAE, but which will be shown later to conform to an African system of behavior.

The majority of the world's languages are tone languages, meaning that tone or tone patterns are as distinctive and important as vowels are in other languages. This is true of most African languages. While AAL has not retained a tonal system from an indigenous African language, tone is used in some interesting and unique ways. For instance, it is sometimes used to convert a word from positive to its negative counterpart, or vice versa. In this way

bad (with low-falling tone) means "not-good," but

bad (with mid-rising tone) means "superior/beautiful."

Similar tonal semantics is operative with pairs like

cool "not warm" and

<u>cool</u> "sharp, in-vogue, highly acceptable," on the one hand, and

<u>cold</u> "heartless" and
<u>cold</u> "outstanding" on the other hand.

In fact, in AAL every adjective has a potential partner with the same sequence of consonants and vowels, but a varying tonal pattern.

The Grammatical System of AAL

PRE-VERBAL ASPECT MARKERS

One of the signature features of the grammatical system of African American Language is the system of pre-verbal aspect markers. Different from SAE, in which tense is the most important dimension of a verbal action, often designated by a suffix on the verb or a different verb form, in AAL the most important dimension might be "frequent/habitual" action or "completedness" of an action. Look at the following examples:

Habitual/Frequent Action, [bi]

Girl, dey [bi] jamming.	"They are always having a good time."
He always [bi] messin wit me.	"He is always teasing/joking with me."
Dey don't [bi] doin' dat.	"They don't usually/ever do that."
Friday nights, Johnny [bi] studying.	"Johnny studies every Friday night."

Completed Action, [d λ n]

Junior [dλn] ate up everything	"Junior has eaten everything."
Y'all [dλn] did it now.	"You have done something that you can't reverse now."
Shanita [dλn] wrote her test.	"Shanita is finished taking her test."
If she [dλn] fixed it, why it don't work?	"If she finished fixing it, why doesn't it work?"

Remote Past Action, [bIn]

I [bIn] knowin' dat.	"I have known that for a long time."
Dat family [bIn] gone.	"That family moved a long time ago."
Jamal [bIn] had dat car.	"Jamal has had that car for a long time."
Marcus [bIn] likin' Shaniqua.	"Marcus has had a crush on Shaniqua for a long time."

PRESENT CONTINUOUS ACTION

There is a zero marker to indicate present continuous action in AAL, as long as the verb carries the -ing form.

Jason readin' the book.	"Jason is reading the book."
Dey playin' at the park.	"They are playing at the park."
You pushin' your luck.	"You are pushing your luck."

By extension, past continuous action is denoted by placing the past marker *was* in front of the verbal in the sentence.

Jason <u>was</u> readin' the book	"Jason was reading the book."
De <u>was</u> playin' in the park.	"They were playing in the park."
You <u>was</u> pushin' your luck.	"You were pushing your luck."

ADJECTIVAL VERBS

In AAL, adjectival notions are communicated by the mere juxtaposition of a noun and its descriptive word (Noun + Descriptor). This is different from SAE, in which this grammatical function has to be carried out by linking the subject noun to the descriptive adjective by a copula verb (to be). Look at the following examples. You will notice that the descriptor in AAL behaves like a verb ("to be X").

She fine.	"She <u>is</u> beautiful."
She <u>ain't</u> so fine.	"She <u>isn't</u> so beautiful." (<u>ain't</u> is NEG. marker)
She [bIn] fine.	"She has always been beautiful."
Man, dey sho ugly.	"Man, they sure <u>are</u> ugly."
Man, dey <u>ain't</u> ugly.	"Man, they <u>aren't</u> ugly."
Man, dey [bIn] ugly.	"Man, they have always been ugly."
Y'all sick.	"You <u>are</u> sick/crazy."
Y'all <u>ain't</u> sick.	"You <u>aren't</u> sick/crazy."
Y'all [bIn] sick.	"You always act crazy."

NEGATIVE HARMONY RULE

A highly stigmatized form of AAL is the frequent appearance of more than one negative word in a sentence, without changing its negative or positive character. Contrary to popular belief, these multiple occurrences of negative words are not random or arbitrary. Instead, the appearance of multiple negation is totally predictable. The rule is bidirectional: (1) if the verb in a sentence is negative, then, any occurrence of indefinite quantifiers (any, anything, anybody, anywhere, anymore) in the sentence must appear in their negative form; and (2) if the subject of the sentence is a negative indefinite quantifier, then, the verb must be marked negative.

I <u>ain't</u> got <u>no</u> money.	"I don't have any money."
She <u>won't</u> give <u>nobody no</u> money.	"She won't give anybody any money."
<u>Nobody ain't</u> gon do <u>nothin'</u> for her.	"Nobody is going to do anything for her."
DeAndre <u>ain't</u> goin' <u>nowhere</u>.	"DeAndre isn't going anywhere."

NON-INVERSION OF SUBJECT + AUXILIARY IN QUESTIONS
In Standard American English, questions are formed by inverting the subject and the appropriate auxiliary verb in the declarative sentence form. For instance, a declarative sentence like <u>He is running</u> is transformed into a question by inverting <u>He</u> and <u>is</u>, producing <u>Is he running?</u> This inversion takes place whether the question is a yes/no question or a WH question. An example of a WH question is as follows: <u>Where is he running?</u> Although this is a simplified presentation of the process, it is easy to see the inversion in basic SAE questions.

By contrast, this subject/auxiliary inversion does not take place in AAL WH questions. Observe the following examples:

<u>AAL</u>			<u>SAE</u>			
How	<u>I'm</u>	gon' buy dat?	"How	<u>am</u>	<u>I</u>	going to buy that?"
	Subj+Aux			Aux	+ Subj	
Why	<u>she won't</u>	see a doctor?	"Why	<u>won't she</u>		see a doctor?"
	Subj + Aux			Aux	+ Subj	

Not surprisingly, in most African languages, no inversion of the subject with an auxiliary or verb marker takes place in the formation of questions. In WH questions, it is the WH word that signals that the sentence is a question. The subject and verbal elements remain in the same order as in declarative statements. In yes/no questions, a rising intonation pattern at the end of the sentence is all that is needed to denote its interrogative nature, although in some languages a question marker might be used to make the question more emphatic. An example from Hausa reveals this typical pattern:

Yaa	tafi	Kano.		"He went to Kano."
(He-Past		go	Kano)	

Yaa	tafi	Kano?		"Did he go to Kano?"

(Rising intonation at end)

Yaa	tafi	Kano	ko?	"Did he really go to Kano?"

(Q-emphatic)

These examples of grammatical patterns in AAL attest to the systematic nature of the language. The fact that AAL differs from SAE in a number of places in which it is very similar to rules and patterns of Niger-Congo languages reveals the degree to which the language of the African American community has preserved its African linguistic character.

Research that points to an African linguistic continuum, from indigenous African languages, through creolized forms of language, to AAL has not been extensive. However, the author (Williams, 1971, 1976, 1977)[21] has demonstrated that the grammar of Sierra Leone Krio is fundamentally Kwa. The functioning of serial verb constructions, the presence of pre-verbal aspect markers, the nature of word creation, and the processes for emphasizing virtually any word in a sentence that are operative in Krio are only a few of the grammatical features that lead to this conclusion. The persistence of many Yoruba lexical items and idioms clinches the argument.

While the African character of AAL is not as transparent as is the case of Krio, a comparison between Sierra Leone Krio, a Creole language with an indisputable African base, and AAL allows us to see the African character in AAL more clearly. Similar to spraying lumenol on a dried blood stain in the dark, the comparison of Krio to AAL exposes the heretofore hidden linguistic identity of AAL. The numerous similarities in phonological features, grammatical features, and semantic concepts can lead one to only one conclusion. Observe the comparison of Krio, AAL, and SAE:

KRIO	AAL	SAE

Phonological Constraints

[#d_____ vs #thorn_____]

Dɛm	[dɛm]	them
dis	[dIs]	this
dat	[dɑt]	that
dɛm wan de	[doz] (ones)	those
dɛm wan ya	[diz] (ones)	these

[_____t/f# vs _____theta#]

wit	[wIt/wIf]	with
tit	[tif]	teeth
MOt	[mouf]	mouth
——	[bof]	both
——	[bafrum]	bathroom

[_____C₁ + C₂# vs _____C₁#]

Lɛf	[lɛf]	left
saful	[sɔf]	soft
pas	[pɑs]	past
fɛn	[fayn]	find
fɔs	[fʌss]	first
fɪf	[fɪf]	fifth

[_____ V + R# vs _____ V#]

brʌda	[brʌδλ]	brother
sista	[sIsta]	sister
afta	[aftλ]	after
po	[po]	poor
minista	[mInIstλ]	minister

Grammatical Patterns

Adjectival Verbs

I fayn lEkE roz.	She fine as she want to be.	She is as pretty as a rose.
Bra, dEm wOwO.	Man, dey ugly.	They are really ugly.
Una sik.	Y'all sick.	You are sick/crazy.
Yu to ful.	You so jive.	You are full of malarkey.

Habitual/Frequentive Action

Sista, dEm <u>kin</u> gladi	Girl, they [<u>bi</u>] jammin'.	They always have a good time.
OltEm i <u>kin</u> ambOg mi.	He always [<u>bi</u>] messin' wit me.	He is always teasing or harassing me.
Dem nO <u>kin</u> du dat.	Dey don' [<u>bi</u>] doin' dat.	They don't usually/ever do that.

Remote Past Action

A <u>bin dOn</u> no dat.	I [bIn] knowin' dat.	I have known that for a very long time.
Dem <u>bin dOn</u> go.	Dey [bIn] gone.	They left a long time ago.
A <u>bin dOn</u> bay da motoka.	I [bIn] had dat car.	I've had that car a long time.

Continuous Action (Present)

A <u>de</u> rid buk.	I readin' a book.	I <u>am</u> reading a book
I <u>de</u> rid buk.	He/she readin' a book.	He/she <u>is</u> reading a book.
Dem <u>de</u> rid buk	Dey reading a book.	They <u>are</u> reading a book.

Continuous Action (Past)

A bin de rid buk.	I was readin' a book.	I <u>was</u> reading a book.
I bin de rid buk.	He/she was readin' a book.	He/she <u>was</u> reading a book.
Dem bin de rid buk.	Dey was reading a book.	They <u>were</u> reading a book.

The reader should not be misled by the fact that the AAL forms and the Krio forms are not identical. What is important here is that the same or similar patterns exist. While Krio uses the pre-verbal marker, <u>kin</u>, to indicate frequent or habitual action, AAL uses <u>bi</u>, but the structure is the same. If one were to extend this analysis further, by looking at the structure of sentences in the creole languages of the Caribbean, one would find the same phenomenon. In fact, Mervyn Alleyne (1980)[22] did a comparison of the creole languages of the Caribbean and found remarkable similarities, both among each other and with the languages of West Africa. Although Alleyne alluded to black English in the United States, his comparative analysis did not include it. The work presented in this chapter completes the picture of the African linguistic global community.

African Language as an Artistic Tool

Although this chapter does not provide an in-depth analysis of the artistic nature of African-based languages, any description of the "African" character of AAL that did not at least mention it would be sorely lacking. The use of language in the African cultural context is as much a performance as it is a communication tool. To peoples of African descent *how* something is said is typically as important as *what* is said. For instance, in a verbal debate, the speaker who is more artful in the use of language and adds a dramatic dimension to the event is likely to be judged the "winner."

In every African community, one finds verbal dueling. In African American society, this verbal dueling is known as "playing the dozens" and is a game, typically between males, in which each tries to socially, emotionally, and linguistically defeat the other through a series of ritual insults. The subject of the verbal insults may begin with the dueling opponent, but eventually escalates into insults against the opponent's relatives and, ultimately, insults against the opponent's mother. In the Sierra Leone Krio community this interaction is called "kOsin." Very little has been written about the traditional African antecedents of these performances. This is fertile ground for future research.

A characteristic mode of communication in African societies is through the use of "indirection." Rather than informing, criticizing, or teasing someone directly, it is done indirectly, often by means of proverbs and sometimes by "signifying." Indirection is used to allow one to get one's message across to another individual without the receiving individual being offended, in many cases allowing the individual to save face in the company of others. Persons who master the proverbs of a society and know the appropriate contexts in which to use them are considered very wise, as well as very skilled.

Finally, there is something in the African personality that loves creating new words and expressions. Each era has had its own set of words that were created for the moment and became the currency of the day. The words "cool," "cold," "hot," "fresh," "slammin'," "jammin'," and "dope" have all carried essentially the same meaning, that being "to be powerfully good, beautiful, or pleasing to the senses." There seems to be a need to define things more emphatically and more dramatically than was possible before. Keeping pace with these new word creations is a measure of belonging to the Black community.

There is a tendency to use body parts to characterize the whole person or to describe a person using body parts. Everyone who has grown up in a black community has been called into the house by his or her mother with the words, "Get yo butt in dIs house!" Commonly heard is the expression, "I don't care what anybody else says, yo mouf bed not be in it." Similarly, a person may ask a girlfiend or boyfriend if he/she wants to "shake a tailfeather," meaning to get on the dance floor. This is a very productive pattern in the African American community. It is also very productive among speakers of Sierra Leone Krio. Someone who is greedy is referred to as [bIg yay], literally "big-eyed." Someone who is stubborn is [traŋa yes], literally "strong/hard ears." A person who is difficult to deal with or who is overly particular is said to [gɛt na an] "have in hand." Krio speakers also use the expression [Im ed gi am], literally "his/her head gives him/her," meaning that the person is somewhat impulsive and acts on his/her thoughts. The similarities here are clear.

Many words in AAL are conversions of words from one part of speech to another, with considerably different meaning. In the context of this word-forming mechanism, a car is called a ride. Simply by placing the verb, ride, in the place reserved for nouns transforms the verb into a noun, without any change in the phonological shape of the word. A relatively recently created expression is my bad, meaning "my fault/error." Here an adjective is placed in an exclusively noun position, creating a new noun. Compare this to the process in Sierra Leone Krio which creates nouns out of verbs. Virtually every verb in the Krio language can be transformed into a noun by placing it as the head of a relative clause. Look at the following examples:

Di bit we i bit am traŋa.
[The beat REL he/she beat him/her was-harsh.]
"She/he gave him/her a sound beating."

Di siŋ we dem siŋ nO fayn.
[The sing REL they sing not good/pleasing.]
"Their singing was not very good."

Based on the productivity of this process in Krio, almost any verb can be transformed into the nominal counterpart of a verb by placing it in a noun position, after the article the, for instance. Thus, the verb it "eat" can be transformed into the noun, "the food" by placing di "the" in front of it, di it. Similarly, the verb kuk "cook" becomes a noun in the phrase, di kuk "the cooking" and was "wash" becomes "the washing" in the phrase, di was.

African Americans often refer to a thing or person by some part or element of it. For instance, "clothes" are referred to as "threads," a hat is referred to as a "brim," and "money" is referred to as "long green." "Girls" may be referred to as "skirts" and a car may be referred to as "wheels." A Black male may ask a friend if he wants to go play "some hoops," meaning "basketball." This is peculiar to the African American community and not found in White America. This raises the question about its origins. Is it uniquely African American or is it yet another example of the African character in the African American speech community that will require further research to uncover.

Conclusion

Too frequently the study of AAL has focused on the linguistically insignificant categorization of this spoken interaction as a "language" or a "dialect." From a scientific perspective, AAL is clearly a discrete linguistic system, with an internally coherent set of phonological, syntactic, and morphological rules that govern the communication between members of that speech community. The language, admittedly, has much in common with SAE because their histories have been inextricably linked to each other. However, the subordinated social, political, and economic status of African Americans, in relation to Anglo-Americans, does not make their linguistic system inferior to that of Anglo-Americans any more than a declaration of war against Iraq makes the Iraqi language inferior to SAE or British Received English. An even closer parallel is one based on race. Just because race can, and is, used as a social, political, and social weapon against people of African descent does not make race a scientifically valid category.

This chapter has identified a number of the areas in which AAL differs, systematically, from SAE. What has been presented here is not an exhaustive study, but rather a demonstrative one. There is much more that could be written on each area discussed herein and many more areas that could be presented. A complete grammar of AAL has yet to be written.

It should be clear from this chapter, however, that a complete grammar of AAL is not needed to determine the African character of the language. Informed comparisons of AAL structures with those from West African languages reveal many similarities, especially when considering structures and features of one of the most prominent African language families, the Niger-Congo Family. The similarities between AAL and Sierra Leone Krio are even closer, revealing the unquestionable continuities found in the African World Speech Community. In fact, the African character of AAL is only speculation without a comparative study of the creolized languages (or Africanized forms of English, French, and Portuguese) spoken on both sides and in the middle of the Atlantic Ocean.

This chapter also sheds light on the mutability of languages over time and under the influence of different cultural forces. AAL does not look or sound exactly like any of the traditional African languages or Sierra Leone Krio. It differs from other languages in the African World Speech Community in varying degrees, depending upon the feature or structure being considered. This is to be expected, just as French differs from Spanish, Portuguese, and Italian, even though they are members of the Romance Language Family. Nuances and innovations can be found not only in languages from the same language family, but also in regional and social variants of the same language. The naming practices in the African American community are innovations based on Niger-Congo phonological restrictions. AAL, as a communication system, has developed in the same way, following the Ghanaian principle of Sankofa, "reaching back into the past in order to advance into the future."

Notes

1. Rober L. Williams is attributed with coining the term *Ebonics* in 1973. He has spoken extensively on his analysis of the language and has published a book on the topic, *Ebonics, the True Language of Black Folks* (1975) through the Institute of Black Studies in St. Louis.

2. In 1963 Daniel Patrick Moynihan and Nathan Glazer published a book entitled *Beyond the Melting Pot*. In that book they stated that "the negro is an American and nothing more. He has no culture to preserve or protect." As noted social scientists of the day, they not only rejected the notion that the African American could have preserved any remnants of African culture, but they also laid the philosophical foundation on this topic for the next generation of social scientists.

3. Niger-Congo arises out of the well-established genetic classification of African languages published by Joseph H. Greenberg in 1963 in his book *The Languages of Africa* (Bloomington: Indiana University Press).

4. See Subira Kifano and Ernie Smith, "Ebonics and Education in the Context of Culture: Meeting the Language and Cultural Needs of English Learning African American Students," *Ebonics in the Urban Education Debate*, ed. J. David Ramirez, Terrence G. Wiley, Gerda De Klerk, and Enid Lee (Long Beach: Center for Language Minority Education and Research, California State University, Long Beach, 2000).

5. See Peter Ladefoged, *A Phonetic Study of West African Languages* (Cambridge: Cambridge University Press, 1968).

6. See William E. Welmers, *African Language Structures* (Berkeley: University of California Press, 1973).

7. See Victoria Fromkin and R. Rodman, *An Introduction to Language* (New York: Holt, Rinehart and Winston, 1993).

8. See Molefi Kete Asante's book *The Book of African Names* (Trenton, N.J.: Africa World Press, 1991).

9. Fromkin and Rodman, op. cit., p. 227.

10. The reference used for Twi examples is J. Yeboa-Dankwa, *Basic Twi for Learners* (Accra, Ghana: Sebewie, 1998).

11. The source of the Wolof examples is Edris Makward, *Wolof Basic Language* (Madison: Department of African Languages and Literature, University of Wisconsin, 1980).

12. Lorenzo Dow Turner's book, *Africanisms in the Gullah Dialect*, first published by the University of Chicago Press in 1949 and republished by University of Michigan Press in 1974, has become a classic in the study of African continuities in the Americas. He provided the foundation for all future research in this area and successfully challenged those who argued that the devastation of slavery had eradicated any semblance of African culture among African Americans.

13. See Marianne Bertrand and Sendhil Mullainathan, "What's in a Name?" *Black Issues in Higher Education* 20(9) (June 2003).

14. See John and Russell Rickford, *Spoken Soul: The Story of Black English* (New York: John Wiley & Sons, 2002).

15. See J. L. Dillard, *The Lexicon of Black English* (New York: Seabury Press, 1977).

16. See Geneva Smitherman, *Black Talk: Words and Phrases from the Hood to the Amen Corner* (New York: Houghton Mifflin, 1994). Smitherman is perhaps best known for her book *Talkin' and Testifyin'* (Boston: Houghton Mifflin, 1977), one of the earliest attempts to describe the multifaceted nature and history of African American Language.

17. See Clarence Major, *Juba to Jive: A Dictionary of African American Slang* (New York: Penguin Press, 1994).

18. See David Dalby, "Americanisms The May Once Have Been Africanisms," the *New York Times*, July 19, 1969. Readers are also directed to Dalby's article "The African Element in American English," *Rappin' and Stylin' Out*, ed. Thomas Kochman (Champaign-Urbana: University of Illinois Press, 1972).

19. See Winifred Kellersberger Vass, *The Bantu Speaking Heritage of the United States*, Monograph Series, Volume 2 (Los Angeles: UCLA Center for Afro-American Studies, 1979).

20. See Selase W. Williams, "Substantive Africanisms at the End of the African Linguistic Continuum," *Africanisms in Afro-American Language Varieties*, ed. Salikoko Mufwene (Athens: University of Georgia Press, 1993).

21. See Selase W. Williams, "Serial Verb Constructions in Krio," *Studies in African Linguistics*, Supplement 2, 1971. This article was a precursor to his doctoral dissertation in which a number of the syntactic and semantic characteristics of the language were explored. The Indiana University dissertation was completed in 1976 under the title, "Linguistic change in the syntax and semantics of Sierra Leone Krio." The reader should also see "The So-Called Relativized and Cleft Predicates in Krio: One Step Closer to

an Understanding of Creolization," *Language and Linguistic Problems in Africa,* ed. Paul Kotey and Haig Der-Houssikian (Columbia, S.C.: Hornbeam Press, 1977). In this article, Williams shows how a powerful nounformation process functions in Krio, similar to a parallel process in Kwa languages, in particular Yoruba and Igbo.

22. See Mervyn C. Alleyne, *Comparative Afro-American* (Ann Arbor, Mich.: Karoma Publishers, 1980).

Contributors

Molefi Kete Asante, Professor of Africology at Temple University, has long had an interest in black language, the African continuity of symbols in the Americas, and Afrocentric cultural analysis. He is the author of thirty-two books, including *The Afrocentric Idea,* and more than one hundred scholarly articles.

George Brandon is Associate Medical Professor of Behavioral Medicine at the City University of New York's Sophie Davis School of Biomedical Education, and also teaches in the Department of Biomedical Engineering at the City College School of Engineering. He is author of *Santeria from Africa to the New World* (Indiana University Press, 1993) and has published studies of African and African American art, music, religion, and traditional healing.

Jessie Ruth Gaston, Professor of African History at California State University, Sacramento, has received numerous awards and fellowships, including an Outstanding Young Women of America Award, the American Association of University Women Fellowship, and the Ford Foundation Middle East and Africa Fellowship.

Robert L. Hall, Associate Professor of African-American Studies and History at Northeastern University, has published several articles and is co-editor of a book, *Holding on to the Land and the Lord* (1982).

Joseph E. Holloway, Professor of Pan-African Studies at California State University, Northridge, is a specialist in cross-cultural studies relating to Africa and Afro-Americana. He is a former Ford and Fulbright Scholar, and is author of *Liberian Diplomacy in Africa, Neither Black nor White: The Saga of an American Family,* and *An Introduction to Classical African Civilizations.* He is co-author (with Winifred K. Vass) of *The African Heritage of American English* (Indiana University Press, 1993), and editor of *The Noble Drew Ali and the Moorish Science Temple Movement* and has published widely on New World Africanisms.

Portia K. Maultsby, Professor of Folklore and Ethnomusicology at Indiana University, was a recipient of a Ford Research Fellowship. She is preparing a book on black popular music and has published many articles on the subject of African American music.

John Edward Philips is Professor on the Faculty of Humanities at Hirosaki University in Japan. He is author of *Spurious Arabic: Hausa and Colonial Nigeria* and co-editor (with Toru Miura) of *Slave Elites in the Middle East and Africa.*

Beverly J. Robinson was at the time of her death a professor in the School of Theater, Film, and Television at the University of California at Los Angeles, where she taught Africana Folklore. She co-edited a two-volume annotated bibliography on African American folk culture and published a life narrative on a South Georgia midwife, *Aunt[Ant] Phyllis: A Biographical Sketch of Mrs. Phyllis Carter,* and *The Life and Work of Oscar Micheaux: Pioneer Black Author and Filmmaker 1884–1951.*

Robert Farris Thompson is Col. John Trumbull Professor of the History of Art and Master of Timothy Dwight College at Yale University. Among his books are *Flash of the Spirit: African and Afro-American Art and Philosophy; Face of the Gods: Art and Altars of Africa and the African Americas;* and *Art from Africa: Long Steps Never Broke a Back.*

Margaret Washington, Associate Professor of History at Cornell University, is author of *"A Peculiar People": Slave Religion and Community-Culture among the Gullahs* (1988).

Selase W. Williams, Dean of the College of Arts and Sciences at California State University, Dominguez Hills, is Principal Investigator on the "Global Diasporas in Southern California Project" funded by the Ford Foundation as part of its Crossing Borders Initiative, and has published on aspects of creolization, sociolinguistics, African American Language, paradigmatic developments in Black Studies, and multicultural/international education.

Index

Page numbers in italics refer to illustrations.

Abrahams, Roger, 6, 305, 375
Aché, 259
Africa: identification with, 15; cultural areas of, 21
Africa Meeting House, 15
African: cowboys, 34; craftsmen, 34; crops in the New World, 45–49; cultural survivals, 384; custom of polygamy, 192; customs in the U.S., 339; dances in North America, 51; day names, 85–86, *85;* deities, 124; Diaspora, 15, 385; ethnicity on the American plantation, 43–45; extended families, 113, 188; languages, 398; religion and spiritualism, 157, 229; rituals, 146, 240; secret societies, 153; social etiquette in the New World, 59; term discussed, 14–16; tribal facial marks, 230; water cults, 207; witchcraft, 381; world view, 154
African American beneficial societies, 194
African American Language (AAL), 8, 397, 398, 406–424; adjectival verbs in, 404, 416; African character of, 397, 413; Consonant Cluster Rule in, 413; copula verb in, 405; grammatical system of, 415; habitual markers in, 404, 415; labio-dental fricative in, 414; negative harmony rule of, 416; phonological rules in, 412; remote past action in,

415; "Theta" sounds in, 413; vocabulary lexicon of, 406, 411, 412, 413; voiced alveolar stop in, 414; voiced interdental fricative in, 414; voiceless th-sounds in, 402
African American music: African features of, 335; black aesthetic expressions in, 334; elements of, 334; evolution of, *327;* folk, 344, 345, 380; forms of, 338; polyrhythmic structure of, 335
The African Background Outlined (Woodson), 4
African Christianity, 340
African cures and medical practices: cures for yaws and syphilis, 53; during slavery, 385; inoculation for smallpox, 53, 364, 385; preventive medicine practice, 365
African Music and instruments: banjo, 392; diasporic music, 338; earth-bow, 379
Africanisms, 255; in African American names, 2, 91; and the black family, 188; in contemporary American English, 59, 93–105; found among white Americans, 59
Africanisms in American Culture (Holloway), 1
Africanisms in the Gullah Dialect (Turner), 2, 5, 82, 406

429

CPSIA information can be obtained
at www.ICGtesting.com
Printed in the USA
JSHW022316281221
21626JS00003B/111